Houses built on sand

MANCHESTER
1824

Manchester University Press

IDENTITIES AND GEOPOLITICS IN THE MIDDLE EAST

Series editors: Simon Mabon, Edward Wastnidge and May Darwich

After the Arab Uprisings and the ensuing fragmentation of regime–society relations across the Middle East, identities and geopolitics have become increasingly contested, with serious implications for the ordering of political life at domestic, regional and international levels, best seen in conflicts in Syria and Yemen. The Middle East is the most militarised region in the world, where geopolitical factors remain predominant in shaping political dynamics. Another common feature of the regional landscape is the continued degeneration of communal relations as societal actors retreat into substate identities, while difference becomes increasingly violent, spilling out beyond state borders. The power of religion – and trans-state nature of religious views and linkages – thus provides the means for regional actors (such as Saudi Arabia and Iran) to exert influence over a number of groups across the region and beyond. This series provides space for the engagement with these ideas and the broader political, legal and theological factors to create space for an intellectual reimagining of socio-political life in the Middle East.

Originating from the SEPAD project (www.sepad.org.uk), this series facilitates the reimagining of political ideas, identities and organisation across the Middle East, moving beyond the exclusionary and binary forms of identity to reveal the contingent factors that shape and order life across the region.

Houses built on sand
Violence, sectarianism and revolution in the Middle East

Simon Mabon

Manchester University Press

Published by Manchester University Press
Oxford Road, Manchester M13 9PL
www.manchesteruniversitypress.co.uk

British Library Cataloguing-in-Publication Data
A catalogue record for this book is available from the British Library

ISBN 978 1 5261 2646 7 hardback
ISBN 978 1 5261 6034 8 paperback
ISBN 978 1 5261 2647 4 open access

First published 2020

Typeset by Newgen Publishing UK

This book is dedicated to my wife, meri douniyeh, Swarnalatha.
It is also dedicated to my family: my parents Sally and George, and my in-laws, Padmavati and Sumohan. Deda, you remain with us, forever.

Contents

Foreword   viii

Acknowledgements   x

    Introduction   1

1   The politics of sovereignty and space   9

2   Letters and declarations   32

3   Ink on paper   62

4   The *dawla* and the *umma*   92

5   Building Beirut, transforming Jerusalem and breaking Basra   125

6   The people want the fall of the regime   149

7   The regime fights back   181

8   Houses built on sand   211

    Conclusion: The end of the dream   235

Selected bibliography   245

Index   248

Foreword

Mehran Kamrava

Scholars have long had a tendency to operate in silos, and those focusing on the Middle East have been no exception. Seldom, in fact, has there been fruitful dialogue between related disciplines. Area studies, including Middle Eastern studies, has been particularly guilty of this sin of omission, as very rarely has it engaged broader theoretical debates about some of the core concepts it employs in its analysis. Concepts such as 'state', 'sovereignty', 'legitimacy', 'revolution' and many others are often employed freely and with little or no attention to their genealogies, their meaning and use in other disciplines and some of the theoretical discussions surrounding them. The present volume is an exception to the rule, situating its subject of study firmly at the crossroads of Middle Eastern area studies and political theory, deftly also drawing from international relations, history and political sociology.

In the pages to come, answers to three key questions are explored: what are the roots of sovereign power and the supporting logic of governmentality in the Middle East; the timing, means and reasons why sovereign power is contested; and implications of the fragmentation of sovereign power for the ordering of space across the Middle East. This ambitious task of interrogating the centrality of sovereignty at the heart of the political history of contemporary Middle East is achieved through meticulous employment of analytical tools from several disciplines. The manuscript begins with an exploration of the links between domestic and regional developments, pointing particularly to the importance of linkages of sovereignty, agency and human action, and the state. Investigations of the region's political history, the role of religion in shaping politics and sovereignty, and pent-up social and political pressures and their eruption in the 2010–11 mass uprisings follow. To bring the journey to a conclusion, the book ends with the responses of local states to the uprisings, and how the ensuing domestic repercussions continue to reverberate and to shape the region's politics.

Trauma can be intergenerational, and from the earliest days of pan-Arabism in the 1950s up until today, the political history of the Middle East has been marked by one traumatic experience after another. Structures and states are important, but so are the memories of the individuals who experience and respond to them. Across the Middle East, the states and political structures that proliferated were invariably authoritarian, shaping both the ways the states sought to legitimise their rule and the responses they elicited in their legitimation efforts. One of the most potent of the responses came from the domain of religion and its articulation of competing claims to authority. Agency, structures, states and conceptions of legitimacy at variance with each other have been the defining forces of Middle East politics, giving rise to geo-sectarian politics and creating zones of possibility and restriction.

These zones, and the unfolding of politics more generally, occur in urban areas. Urban design and architecture, intentional or accidental, and transformative processes such as gentrification, shape both the ways in which life can be regulated and the popular responses that structures and sources of authority elicit. These responses have led to a long history of urban political unrest across the region, culminating with unsurpassed contagion in what optimistically came to be called the Arab Spring. The Spring was not to be, however, soon reversed by the forces of violence, war and army coups. The outcome, ultimately, was no better than what had been replaced: houses built on sand, geopolitical sectarianisation, realignments and an American president globally plying his trade of commerce, his only trade, along with a young and ambitious prince determined to put his mark on Middle Eastern history. Indeed 'end of a dream', as the book soberly concludes.

What we have before us here is a rich text, informed by meticulous scholarship, extensive fieldwork and meaningful engagement with existing scholarship in the field. More importantly, the volume is theoretically informed, presenting new insights and interpretations, and examines, in both subtle and overt manners, the struggle over sovereignty, and its meaning and consequences, that has shaped so much of contemporary politics in the Middle East. One only hopes the present volume becomes a model for future generations of scholars to follow. As such, it serves as an excellent inaugural volume for the *Identities and Geopolitics in the Middle East* series.

Acknowledgements

Although this book has been four years in the making, its roots date back to my time as a philosophy undergraduate student where I encountered a paradox that articulates problems with defining vague predicates. As my journey into academia progressed, I later returned to the sorites paradox in an attempt to work through problems of borders, contestation and the limits of sovereign power in the Middle East where state power was becoming increasingly contested. It is the memory of a paradox that set me on this journey.

While focusing on the Middle East, this book was written in countless countries where I have had the benefit of engaging with many people from different backgrounds whose continued support has enriched the project and although some may disagree, kept me sane. I have been fortunate to have spent a good deal of time travelling across the region where I have, on the whole, been met with incredible kindness. A number of people gave up time to be interviewed and I am incredibly thankful for to everyone who spoke with me.

I have been lucky enough to present parts of this work at a range of institutions including Oxford, Harvard, St Andrews, King's College, Georgetown Doha, George Mason, the LSE, Aarhus, Brookings, People's College Nanded, Stockholm, Copenhagen and others, where I have received invaluable feedback. I am grateful to Carnegie Corporation for funding 'Sectarianism, Proxies and De-Sectarianisation' (SEPAD) and allowing me to explore particular aspects of this project, the wonderful team of SEPAD fellows whose presence on the project has facilitated my intellectual development and provided huge levels of emotional support.

At Lancaster University, I have been able to count on a number of wonderful colleagues and a cohort of incredible PhD students who have read parts of this work. In particular, I must thank Rashed Al Rasheed, Meysam Tayebipour, Ali Seyadrazaghi, Adel Ruished, Amel Houna, Bekir Varoglu, Thanos Trappelides, Elias Ghazal, Ana Kumarasamy, Samira Nasirzadeh, Sukru Cildir, Eyad Al Refai, Mike Todman and David Waines who worked through the book in a reading group. Edith Szanto read through my engagement with Agamben and provided invaluable encouragement. Of course, any mistakes remain mine alone.

I must also thank a number of people who have welcomed me into their homes and humoured me while I shut myself away to write. In particular, Amu, Chris and their cats were wonderful hosts, plying me with coffee and all manner of sweet things, although they were of little use helping us escape a locked room. Others including Mark (my Impact Narrative co-host), Matt, Nupa, Joe and Upasna, Robert, Momma (and Jazz!), Mukti, Brian and Sarah, Robert and Sigrun, Shantanu, Chris and Supri offered welcome distractions from the difficult times.

I must thank Rob Byron and Tony Mason at Manchester University Press who have been wonderful to work with, offering a huge amount of support for the project and my work more broadly. Tony expressed a great deal of support for the idea in its infancy while Rob later guided it through the treacherous ground of completing the manuscript and I am forever thankful for their support.

I must thank my family who have been everything that anyone could have wished for and much, much more. I am blessed to have an incredibly supportive family that while spread across the world, comes together incredibly well. A good chunk of this book was proofread as we were celebrating our Indian wedding in 2018 in Hyderabad and Goa where I was fortunate to draw support from Lynne, Sylvia, Ed, John, Andrea, Trudi, Dave, Sakshi, Rucha, Sutti, Sandesh, Teja, Tarun, Ami and Ramya. I was also able to draw inspiration from spending time with our wonderful nephews and nieces, Pingu, Simba and Bambi.

Lastly, I must thank my immediate family who helped me survive an incredibly difficult few years. They have been a constant source of support in the writing process and life more broadly. I am deeply sad that Deda is not here to see the finished version of the book, but I am proud that I was able to talk at the People's College, Nanded – in his presence – the place where his father taught astrophysics. Finally, I must thank my wife, to whom this book is dedicated. She has offered endless support, enthusiasm, criticism, distraction, praise and love. She is the person who has supported me throughout this project but must importantly, has helped me to navigate the precarious terrain of life. I am eternally thankful to her for her presence in my life.

All of this has seen me through; until the next one.

Thank you.

Introduction

Crossing a street in Dahiyeh, a suburb of Beirut in the summer of 2015 should have been simple. It was Ramadan 1436 and the streets were adorned with colour to go with images of Hassan Nasrallah, Ruhollah Khomeini and Ali Khamenei. Destroyed in 2006 after the thirty-four-day war with Israel, Dahiyeh has since been rebuilt in a way that reflects the area's Shi'a, Arab roots, rather than the European influences that help define other parts of Beirut.

Taking all of this in, I failed to notice the SUV that had turned off Ayatollah Khomeini Street, but I was quickly aware of the men who jumped out of it, shouting at me in Arabic and Spanish, somewhat bizarrely: Who was I? What was I doing there? Who did I work for? Shortly thereafter, I was left to go on my way, heading back to the safety of my hotel. A couple of metres towards my destination, another car screeched to a halt and three policemen got out. Again, the questions came and the trepidation built.

Speaking with the police, it transpired that they had been asked to find out who I was by people who regulated life across that part of town: Hizballah. Cameras had been installed across Dahiyeh out of fear that there would be an attack and there was a liaison agreement in place between the Lebanese state police and Hizballah concerning security in that part of Beirut and power lay with the latter. After answering a few questions, I was once again free to go. This time, I took a taxi back to my hotel in Hamra, where I remained for the afternoon. On 12 November 2015, less than four months after my visit, a devastating suicide attack killed 43 people and injured a further 200. The attack was claimed by Da'ish.

My experiences in Beirut provided a first-hand account of how sovereign power in Lebanon is contested. Hizballah is often referred to as a 'state within a state', but in this case the *quasi* state was collaborating with formal state institutions to maintain its security. For a state that had endured a fifteen-year long civil war in the not too distant past, such collaboration appeared promising. Yet the Party of God's involvement in the Syrian war in support of the embattled President, Bashar Al Assad, proved deeply unpopular back home, increasing fears of a retreat back into sectarian violence.

Lebanese politics has long been characterised by religious difference that is built into the very fabric of the state, embedded in a constitution that shares power along sectarian lines. This organisation of political life has left the state open to the geopolitical aspirations of others, leading to the penetration of Lebanese politics by Syria, Iran, Saudi Arabia, Israel and others, resulting in the conflation of domestic and regional politics. Regulating life, a key part of a sovereign's responsibilities, becomes increasingly difficult in such contexts, where the spread of identities and religious groups provides opportunities for a range of actors to wield influence and highlights the fragility of states across the region. It is this struggle to regulate life amid instances of contested sovereignty across the Middle East that is the main focus of this book.

A growing body of work quickly emerged in the aftermath of the Arab Uprisings, the spate of protests that cut across the Middle East in early 2011. The literature on the uprisings spans a range of different theoretical, ontological and epistemological positions, raising a number of important questions about the hows, whys and whens of the recent past. While each set of protests was driven by the theme of human dignity and greater political access, demands were shaped by local context. Economic concerns, contested ruling bargains, seemingly endemic corruption and deepening ties between regimes and Western states all increased anger and discontentment among peoples, but with particular grievances serving to mobilise people. In spite of this contextual difference, the target of the protesters' ire was largely the same: the state. With this in mind, to understand the onset of the Arab Uprisings, we must begin by exploring ideas of sovereignty and political organisation in the form of the state.

While a great deal of work has focused upon questions of (in)security, a growing body of literature across a range of disciplines questions the centrality of *the state* and the role of *religion* within political life. It is here where I situate this book, albeit with a slightly different focus. The role of the state in the contemporary Middle East has long been contested, from the suggestion that its importance as a form of political organisation has been imposed or overstated, to the Realist position that places the state as central to all of political life.

A growing body of literature emerges that talks about the (re)emergence of the 'weak' Arab state amid myriad challenges to its sovereignty, from both above and below. As Bassel Salloukh has noted, the overlapping of domestic, transnational and geopolitical factors has created a scenario where as states consolidated, they not only had to balance against material threats but also against ideational threats. Such overlapping had been commonplace during the 1950s and 1960s but following the 2003 US-led invasion of Iraq, the regional landscape took on many of those characteristics.[1] In the years after the Arab Uprisings, such pressures increased as states became increasingly unable to address – and balance – the competing pressures, fragmenting and creating opportunities for others to interfere within their borders.

Geopolitical struggles for Syria, Yemen and Iraq pitted regional and international powers against each other, with a devastating impact on local politics penetrated by actors and their allies. This transformation was fuelled by increasingly vitriolic difference that took on new meaning with the emergence of a geopolitical struggle between Saudi Arabia and Iran that conflated regime interest with religious identity.[2]

It is easy to reduce the contemporary Middle East to a struggle between Sunni actors led by Saudi Arabia and Shi'a actors led by Iran, but the region is far more complex than this,[3] where local identities interact with national, ethnic and religious denominations, while underpinned by class and ideology. Moreover, we must be careful not to deny local agency within the environment of this regional struggle. Instead, as we shall see, space is shaped by the complex interaction of regional and local actors, meaning that domestic political wrangling takes place within the context of geopolitical struggles between actors whose networks transcend state borders, often underpinned by shared religious values.

With this in mind, it is important to consider the role of religion within society, which raises a number of important philosophical and practical considerations. Scholars as far back as Ibn Khaldun have focused upon the social power of religion, which, as the twentieth century developed, became increasingly important. At the turn of the century, religion was largely seen as a private matter, yet in the postcolonial period, a number of regimes used the legitimising ideologies of religion to support their claims to self-determination. Religion took on an increasing *political* importance, leading to the emergence of competition between the nationalist movements of pan-Arabists who advocated the supremacy of the state and the Islamists who argued that sovereignty was found in God.

This religious revival challenged the fragile relationship between peoples and their nascent national projects, also serving as an outlet for political dissent. This struggle would be at the heart of political life in the years that followed. Yet this was not a singular struggle between those advocating the sovereignty of the state and those espousing the sovereignty of God, but complicated by a range of often competing interpretations about the role of Islam within political life.

Islamists, broadly speaking, believe that Islam and Islamic values should play a central role within public life. Although a broad phenomenon, we can view Islamists as those who hold that their faith provides strong political and legal guidelines beyond the moral code adhered to by all Muslims. Becoming an Islamist is a conscious act, affirming membership to a particular ideology. It is not just a response to modernity but it is also a product of it. The basic premise of Islamist movements is to locate Islam and its moral and legal codes with the fabric of the nation state. What that looks like in practice is a consequence of context and contingency, determined by the socio-economic politics of the state and the power of the group itself. As such, Islamists in Iran, Gaza, Lebanon and Saudi Arabia have vastly different visions of the relationship between Islam and the state, shaped by context and contingency. Difference is a consequence of the interaction of various factors that are context specific, such as class, nationality and ethnicity alongside the individual – and community's – interpretation of Islam, and right to do so.

Some Islamists also possess cross-border networks and aspirations, challenging political organisation across the Middle East in the process. Although groups including the Muslim Brotherhood (and its affiliates) and Hizballah (and its networks) both operate across the region, they fall broadly within the rubric of the sovereign state's system and engage in electoral politics. Other groups who also fall within broad definitions of

Islamism include those who conduct what they hold to be religiously sanctioned warfare as a consequence of their obligations. Even those who carry out such acts range from those with a fundamentalist Salafi vision to the Sufis, via those who lack a classical Islamic education.

Perhaps the most obvious point of tension, however, is the emergence of politically, economically and socially charged sectarian difference across and within spatial borders. The struggle between Sunni and Shi'a communities is politically charged, fusing faith with political identities and geopolitical aspirations. Competing views of sectarian difference exist, from the primordialist who reduces difference to faith, to the constructivist who views identities as constructed phenomena. Yet this is not purely an academic debate. Speaking in 2013, President Obama referred to 'ancient hatreds' in explaining the underlying reasons for the Syrian conflict, ignoring the lack of political space and the increasing barbarism of the regime.

Writing in 2015, Naser Ghobadzdeh and Shahram Akbarzadeh noted that,

> Once othering becomes part of politico-religious discourse, it moves to all levels of society, transforming itself into as much a bottom-up as a top-down process. Over the course of time, othering rhetoric has expanded beyond theology to become a decisive part of political, social, religious and economic reality.[4]

Ghobadzdeh and Akbarzadeh's point is astute. The politicisation of sectarian difference has given such identities almost existential importance within – and across – territorial borders, resulting in not only top-down but bottom-up constructions of othering, shaped by context-specific contingent factors. Put another way, the factors that shape sectarian difference are radically different in Lebanon than they are in Bahrain, Egypt, Jordan or Saudi Arabia. In each of these states, local historiographies give particular meaning to communal groups – shaped by social, political and economic contexts – which can result in distinct manifestations of difference when interacting with sectarian meta-narratives. There is, of course, a marked difference between the two sects and people who bear those identities, but there is nothing inherently violent about such difference. Instead, sectarian difference appears to be an inescapable phenomenon that *ignites* amid socio-political upheaval, uncertainty and fear, finding traction amid fragmentation.

As Fanar Haddad observes, the concept of sectarianism appears to be merely a *slogan*, deriving meaning in the eye of the beholder. In a powerful piece that documents the use of over a hundred scholarly sources on the subject of sectarianism, Haddad argues that the concept 'lacks and eludes definition', giving it an amorphous quality that allows it to be used almost indiscriminately to label anything related to sect identity.[5] A great deal of this scholarly literature seeks to define the concept, although a large body of literature follows Haddad's lead and chooses not to define a concept that has become too politicised and emotionally charged to possess analytic clarity. Locating myself in this camp, I follow Haddad by deploying the term *sectarian* with an adjoining word when necessary but aiming for the greatest level of precision and analytic clarity as possible.

A deeper problem of latent Orientalism within Western analysis of the Middle East adds to these problems. As Geneive Abdo observes, Western analysis is beset by two serious problems. The first is a 'flagrant tendency' to dismiss the abiding importance of religion. The second is the continued desire to view the nation-state model as the 'proper vehicle' of political organisation.[6] Both views emerge from post-Enlightenment European history, ignoring the local historiographies of the region and projecting norms on to a region with its own unique normative and cultural history. Such issues, both philosophical and empirical, are prevalent across a great deal of the literature written in the recent past. In times of crisis and uncertainty, political landscapes and social contracts are redrawn. The toppling of a number of Arab leaders in the aftermath of the popular protests in 2011 prompted a burgeoning literature detailing the events and the violence that swiftly followed.[7] Yet very little work has been undertaken placing the protests within the context of political dissent and contestation across the Middle East in the twentieth and twenty-first centuries.

In George Orwell's magnum opus *1984*, the Party slogan, 'Who controls the past controls the future. Who controls the present controls the past', seeks to restrict agency. Such comments also evoke memories of Walter Benjamin, who noted that history is written by the victors. History is important. History provides a narrative that justifies action, which supports claims to legitimacy and, ultimately, power. Often this involves attempts to rewrite history, such as the order given by the Egyptian President Gamal Abd Al Nasser to destroy all evidence of Egypt's military activity in Yemen.

Political projects are amorphous entities, constructed and shaped through the interaction of countless actors and social forces. Understanding the emergence of political projects and the sovereign claims that underpin them requires an exploration of the processes of state building. Such mechanisms have rarely proved inclusive; instead, they have typically been inherently exclusionary, leading to people struggling for basic needs. Complicated by the precariousness of modernity, the struggle for certainty pushes people to a range of different identities and ideologies in search for meaning. Amid such factors, regimes seek to maintain power, using a range of logics of governmentality to do so. To understand such techniques, I draw on the work of a number of scholars including Giorgio Agamben, Hannah Arendt, Gilles Deleuze and Felix Guattari, Achille Mbembe, Khaldun, Robert Cover and Peter Berger, whose work allows for rigorous exploration of the relationship between rulers and ruled and the construction of political projects.[8]

In order to achieve this task, it is necessary, at times, to paint with a broad brush, meaning that a number of important incidents are either covered briefly or not at all. This is not a reflection of the importance of such events but rather, the need to be selective in the examples considered to facilitate analysis of events across the region. I have deployed a broad but implicit comparative framework where I select events not only based on similarity but also difference to provide a region-wide analysis of events. Although the Arab Uprisings were trigged by the actions of a Tunisian street vendor, this book does not engage with events in North Africa, for reasons of scope and analytical clarity.

In support of this, I draw upon fieldwork conducted across the Middle East between 2011 and 2018, along with interviews conducted with a range of people via phone, Skype and email from a range of groups in an effort to understand their relationship with political structures. All names have been removed to maintain anonymity and after a number of worrying events, locations have also been removed in an attempt to ensure safety. This empirical material is supported by tweets, diplomatic cables (released by WikiLeaks), speeches, constitutions and secondary literature in English, Arabic and Persian. I also draw upon material from my time as specialist advisor to the House of Lords International Relations Committee, which produced a report on the UK's relationship with the Middle East entitled *Time for a New Realism*. In this role I was involved in selecting expert witnesses and writing questions for witness sessions. The committee drew expert testimony from ambassadors, civil society leaders, academics, policymakers, and a round table of 'young people'. I have not included any confidential material or referred to private sessions of the committee.

At times, this book seeks to offer a historiography of claims to sovereignty, yet it should not be read solely as such. Nor should it be taken as purely a work of political theory. Instead, I seek to combine the two to offer an approach to understanding the contemporary Middle East that uses political theory to deconstruct claims to sovereignty. In doing this, I hope to explore the claims and mechanisms through which life is regulated. Central to this are the following questions:

- What are the roots of sovereign power and what are the logics of governmentality that support it?
- When, how and why is sovereign power contested?
- What implications does the fragmentation of sovereign power have on the ordering of space across the Middle East?

With this in mind, the book is split across eight chapters. Chapter 1 engages with debates about sovereignty in the contemporary Middle East, interrogating ideas of *space* and *nomos* in the process of suggesting that amid shared normative environments, what happens within the borders of one state can have repercussions beyond the state. Chapter 2 offers a genealogy of states across the twentieth and twenty-first centuries, focusing upon the establishment of states amid competing pressures of decolonisation, pan-Arabism, pan-Islamism and nationalism. It then considers how political projects exist and operate amid regional and international pressures such as the War on Terror and the Arab Uprisings.

Chapter 3 explores the development of political structures and the means through which regimes exert sovereign power, through cultivating the ban, exclusion and eviscerating political meaning from life. Chapter 4 engages with the role of religion within political life and sovereign projects broadly. It interrogates a key source of sovereign tension and the space of possibility that emerges as a consequence. Chapter 5 looks at the urban environment. With a large majority of the region's population living in cities, urban landscapes become a prominent arena through which politics plays out.

Chapter 6 explores the Arab Uprisings, placing them in historical context and suggesting that they are the latest manifestation of long-standing grievances that have emerged as a fundamental consequence of building political projects. Chapter 7 looks at regime responses to the Arab Uprisings, ranging from reform and the stripping of meaning from political life to the emergence of war machines. Such variety reveals the multifarious stresses and pressures on regimes seeking to maintain power amid an array of societal pressures. Chapter 8 locates the domestic repercussions of the Arab Uprisings and their aftermath within broader Middle Eastern geopolitical and normative environments.

Central to all chapters is a focus upon the role of agency. The uprisings were triggered by the actions of a single individual whose act of resistance inspired the region-wide contestation of sovereign power. In the face of biopolitics and necropolitics, the power of agency appears limited, yet we should never underestimate the ability of one person or one idea to facilitate change. Fundamentally, the book argues that the Arab Uprisings were (the latest) manifestations of sovereign contestation that can be traced across state-building projects in the Middle East.

Notes

1 Bassel Salloukh, 'Overlapping Contests and Middle East International Relations: The Return of the Weak Arab State' (POMEPS, 12.08.15), available at https://pomeps.org/2015/08/12/overlapping-contests-and-middle-east-international-relations-the-return-of-the-weak-arab-state/#_edn13 (accessed 18.08.15).
2 Simon Mabon, *Saudi Arabia and Iran: Soft Power Rivalry in the Middle East* (London: I. B. Tauris, 2013).
3 Curtis Ryan, 'The New Arab Cold War and the Struggle for Syria', *Middle East Report*, 42 (2012), 262, available at www.merip.org/mer/mer262/new-arab-cold-war-struggle-syria (accessed 06.01.03).
4 Naser Ghobadzadeh and Shahram Akbarzadeh, 'Sectarianism and the Prevalence of "Othering" in Islamic Thought', *Third World Quarterly*, 36 (2016), 700.
5 Fanar Haddad, '"Sectarianism" and Its Discontents in the Study of the Middle East', *Middle East Journal*, 71:3 (2017), 363.
6 Geneive Abdo, *The New Sectarianism: The Arab Uprisings and the Rebirth of the Shi'a-Sunni Divide* (Oxford: Oxford University Press, 2017), p. 9.
7 See Marc Lynch, *The Arab Uprising: The Unfinished Revolutions of the New Middle East* (New York: Public Affairs, 2012); Tariq Ramadan, *Islam and the Arab Awakening* (Oxford: Oxford University Press, 2012); Mehran Kamrava, *Inside the Arab State* (London: Hurst, 2018); Yassin Al Haj Saleh, *The Impossible Revolution: Making Sense of the Syrian Tragedy* (London: Hurst, 2017); Hamid Dabashi, *The Arab Spring: The End of Postcolonialism* (London: Zed, 2012); Asef Bayat, *Revolution Without Revolutionaries: Making Sense of the Arab Spring* (Palo Alto, CA; Stanford University Press, 2017); Toby Matthiesen, *Sectarian Gulf: Bahrain, Saudi Arabia and the Arab Spring That Wasn't* (Palo Alto, CA; Stanford University Press, 2013); Kristian Coates Ulrichsen, *Qatar and the Arab Spring* (London: Hurst, 2014); Christopher Davidson, *After the Sheikhs: The Rise and Coming Fall of the Arab Gulf Monarchies* (London: Hurst, 2012); Nimer Sultany, *Law and Revolution: Legitimacy and Constitutionalism After the Arab Spring* (Oxford: Oxford University Press, 2017); Nader Hashemi and Danny Postel (eds), *Sectarianization: Mapping the New Politics of the Middle East* (London: Hurst, 2017); André Bank, Thomas Richter and Anna

Sunik, 'Durable, Yet Different: Monarchies in the Arab Spring', *Journal of Arabian Studies*, 4:2 (2014), 163–79; Asef Bayat, 'Arab Revolutions and the Study of Middle Eastern Societies', *International Journal of Middle East Studies*, 43:3 (2011), 386; Eva Bellin, 'Reconsidering the Robustness of Authoritarianism in the Middle East: Lessons from the Arab Spring', *Comparative Politics*, 44:2 (2012), 127–49; Nathan Brown, 'Remembering Our Roots', *International Journal of Middle East Studies*, 43:3 (2011), 388; Francesco Cavatorta, 'No Democratic Change … and Yet No Authoritarian Continuity: The Inter-Paradigm Debate and North Africa After the Uprisings', *British Journal of Middle Eastern Studies*, 42:1 (2014), 1–11; Vincent Durac, 'Protest Movements and Political Change: An Analysis of the "Arab Uprisings" of 2011', *Journal of Contemporary African Affairs*, 31:2 (2013), 175–93;
Tamirace Fakhoury, 'Do Power-Sharing Systems Behave Differently Amid Regional Uprisings? Lebanon in the Arab Protest Wave', *Middle East Journal*, 68:4 (2014), 505–20; F. Gregory Gause III, 'Why Middle East Studies Missed the Arab Spring: The Myth of Authoritarian Stability', *Foreign Affairs*, 90:4 (2011), 81–90; Shadi Hamid, 'The Rise of the Islamists: How Islamists Will Change Politics, and Vice Versa', *Foreign Affairs*, 90:3 (2011), 40–7; Sari Hanafi, 'The Arab Revolutions: The Emergence of a New Political Subjectivity', *Contemporary Arab Affairs*, 5:2 (2012), 198–213; Adam Hanieh, 'Shifting Priorities or Business as Usual? Continuity and Change in the Post-2011 IMF and World Bank Engagement with Tunisia, Morocco and Egypt', *British Journal of Middle Eastern Studies*, 42:1 (2014): 1–16; Raymond Hinnebusch, 'Historical Sociology and the Arab Uprising', *Mediterranean Politics*, 19:1 (2014), 137–40; Raymond Hinnebusch, 'Syria: From "Authoritarian Upgrading" to Revolution?', *International Affairs*, 88:1 (2012), 95–113; Raymond Hinnebusch, 'Change and Continuity After the Arab Uprising: The Consequences of State Formation in Arab North African States', *British Journal of Middle Eastern Studies*, 42:1 (2014): 1–19.

8 Although incredibly powerful, the ideas of these scholars have only sparingly been applied to the Middle East and, when they have, they typically take place looking at specific issues rather than a broader engagement with political life and sovereign power more generally. This reveals a desire to focus upon particular manifestations of *the camp* – a key theme in Agamben's work – rather than a broader exploration of the camp as the hidden paradigm of modernity. For example, Agamben's work has been used to explore refugee camps in Palestine and Lebanon – spaces of exception – but has not yet been applied more broadly while Mbmembe's work has been used to explore life in Palestine. See for example: Adam Ramadan 'Destroying Nahr el-Bared: Sovereignty and Urbicide in the Space of Exception', *Political Geography* 28:3 (2009), 153–63; Sara Fregonese, 'The Urbicide of Beirut? Geopolitics and the Built Environment in the Lebanese Civil War (1975–1976)', *Political Geography*, 28:5 (2009), 309–18; and Eyal Weizman, *Hollow Land: The Architecture of Israel's Occupation* (New York: Verso, 2012), among others. Although questions about the use of such a plurality of theoretical positions are legitimate, these authors are broadly interested in the same type of questions and Agamben, Arendt, Mbembe, Deleuze and Guattari all work from the same ontological position.

1

The politics of sovereignty and space[1]

Politics, for the Arab philosopher Khaldun, concerns 'the administration of home or city in accordance with ethical and philosophical requirements, for the purpose of directing the mass toward a behaviour that will result in the preservation and permanence of the (human) species'.[2] This quest for survival, at the heart of Khaldun's understanding of politics, raises a number of fundamental questions about space, law, security and ultimately survival, which remain pertinent today. The questions emerging from Khaldun's work are certainly apt when discussing the contemporary Middle East, where the construction of political organisation has been directed towards the regulation of life. This chapter explores the way in which life has been regulated across the space of sovereign states, drawing on the work of Giorgio Agamben, Hannah Arendt, Robert Cover, Gilles Deleuze and Felix Guattari.

Although the concept of the sovereign state is one that is traditionally associated with European political philosophy, states have manifested across the region as the contemporary form of political organisation, replacing the tribe, *umma*, *khalifa* and sultanate, which had regulated life prior to the demise of the Ottoman Empire. According to Charles Tilly, the dominance of the European view is a consequence of three hundred years of Europeans and their descendants imposing their system on the world.[3] Of course, states that were imposed three hundred years ago are vastly different to their modern relations, stemming from developments in all forms of life; the modern nation state is an altogether different beast albeit one that continues to interact with the legacy and memory of what came before.

Debate over the imposition and the creation of artificial political projects by external powers – referred to as 'the original sin of state creation' by Ghassan Salame – has been a prominent feature of discussions of state formation and state building in the politics of the region.[4] While often viewed as artificial entities and condemned as impotent, states largely remain intact into the twenty-first century, predicated upon a range of context-specific contingent factors that shape the nature of social contracts and political life. Yet questions about the very nature of the state and sovereignty continue to dominate intellectual discussion.

A great deal of work has been undertaken on states and their claims to sovereign power. Focusing on the Middle East, scholars including Nazih N. Ayubi, Roger Owen, Lisa Anderson, Charles Tripp, Sami Zubaida, Fred Halliday, Philip S. Khoury, Joseph Kostiner, Raymond Hinnebusch and Fouad Ajami (among others) have all engaged with such projects with a variety of different conclusions.[5] Although taking divergent theoretical, ontological and conceptual approaches, these works trace the development and interaction of states, peoples, bureaucracies and ideologies, focusing upon different loci of power and the spatial repercussions of such projects.

Acknowledging the important contributions made by these authors, I endorse Joel Migdal's definition of the state as:

> [An] organization, composed of numerous agencies led and coordinated by the state's leadership (executive authority) that has the ability or authority to make and implement the binding rules for all the people as well as the parameters of rule making for other social organizations in a given territory.[6]

Following Charles Tripp, I also view the state as a consequence of performability, an ongoing process that refutes the 'fixed' nature of states. In accepting this, I view states as political projects that are shaped and reshaped by the context and contingency of spatial dynamics. In times of crisis, performances draw upon a range of different forms of symbolic capital to maintain or re-establish the state, yet such processes often lead to contestation within domestic borders and across the region.

State-building processes are typically understood by considering the work of Charles Tilly, whose thesis 'war made the state and the state made war' offers a convincing account of the development of state institutions.[7] Within debate and reflection on the nature of statehood, comparisons are often made with European states and the Weberian 'ideal' type, which bring together concepts of security, welfare and representation. Yet as Rolf Schwarz argues, perhaps this ideal type is the exception, not the rule; instead, regulating interactions in a number of context-specific ways.[8] While the Middle East has been shaped, and perhaps in the middle of the twentieth century characterised, by violent conflict, territorial gain was not always the primary goal.[9] The rapid militarisation of the Middle East supports this premise, increasing insecurity as a consequence, yet closer examination reveals that conflict has been facilitated by the massive extraction of rent derived from natural resources[10] often viewed as 'the gift from nature' facilitating regime survival.

Within debate on political systems and state–society relations in the Middle East there is typically a conflation between state, sovereign, government and regime. This is deeply problematic and before we move forward, we must quickly distinguish between different typologies. Regimes are more permanent representations of political organisation than governments or leaders, but they are less permanent than the state. Regimes typically pre-date both the state and nation[11] thus state- and nation-building projects are driven by regimes, with their own survival at the forefront of political projects. They are a product of their historical environment, shaped by the interaction of a number of competing identities and ideologies. With this in mind, the state is taken as a 'more permanent structure of domination and coordination including a coercive apparatus and the means to administer a society and extract resources from it'.[12] Thus, domestic sovereignty is the ability to regulate life based upon the context-specific relationship between ruler and ruled that is shaped by a range of contingent factors. Thus, to understand the emergence of states across the Middle East we must follow Albert Hourani's lead and retain that which was previously discarded.[13]

While discussion of statehood is certainly of paramount importance, it is here where I depart from other scholars, choosing instead to focus upon the concept of sovereignty as the lens through which interactions are regulated rather than discussing typologies of political organisation. As Talal Asad articulates, the state, 'independently of the entire population, embodies sovereignty'[14] but the separation of sovereignty from state poses a range of challenges. As Lisa Anderson notes in a brief bibliography on the concept of the state in the Arab world, this approach of ungluing sovereignty from statehood is potentially disconcerting on normative grounds as sovereign power may be 'reattached' to monarchs, princely families or even firms.[15] I do not go quite so far in my analysis. Instead, I argue that such an approach is necessary to understand the claims to power made by regimes and from this, the way in which political life is contested. Ultimately, focusing on sovereignty allows for exploration of political communities and their relationship with both territory and regional dynamics.

Inherent to the parabolic pressures that forge states are innumerable forms of contestation. To ensure survival, rulers have imposed political, legal and economic structures to secure their rule, creating order within space while also cultivating narratives to increase legitimacy and recognition among both internal and external audiences. Several states have referred to pan-state ideologies – Arabism and Islamism – in an effort to unite peoples across the region, which has often been driven by national interest.[16] More recently, ideas of sectarian unity have been used to construct membership of a shared community against an 'other' that is often perceived to possess nefarious intent. This reference to pan-state ideologies which transcend state borders and political organisation reveals the presence of a shared normative environment, which poses serious challenges to state sovereignty and the Westphalian principle of 'non-interference'.[17] Referring to leadership of the *umma*[18] has led some to suggest that *dawla* (states) have no real power and that true authority – sovereignty – can only be found in God and membership of the *umma*.

Such challenges emerging from the relationship between religion and politics are not restricted to Islam and are perhaps more obvious in the complex relationship between the state of Israel and myriad sects of Judaism, where competing visions of political organisation define the spatial limits of the state. The most prominent example of such contestation is apparent in the building of settlement outposts in the West Bank. which is sometimes undertaken by the state but also undertaken by groups contesting the state's authority. Organisations such a Gush Emunim and the Hilltop Youth have conducted 'price tag' attacks against the state and Palestinians while also rejecting the legitimacy of the state of Israel, in a number of cases, seeking to bring about its downfall. Recent estimates suggest that over five hundred thousand people live in settlements – some of which are sanctioned by the state – in the West Bank, with a growing number living in Area B, in breach of the Oslo Accords.[19] Of course, questions about the territorial limits of political organisation play an increasingly important role in the nature of state sovereignty and the relationship between regimes and people, within and across space.

From the Sykes–Picot agreement until the present day, external powers have played a prominent role in shaping the nature of regional politics and the daily life of individuals, albeit with tensions emerging between states and global economic forces.[20] The legacy of colonialism is easily seen in the development of political organisation across the region. From the residue of the Ottomans to mandates and the role of British agents across the Gulf, the prominence of external actors in shaping political structures must not be ignored.[21] For some, the very existence of the state is evidence of this colonial legacy, viewing the emergence of the contemporary state as the impact of Western forces. Yet in acknowledging such a position, one has to be careful not to deny native agency to those involved in political life, as local contexts feature prominently in the construction of political life and the regulation of space.

Penetration also takes place through the emergence of a global economy and actions of private companies and individuals who continue to reproduce economic, political and legal structures that feed into the (re)construction of the sovereign state. While the discovery of oil was heralded to facilitate autonomy and strength across the region, the patron–client relationships that emerged contributed to economic structures shaping dependency across the region.[22] Over time these relationships have changed, but patron–client relations continue to penetrate – and shape – the region, through helping define the spatial limits of political projects but also the capacity of sovereign power itself.[23]

The history of an idea

If one is asked to trace the roots of the sovereign state, one typically begins with the 1648 Peace of Westphalia, which established the principle of non-interference based upon the premise of states possessing exclusive authority within their territorial borders.[24] The peace treaties signed at Munster and Osnabruck established the inviolable norm of non-interference within the domestic affairs of other states, enshrining borders, security and order within relations between different states defined by spatial boundaries. Of course, the structure of such forms of organisation differs, shaped by time, space and local traditions, yet the principle of non-interference remains central.

Over the years, scholars have sought to trace the philosophical roots of sovereignty and with it, constituent parts of the idea, with a recent focus on the ordering of life. The opening line of *Political Theology*, Carl Schmitt's seminal work that would shape scholarly work on the concept of sovereignty in the coming years, clearly articulates his position: 'Sovereign is he who decides on the exception'.[25] Schmitt's thought posits the state of exception as a paradigm of government that, as Agamben later suggests, 'has today reached its full development'.[26]

Building upon Schmitt and Foucault – along with others including Hannah Arendt and Walter Benjamin – Agamben's *Homo Sacer* project is grounded in biopolitics, concerned with the organisation and control of human life through the governance power of the state. Ultimately, it is an approach concerned with inclusion through exclusion. Fundamental to this is the sovereign decision over where the law applies and where it does not. For Agamben, 'the rule, suspending itself, gives rise to the exception and, maintaining itself in relation to the exception, first constitutes itself as a rule'.[27]

Within this 'paradigm of government', Agamben suggests that the law 'encompasses living beings by means of its own suspension', controlling life through locating *bare life* at the forefront of politics, rejecting the rule of law in the process.[28] Fundamental to this line of thought is the idea that 'the state of exception is the preliminary condition for any definition of the relation that binds and at the same time abandons the living being to the law',[29] deciding which forms of life are worth living in the process.

As Agamben argues,

> [T]he realm of bare life – which is originally situated at the margins of the political order – gradually begins to coincide with the political realm, and exclusion and inclusion, outside and inside, *bios* and *zoe*, right and fact, enter into a zone of irreducible indistinction. At once excluding bare life from and capturing it within the political order, the state of exception actually constituted, in its very separateness, the hidden foundation on which the entire political system rested.[30]

Within the state of exception, the sovereign differentiates between the realms of *bios* and *zoe*, creating a binary distinction between those recognised as fully human through their participation in political life and those who are outside, where political life and meaning is stripped from them, creating a zone of indistinction and bare life. The marginalisation of people into the condition of bare life can occur as a consequence of a number of different processes, yet in attempting to escape these conditions, violent dislocations occur between regimes and society.

Central to Agamben's project is the idea of the camp, the 'hidden paradigm of the political space of modernity', a site of possibility as well as a specific area within which life is stripped of meaning.[31] The camp is a spatial-ontological arena, a space of possibility and the link between localisation and ordering. Fundamentally it is a spatial construct, existing beyond the normal juridical and governmental order, with implications for ordering international politics.[32] The camp emerges when the exception becomes the rule, in specific sites but also as a broader space of metaphysical possibility, which creates the conditions within which human life may be reduced to bare life.[33] Although a space of exception, the physical manifestation of the camp exists as a territorial area that lies beyond the juridical order, the production of a spatial exception, inscribing exclusion through inclusion.[34]

In *The Kingdom and the Glory*, Agamben builds upon these ideas, arguing that '*the real problem, the central mystery of politics is not sovereignty, but government ... it is not the law, but the police – that is to say, the governmental machine that they form and support*' (emphasis in original).[35] In a complex yet persuasive argument, he suggests that politics is comprised of the constituent parts of government structures that build the mechanisms of the state. Identifying and engaging with these structures is then imperative when considering political change and its processes.[36] This distinction between government machinery and those constrained by it provides an opportunity to differentiate between rulers and ruled, between regimes and society and it is here where we can build upon Agamben's work to allow for greater discussion of the contemporary Middle East.

In such conditions, the metaphysical constitution of the state, encapsulated in the concept of sovereignty, 'gives birth to law'[37] and ultimately, the state of exception and the ban. Legal structures, institutions and the zone of indistinction do not exist in a vacuum; rather, they are contingent upon and shaped by conditions and cultural relations that are prominent features of political organisation. Efforts to understand such dynamics in the aftermath of state formation have been all too quick to discard the legacy of tradition, as Hourani argues, disregarding what was retained[38] and what continued to shape interactions within the political and institutional fabric of the state. Such a position stresses the importance of considering both formal and normative structures in shaping the ban and the regulation of life.[39]

Yet in cases of severe contestation, the regulation of life is not sufficient as a means of articulating sovereign power. Although sovereign power exists within localised and ordered space, when spatial borders and the means through which space is ordered become contested, sovereign power too is called into question. An alternative logic of governmentality is posed by Achille Mbembe, who argues that in such cases, sovereign power is not just about the regulation of life but it is also the power over death, the systematic destruction of people and the subjugation of life to death, as 'the living dead'.[40] Central to Mbembe's theorisation is consideration of the following question: 'Under what practical conditions is the right to kill, to allow to live, or to expose to death exercised?'[41] This approach, referred to as *necropolitics*, builds on similar foundations to Agamben, taking it a step further to exert the power to control those who live and die.

The increasing prominence of work by scholars such as Agamben and Mbembe within international relations has stimulated a vibrant debate over the application of such ideas to the contemporary world.[42] One of the main points of tension in Agamben's work is concerned with his understanding of biopolitics, which builds upon Foucault's engagement with the term, seeking to 'correct' a number of factors, notably the idea that the rise of biopower heralded the emergence of modernity.[43] Instead, Agamben argues that politics is always biopolitical, as the political is shaped by the state of exception and its production of bare life. Another point of contention concerns the lack of development of this monolithic construction of bare life,[44] which can differ depending upon context and conditions. Nor does Agamben differentiate between liberal democratic regimes and totalitarian regimes; rather, he suggests that it is the division between *bios* and *zoe* that is the most important characteristic of political life.[45]

Perhaps the most damning criticism of Agamben's work concerns the role of agency and scope for resistance against structural conditions.[46] It is clear that structural factors are central to discussions of sovereignty and that agency operates within the confines of structural parameters. Yet Agamben's approach is guilty of restricting agency, removing socio-economic contexts that are essential for understanding the contingency and relativity of different situations. Even within restrictive conditions, individuals have the capacity to exercise agency, no matter how remote the possibility; and as a number of scholars note, even the refugee can exercise agency.[47] From this, amid the increasingly restrictive conditions of authoritarian rule, we can still speak of agency and the exception.

Agamben responds to this criticism by suggesting that agency is reasserted by taking ownership of the condition, as 'putting life into play'.[48] To claim ownership, one has to accept the conditions of 'being thus' and to acknowledge the conditions within which one exists. Even this lacks methodological development, failing to adequately explore the impact of agency upon structures, as agency also operates prior to being and both prior to and post restructuring. Returning agency to the discussion allows for a greater analysis of political activity and consideration of structural changes within society.

Agamben speaks of the destruction of identities (and agency) through desubjectivation and resubjectivation, the reshaping of destroyed identities. If individuals exercise agency then this is a resubjectivation of the self. In Agamben's work, sovereignty is fully constituted as the only conceptual space within which the logic of sovereignty is sound but this concept merges potentiality and being, where potentiality can only be viewed retroactively.[49] Slavoj Žižek's response to this is to suggest that there must be an act prior to being, 'overlooking the fact that the order of being is never simply given, but is itself grounded in some preceding Act'.[50] By accepting Žižek's point, we take sovereignty as a process that is ongoing in order to maintain logical consistency and by focusing upon the act, we are able to return agency to our project, albeit shaped by context and contingency.

In *The Use of Bodies*, Agamben engages with ontology and potentiality to suggest that sovereignty should be a process, an act that repeats itself, which supports both the need to do this and the scope for us to do so. With that in mind, the *process* of sovereignty is ongoing, continually regulating life, yet amid the fragmentation of political organisation, this regulation evolves into the subjugation of life to death. Ultimately, what remains central are regime struggles to retain power and exert sovereignty, using a range of different logics of governmentality. When it is contested, the mere regulation of life through the ban and exception suffice, yet when this contestation escalates, the regulation of life turns to subjugation of death. While sovereign projects are typically associated with territorial spaces that are central to the Westphalian state, amid fragmentation and contestation the parameters of space become disputed. As Mbembe suggests, space is 'the raw material of sovereignty and the violence it carried with it'.[51]

The fragmentation of sovereignty can result in existential transformation as life is displaced, often stripped of political meaning and reduced to bare life. It is within such conditions that we see the emergence of *war machines*, entities that challenge the rule-based form of political organisation. Developed by Gilles Deleuze and Felix Guattari, the concept of the war machine sits in opposition to the state, which exists as an apparatus of power distinct from societies. Seeking to reject the power of the state, particularly amid conditions of fragmentation, Deleuze and Guattari suggest that a new form of war emerges, akin to that conducted by nomads. The analogy used to denote this is between a game of chess and Go where the former codes and decodes space while the latter seeks to *territorialise* or *deterritorialise*.[52]

This form of war is often in tension with state apparatus but is also counter-hegemonic, applying as much to intellectual debate as to conflict.[53] War machines exist as the manifestation of disruption, operating against states, but also with the possibility of being incorporated into state structures. Within sites and spaces of exception, power is 'contracted' out, functioning as private organisations one stage removed from the state. The idea of the war machine evokes memories of a Hobbesian 'war of all against all' following the descent into the state of nature, particularly amid the fragmentation of political organisation.

The goal of the war machine is to bring everything back to the 'empty space' of what is seen as the primordial *tabula rasa*. As Deleuze and Guattari suggest, the war machine is 'a pure form of exteriority, whereas the State apparatus constitutes the form of interiority', the means through which space is coded and decoded: 'It is the State that makes possible the distinction between governors and governed'.[54] Fundamentally, 'the concern of the State is to conserve'[55] while the war machine aims to deterritorialise, seen in the *nomad* who challenges 'the rules and structures of the sedentarised form of political life, existing as a fundamental challenge to states, for whom a vital concern is to vanquish nomadism' and to 'establish a zone of rights over an entire "exterior"'.[56]

Operating through interaction with the state, the war machine challenges the ordering of space. The unappropriated war machine

> has as its object not war but the drawing of a creative line of flight, the composition of smooth space and of the movement of people in that space. At this other pole, the machine does indeed encounter war, but as its supplementary or synthetic object, now directed against the State and against the worldwide axiomatic expressed by the States.[57]

The manifestation of a war machine is irreducible to the state apparatus although, as we shall see, it may be appropriated by states, wherein previously autonomous social movements are harnessed by a regime, losing their deterritorialised essence in the process and embracing purposeless destruction.[58] It is beyond the scope of our project to go into these concepts in more detail, but the idea of war machines offers a conceptual tool to discuss mobilisation against state power – as a manifestation of exterior against interior – which, as we shall see in later chapters, plays a prominent role in times of contestation.

Space and *nomos*

While politics is inherently about people, space is the theatre within which interactions take place. It is simultaneously a physical environment, a semiotic abstraction, and relational.[59] These interactions exist within one another and coexist within power relations and social practices. Each society produces a space of its own nature along with a set of rules that regulate behaviour within space. The concept of space is deeply contested among scholars yet is central to understanding contemporary political organisation, from the camp to the city to the state. Each different definition contains within it sets of interactions and struggles for domination, which are context specific and shaped by a range of different contingent factors. Such a position bears the hallmarks of the work of Doreen Massey, who in *For Space* sets out three propositions that are central to our project. First, space is the product of a set of interactions and struggles that range from the 'intimately tiny' to the global. Second, space should be viewed as a sphere of possibility, heterogeneity and multiplicity. Third, that space is in a constant state of construction.[60] Through these interactions, what happens in one space can have implications for other spaces, transcending both political and normative environments.

The establishment of boundaries is fundamentally an attempt to stabilise meaning within space and time, although such efforts are sites of contestation, 'battles of the power to label space-time, to impose the meaning to be attributed to space'.[61] They are sites of contestation, arenas within which power is exerted.[62] Yet such things are not truly bounded, but rather in flux, ongoing processes of movement and evolution; social and dynamic, with scope for reproduction and transformation.[63] People operate and exist within such spaces, regulated by power relations and given meaning amid contestation and the definition of community by articulating an outside against which one is closed off, although amid fluid boundaries this closure is increasingly problematic. Although regimes and states are the actors that predominantly regulate space, they are not alone. When meaning is rejected it becomes contested amid efforts to (re)appropriate space. In doing this, rights become asserted through the performance of a new spatiality by contesting the regulatory mechanisms – the governmentality – of such spaces.

Agamben's *Homo Sacer* project is one that engages with profoundly spatial questions. Central to discussions of space and political life is *nomos*, a foundational ancient Greek concept used to denote 'a range or province, within which defined powers may be legitimately exercised'.[64] *Nomos* is subject of a range of (often competing) interpretations that facilitate the interrogation of *order*, *life* and existence.[65] Agamben's reading of *nomos* is influenced by Schmitt, whose treatise *The Nomos of the Earth* set out a view of world order that roots law to land, stressing fundamentally spatial characteristics through the interaction of *ortung* (localisation) and *ordnung* (ordering).[66] Schmitt's understanding of *nomos* views it as 'the original spatial order, the source of all further concrete order and further law. It is the reproductive root in the normative order of history'.[67]

Schmitt's ideas come out of the end of the Second World War and are underpinned by his views on *the political* and a fundamental concern with order. In his view, politics was the 'art of *ordering*' (emphasis in original), the localisation and ordering of space.[68] This, for geographers such as Claudio Minca and Rory Rowan, demonstrates Schmitt's spatial turn, as such events take place *within* space, but also *shape* space. In this view, land appropriation was the foundational act of existence, resulting in the belief that the *nomos* was a fundamentally ontological act, an original spatialisation.[69] Schmitt's work suggests that *nomos* is a consequence of the interaction between *ordnung* and *ortung*, between space and ordering and while this interaction is important, it suffers through Schmitt's failure to acknowledge both the importance of agency and norms. Indeed, as John Agnew argues, the very idea of the state as the manifestation of political organisation requires drawing upon shared histories and cultural legacies in an attempt to create order within space.[70]

In contrast, for Agamben, *nomos* is the localisation of the unlocalisable, the immediate form through which Schmitt's axiom that 'the political and social order of a people becomes spatially visible' rings true.[71] Concepts of *polis* and *nomos* are thus fundamentally interrelated, shaped by spatial concerns. As Deleuze and Guattari argue,

> [T]he State itself has always been in a relation with an outside, and is inconceivable independent of that relationship. The law of the State is not the law of All or Nothing (State-societies *or* counter-State societies), but that of interior and exterior. The State is sovereignty. But sovereignty only reigns over what it is capable of internalizing, of appropriating locally.[72]

Building on Schmitt, Agamben adds the nation as an additional dimension of discussions about the *nomos*,[73] suggesting that the global *nomos* is a product of neo-liberal modernity, the spatial manifestation of the unlocalisable exception. Yet within this global *nomos* are individual spatial orderings – *nomoi* – characterised by the global *nomos* yet given meaning by the context and contingency of space and local agency.[74] Countless identities, ideologies and beliefs exist often with competing views of political organisation, emerging in the relationships that people have to the governance structures of the state and the way in which people live their lives. Such a view means that although existing within a global *nomos*, there are other *nomoi* – with spatial characteristics – that order communities; it is the spatial characteristic that differentiates *nomos* and *nomoi* from norms. The manifestation of sovereign power is contingent on the organisation of such spaces – particularly in the postcolonial world – brought to life by Schmitt's ideas about the interaction between *ordnung* and *ortung*. This position suggests that we must not only focus more on the normative aspect of *nomos* but also engage with questions about the very concept of community.

Communities are central not only to discussions of *nomos* but also to the very nature of political organisation. As Hans Lindahl argues, 'no political community is imaginable … that does not close itself off as an inside over against an outside. Moreover, and no less importantly, by closing itself off as an inside with respect to an outside, a community posits a space as its own'.[75] Here, not only does the closing off define the metaphysical aspects of a community and with it, the rules that regulate it, but also the space that a community resides in. Such a definition is not fixed, however, but is predicated upon ongoing subjective interactions that establish principles and institutions.[76] Moreover, in closing off space against an outside, the possibility of citizenship is conditioned through membership of a shared community.

For Hannah Arendt, 'all legislation creates first of all a space in which it is valid, and this place is the world in which can move in freedom. What lies outside this space is lawless and properly speaking without a world'.[77] In *On Revolution*, the importance of spatially bounded territory for the establishment of a political community and the rules that regulate life are acknowledged.[78] Here, however, we can see parallels with the work of Khaldun, who makes similar claims about the importance of boundaries and the normative ordering of space:

> [1] The world is a garden the fence of which is the dynasty. [2] The dynasty is an authority through which life is given to proper behaviour. [3] Proper behaviour is a policy directed by the ruler. [4] The ruler is an institution supported by the soldiers. [5] The soldiers are helpers who are maintained by money. [6] Money is sustenance brought together by subjects. [7] The subjects are servants who are protected by justice. [8] Justice is something familiar, and through it the world persists. The world is a garden.[79]

This approach evokes ideas of the need for a reflexive reading of *nomos* of the sort advocated by Hans Lindahl, stressing the ongoing relationship of *ordnung* and *ortung* and between *nomos* and *nomoi*. This dialectic relationship has occupied a central role in the establishment and evolution of political projects across the past century.

Building on this and the notion that the closure of space conditions the possibility of citizenship, Arendt argues that the world gains meaning through the interaction of people, their words and deeds.[80] This world building is an essential part of the closure of an inside against an outside, stressing the importance of the normative within *nomos* and political community. Put another way, as Robert Cover argues, 'to inhabit a *nomos* is to know how to *live* in it'.[81] Knowing how to live requires awareness of both the formal and normative structures that can regulate life: the political, legal and economic structures that are designed and implemented by regimes, along with the normative structures that can be harnessed by both regimes and communities for a range of ends. In harnessing the normative, myths, narratives and histories can be moulded and put to use in 'meaningful patterns' to regulate behaviour and can be passed across generations, learned, developed and moulded.

Yet as Cover acknowledges, the establishment of such a *nomos* brings with it its own unavoidable demise, amid debate around interpretation, creed, identity and practice. Thus, a fleeting instant of emergence as objective meaning creates a template for 'a thousand real integrations'.[82] Take, for example, faith and membership of a religious community. Beyond that immediate moment of shared belief, a plurality of interpretations exist that differ in practice, leading to contestation and a struggle to regulate political life and meaning. For Cover,

> Legal precepts and principles are not only demands made upon us by society, the people, the sovereign, or God. They are also signs by which each of us

communicates with others. There is a difference between sleeping late on Sunday and refusing the sacraments, between having a snack and desecrating the fast of Yom Kippur, between banking a check and refusing to pay your income tax. In each case an act signifies something new and powerful when we understand that the act is in reference to a norm. It is this characteristic of certain lawbreaking that gives rise to special claims for civil disobedients. But the capacity of law to imbue action with significance is not limited to resistance or disobedience. Law is a resource in signification that enables us to submit, rejoice, struggle, pervert, mock, disgrace humiliate, or dignify.[83]

Similar arguments can be made about Islam and interpretations of Quran, Sunna and hadith. While some claims are fundamental – such as *tawahid*, the oneness of God – transgression is also justified within the Quran, leading to numerous possible interpretations.[84]

Of course, different contexts and their socio-economic, historical, cultural contingencies only serve to facilitate transgression and diffusion; for example, a Muslim in the UK has a different set of experiences and context-specific practices to a Muslim in Indonesia, while a Muslim in Israel has a different way of life to a Muslim in Oman. At a more micro level, a Sunni Muslim in Saudi Arabia will have a different set of beliefs, practices and experiences to a Shi'a Muslim from the same state. The *nomos* then becomes the arena for the interaction of a set of normative structures predicated upon a shared belief and fleeting moment of unity, resulting in a process of tension and reconciliation that plays out in the community. From this we can see how ideas easily transcend the territorially grounded *polis*, leading to challenges to the sovereign state, the global *nomos* and competing interpretations of *ordnung* and *ortung*, although this challenges the idea of a political community as closed off as an inside against an outside, contesting sovereign power in the process.

Yet when considering how different communities emerge that seek to close themselves off as an inside against an outside, tensions arise between different visions of the inside and the extent to which normative ordering finds traction in space. Such an extension can be applied to the building of collective identities, although tensions can emerge when state formation clashes with tribal or religious loyalties. Here, much like Sophocles' *Antigone*, individuals may find themselves caught between the law of the state and the normative values that regulate life.[85] Moreover, when groups seek to close themselves off against an *outside* within the *inside*, political projects face existential challenges. Here, competing visions of the ordering of space emerge from within, stemming either from the transient nature of *nomos* or from competing efforts to order space. This problem was identified historically by Khaldun who stressed the importance of *asabiyyah* as a form of *collective* membership, transcending the loyalty to family and group.[86] Of course, amid contestation and fragmentation, *asabiyyah* breeds *asabiyyah* as family, tribe and group become pitted against each other.

Yet Arendt's words can be applied on a grander scale: 'the organisation of the people as it arises out of acting and speaking together, and its true space lies between people living together for this purpose, no matter where they happen to be … can find its proper location almost anytime and anywhere'.[87] Rather than people directly living together, it can be applied to people living *according to the same rules* regardless of the spatial location and the contingent factors that shape those rules. The concept of *nomos* helps us to understand membership of this type of community, not necessarily territorially grounded, but underpinned by a set of normative beliefs that regulates life and shapes political behaviour, closing off a metaphysical inside against an outside with implications for the spatialised *nomos*.[88]

A final observation must be made about the impact of closing off an inside against an outside on the construction of citizenship and the ordering of space. Fundamentally, *nomos* cannot include without *excluding* and while this predominantly takes place against other communities, it can also concern individuals who are displaced from the inside. While citizenship is the manifestation of inclusion, *statelessness* is the dominant form of displacement, facilitated by racial undertones.[89] There is no form of self-inclusion without a measure of self-exclusion.[90] Here we see how sovereign power can operate and order space, giving life meaning through inclusion within the political life of a community, but also stripping it of this meaning through a form of exclusion.

As we shall see in the coming chapters, *nomos* is shaped by local context and contingency, which in the Middle East results in challenges to the spatial and ordering aspects of the regulation of life. Authority can be claimed by various individuals and groups, including family hierarchies, tribal leaders, religious officials, regional officers, employers and rulers but when applied to the sovereign state, it is assumed that these forms of authority have coalesced into a hierarchical structure within a particular territory. Across the Middle East, regime authority – and autonomy – can be challenged by actors operating both at a sub-state and supra-state level who are often able to lay more convincing claims to authority, legitimacy or power. With a rich normative environment serving as a means of legitimising rule that does not directly correspond with the geographic spaces of the sovereign state, what happens in domestic spaces can – and does – have regional consequences.

A further challenge emerges where regimes are unable to compete with strong societies in what Joel Migdal termed a struggle between *strong societies* and *weak states*.[91] Weak states are those who are unable to enforce governance structures, to '*penetrate* society, *regulate* social relationships, *extract* resources, and *appropriate* or use resources in determined ways' (emphasis added), where social forces stymie efforts at exerting authority.[92] It should be noted that structures that regulate authority can be both formal and normative – including but not limited to political, legal, economic, normative and religious – stemming from a range of sources. Essentially, the crux of Migdal's claim is that states and societies compete for social control, practices and norms, influencing each other in the process.

As Marisela Montenegro and Joan Pujol suggest, contemporary manifestations of governmentality resort to different logics of sovereignty in an attempt to maintain power and order. For Montenegro and Pujol, this modern governmentality

combines biopolitical and necropolitical logics to establish social, political and physical borders that classify and stratify populations using symbolic and material marks ... The safeguarding of worthy populations is enacted and justified by pointing to potentially threatening events and declaring 'state of exception'.[93]

Thus, we can see how sovereign and governmental logics set out by Agamben and Mbembe can be taken alongside one another, contingent on the intricacies of time and space. Underpinning these approaches, however, is the cultivation of an other, a racism that in Mbembe's words, can 'regulate the distribution of death and to make possible the murderous functions of the state'.[94] A direct consequence of this is the creation of new forms of subjugation.

Sovereignty, space and *nomos* in the Middle East

The history of political organisation across the Middle East is one of contestation. Efforts to maintain control amid an array of competing pressures from various locations reveals a range of different logics of governmentality that are key to ensuring survival. Interrogating these techniques and strategies helps to understand the contemporary Middle East and, ultimately, instances of violence and revolution such as those seen in 2011. From the regulation of life to the subjugation of life to death, a range of mechanisms of governance and governmentality exist to provide regimes with the ability to exert power, albeit not without contestation, as competing groups seek influence through laying claim to social norms, practices, economies and claims to sovereignty, with spatial consequences.

The interaction of these factors and the closing of an inside off against an outside show how people can become marginalised from political communities and exist within bare life, reintroduced into yet excluded from politics through the declaration of a state of exception. Within this context, political life was stripped from large numbers of people across the Middle East, where lives became expendable as government machinery attempted to retain control. Such processes are ongoing as regimes seek to maintain power and people engage with the structures of politics. Following decades of exception and bare life, the Arab Uprisings became an outlet for much of the frustration people had with governance structures regulating life, resulting in a struggle between regimes and societies and the (further) marginalisation of particular identities for domestic, regional and international audiences.

Put another way, the state of exception begot the state of exception, while bare life begot bare life. As noted in *The Kingdom and The Glory*, to understand politics – and the Arab Uprisings – it is imperative to look at government and governance structures within a state that serve the biopolitical project. The need to do this is supported by the 2016 Arab Human Development Report, which argues that 'the events of 2011 and their ramifications are the outcome of public policies over many decades that gradually led to the exclusion of large sectors of the population from economic, political and social life'.[95]

Nomoi are not limited to the nation-state but can exist across space. The pan-Arab movement with Gamal Abdl Nasser at its vanguard suggested that the Arab states were subservient to a larger collective, to *umma arabiyya wahida dhat risala khalida*, the 'one Arab nation with an immortal mission'.[96] This vision eviscerated states and societies and eroded their agency, claiming to speak for the *vox populus*, leaving the nation state in its wake. Rulers aware of the power of this narrative would tap into a source of legitimacy that transcended domestic reserves, despite its threat to the survival of the sovereign state and used its symbolic power in an effort to engender popular support.[97]

The birth of pan-Islamism stemmed from a desire to challenge the pan-Arab discourse and Saudi Arabia's attempt to counter the rising power of Nasser's Egypt by stressing the importance of Islamic unity,[98] along with the proselytising of a Wahhabist vision brought about through the development of the Islamic University of Medina and provision of training and funding to Imams from across the world.[99] A pure pan-Islamist vision also held Middle East states to be transient entities working towards the unification of the Muslim world, yet much like Arabism before it, the ideology was increasingly used for political ends, leading to political rivalry between states, with domestic and regional repercussions.[100] Ultimately, both ideological movements were brought down by the enduring power of the nation-state,[101] yet the nature of global political life means that the state once more appears to be contested and the legacy of these movements remains.

Such movements also challenged the spatial aspects of the sovereign state that had come to dominate the international system, a site of contestation between regimes and broader populist movements that derived legitimacy from a greater, collective movement not confined to the borders of the sovereign state. Both pan-Arabism and pan-Islamism appealed to a sense of *asabiyyah* among the people of the region, drawing upon shared normative views – albeit in a number of different forms – in an attempt to construct a broad community of support against an outside, which were traditionally colonial agendas and the establishment of Israel. In recent years, this 'outside' has been constructed as Shi'a and Persian.

Yet the instrumentalised use of such narratives was not without problems, as Michael Barnett reveals in *Dialogues in Arab Politics*.[102] Such ideologies also provided domestic support against the Communists and Leftist movements as regimes across the Gulf sought to empower groups such as the Muslim Brotherhood to counter the perceived threat posed by Communism. Longer term, regimes implemented structures that sought to restrict the possibility of agency, while holding together the fabric of political organisation. State-building processes seek to circumvent these challenges and establish a framework ensuring regime security and stability while the existence of structures to circumvent challenges results in a range of different structural pressures across states, which resulted in violence in times of severe contestation. Moreover, the location of states within shared normative environments means that events in one state can reverberate across the region, having an impact upon the domestic affairs of others.

Amid a range of challenges including but not limited to Western military engagement, global financial crises, a growing middle class[103] and huge demographic changes, notably a youth boom and a population increase of 53% between 1991 and 2010, along with waves of urbanisation,[104] social contracts and ruling pacts began to fragment. Before the uprisings, middle classes were largely stable, albeit subjected to a range of governance strategies, yet political marginalisation and the rising price of essentials – especially bread – altered this stability. A Human Development Report that tracked change between 2009 and 2014 offers greater insight into events at this time, noting a positive change of +10 in Saudi Arabia, facilitated by the $96 billion package of social reform, and a negative change of -15 in Syria.[105] With the emergence of states of exception across the region, perhaps best characterised in Egypt's *Emergency Laws*, people were marginalised by legal and political structures and political meaning was stripped from life. From this, in order to understand the uprisings, we must identify both the conditions and the structures that facilitated the biopolitical project and ultimately, bare life.

As the uprisings continued across the region, revolution and counter-revolution vied for control. In Egypt, the end of the Mubrak era resulted in a democratically elected Muslim Brotherhood regime under the leadership of Mohammad Morsi, which also stressed the need for emergency legislation to maintain security and stability.[106] The counter-revolution that toppled Morsi violently banned the group's supporters from political life in Egypt, imprisoning thousands of Muslim Brothers and their followers, along with the massacre of over a thousand of the group's supporters on 14 August 2013 in Cairo. Those states who had supported the Morsi presidency were subjected to geopolitical punishment, as a Saudi-led bloc sought to regulate life not only within their states but also across the Middle East.

The fragmentation of states and their structures resulted in the erosion of sovereignty, necropolitics, war machines and conditions of bare life across the region. Amid such conditions, the emergence of social movements – war machines – that challenged the power of the state was hardly surprising. During times of conflict across the region, war machines have emerged as a means of contesting the power of the state, albeit occasionally co-opted into those structures. In some cases, this resulted in the erosion of political projects driven by irredentist and secessionist movements. As Ariel Ahram notes, much of the focus on political projects in the Arab world presumes *the state* to be 'immutable and fixed', albeit 'fierce but weak',[107] yet amid contestation and fragmentation to hold such a position is infelicitous. Such a position is especially troubling when faced with secessionist and irredentist movements in Syria, Iraq, Iran, Turkey and Yemen. From numerous forms of competition to sovereign power, a plethora of possible outcomes emerge, contingent upon time and space, requiring analysis of the relationship between rulers and ruled.

Within the context of fragmenting sovereignty that left states vulnerable to the political ambitions of others, regimes manipulated events to ensure their own survival. Islamic rhetoric was increasingly used as a cloak for geopolitical agendas, best seen through Iranian and Saudi Arabian efforts to increase the legitimacy and vitality of their own rule for internal and external audiences.[108] Schisms within the Muslim world also served as a means of undermining governmentality, authority and autonomy, as individuals faced often-contradictory guidance from competing sources of authority. Religious difference led to securitised divisions while also proving to be a useful tool in efforts to retain security after the Arab Uprisings.

Conclusions

Questions about sovereign power remain central to understanding the nature of political organisations. To understand political life, one must understand the manifestation and contestation of sovereign power. Within such projects, the role of the state occupies a central role, albeit one that is increasingly contested within a global *nomos* that is defined by spatial exception and underpinned by neo-liberal modernity. Within this *nomos*, the localised unlocalisable becomes contested as context and contingency challenge the relationship between *ordnung* and *ortung*, with serious consequences for sovereign projects and the organisation of communities.[109] The process of defining an inside against an outside is central to the establishment of communities that then regulate life according to their normative codes. Yet competing visions of how to live and the values that structure such visions do not always coalesce with state sovereignty, resulting in challenges to the sovereign order.

Although deploying a number of theoretical positions in pursuit of answers, these approaches fit together neatly, sharing similar ontological foundations. Consideration of sovereign power allows for a greater focus on agency and human action. Fundamentally concerned with the regulation of life, sovereignty seeks to ensure regime survival through the removal of political meaning from life and creating conditions of bare life, or by controlling life by subjugating it to death. In opposition to regime power, war machines emerge that contest the organisation of political life. These interactions all take place within space, bringing together regional dynamics with intimately small local dynamics. Understanding the ordering of space goes some way in understanding political action and here *nomos* helps to understand the regulation of political organisation. Taken together, we have a rich tapestry that allows us to understand the manifestation of sovereign power, the areas in which such power is exerted and the means through which it is contested.

In spite of ongoing contestation, the state remains the central focus of our exploration, albeit in many forms. What we shall see, however, is that amid a fundamental struggle to exert sovereign power through the regulation of life, the repercussions are felt across space and time. In the contemporary world, these repercussions of political action are felt beyond state borders, while the harnessing of competing sovereignties locates political struggles within broader geopolitical and normative environments. While the state is often taken as a distinct unit, closer examination leaves it comprised of a number of different factors, existing across different spaces, shaped by the interactions that construct space.

The sovereign state is inherently an exclusionary concept and the need to define, redefine and maintain the exception exposes the power of the state. To understand political spaces, we must consider not only the relationship between rulers and ruled – and thus included and excluded – but also technologies of exclusion, which are (re)negotiated in response to context-specific contingent factors. Although we are concerned with the contestation that occurs within the state, tensions between loyalty to the state and to the *nomos* means that we have to locate our exploration within spatial dynamics across the Middle East, replete with contestation. As our journey continues, we must locate the state – and its discontents – within broader geopolitical and normative environments. By doing this we are better placed to engage with the regulation of life and the subjugation of life to death.

Notes

1 This chapter is a modified version of an article originally published in *Third World Quarterly*. I thank the editors for permission to reuse it here.
2 Ibn Khaldun, *The Muqaddimah: An Introduction to History* (Franz Rosenthal trans.) (Princeton, NJ: Princeton University Press, 1967), p. 39.
3 Charles Tilly, *The Formation of Nation States in Western Europe* (Princeton, NJ: Princeton University Press, 1975), p. 45.
4 Ghassan Salame, *Introduction*, in Ghassan Salame (ed.), *The Foundations of the Arab State* (Oxford: Routledge, 1987), p. 3.
5 See, among others, Talal Asad, 'Where Are the Margins of the State?', in Veena Das and Deborah Poole (eds), *Anthropology in the Margins of the State* (Santa Fe, NM: School of American Research Press, 2004), pp. 279–88; Nazih N. Aubui, *Over-Stating the Arab State* (London: I. B. Tauris, 1995); Roger Owen, *Rise and Fall of Arab Presidents for Life* (Cambridge, MA: Harvard University Press, 2012); Roger Owen, *State, Power and Politics in the Making of the Modern Middle East* (Oxford: Routledge, 2004); Lisa Anderson, 'The State in the Middle East and North Africa', *Comparative Politics*, 20:1 (1987): 1–18; Charles Tripp, 'The State as an Always-Unfinished Performance: Improvisation and Performativity in the Face of Crisis', *International Journal of Middle East Studies*, 50 (2018), 337–42; Fred Halliday, *The Middle East in International Relations: Power, Politics and Ideology* (Cambridge, UK: Cambridge University Press, 2005); Philip S. Khoury and Joseph Kostiner (eds), *Tribes and State Formation in the Middle East* (Berkeley: University of California Press, 1990); Fouad Ajami, *The Arab Predicament: Arab Political Thought and Practice since 1967* (Cambridge, UK: Cambridge University Press, 1992); Joel Migdal, *Strong Societies and Weak States* (Princeton, NJ: Princeton University Press, 1988).
6 Migdal, *Strong Societies and Weak States*, p. 19.
7 Tilly, *The Formation of National States*, p. 42.
8 Rolf Schwarz, *War and State Building in the Middle East* (Gainesville, FL: University of Florida Press, 2012), p. 18.
9 Lisa Anderson, 'The State in the Middle East and North Africa', p. 74.
10 Yahya Sadowski, *Scuds or Butter? The Political Economy of Arms Control in the Middle East* (Washington, DC: Brookings, 1993). The idea of the rentier state was a prominent feature of early work on the contemporary Middle East, driven by the ideas of Beblawi and Luciani in particular. See Hazem Beblawi, 'The Rentier State in the Arab World', in Giacomo Luciani (ed.), *The Arab State* (London: Routledge, 1990), pp. 85–98; and Giacomo Luciani, 'Allocation vs Production States: A Theoretical Framework', in Giacomo Luciani (ed.), *The Arab State* (London: Routledge, 1990), pp. 65–84.
11 Russell E. Lucas, 'Monarchical Authoritarianism: Survival and Political Liberalization in a Middle Eastern Regime Type', *International Journal of Middle East Studies*, 36 (2004), 106.

12 Robert M. Fishman, 'Rethinking State and Regime: Southern Europe's Transition to Democracy', *World Politics*, 42:3 (1990), 428.

13 Albert Hourani, 'How Should We Write the History of the Middle East?', *International Journal of Middle East Studies*, 23 (1991), 125–36.

14 Asad, 'Where Are the Margins of the State?', p. 281.

15 Lisa Anderson, 'Essential Readings: The Arab State' (Middle East Pedagogy Initiative, 19.06.18), available at www.jadaliyya.com/Details/37665/Essential-Readings-The-Arab-State (accessed 19.07.18).

16 See Michael Barnett, *Dialogues in Arab Politics: Negotiations in Regional Order* (New York: Columbia, 1998); and Malcolm Kerr, *The Arab Cold War: Gamel 'Abd Al-Nasir and His Rivals, 1958–70* (Oxford: Oxford University Press, 1972).

17 Toby Dodge, ' "Bordieu Goes to Baghdad": Explaining Hybrid Political Identities in Iraq', *Journal of Historical Sociology*, 31 (2018), 25–38.

18 Taken to be the worldwide community of Muslims.

19 B'Tselem, an Israeli human rights organisation, puts this number at 547,000 people living in 125 government-sanctioned settlements in the West Bank and a further 100 settlement outposts. See B'Tselem, *Statistics on Settlements and Settler Population* (Jerusalem: Israeli Information Center for Human Rights in the Occupied Territories, n.d.). The designation of Areas A, B and C was an attempt to facilitate the Israeli military withdrawal from the West Bank and the transfer to the Palestinian Authority as part of the peace process. According to Dror Etkes, an anti-settlement activist, 'the takeover of land in Area B is a combination of unbridled thievery by settlers and impotence on the part of the Israeli authorities'.

20 Fred Halliday, 'The Middle East and the Politics of Differential Integration', in Toby Dodge and Richard Higgot (eds), *Globalisation and the Middle East: Islam, Economics Culture and Politics* (London and Washington, DC: Royal Institute of International Affairs and Brookings Institution Press, 2002); and Raymond Hinnebusch, 'The Middle East in the World Hierarchy: Imperialism and Resistance', *Journal of International Relations and Development*, 14:2 (2011), 232.

21 Although a number of academic outlets have begun to contest colonial history. A number of years ago, an article of mine was rejected by a prominent international relations journal on the grounds that 'the Middle East had no colonial legacy'.

22 See Simon Bromley, *American Hegemony and World Oil: The Industry, the State System and the World Economy* (University Park, PA: Penn State University Press, 1991); and A. Alnasrawi, *Arab Nationalism, Oil and the Political Economy of Dependency* (New York: Greenwood Press, 1991).

23 See Simon Bromley, *Rethinking Middle East politics* (Austin, TX: University of Texas Press, 1994).

24 Steven Krasner, 'Compromising Westphalia', *International Security*, 20:3 (1995–96), 116.

25 Carl Schmitt, *Political Theology. Four Chapters on the Concept of Sovereignty.* (Chicago: University of Chicago Press, 2005).

26 Giorgio Agamben, *State of Exception* (Chicago: Chicago University Press, 2005), p. 33.

27 Giorgio Agamben, *Homo Sacer, Sovereign Power and Bare Life* (Stanford, CA: Stanford University Press, 1995), p. 18.

28 Agamben, *State of Exception*, p. 3.

29 Ibid., p. 23.

30 Ibid., p. 9.

31 Ibid., p. 123.
32 Ibid., p. 169.
33 Bulent Dilken, 'Zones of Indistinction: Security, Terror and Bare Life', in Anselm
    Franke and Kunst-Werke Berlin (eds), *Territories: Islands, Camps, and Other States of
    Utopia* (Berlin: Verlag der Buchhandlung Walther König, 2003), pp. 42–51. A similar
    point is made by J. Edkins and V. Pin-Fat, 'Introduction: Life, Power, Resistance',
    in J. Edkins, M. J. Shapiro and V. Pin-Fat, *Sovereign Lives: Power in Global Politics*
    (New York: Routledge, 2004), p. 9.
34 Derek Gregory *The Colonial Present: Afghanistan, Palestine, Iraq* (Oxford: Blackwell,
    2004), p. 258.
35 Giorgio Agamben, *The Kingdom and the Glory*, Palo Alto, CA: Stanford University
    Press, 2011), p. 276.
36 Giorgio Agamben, *The Use of Bodies* (Palo Alto, CA: Stanford University Press, 2016).
37 Wael Hallaq, *The Impossible State* (New York: Columbia University Press, 2013), p. 29.
38 Hourani, 'How should we write'.
39 An obvious criticism emerges when considering the application of a Western theory to
    the Middle East. Initially, such an attempt may fall foul of intellectual neo-colonialism
    and essentialism, yet when looking at the work of Wael Hallaq, particularly in *The
    Impossible State*, one can make the case that the metaphysics of states in the region
    share a number of characteristics with states across the world.
40 Achille Mbembe, 'Necropolitics', *Public Culture*, 15:1 (2003), 11–40.
41 Ibid., p. 12.
42 See Angharad Closs Stephens and Nick Vaughan-Williams (eds) *Terrorism and the
    Politics of Response* (Oxford: Routledge, 2009); Edkins et al., *Sovereign Lives*; Sergei
    Prozorov, 'Three Theses on "Governance" and the Political', *Journal of International
    Relations and Development*, 7:3 (2004), 267–93.
43 For purposes of brevity, the debate about the validity of Agamben's claims will be
    left to other scholars. For an introduction, see Patricia Owens, 'Reclaiming "Bare
    Life"?: Against Agamben on Refugees', in *International Relations*, 23:4 (2009),
    567–82.
44 C. Levy, 'Refugees, Europe, Camps/State of Exception: "Into the Zone": The European
    Union and extraterritorial Processing of Migrants, Refugees, and Asylum-Seekers
    (Theories and Practice)', *Refugee Survey Quarterly*, 29:1 (2005), 26–59.
45 Thomas Lemke, ' "A Zone of Indistinction": Critique of Giorgio Agamben's Concept of
    Biopolitics', *Outlines: Critical Practice Studies*, 7:1 (2005), 8.
46 William Walters, 'Acts of Demonstration: Mapping the Territory of (Non-) Citizenship',
    in E. Isin and G. Neilson (eds), *Acts of Citizenship* (London: Zed Books, 2008), pp.
    182–207.
47 Dan Bousfield, *The Logic of Sovereignty and the Agency of the Refugee: Recovering
    the Political from 'Bare Life'* (YCISS Workling Paper Number 36, October 2005); and
    Owens, 'Reclaiming "Bare Life"?'.
48 Agamben, *Profanations* (New York: Zone Books, 2007).
49 Agamben, *Homo Sacer*, p. 45.
50 Žižek, *The Ticklish Subject The Absent Centre of Political Ontology* (New York: Verso,
    1999), p. 238.
51 Mbembe, 'Necropolitics', p. 26.
52 Gilles Deleuze and Felix Guattari, *Nomadology: The War Machine* (South Pasadena,
    CA: Semiotext(e), 1986).

53 Although the name suggests otherwise, the *war machine* need not necessarily be violent, but rather something that contests the formal power of the state.

54 Deleuze and Guattari, *Nomadology*, p. 13.

55 Ibid.

56 Ibid., p. 59.

57 Gilles Deleuze and Feliz Guattari, *A Thousand Plateaus* (London: Continuum, 1987), pp. 422–526.

58 See Eyal Weizman, 'The Art of War: Deleuze, Guattari, Debord and the Israeli Defence Force' (*Mute*, 03.08.06), available at www.metamute.org/editorial/articles/art-war-deleuze-guattari-debord-and-israeli-defence-force (accessed 10.10.12).

59 Henri Lefebvre, *The Production of Space* (Oxford: Blackwell, 1974).

60 Doreen Massey, *For Space* (London: Sage, 2005), pp. 9–11.

61 Ibid., p. 5.

62 Lefebvre, *The Production of Space*.

63 Kim Knott, 'Religion, Space and Place: The Spatial Turn in Research on Religion', *Religion and Society: Advances in Research*, 1 (2010), 40.

64 F. M. Cornford, *From Religion to Philosophy: A Study in the Origins of Western) Speculation* (New York: Harper Torchbooks, 1958), p. 30, cited by Hannah Arendt in *On Revolution* (Harmondsworth, UK: Penguin Books, [1963] 1990), pp. 186–7.

65 M. Ostwald, *Nomos and the Beginnings of Athenian Democracy* (Oxford: Clarendon Press, 1969), p.20

66 Carl Schmitt, *The Nomos of the Earth in the International Law of the Jus Publicum Europaeum* (New York: Telos Press, 2003).

67 Ibid., p. 42.

68 Claudio Minca and Rory Rowan, 'The Question of Space in Carl Schmitt', *Progress in Human Geography*, 39:3, 268–89.

69 Claudio Minca, 'Carl Schmitt and the Question of Spatial Ontology', in Stephen Legg (ed.), *Spatiality, Sovereignty and Carl Schmitt: Geographies of the Nomos* (London: Routledge, 2011), p. 168.

70 John Agnew, 'Territory', in Derek Gregory, Ron Johnston and Geraldine Pratt (eds), *The Dictionary of Human Geography* (Chichester, UK: Wiley- Blackwell, 2009), pp. 746–7.

71 Ibid.

72 Deleuze and Guattari, *Nomadology*, pp. 15–16.

73 Mitchell Dean, 'A Political Mythology of World Order: Carl Schmitt's Nomos', *Theory, Culture and Society*, 23:5 (2006), 1–22.

74 Humphrey acknowledges the existence of 'localised forms of sovereignty', 'nested' within 'higher sovereignties'. From this, it is possible to extrapolate and envisage *nomoi* 'nestled' within 'higher *nomoi*'. C. Humphrey, 'Sovereignty', in D. Nugent and J. Vincent (eds), *A Companion to the Anthropology of Politics* (Oxford: Blackwell, 2004), pp. 418–36.

75 Hans Lindahl, 'Give and Take: Arendt and the *nomos* of Political Community', *Philosophy & Social Criticism*, 32:7 (2006), 882.

76 Anna Jurkevics, 'Hannah Arendt Reads Carl Schmitt's *The Nomos of the Earth*: A Dialogue on Law and Geopolitics from the Margins', *European Journal of Political Theory*, 16:3 (2017), 345–66.

77 Arendt, *Was ist Politik? Fragmente aus dem Nachlaß* (Ursula Ludz, ed.) (Munich: Piper, [1993] 2003), p. 122.

78 Arendt, *On Revolution* (New York: Penguin, 2006), p. 275.

79 Khaldun, *The Muqaddimah*, 1:82.

80 Hannah Arendt, *The Human Condition* (Chicago: Chicago University Press, 1998), pp. 197–8, 207.

81 Cover, 'The Supreme Court, 1982 Term – Foreword: Nomos and Narrative', *Faculty Scholarship Series* (1983) Paper 2705, p. 10.

82 Ibid. p. 15.

83 Ibid. p. 8.

84 Quran 2:173.

85 The story of Antigone reveals a fundamental tension between obeying the laws of the sovereign or following the norms of one's faith, bringing to light the contestation of competing orderings.

86 Khaldun, *The Muqaddimah*.

87 Arendt, *The Human Condition*, pp. 197–8.

88 Simon Mabon, 'The World Is a Garden: *Nomos* and the (Contested) Ordering of Life', *Review of International Studies* (forthcoming).

89 Of Arab fears of Persian and vice versa.

90 For a detailed discussion of this and Arendt's work on *nomos* more broadly, see Lindahl, 'Give and Take'.

91 Migdal, *Strong Societies and Weak States*.

92 Ibid., p. 4. While some may draw parallels with ideas of hybrid sovereignty, such a concept struggles to adequately take into account the interaction of formal and normative structures, particularly the implications of such a struggle for space and the regulation of life.

93 Marisela Montenegro and Joan Pujol, 'Introduction: Bordering, Exclusions and Necropolitics', *Qualitative Research Journal*, 17:3 (2017), 143.

94 Mbembe, 'Necropolitics', p. 17.

95 United Nations, *Arab Human Development Report 2016: Youth and the Prospects for Human Development in a Changing Reality* (New York: United Nations, 2016), p. 17.

96 Fouad Ajami, 'The End of Pan-Arabism', *Foreign Affairs*, 57:2 (Winter 1978–79). 355.

97 Barnett, *Dialogues in Arab Politics*.

98 Martin Kramer, 'Muslim Congresses', in *The Oxford Encyclopedia of the Modern Islamic World* (John L. Esperito, ed.) (Oxford: Oxford University Press, 1995), p. 309.

99 See Michael Farquar, *Circuits of Faith: Migration, Education, and the Wahhabi Mission* (Palo Alto, CA: Stanford University Press, 2016); and Michael Farquhar, 'Saudi Petrodollars, Spiritual Capital, and the Islamic University of Medina: A Wahhabi Missionary Project in Transnational Perspective', *International Journal of Middle East Studies*, 47:4, 701–21.

100 Simon Mabon, *Saudi Arabia and Iran: Soft Power Rivalry in the Middle East* (London: I. B. Tauris, 2013).

101 See Martin Kramer, *Ivory Towers on Sand: The Failure of Middle Eastern Studies in America* (Washington, DC: Washington Institute for Near East Policy, 2001).

102 Barnett, *Dialogues in Arab Politics*.

103 In Syria this was 56.5%, in Egypt 55% and in Yemen 31.6%. See United Nations Economic and Social Commission for Western Asia, Arab Middle Class: Measurement and *Role in Driving Change* (New York: United Nations, 2014).

104 International Labour Organization, 'Rethinking Economic Growth: Towards Productive and Inclusive Arab Societies' (ILO, 2012), available at www.ilo.org/wcmsp5/groups/public/---arabstates/---ro-beirut/documents/publication/wcms_208346.pdf, pp. 6, 47.
105 United Nations, *Arab Human Development Report 2016*, table 2.
106 Mara Revkin, 'Egypt's Untouchable President' (*Foreign Policy*, 25.11.12), available at https://foreignpolicy.com/2012/11/25/egypts-untouchable-president (accessed 25.11.12).
107 Ariel Ahram, 'On the Making and Unmaking of Arab States', *International Journal of Middle East Studies*, 50:2 (2018), 323–7. See also Ariel I. Ahram, *Break all the Borders: Separatism and the Reshaping of the Middle East* (Oxford: Oxford University Press, 2019).
108 Mabon, *Saudi Arabia and Iran*.
109 Mabon, 'The World Is a Garden'.

2

Letters and declarations

The nature of this melancholy becomes clearer, once one asks the question, with whom does the historical writer of historicism actually empathize. The answer is irrefutably with the victor. Those who currently rule are however the heirs of all those who have ever been victorious. Empathy with the victors thus comes to benefit the current rulers every time.

Walter Benjamin, *Illuminations*

The development of a political community is an inherently exclusionary project based upon a particular vision of the organisation of life. The establishment of bureaucratic structures that facilitate the regulation of life flows from the enactment of this idea. As we have seen, definitions of statehood and sovereignty differ greatly, but it is evident that in order for a state to be considered as such, a number of characteristics must be met, including the existence of a people residing within a particular territorial area with a shared identity and a system of governance to facilitate the survival of their project. Fundamentally, as Khaldun suggested, politics is the survival of the species.

This chapter engages with attempts to establish political projects, driven by actors both within and beyond territorial borders. In many cases, such efforts were revolutionary, violent dislocations between past and future that radically altered the ordering of space within a particular area. Yet such transformations also possessed an economic dimension as foreign powers sought to capitalise on opportunities provided by domestic upheaval, while political elites began processes of modernisation as they sought to forge states from the embers of uncertainty. The neo-liberal modernity that underpins Agamben's spatialisation of the exception shapes the local manifestations of *nomos* and while context and contingency create unique peculiarities, there are underlying structural similarities that shape the exception. Although offering a brief genealogy of the establishment of states, this chapter should not be viewed as a complete history of the contemporary Middle East. Instead I seek to offer an account of the interaction between internal and external forces – material and ideational – that facilitated the establishment of states and *nomoi*, through the interaction of *ordnung* and *ortung*.

Amid a range of parabolic pressures, the Arab state continues to face a range of pressures.[1] From this, tensions emerge between loyalty to particular communities and projects. Such projects are also shaped by global and regional events; space is (re)constructed through the interaction of the global with the local, with implications for the interaction of *ordnung* and *ortung* constituting both *nomos* and *nomoi*. In a normative environment that draws members from different states, the interaction of regional, global and local issues is hardly surprising. For Paul Noble, this shared environment created a 'vast sound chamber in which information, ideas, and opinions have resonated with little regard for state frontiers'.[2]

Emerging from the demise of the Ottoman Empire, the contemporary regional states system underwent a period of (re)construction forged by an array of domestic and regional struggles, amid the penetration of the Middle East by external powers. As Agamben suggests, all states operate within the global *nomos* of a spatialised exception that is underpinned by neo-liberal modernity, but such localised exceptions are shaped by local context and contingency. There is then a two-tier dimension to *nomos*: the global ordering of spatial exceptions that is viewed as the apparently universal concept of the sovereign state, alongside the localised spatial exception, where *nomos* emerges through the interaction of *ordnung* and *ortung*.

Challenges facing rulers across the twentieth century were multifaceted, yet predominantly revolved around efforts to bring dislocated peoples together to ensure the survival of the collective.[3] The quest for a national identity involved harnessing a number of historical narratives, cultural norms and tribal values in an attempt to create a convincing narrative of how the political vision should be expressed. Of course, by its very nature, such projects are exclusive and required the rejection of other narratives. Exclusion fed into already existing socio-economic grievances, creating fertile breeding ground for a range of different ideologies including Arabism, Ba'athism, Islamism, Communism, along with incarnations of nationalism defined within territorial borders. Following a spate of *coups d'état* across the 1960s and 1970s, new leaders put 'coup-proofing' strategies in place to ensure the survival of regimes within specific territorial boundaries, seeking to withstand pressures from above and below.[4]

These strategies established a range of different relationships including between the family, tribe, sect, city and ethnic group, designed to draw support from a number of different constituencies, with the by-product of widespread exclusion.[5] Processes designed to include/exclude groups from the political sphere also had serious repercussions across the region, as a consequence of the spread of identities across the Middle East, meaning that what happens within the borders of one state can have consequences elsewhere.

Reverberations from events such as the establishment of the state of Israel, the Suez Crisis, the 1967 war, the Iranian Revolution, the 2003 invasion of Iraq, the 2005 Cedar Revolution and the Arab Uprisings were felt across the Middle East, shaping the regional security environment. The establishment of states, either in an attempt to politically represent an existing nationality, or to simultaneously create a national identity and state, take place within the context of this broader regional environment, deriving legitimacy through recourse to the norms of the environment.

A key part of efforts to survive was the ability to lay claim to legitimacy. Academic discussions about legitimacy rarely find consensus but it is generally accepted that in the Middle East, legitimacy deficits are responsible for malaise and political instability. In a groundbreaking discussion of legitimacy in the Arab world, Michael Hudson identified legitimacy deficits as responsible for a range of the region's ills, from instability to repression, via cynicism, inefficiency and corruption.[6] Legitimacy, for Hudson, stemmed from four main sources of authority: patriarchal, consultative, Islamic and feudal. Scholars of the Middle East will note that successful leaders create reserves of legitimacy through strategies that draw upon these different sources, providing leaders with the means through which to secure their rule and improve their standing across regional politics.[7]

Reserves of legitimacy are not restricted to territorial borders. In *Dialogues in Arab Politics*, Michael Barnett's constructivist interpretation of the impact of pan-Arabism on regional politics, shared ideological movements provide opportunities to increase reserves of legitimacy. Times of crisis then serve as opportunities to reshape the regional order, where regimes lay claim to ideological membership as a mechanism of improving their legitimacy and position in the regional order. As Barnett argues,

> Arab states have had strikingly different views of the desired [regional order] Although such differences might be attributed to principled beliefs, the more prominent reasons were regime interests, beginning with but not exhausted by survival and domestic stability. As a consequence, over the years Arab leaders have vied to draw a line between the regimes' interests, the norms of Arabism, and the events of the day.[8]

For Barnett, events occur within normative environments that allow actors to derive meaning and interpret events in different ways. Much like our understanding of *nomos*, Barnett's approach demonstrates that events serve as a mechanism through which regimes gain legitimacy but also shape their environments, providing transformative opportunities to reshape regional dynamics. Periods of crisis both national and regional thus provide opportunities for political elites to increase their legitimacy – beyond their capacity to govern – and strengthen their positions vis-à-vis the regional order.

Versailles and the League of Nations

> Oh, if we can pull this thing off! Rope together the young hot-heads and the Shi'ah obscurantists, and the enthusiasts ... if we can make them work together and find their own salvation for themselves, what a fine thing it will be. I see visions and dream dreams.[9]

In *Arab Awakening*, George Antonius' seminal – albeit problematical – study of the Arab Revolt, the roots of Arab nationalism are traced back to Beirut in 1875, where the ideas of five young Christian men that would shape Arab politics in the following century were forged. Amid the strict enforcement of Ottoman law, the five engaged in seditious activity, placing placards around the streets of Beirut that contained 'violent denunciations of the evils of Turkish rule' and called for rebellion.[10] Although initially unsuccessful, the events of 1875 created a movement that would have a lasting impact on regional politics in the following century. Over the coming decades, amid the turbulence of political upheaval, Arab nationalism was developed and debated, driven by intellectuals but played out across the streets of the region.

The most important incident in the formative years of calls for Arab nationalism was the demise of the Ottoman Empire at the end of the Great War in November 1918, following widespread unrest among Arab populations who had grown frustrated at long-standing persecution under the Young Turks,[11] culminating in the Arab Revolt and the ensuing efforts of external powers to shape the actions of local agency.[12] The Arab Revolt sought to overthrow the yoke of the Ottoman Empire, albeit supported by a different colonial power. Although initially confined to the Hejaz, the revolt spread across the region and while Sharif Hussayn was able to draw upon a relatively large army, they were poorly armed. The political fallout from the establishment of a mandate system – and location of a strong international presence in the region – had serious repercussions for the ordering of space, which, in turn, determined the capacity of indigenous Arab movements to shape their own political futures.[13]

During the war, British and French diplomats became involved in detailed discussions about the reorganisation of the Middle East following the expected demise of the Ottoman Empire. Diplomatic wrangling led Sir Marc Sykes and his French counterpart François Georges Picot to divide the region into spheres of influence, seemingly disregarding indigenous political organisation. Sykes expressed that to divide the region, he 'should like to draw a line from the *e* in Acre to the last *k* in Kirkuk'.[14] The agreement stated that 'in the blue area France, and in the red area Great Britain, shall be allowed to establish such direct or indirect administration or control as they desire and as they may think fit to arrange with the Arab state or confederation of Arab states'.[15] Although the Sykes–Picot agreement of 1916 was never directly implemented, it had a lasting legacy upon the region, according a great deal of power to the two remaining European powers and locating the idea of partition within future diplomatic initiatives such as the Treaty of Sèvres and the San Remo Agreement.

With the signing of the Treaty of Sèvres, the dissolution of the Ottoman Empire was complete. Article 22 of the League of Nations Covenant established mandates in the Middle East, where 'their existence as independent nations can be provisionally recognised subject to the rendering of administrative advice and assistance by a mandatory unit until such time as they are able to stand alone'.[16] Powers responsible for regulating the mandates were seen to be 'trustees', wherein they would administer life 'within such boundaries as may be fixed by them'.[17]

Reconstruction efforts had previously taken place between British officials and Arab leaders directly, where concessions over territorial control were made in return for political support. An earlier exchange of letters between the British High Commissioner to Egypt Sir Henry McMahon and Hussein bin Ali, Sharif of Mecca, revealed how a territory 'in the limits and boundaries proposed by the Sharif of Mecca' was offered in exchange for starting the Arab Revolt.[18]

At the end of the war, the Ottoman Empire was divided into mandates that were later shared between the British and French. Once established, mandates became sites of contestation, with local agency posing serious challenges to colonial overlords. Iraq provides perhaps the most obvious example of the challenge of state building at this point, as newly installed political elites had to balance myriad forms of indigenous political organisation, religious networks, strong tribal groups and a severe disparity between urban and rural populations, manifesting in tensions between tradition and modernity. Competing narratives and efforts to facilitate inclusion emerging from the *nomos* shaped the political trajectory, resulting in cycles of marginalisation, persecution and violence.

Tribal, religious and class divides posed serious problems for state building in the formative years of Iraq. As outlined in Hanna Batatu's magisterial study of twentieth-century Iraq, Iraqis were not one community but were comprised of members from disparate ethnic and religious nationalities. As Batatu argues, the Arabs of Iraq were 'a congeries of distinct, discordant, self-involved societies', dissected by serious class schisms most obviously manifesting in the distinction between rural and urban societies.[19]

Central to the political decisions taken in both Baghdad and London was a British archaeologist from County Durham by the name of Gertrude Bell. An intrepid explorer, Bell's exploits across the Middle East rival that of T. E. Lawrence. One of Churchill's representatives at the 1921 Cairo conference, a witness to the Armenian genocide and officially recognised by Sir Percy Cox as 'Oriental Secretary', Bell played a prominent role in the establishment of Faisal as King and the formative years of the Iraqi state. In a political vacuum following the Ottoman defeat, religion played an important role in the formative years of the Iraqi state. Accordingly, the role of clerics was central to political life in southern Iraq, which worried many in the British administration, fearing an open door to external influence. For Bell, the proximity of Persia and the presence of key Shi'a shrines in Karbala and Najaf 'brought the country much under Persian influences'.[20]

Such perceptions were central in shaping the decisions taken by the British and Faisal. The installation of a Sunni monarch to rule over a Shi'a majority was a consequence of the desire to work with the wealthy, military trained urban elites deemed more sympathetic to the British cause, but also to uphold Iraqi sovereignty and avoid the penetration of the nascent state by external powers. In the following decades, Iraqi leaders shared similar concerns about the loyalties of Shi'a communities and in an attempt to prevent unrest – and ultimately to retain power – political and legal structures were created to continue the process of marginalisation and remove political meaning from the lives of the Shi'a; at this point political institutions enshrined difference. As a general rule, no Shi'a was accepted into military college or bureaucracy, while accessing high school was problematic, creating deep grievances among Shi'a communities.[21]

Economic and tribal differences played a prominent role in shaping the early years of the state, amid competing normative agendas and visions of what such a project would look like.[22] Difference required regulation and the co-opting of tribal groups into nascent forms of political organisation, much to their chagrin.[23] Urbanisation processes included the abolition of the 1933 Law Governing the Rights and Duties of Cultivators, allowing tribes to move to cities, although by 1965 some 50% still lived in rural areas.[24] Unsurprisingly, oil dramatically altered the economic capability of the country, accounting for 60% of the budget by 1959.[25] Land ownership thus became a key component of the social fabric of the state[26] and a prominent site of political contestation in the coming decades.

Across the Levant, state formation was a shaped by the interaction of domestic social forces with the far more powerful exogenous forces, in what Nazih Ayubi referred to as 'a disintegrative political process imposed "from without"'.[27] Here, states were established as arbiters among competing groups that sought to pacify groups through the instruments of central rule, notably the army and bureaucracy. Such an approach does little to facilitate harmony and integration but rather isolates and separates groups within the state. Governance was achieved through alliances between blocs that are community based and retain all of their characteristics as they come into power. Such an approach deepened political, economic, social and community divisions, facilitating grievance and distrust that would manifest in violence across the century.[28]

Perhaps the most important mandate for future stability across the Middle East was the League's recognition of the British Mandate over Palestine, which used the Jordan river to divide the land in two, into Palestine to the West and Transjordan to the East. At this time, the Hashemites occupied three thrones across the region, with Faisal in Iraq, Abdullah in Transjordan and Hussein in the Hijaz. Yet the movements of Abdul Aziz Ibn Saud across Arabia put an end to broader Hashemite aspirations with the establishment of Saudi Arabia within the decade.

The emergence of a state under the leadership of Abdul Aziz Ibn Abd Al Rahman Al Saud in 1932 occurred after the unification of disparate tribal groups across the Arabian Peninsula into a sedentary form of political organisation over the previous decades. This process of sedentarisation and economic development continued over the coming years, but the transition from a nomadic, rural population to an urban dwelling population was central in securing the territorial borders of the state, a prime example of the relationship and interaction between *ordnung* and *ortung*, the harnessing of regulatory power to create spatial order. Fundamental to the state-building process was a centuries old alliance between the Al Saud tribe and the puritanical Wahhabi sect of Islam, but it was also facilitated by support from the British, although it was the Soviet Union that first recognised Ibn Saud as the King of the Hejaz and Sultan of the Nejd in 1926.[29] Tribal developments aided the evolution of the political project, not only from rural to urban but also in providing Ibn Saud with the cultural and symbolic characteristics to regulate life.[30]

Islam played a prominent role within the nascent political project. Not only was Ibn Saud's standing army the *ikhwan*, a group of devout Muslims, central to the expansion of the borders of the state, Islam was positioned centrally within the fabric of political organisation. The relationship with the Wahhabi *ulema* offered a degree of legitimacy for Ibn Saud's rule. The importance of Islam was not restricted to the kingdom's borders, however, as Ibn Saud offered financial support to the newly established Muslim Brotherhood and when the King met Hassan Al Banna in 1936, he jokingly said 'we are all Muslim Brotherhood'. In the coming years Al Banna was offered protection by the Al Saud amid suggestions that the Egyptian regime planned to assassinate him, but as the century developed, the relationship became more complex as we shall see.

Although largely successful, Saudi expansion during the 1920s was not without resistance. Having crossed into what is now Kuwait, *ikhwan* fighters were met by a small force and in what became known as Battle of Jahra where, in 1920, the *ikhwan* were defeated.[31] The battle offers important insight into the complexity of political dynamics at the time, as members of the Al Mutair tribe could be found on both sides of the conflict, revealing a burgeoning attachment to the land among those fighting on the Kuwaiti side.[32] This burgeoning loyalty to land led to the evolution of political organisation, transforming the way in which life was organised and ordered, within clearly defined political spaces. In later years, tribes would be essential in the development of states across the Gulf, protecting oil installations, pipelines and ports, which were essential to provide the financial might to facilitate socio-political transformations. Of course, the tribal sheikhs were handsomely rewarded for such practices and were thus brought into the political and infrastructure of the new state, creating an interaction between *ordnung* and *ortung*.

The embers of the Ottoman Empire created opportunities for the reorganisation of territory across the Middle East. While the aftershocks were felt across the region, the epicentre was Turkey. Under Mustafa Kemal Ataturk, a new republic was founded in 'revolutionary style', transforming citizens of the Ottoman Empire into Turkish citizens amid the widespread removal of religion from public life. The establishment of the Turkish state necessitated eradicating the residue of Ottoman rule and the creation of state apparatus and institutions.[33] This project initially abolished the Sultanate before co-opting support from the royalists and religious clerics alike by appointing an Ottoman prince as caliph, albeit before abolishing the caliphate completely in 1924 and the *azzam* in the following years as part of a secularising move. Unlike other identity-building projects in the region that had to begin from scratch, Turkish nationalism had linguistic and literary roots in the middle of the nineteenth century[34] but it was the nascent Ataturk regime that enshrined such sentiments into the state project.

As the historian Bernard Lewis notes, this process was not without challenges, demonstrated by new frontiers, the rejection of religious and dynastic royalties and a lack of emotional attachment.[35] Over time, the Republican People's Party worked towards enshrining Ataturk's vision within new political structures. Perhaps the most important aspect of this was the establishment of the military, who were heavily involved – much as in other states across the region – within the domestic political climate as well as broader regional dynamics. It was not a project without difficulty, however, as loyalty to the former caliph and caliphate remained strong among the population. One of Ataturk's closest advisors is reported to have confessed that it was his duty to 'remain loyal to the sovereign: my attachment to the Caliphate is imposed on me by my education … To abolish this office and try to set up an entity of a different character in its place, would lead to failure and disaster'.[36] This opened up a key source of tension and competition over loyalty to the two distinct sovereigns.

In spite of such traces of loyalty to the erstwhile caliph, competing nationalist sentiments were rife due to the spread of different identities and political aspirations that had previously been co-opted by the Ottomans. One aspect of the nationalist project was the creation of a new system of language, which ensured that future generations would share the nationalist vision. The new Turkish language was prioritised over all other regional languages, marginalising minorities further and feeding into the cultivation of inclusion and exclusion. A new national vision was put forward that drew upon the past to shape the future.

Similar processes occurred in Persia, where Reza Khan sought to transform political organisation from the Persian Empire into a new, *modern* Iran. Amid the fallout from both the Constitutional Revolution and the aftermath of the Great War, Reza Khan established a dominant, personality-driven form of politics that succeeded in pushing both ethnic minorities and the Shi'a clerics to the margins of society. The political turmoil that followed reflected the struggle to shape the nature of the state in the move from empire to nation state, perhaps best seen in the reframing of Persia as Iran.

The speed of transformation across the Middle East was astounding. For George Antonius, these transformative processes created 'new forces and tendencies which were not inherent in the trends of the national movements'.[37] Antonius is correct in this observation, particularly when considering that transformation and dislocation would also result in pushback against these movements, but also in inertia and competition among existing institutions designed to implement such strategies. Perhaps the most severe of all points of dislocation from the fall out of the Great War was found in the establishment of the state of Israel.

The Palestinian mandate and the state of Israel

While European powers were operating across the Middle East, populations of these – and indeed other states – had become increasingly restless. Widespread anti-Semitism, reflected in incidents such as the Dreyfus affair, cultivated political support for what became known as the Zionist project that would eventually call for a *return* to the ancient land of Israel. The emergence of the Zionist movement in the late nineteenth century was itself a consequence of particular socio-political experiences. Central to the burgeoning movement was *The Jewish State*, written by Theodore Herzl, whose words called for 'sovereignty [to] be granted us over a portion of the globe large enough to satisfy the rightful requirements of a nation'.[38]

In spite of the growing popularity of the Zionist movement, it took a 67-word declaration of support from the British Foreign Secretary published on 2 September 1917 to firmly locate the matter within the realm of international politics.

His Majesty's government view[s] with favour the establishment in Palestine of a national home for the Jewish people, and will use their best endeavours to facilitate the achievement of this object, it being clearly understood that nothing shall be done which may prejudice the civil and religious rights of existing non-Jewish communities in Palestine, or the rights and political status enjoyed by Jews in any other country.[39]

While the Balfour Declaration expressed support for creating a 'national home' for Jewish people in Palestine, the wording of the declaration was deliberately ambiguous. For many at the time, the concept of a national home was coterminous to a state, although some such as Winston Churchill and Neville Chamberlain were largely of the opinion that a Jewish state would occur in due course; such a view helped generate a sense that the declaration was in British interests to curry favour with Jewry across the world during the war.[40] At the same time, many Arabs were of the view that the British had also promised them a state, as a reward for their involvement in defeating the Ottoman Empire.[41] British policy was convoluted, seeking to support both Arabs and Jews, leaving both firmly of the opinion that they had London's support.

Before the Second World War, five distinct waves of *aliyah* (the immigration of Jews from across the diaspora to the land of Israel) had brought almost four hundred thousand Jews to Palestine. Once settled, institutions were formed – in parallel with mandatory governance structures – to provide support to Jewish settlers in what Mehran Kamrava has referred to as a 'state within a state', a common theme that emerges amid contestation.[42] After *aliyah* came the process of transforming land into a state for the incoming settlers, at the expense of the indigenous Palestinian communities. Such processes occurred physically and intellectually, transforming the soil in accordance with particular political visions, along with creating a new ordering of space.

The need for expropriation and removal was quickly acknowledged, first by Theodor Herzl, albeit 'discreetly and circumspectly'.[43] In contrast, the first Prime Minister of Israel, David Ben Gurion, argued that 'there were no others'[44] and ultimately that Palestine was the ideal choice for settlement.[45] Yet it was the transformation of life on the ground that would have the most lasting impact, as land was bought by Zionists while more directly, groups such as the Haganah, Irgun and Stern Gang engaged in violence against Palestinian Arabs.

After the establishment of the United Nations (UN), a partition plan for Palestine was approved by UN General Assembly Council Resolution 181 on 29 November 1947, which called for the partition of Palestine into eight parts: three to the Arab state; three to the Jewish state; one, the town of Jaffa, was to be an Arab enclave in the Jewish territory; and Jerusalem was to remain under international control, administered by the UN.[46] This plan was accepted, pragmatically, by the Jewish leaders, but rejected by Arab leaders who were loath to cede such an amount of territory and argued that it was in violation of their right to self-determination.[47]

The Declaration of the State of Israel on 14 May 1948 was the culmination of Herzl's vision. In the years that followed, erstwhile Mandatory Palestine was existentially transformed as indigenous communities were 'systematically extinguished' to allow for the establishment of the state of Israel.[48] After the declaration of statehood, armies from neighbouring Arab armies invaded. In spite of a huge disparity in the number of troops, the newly established Israeli Defence Force (IDF) ultimately proved victorious, feeding into an environment where seven hundred thousand Palestinians were expelled from their homes on 15 May 1948 in what would become known in Palestinian history as the *nakba*, the catastrophe.

Efforts to establish the state of Israel required engagement with a number of competing historiographies, each laying claim to land and its history. Such contestation has routinely been acknowledged by Israeli leaders along with the construction of a historiography of Jewish claims to the land, which was later powerfully destroyed by Shlomo Sand, an Israeli academic working at Tel Aviv University.[49]

Nasser, pan-Arabism and Ba'athism

The failure of Arab armies to defeat Israel on the battlefield and the continued presence of colonial powers helped ferment widespread nationalist support for a pan-Arab movement that challenged the ordering of the states system. This was both physical and intellectual, as a large number of people found solace in the ideological movement. In such conditions, radical ideas quickly began to spread.[50] Long-standing tensions within the mandate programme erupted as burgeoning movements for self-determination clashed with colonial overlords amid the fallout from the declaration of the State of Israel. Political institutions established as part of mandatory control fed into the cultivation of nationalist programmes. Questions about the regulation of life and its spatial ordering became prominent within political discourse, often facilitated through colonial structures. This was a time of serious turmoil where local populations began to 'awaken to their full potential'.[51]

Although Egypt had been under occupation since before the establishment of the mandate system, an increasingly turbulent period would lead to a form of quasi independence, albeit on the condition that Britain retained control of the canal zone, foreign policy and security.[52] It was within this context that a school teacher from Cairo named Hassan Al Banna formed the Muslim Brotherhood. Al Banna's vision for the Brotherhood included the provision of social goods and services that the state failed to provide, resulting in a deeply fractious relationship between the regime and the *ikhwan*.

For many scholars, with the toppling of King Farouk in 1952 and the birth of the Egyptian Republic, the modern Middle Eastern state was born. In previous decades, tensions between political elites and burgeoning nationalist movements began to manifest in countless forms but it was the alliance of the nationalist movement with members of the Muslim Brotherhood that was fundamental to the establishment of the new Egyptian Republic. This alliance proved to be short-lived amid serious personal, political and ideological tensions between the nationalists and the Islamists. The fallout established two populist strands in the Arab world and pitted them against each other over the regulation of life and ultimately, the roots of sovereign power. In doing so it resulted in the establishment of authoritarian structures and the deep state that continues to dominate Egyptian politics to this day.[53]

The roots of Arab nationalism were found within colonial residue across the Middle East and efforts to facilitate political development amid a fragmenting post-Ottoman landscape.[54] Ideas of this shared vision reveal serious tensions between conceptions of the state and the broader Arab nation, based initially upon a shared linguistic vision, but also upon a mercantile integration of the region.[55] For some like Nazih Ayubi, the decline in this trade prevented the emergence of a strong class dimension to drive the movement, furthered by regional disintegration as a consequence of assimilation into capitalist systems by colonial actors.[56]

Of course, the very concept of Arab nationalism is contested both philosophically and politically as a consequence of context and contingency.[57] Political manifestations of the concept varied from efforts to create a shared territorial entity such as the short-lived United Arab Republic (UAR) and the broader goal of unity between all Arab states, or the much less ambitious aspiration of collectivity and coordination. Seen in a range of different ways, there is little doubt that Arab nationalism was a radically new way of *doing* politics, which resulted in a populist movement that threatened the conservative status quo of 'old style notables, large merchants and landowners'.[58] The emergence of the Arab nationalist movement provoked questions about the ordering of space and the means through which life was regulated, creating friction between *ordnung* and *ortung* once again.

This new way of doing politics led to the emergence of different forms of political organisation, perhaps most notably in Syria under the leadership of Hafez Al Assad in 1971; the ensuing transformation of the Syrian state was described by one scholar as a process of turning the state's social and political structures 'upside down'.[59] The Ba'ath ideology played a key role in the development of the state and Assad occupied a prominent role in 'defending its cause on the streets', which nearly cost him his life when he was stabbed by a member of the Muslim Brotherhood.[60]

The early years of Assad's rule sought to ensure the survival of the Ba'ath regime amid a range of *coups* – and counter *coups* – *d'état*, resulting in the widespread restriction of opposition and dissent. As part of this process, former members of the Muslim Brotherhood were asked to provide documentary evidence of their withdrawal from the organisation within a month; according to Law 49, anyone unable to provide it would be sentenced to death. Such measures had a dramatic impact upon political opposition across Syria. The years after the writing of the 1973 constitution were plagued by protest and violence, but the Hama massacre of February 1982 which killed an estimated thirty thousand people removed all space for public and private dissent, revealing the ferocity of the Assad regime and hinting at the characteristics of necropolitics to come.[61]

Yet this was just one strand of Arab nationalism. Jalal Al Sayyid, one of the prominent Arab nationalist figures – and later a founding member of the Ba'ath party – distinguished between these different strands:

Arab nationalism is the sum total of characteristics, qualities and hallmarks which are exclusive to the collectivity called the Arab nation, Arab unity is a modern notion, which stipulates that all disparate Arab countries should be formed into one single political system under one single state … the Arab nation is that human collectivity which speaks the Arabic language, inhabits a territory called the Arab lands and has a voluntary and spontaneous felling of belonging to that nation.[62]

These views have their roots in the late nineteenth century, where education played a prominent role through both the establishment of institutions and the historiographies taught.[63] Such views are supported by Youssef Choueiri who argues that a number of local histories provided by the likes of Muhammad Izzat Darawazh, Darwish Al Miqdadi and Shafiq Ghurbal can be seen as part of broader pan-Arab trends, albeit shaped by local context.[64] Fundamentally, for Choueiri, nationalism is a process that is a consequence of modernity, stemming from the interaction of global and regional factors and the institutionalisation of Arab culture and language within the fabric of states, leading to a range of different interpretations.

A shared language was key to establishing unity amid such difference and Arabic was the vehicle through which culture and history could be developed, distinct from their Ottoman and Persian neighbours. Yet questions about the role of religion within the movement offered an area of dissent, where prominent thinkers wavered in the loyalty afforded to Islam or nationalist goals. Intellectuals such as Rashid Rida, – who we shall return to in Chapter 4 – Amir Shakib Arslan, Ma'ruf Al Arnawut and Darwish Al Miqdadi differed over the role of Islam in Arab nationalism. Ultimately, it was down to a Christian, Qustantin Zurayq, to argue that religion provided a source of ethics and culture that were integral to the nationalist cause. Yet with economic malaise and the burgeoning influence of socialism from interaction with European powers, a more secular form of nationalism began to dominate Arab political discourse.[65]

In spite of a plurality of views, the movement gained a great deal of traction as ideas spread across the Middle East. Yet unlike the Zionist movement that was immediately concerned with the establishment of a state project, pan-Arabism was characterised by a range of philosophical questions about its nature.[66] Different visions of the Arab project emerged across the region, shaped by context-specific contingent factors and the lack of intellectual and political coherence ultimately prevented its development. Regime interests routinely trumped commitment to this shared ideological vision, resulting in competition between the members and a process of one-upmanship in a struggle over spatial ordering.[67]

In spite of these tensions, nationalist movements possessed a strong social core. While in power, Nasser sought to bring about social justice and the development of the Egyptian economy, albeit largely unsuccessfully as a consequence of tensions between political and economic capabilities.[68] Similar tensions were found across the Middle East at this time as states sought to regulate all aspects of life, albeit to the detriment of their economies, eroding their ideological visions in the process. The dominance of private interests over public to the benefit of particular groups at this point served to further embed patrimonial networks into the fabric of the developing states.

Central to the political and economic development of states at this time was their continued assimilation into the capitalist system and world politics. Underpinning such calculations was the emergence of a Middle Eastern 'front' in the Cold War, as concern about the spread of Communism and the location of vast reserves of oil and gas focused the attention of the super powers on the region.[69] A raft of policies were drafted in Washington, DC designed to curtail the Communist influence, most obviously seen in the Truman Doctrine and the Marshal Plan, while the UK and France sought to retain their role on the world stage amid burgeoning nationalist movements and decolonisation.

Containment policies resulted in the establishment of the Baghdad Pact and later the Eisenhower Doctrine, which attempted to secure pro-Western regimes and maintain their anti-Communist stance. Later, these efforts would result in direct interference in the domestic affairs of states across the region. A British and US sponsored *coup d'état* removed the first democratically elected Prime Minister of Iran, Mohammed Mossadegh, and returned Reza Shah to power.[70] The perceived success of the coup prompted the CIA to attempt to overthrow the Syrian government in 1957, but the plan was discovered before it could be enacted.[71] In neighbouring Iraq, a 1958 *coup d'état* removed the Hashemite dynasty, creating a period of instability and fertile ground for the Ba'ath party, particularly amid the widespread dissatisfaction with Nouri Al Said, the Prime Minister at the time, and his apparent pro-Western leanings.[72]

Perhaps the most important incident during the Cold War in the Middle East was the Suez Crisis of 1956, which not only signalled the end of British influence across the world but also demonstrated the vitality of the Arab nationalist movement.[73] Britain's presence in Egypt in the late nineteenth and early twentieth centuries had a key role to play in shaping the establishment of the Muslim Brotherhood and the emergence of the Arab nationalist beacon, Gamal Abd Al Nasser. In addition to their involvement in Palestine and Iraq, Egypt was of paramount importance to the British, where the Suez Canal was described by Anthony Eden as the 'back door to the East and swing door of the British Empire'.[74] The need to defeat Nasser related not only to British goals in the Middle East but also to its position in the world. As one minister suggested, 'If we lose the [Middle East] we are finished'.[75]

After the successful handling of the Suez Crisis, Nasser's popularity was at an all time high, but this would be eroded by military defeat to Israel amid an array of domestic and regional mistakes in the years leading up to his death in 1970. The starting point of this decline was the short-lived UAR, a union between the pan-Arab visions of Nasser's Egypt and the Syrian Ba'ath regime. The Ba'ath party was inspired by the metaphysical vision of the Syrian Zaki Al Arsuzi, but its main ideologue was the Arab nationalist Michel Aflaq, who formed the party in 1943 along with Salah Al Bittar and members of the local intelligentsia. Aflaq's vision was based upon a shared language that would eventually forge a stronger bond over time, underpinned by love, thought and sentiment.[76]

This vision was grounded in socio-economic concerns and rapidly became fused with socialism, which helped stress the importance of both the broader collective and territorial state. Although he acknowledged the role of the state in the shared Arab vision, Aflaq stressed the importance of the party that represented 'the whole of the nation which is still slumbering in self-denial of its own reality and forgetfulness of its own identity'.[77] At a time of bickering among Arab states, the Ba'ath slogan of 'common Arab destiny' began to resonate among the peoples of the region.[78]

Yet in spite of a shared commitment to Arab unity, the UAR was undermined and ultimately decimated by political wrangling and competing political visions; Nasser later expressed that the union was against his better judgement, revealing the amorphous character of Arab nationalism.[79] Local contexts also differed greatly. In Syria, anti-Egyptian sentiment was rife – some referred to 'Egyptian colonialism' – and the commercial bourgeoisie remained active unlike in Egypt, where state control of both the economy and political sphere were rapidly increasing.[80]

Political instability was not limited to the UAR but was rife amid the penetration of the region by global forces, perhaps best seen in North Yemen as civil war pitted royalists against republicans, triggered by a series of *coups d'état* that drew in states from across the region into what Malcolm Kerr later termed the Arab Cold War.[81] While Egypt supported the republicans, Saudi Arabia, Iran, Jordan and others offered military aid to the royalists out of fear at the potential revolutionary repercussions along with the nationalist aspirations of Nasser.[82] A porous border between Saudi Arabia and Yemen helped Saudi forces cross into the country which increased the severity of the task facing the Egyptians in the process. What initially began as an opportunity for Nasser to regain credibility across the Arab world proved, as Anthony Nutting suggests to be his Vietnam.[83]

Beyond Egypt, the case of Jordan reveals the precarious challenge of balancing domestic and regional pressures. Political wrangling in the country pitted the Hashemites against the vociferous Ba'athists and Nasserists, leading to the formation of an anti-Western government led by Suleiman Nabulsi, which left the kingdom occupying a contradictory position on the world stage. This situation was ultimately resolved by Hussein dissolving parliament and restricting political space across the kingdom, allowing only the Muslim Brotherhood to operate, given their strong anti-Nasser sentiment; such a move later helped assuage concerns that the Hashemite monarchy was merely a Western pawn.[84] Yet Jordan remained trapped by regional forces. Although the Hashemite kingdom decided against joining the Baghdad Pact, it felt compelled to participate in the 1967 war with Israel, alongside a number of republics who had conspired against it. Such a position appears counter intuitive, but as Michael Barnett persuasively argues, King Hussein was trapped in the parabolic pressures of the Arab sound chamber: '[I]f he went to war with Israel, the most he would lose would be the West Bank and Jerusalem, but if he stayed on the sideline he would probably lose his crown and country.'[85]

The death knell of Arab nationalism rang in the summer of 1967 when Israeli forces decimated the combined armed forces of Egypt, Jordan and Syria, resulting in the deaths of twenty thousand Arabs and the creation of a further five hundred thousand refugees. Perhaps most significantly – and indeed symbolically – however, the war resulted in the Israeli capture of Jerusalem along with the West Bank, Sinai Peninsula and the Golan Heights.

Prior to the war, an air of confidence breezed across the Arab world. Newspapers such as *Al-Ahram* published opinion pieces by commentators including Mohammed

Hassanein Heikal who argued that 'Whatever happens, and without trying to anticipate events, Israel is drawing near almost certain defeat … whether from the inside or the outside.' Others claimed that Israel could be crushed 'in a matter of hours'. Reporting on the battle, the BBC proclaimed Israeli successes as 'the swiftest victory the modern world has known'.[86] The defeat ushered in widespread recrimination and criticism of political elites through with a wave of literary works across the Middle East that framed regimes as *anzimat al-hazima*, or 'regimes of defeat'.[87] This was a seismic reframing of political leadership across the Middle East. In a damning critique of Arab states, Fouad Ajami argued that the defeat revealed that 'the Arab revolution was neither socialist nor revolutionary: The Arab world had merely mimicked the noise of revolutionary change and adopted the outside trappings of socialism; deep down, under the skin, it had not changed'.[88] Fundamentally, for Ajami, the defeat showed the bankruptcy of Arab unity.[89]

Even the establishment of the Arab League was wracked by competing visions and political difference. Although the League was able to draw upon states from across the Middle East and North Africa and also oversaw inter-governmental organisations, it was largely the victim of regional rivalries. Perhaps the League's biggest success was at the 1967 summit in Khartoum, which ended Saudi and Egyptian proxy involvement in the Yemen civil war amid shared animosity towards Israel. The Yemen war was emblematic of issues that had created schisms across the Arab world, stemming from competing visions of Arab nationalism and its relationship with the sovereign state.[90] Yet the Khartoum Summit did not end the fighting in Yemen, nor did it lead to the establishment of a unified Yemeni state. While the Republic of North Yemen was established in 1962, the People's Republic of South Yemen was established in 1967, supported by the Soviet Union, while full unity was only achieved in 1990.[91]

A second feature of the summit was debate about how to engage with Israel. Defeat in the 1967 war had escalated divisions across the Arab world while stressing the importance of a shared position on Israel. The Khartoum summit emphasised the importance of the sovereign state across the region, while also acknowledging the need for unity. Yet such unity was constrained by the personalities of rulers from states across the region, albeit alongside a pragmatic agreement not to undermine the regional order.[92] The summit also established the principle of 'three nos' in dealing with Israel: no negotiation, no recognition and no peace, which was seen by some to be a diplomatic success.

Others were less convinced, believing that the summit signalled the victory of conservative politics over radical. This conservativism was coupled with the vulnerability of the Arab order, which meant that the revolutionary philosophies of the likes of George Habash and Nayef Hawatmeh were largely ignored. Such a conclusion helped empower a range of other actors and, ultimately, created fertile ground for the emergence of Islamist movements in the coming decade.

While Ajami's words reflect the perceptions in the Middle East towards their leaders, the geographic landscape of the region had dramatically shifted. One response to this was UN Security Council Resolution 242 passed in November 1967, which called for 'respect for the acknowledgement of the sovereignty, territorial integrity and political independence of every state in the area to live in peace within secure and recognised boundaries free from threats or acts of force'.[93] The resolution brought with it tacit acceptance of the state of Israel's existence and established the idea of 'Land for Peace', which became implicit within all future peace processes.[94]

The response from Palestinian resistance organisations was to increase the ferocity of their campaign against the Israeli state with high-profile attacks including those at the Munich Olympics. By now the world was aware of the plight of the Palestinians and the UN invited the leader of the Palestine Liberation Organization (PLO), Yasser Arafat, to speak to the General Assembly in 1974. Arafat appealed to the delegates to 'enable our people to establish national independent sovereignty over its own land'.[95] With the failure of the Arab states to address the Palestinian question, it became the *cause célèbre* of liberation movements across the world.

In spite of the increasing popularity of their cause, Palestinians struggled to integrate into Jordanian society forcing them to move to Lebanon. Once again they would struggle to assimilate, particularly with the outbreak of civil war during which massacres took place at the Sabra and Shatilla refugee camps, committed by the Lebanese Phalanges Party, but according to recently released documents with the support of the IDF.[96] Beyond this, a number of Arab leaders sensed an opportunity to capitalise upon Nasser's weakness while also addressing serious domestic problems through the instrumentalised use of Islam. The (re)birth of the pan-Islamic movement provided another means through which political elites could increase their legitimacy and speak to populations at home and abroad.

Six years after the 1967 war during the Jewish festival of Yom Kippur, Egyptian forces and their Syrian counterparts launched a strike against Israeli targets, quickly regaining control of the Golan Heights and Sinai. After this initial period of Arab success, Israeli forces turned the tide of the war, albeit with help from the United States, and regained control of both the Golan Heights and Sinai Peninsula. It is widely accepted that Egyptian President Anwar Sadat began the war to try and strengthen his hand in negotiations with Israel and following a ceasefire on 22 October, he was heralded as the *batal al ubur*, the Hero of the Crossing, the one responsible for healing the wounds of Egyptian nationalism. A year later Egypt and Israel signed a disengagement agreement and, six years after the war, the Camp David Accords resulted in a peace deal between Israel and Egypt. As a consequence of the deal – and the rejection of the three nos – Egypt was isolated from the Arab world and faced sanctions from the Arab League.[97]

In Egypt the years after the war were characterised by increasing repression and authoritarianism, resulting in serious economic challenges and widespread vitriol directed against Sadat. The peace deal was viewed as a betrayal of Arab, Palestinian and Muslim causes and for Egypt to be the first Arab state to make peace was an affront to many across the state. At this time the Muslim Brotherhood began to play a more prominent role in Egyptian life and amid rising violence emerging during criticism of Egypt's peace treaty with Israel – signed under US auspices after Sadat visited Jerusalem – debate about the nature of Egyptian society and celebrations of the 1973 war, Sadat was assassinated. The failure of the Arab nationalist dream – in part because of the military defeat to Israel, yet equally as a consequence of domestic repression and rising authoritarianism – meant that political forms of Islam became increasingly popular as a way of ordering regional politics.[98]

Islamic revivalism

The repercussions of the demise of the pan-Arab movement were felt far beyond the borders of Egypt. Tensions over the construction of identity amid changing regional dynamics helped create the space and context for the emergence of an increasingly politicised form of Islam. After the failure of the pan-Arab project, Islam offered the most potent form of resistance, opening up schisms in the relationship between rulers and ruled as messages were spread through mosques, largely circumventing state censorship. Religious identity had long been a key component of Arab nationalism, with the perception that to be an Arab meant that one should also be Muslim.[99] Shared cultural aspects underpin both identities that are formed within the context of particular histories and following the fragmentation of the Arab nationalist vision, an Islamic revival was hardly surprising.

It is within this context that the British government made the decision to withdraw from 'East of Suez' and by 1971, all British forces had been removed from the Gulf. This withdrawal created space for independence movements to find traction, ultimately resulting in the establishment of Bahrain, Kuwait and the United Arab Emirates (UAE). Yet British involvement in the Gulf continued. In Bahrain, Ian Henderson, a colonial policeman awarded the George Medal for his role in quashing the Mau Mau rebellion, was installed as the head of security in 1966. Henderson retained his position for thirty years amid wide-ranging allegations of torture during his tenure.[100] Even after formal withdrawal, British involvement in Bahrain remained strong, continuing to head up key security portfolios and using an array of strategies perfected amid counter-insurgency campaigns.[101] Although British involvement remained, political tensions were exacerbated by increased Iranian activity on the archipelago, reviving historical Persian claims to sovereignty over Bahrain that were later rejected in a UN-supported plebiscite.[102]

The following years were shaped by global concerns about oil, resulting in the Organization of the Petroleum Exporting Countries (OPEC) crisis of 1973. At this time, the power of ideology had given way to the economic might of states across the Gulf who, other than Saudi Arabia, were little more than city states at this time and thus were sarcastically referred to as al-dawla al-bi'r, the oil-field/well states.[103] Yet such states would exercise a great deal of power and influence in the coming years, as events across the Gulf began to be felt across the Middle East.

Revolution in Iran resulted in a serious dislocation of the regional order.[104] While under the Shah Iran worked closely with Saudi Arabia and other Arab Gulf states on regional security, the revolution and ensuing establishment of the Islamic Republic put an end to this cooperation. It also added an explicitly sectarian dimension to the foreign policies of the Persian Gulf states,[105] alongside a strong Iranian desire to provide financial, logistical and ideological support to marginalised groups across the region.

The aftershocks were felt across the region as revolution left 'a trail of devastation in regional relations, littered with spontaneous utterances and unfettered intervention in neighbouring states'.[106]

A great deal has been written about the revolution in Iran, but a few points are worth repeating. Widespread unrest stemming from a history of persecution and draconian policies had ostracised large aspects of society who took to the streets after protest groups were brutally repressed. Ruhollah Khomeini had been viewed by many as the figurehead of opposition to the Pahlavi regime, returning from exile shortly after the Shah had abdicated. The system of *veleyat-e faqih* was quickly established, creating an Islamic system of government ruled, in the absence of the missing twelfth Imam, by Khomeini.

At this point, ideas once again took on a central role in the organisation of regional politics in the guise of pan-Islamism. Much like Arab nationalism before it, visions of pan-Islamism required demonstrations of *adherence* to – and *purity* of – Islamic messages in an attempt to speak to members of the global *umma*. Once again, regime interest began to manifest in such claims, as Saudi Arabia sought to frame Iran as a Shi'a state, reducing its appeal to Sunni Muslims, while also stressing the Persian nature of the revolution. In contrast, Tehran sought to portray the Al Saud as unpious and not worthy of being the guardians of the two holy places.[107]

Domestic unrest also began to increase amid the rising prominence of Islam within politics. The same year, on the eastern and western coasts of the kingdom, unrest was brewing. On the western coast in the largely Shi'a areas, political unrest among the marginalised Shi'a groups, long persecuted by the state on the grounds of their sect had been empowered by events in Iran. On the opposite coast, during the pilgrimage season, a descendent of the Saudi *ikhwan*, Juhayman Al Utaybi, seized the Grand Mosque of Mecca in protest at what was seen to be the 'moral laxity and degeneration of the Saudi rulers'.[108] While ended by military force, the symbolic ramifications of events demonstrate different interpretations of Wahhabist doctrine within Saudi Arabia.

The events of 1979 demonstrate the symbolic importance of religion within regional – and global – politics, particularly in light of the Soviet invasion of Afghanistan and ensuing flow of Muslims to the country to fight for the Western-backed *mujahedin*. While some scholars reduce the rivalry between Saudi Arabia and Iran to a sectarian schism,[109] a more nuanced reading of events suggests that religion has taken on additional political meaning within the context of increasingly vocal sectarian divisions.[110] In a reading of events similar to that put forward by Barnett to describe the regional influence of Arabism, Islam thus took on a symbolic role, serving as a source of legitimacy for audiences across the region. From this, religion also became a source and arena of competition and rivalry, resulting in the politicisation of religion and the conflation of politics with religion.

In Lebanon, the collision of religion, politics and geopolitics resulted in the establishment of Hizballah, the Party of God, which was formed with Iranian support, both financial and ideological, for Shi'a communities across the south of the state. In the following decades Hizballah would go on to become a prominent Iranian ally, but as we shall see, context and contingency were central to the group's formation.[111] While the new Islamic Republic was central to the emergence of the Party of God, we must also recall the importance of the Israeli invasion of Lebanon in 1982 in response to continued attacks from the PLO. The importance of the Israeli invasion in creating Hizballah was acknowledged – and perhaps overstated – by former Israeli Prime Minister Ehud Barak, who argued that 'it was our presence there that created Hezbollah'.[112]

It was hardly surprising that war quickly followed the declaration of the Islamic Republic. Iraqi armed forces invaded Iran on 22 September 1980 and began an eight-year conflict that resulted in a catastrophic loss of life and drew in other Gulf states, demonstrating the regional importance of the war amid widespread fear of Iranian intentions.[113] Khomeini's rhetoric only served to fuel such concerns by stressing a desire to export the revolution and to provide support for oppressed Muslims across the world. The use of religious rhetoric threatened to open up the regional order, leading to the fear that minority Shi'a groups – many of whom had experienced discrimination throughout state-building processes – would side with Iran.

Shared religious and ethnic ties across the border between the two states meant that in both Tehran and Baghdad, ethno-religious minorities were perceived as fifth columns and subject to discrimination and marginalisation from state projects. In Iraq, Saddam Hussein had risen to power in 1979 after a bloodless coup toppled Ahmed Hassan Al Bakr. At this point tensions between ruler and ruled resulted in a violent society and the widespread repression – and murder – of Shi'a political and religious figures. Minority groups were violently repressed, most notably in the al-Anfal genocide and the Halabja massacre which resulted in the deaths of over a hundred thousand Kurds.[114]

Following the end of the war, circumstances facilitated moves towards rapprochement between Iran and Saudi Arabia following a catastrophic earthquake in Iran and continued fear about the aspirations of Saddam Hussein. The annexation of Kuwait as the nineteenth province of Iraq in 1991 was the manifestation of such fears, exacerbated by Saddam's weapons of mass destruction (WMD) programme. The invasion quickly topped the regime of Sheikh Jaber Al Sabah, who fled to Saudi Arabia, but a week after Operation Desert Storm was launched, the Iraqi military was decimated but the Ba'ath party rule continued.

Political turmoil was not restricted to the Gulf. The struggle between Israelis and Palestinians erupted once again in 1987 with the first *intifada* (uprising) comprised of widespread acts of civil disobedience and resistance across the West Bank and Gaza. The events lasted until 1991 with the Oslo Accords but marked a significant turning point in the Palestinian cause as local agency began to act independently of regional Arab states. The Oslo Accords sought to restart the peace process and move toward a two-state solution, based on the 1978 Camp David Accords but predicated upon mutual recognition and the right of Palestinians to self-determination as documented in UN Security Council Resolutions 242 and 338. Signed on the White House lawn on 13 September 1993, the accords put a road map towards a two-state solution in place, which was halted in 1995 with the assassination of Yitzak Rabin by Yigal Amir, an Israeli citizen who rejected peace with the Palestinians. Showing the power of ideas and ideology and their interaction with political projects, at his trial, Amir claimed that he was acting in accordance with Jewish Law, which was rejected by the judges.[115]

The War on Terror

The events of 11 September 2001 dramatically altered the nature of international politics, creating more conducive conditions to spatialise the exception. The declaration of War on Terror called for the eradication of violent Islamic fundamentalism and the safe havens that allowed such groups to flourish. Across the region, the narrative of the War on Terror provided scope for leaders to frame dissent as terrorism and draw upon US support in the process. In framing political struggles as part of this broader struggle, regimes were able to conduct military campaigns that involved emergency powers, derogation from legal structures and, also, to transgress humanitarian concerns.[116]

In the State of the Union speech that followed the 9/11 attacks in early 2002, President Bush positioned Iran and Iraq as part of an 'axis of evil' that would shape the contemporary world order. Although eleven of the nineteen hijackers were Saudi citizens, the alliance between Saudi Arabia and the United States remained positive amid strong personal relations between kings and presidents.[117] Regional security calculations were a central part of tensions across the Persian Gulf, with Saudi Arabia reliant upon the United States for security while Iran deemed itself uniquely qualified to preserve the regional status quo.[118]

A year later, a US-led military force invaded Iraq, albeit with limited international support and without a UN Security Council Resolution. There is little doubt that the invasion and its aftermath had a catastrophic impact upon Iraq as it quickly became the site of a struggle for political power and a broader conflict that drew in a range of regional actors not only in response to the invasion, but also in an attempt to shape the post-war landscape of the country. Abu Al Zarqawi, the leader of Al Qa'ida in Iraq, suggested that the fight against coalition forces in Iraq would play an important role in the group's larger struggle: 'the spark has been lit here in Iraq, and its heat will continue to intensify – by Allah's permission – until it burns the crusader armies in Dabiq'.[119]

Post Saddam, politics in Iraq became shaped by a range of parabolic pressures that thrust the indigenous alongside the regional and the international, with Iran in a position of influence.[120] For many Arab leaders, the idea that Iran would gain a foothold in the Arab world was a source of great concern. Saudi Arabia was especially worried, urging US officials not to 'leave Iraq until its sovereignty has been restored, otherwise it will be vulnerable to the Iranians'.[121]

Iraq quickly become the main arena of the rivalry between Saudi Arabia – along with other Sunni Arab states – and Iran, although the struggle was not limited to Iraq's territorial borders, opening up space for a regional competition. The rivalry was escalated by King Abdullah of Jordan's claims about a 'Shi'a Crescent' that framed Shi'a communities across the region as fifth columnists, doing the nefarious bidding of Iran.

Efforts to frame regional politics along sectarian lines began in earnest after the 2003 war, yet these narratives struggled to find traction across the region, where President Mahmoud Ahmadinejad of Iran had become one of the most popular figures through his anti-imperialist stance.

Ahmadinejad's popularity was matched by that of Hassan Nasrallah, the leader of Hizballah, whose actions in the 2006 war with Israel were well received by populations across the Middle East. Only a year before conflict, Hizballah's power in Lebanon appeared to be in jeopardy following the assassination of Rafik Hariri, the Lebanese Prime Minister – allegedly by Hizballah and Syrian actors[122] – which resulted in the withdrawal of Syrian troops from the state who had been in Lebanon since the start of the civil war.[123] Yet within the space of a year, the Party of God fought a thirty-four-day war with Israel in south Lebanon, which resulted in the punitive destruction of the Beirut suburb of Dahiyeh but was framed as a success for Hizballah and, by extension, Iran.[124] As a consequence, Hizballah's popularity increased dramatically across the region, laying bare a dilemma in Arab leadership: to support groups that opposed Israel, or to oppose Shi'a groups across the region and, by extension, Iran.

Post 2003, scholars began to view a new form of regional organisation through the lens of a 'normal' Westphalian system, where states were driven by *raisons d'état*.[125] With the increased prominence of non-Arab players within regional politics the move to a 'post-Arab system' appeared in motion. At this point, as scholars such as Vali Nasr suggested, sectarian identities began to shape the region, not Arabism.[126] Yet as Morten Valbjørn and André Bank stress stress, Arab politics became shaped by a 'new' form of competition over the meaning of Arab nationalism. Evoking Malcolm Kerr's work on the *Arab Cold War* and Jerrold Green's assertion that 'Arab politics is still Arab',[127] Valbjørn and Bank argued that this new form of Arab nationalism played out over Arab symbols, allowing for analysis of the rivalry between Saudi Arabia and Iran.[128] Yet with the Arab Uprisings of less than a decade later, the ordering of space took on a different form, shaped by the interaction of Arabism with Islamism, taking place within arenas that were not traditionally associated with the Arab cause[129] and cultivating sect-based cleavages.

In December 2010, the actions of a Tunisian street vendor triggered a tidal wave of protests across the region that toppled long-standing authoritarian regimes in Tunisia, Egypt, Yemen and Libya. The Arab Uprisings eviscerated regime–society relations, opening up deep schisms within the fabric of political projects and revealing traumatic memories across the region's history. The spread of protests across the region driven by a dissatisfaction with the economic climate and frustration at the nature of regime–society relations is the focus of later chapters, but it is important to note that the spread of these grievances from Tunisia to Bahrain shows the capacity of ideas and movements to transcend state borders. The emergence of regional grievances created conditions of uncertainty that placed serious pressure on regimes across the region, resulting in fragmentation and reframing the relationship between *ordnung* and *ortung*, with broader regional consequences.

The uprisings also impacted upon relations between states as a number became embroiled in proxy conflicts in pursuit of their foreign policy goals.[130] Other states affected by the uprisings were able to avoid widespread destruction yet claims to sovereignty and legitimacy had been damaged by the unrest. This unrest put serious pressure on regime–society relations and the ability of a state to withstand this reveals a great deal about the state-building process. It also opened up schisms within these processes, particularly over the role of religion within political life. While suspicion at Iranian involvement had escalated into proxy conflicts across the region, it later transpired that groups such as the Muslim Brotherhood had received support for Qatar, leading to a Saudi-led land and sea blockade.

The blockade shortly followed the withdrawal of Saudi, Bahraini, Emirati and Sudanese ambassadors, posing a serious challenge to the very survival of the Gulf Co-Operation Council (GCC).[131] The GCC had been formed in the midst of the Iran–Iraq War to maintain security and stability across the Persian Gulf, but was predominantly formed to counter threats from across the Gulf. Yet Qatar's apparent counter-hegemonic behaviour across the post-Arab Uprisings region including the funding of violent groups, support for Islamist movements and Al Jazeera's anti-status quo coverage of the uprisings created serious schisms within the organisation. The blockade continued over the summer of 2018, echoing a similar withdrawal of ambassadors in 2014 and resulting in tenders being placed to create a canal zone between Qatar and the mainland.

Perhaps the biggest impact on the territorial construction of the Middle East, however, was the emergence of Da'ish in the summer of 2014. The declaration of the caliphate spanning territory in both Iraq and Syria was heralded by a video posted on YouTube by Bastian Vasquez, a Chilean-Norwegian man, stood on the border between Iraq and Syria. The video, entitled 'The End of Sykes–Picot' shed light upon the intentions of the group, rejecting the 'so-called border of Sykes–Picot' and articulating widespread anger and frustration at the legacy of state formation across the region.[132] Despite the inaccuracy of the claims, the Sykes–Picot narrative proved to be a powerful vehicle for demonstrating the legacy of external interference across the region. Although defeated through a loose alliance of forces from Iraq, Popular Mobilisation Units (PMUs), Iran, Hizballah, Syria, the United States, Russian, UK and Turkey, the legacy of the caliphate remains, as post-conflict reconstruction efforts play out across Iraq and conflict continues in Syria.

Conclusions

Results from a 2015 study undertaken by a research team at Mount Sinai hospital in New York found that trauma from the Holocaust with epigenetic alterations can be seen in both parents and offspring. The conclusions of the study suggest that trauma can be intergenerational and similar conclusions can be derived about how memory can be shared across communities.[133] From this, historical experience has an undeniable role in shaping the present. Thus, the establishment of political organisation across the region should not be viewed in isolation. Rather, we should place the emergence of states and groups within context, through which rules and norms are established and ultimately, one learns how to live. Interpretations of history result in the cultivation of particular forms of identities and political organisation, shaped by the residue of history.

Tensions over memories and the political actions that they provoke can cause rifts within and between states, leaving regimes open to criticism, which itself creates space for new arrangements of political life, as we see in the cases of Arabism and pan-Islamism. Thus, events occur within the context of history and memory and how people act at such points is a consequence of their engagement with both the *nomos* and the political structures of the state, which may not be aligned.

Structures also exist between states, as collective memory and experience operates within ethnic groups, sects, religions or broad ideological positions, setting rules on how to live and defining spatial borders. Ultimately, a dialectic relationship between agency and *nomos* means that political actions have metaphysical consequences with longer-term repercussions. Such structures impact on the ability to act in particular ways, creating, replicating or moulding grievances across time. Structures can exist within states, for instance across history, reflecting the challenges that the state has gone through, along with the type of nation building and the assimilation of others into national projects.

A central tension emerges from the interaction of *nomos* and *nomoi* that exist within powerful currents, driven by nationalist, tribal and religious sentiments. While the global *nomos* offers a form of political ordering, the interaction of *ordnung* and *ortung* that defines *nomoi* can create myriad forms of political life amid parabolic pressures and currents. Such currents posed challenges for the development of political organisation, seen in Migdal's ideas about the role of the state in society and the inability to penetrate and regulate social relationships.

The presence of 'weak states' and a shared normative environment means that regional security machinations have domestic repercussions. Fearing increased Iranian involvement, regimes typically respond with restrictive strategies and securitisation, resulting in conditions of bare life and necropolitics as a consequence of regional events. Of course, this is not a region-wide strategy, as we shall see in Kuwait, but it is common in Saudi Arabia, Bahrain, the UAE, Qatar, Egypt, Jordan, Syria, Lebanon, Yemen and Israel. Opposition is often framed within the context of an existential struggle for survival in an attempt to justify recourse to emergency legislation. For many states, this transcends conflict and also exists within the context of a process of securitisation, often along sectarian lines and thus, occurring across borders. Framing political tensions in such a way removes agency from domestic groups while also consolidating the support base of a ruling elite and eroding the traction of socio-economic protest movements. Within this process, regimes create the conditions of bare life and necropolitics in an effort to ensure their own survival, while securing regional alliances in the process. Yet the onset of the uprisings suggests that it is not enough to focus solely upon structure; we must also consider the role of agency in political activity.

As we move forward, it is important to remember the legacy of this experience as residue feeds into quasi-normative structures such as memory, trauma and empowerment, shaping the behaviour of actors. Indeed, the interaction of material and ideological structures shapes the capacity and desire of actors to behave in particular ways. Yet we must also note that state experience – and from this, the experience of individuals and groups within the state – differ, shaped by contingent facts. Such experiences create normative environments that regulate life, but also provide opportunities for regimes to derive legitimacy from times of contestation.

Notes

1 Ariel I. Ahram and Ellen Lust, 'The Decline and Fall of the Arab State', *Survival*, 58:2 (2016), 7–34.
2 Paul Noble, 'The Arab System: Pressures, Constraints, and Opportunities', in Bahgat Korany and Ali E. Hillal Dessouki (eds), *The Foreign Policies of Arab States* (Boulder, CO: Westview, 1991), p. 57.
3 Bahgat Korany, Paul Noble and Rex Brynen (eds), *The Many Faces of National Security in the Arab World* (New York: Palgrave Macmillan, 1993).
4 See James Quinlivan, 'Coup-Proofing: Its Practice and Consequences in the Middle East', *International Security*, 24:2 (1999), 131–65; Owen, *State, Power and Politics* and *Rise and Fall*.
5 See Khoury and Kostiner, *Tribes and State Formation in the Middle East*.
6 Michael C. Hudson, *Arab Politics: The Search for Legitimacy* (New Haven, CT: Yale University Press, 1977), p. ix.
7 Ibid., p. 83.
8 Barnett, *Dialogues in Arab Politics*, p. ix.
9 Gertrude Bell, *A Woman in Arabia: The Writings of the Queen of the Desert* (New York: Penguin, 2015), p. 195.
10 George Antonius, *Arab Awakening: The Story of the Arab National Movement* (New York: Capricorn Books, 1965), pp. 79–100.
11 Nasif Nassar, Tasawwurat al-'umma al-mu'asira [Perceptions of the Contemporary Nation in Modern Arabic Thought] (Kuwait: Mu'assasat al-Taqaddum al-Ilmi, 1986).
12 R. Palme Dutt, *World Politics 1918–1936* (New York: Random House, 1936).
13 David Fromkin, *A Peace to End All Peace: The Fall of the Ottoman Empire and the Creation of the Modern Middle East* (New York: Henry Holt & Company, 1989).
14 James Barr, *A Line in the Sand: Britain, France and the Struggle that Shaped the Middle East* (London: Simon & Schuster, 2011), ch. 1.
15 Full text available at http://avalon.law.yale.edu/20th_century/sykes.asp.
16 Quoted in Peter Mansfield, *The Ottoman Empire and Its Successors* (New York: Macmillan, 1973), p. 50.
17 Quoted in Joshua Baylson, *Territorial Allocation by Imperial Rivalry: The Human Legacy in the Near East* (Chicago: University of Chicago Press, 1987), p. 104.
18 Memorandum by the Secretary of State for Foreign Affairs (Lord Halifax), January 1939, UK National Archives, CAB 24/282/19, CP 19 (39).
19 Hanna Batatu, *The Old Social Classes and the Revolutionary Movements of Iraq: A Study of Iraq's Old Landed and Commercial Classes and of its Communists, Ba'athists and Free Officers* (Princeton, NJ: Princeton University Press, 1978), p. 13.
20 Bell, *Woman in Arabia*, p. 169.
21 Adeeda Dawisha, *Iraq: A Political History from Independence to Occupation* (Princeton, NJ: Princeton University Press, 2013), p. 72.

22 Batatu, *The Old Social Classes*.
23 Amatzia Baram, 'Neo-Tribalism in Iraq: Saddam Hussein's Tribal Policies 1991–96', *International Journal of Middle East Studies*, 29:1 (1997), 3.
24 Batatu, *The Old Social Classes*, p. 82.
25 Charles Issawi and Muhammed Yeganeh, *The Economies of Middle Eastern Oil* (New York: Praeger, 1962), pp. 143–7.
26 Batatu, *The Old Social Classes*, p. 87.
27 N. N. Ayubi, *Overstating the Arab State* (London: I. B. Tauris, 1995), p. 108.
28 Waddah Sharara, *Isti'naf al-bad'* [Resuming the Start: Essays on the Relationship Between Philosophy and History] (Beirut: Dar al-Hadatha, 1981), pp. 104–12 (cited in Ayubi, *Overstating the Arab State*, p. 109).
29 Salafism is broadly speaking a fundamentalist movement that espouses a literal application of the Quran in a quest to emulate the 'pious predecessors'. Joas Wagemakers, 'Defining Salafism', in *Oxford Research Encyclopedia*, available at http://religion.oxfordre.com/view/10.1093/acrefore/9780199340378.001.0001/acrefore-9780199340378-e-255 (accessed 15.10.17). It is generally accepted that there are three strands within Salafism: quietist, political and jihadi. For a discussion of the recognition of Saudi Arabia by the USSR see Yury Barmin, 'How Moscow Lost Riyadh in 1938' (*Al Jazeera*, 15.10.17), available at www.aljazeera.com/indepth/opinion/moscow-lost-riyadh-1938-171014113525997.html (accessed 15.10.17).
30 Ernetst Gellner, *Nations and Nationalism* (Ithaca, NY: Cornell University Press 1983), pp. 436–48.
31 Anthony B. Toth, 'Tribes and Tribulations: Bedouin Losses in the Saudi and Iraqi Struggles Over Kuwait's Frontiers, 1921–1943', *British Journal of Middle Eastern Studies*, 32:2 (2005), 145–67.
32 Interview with Kuwaiti academic, 2018.
33 S. N. Eisenstadt, 'The Kemalist Regime and Modernization: Some Comparative and Analytical Remarks', in Jacob Landau, *Ataturk and the Modernization of Turkey* (Boulder, CO: Westview Press, 1984), pp. 7–9.
34 Niyazi Berkes, *The Development of Secularism in Turkey* (Montreal: McGill University Press, 1964), pp. 129–93.
35 Bernard Lewis, *The Emergence of Modern Turkey* (2nd ed.) (New York: Oxford University Press, 1968), p. 354.
36 Quoted in Ahmad Feroz, *The Making of Modern Turkey* (London: Routledge, 1993), p. 15.
37 Antonius, *Arab Awakening*, p. 325.
38 Quoted in Walter Laqueur and Barry Rubin (eds.), *The Israeli-Arab Reader: A Documentary History of the Middle East Conflict* (5th ed.) (New York: Penguin Books, 1995), pp. 5–10.
39 'The Balfour Declaration' (Israel Ministry of Foreign Affairs, 02.11.17), available at www.mfa.gov.il/mfa/foreignpolicy/peace/guide/pages/the%20balfour%20declaration.aspx (accessed 17.11.17).
40 Jon Kimche, *The Unromantics: The Great Powers and the Balfour Declaration* (Liverpool, London and Prescot, UK: C. Tinling & Co., 1968).
41 Elie Kedourie, *Politics in the Middle East* (Oxford: Oxford University Press).
42 Mehran Kamrava, *The Modern Middle East: A Political History Since World War I* (Berkeley: University of California Press, 2013), p. 74.

43 Quoted in Edward Said, *The Question of Palestine* (New York: Random House, 2003), p. 13.

44 David Ben Gurion, *Memoirs* (New York: World, 1970), p. 26.

45 W. T. Mallison, Jr., 'The Balfour Declaration: An Appraisal in International Law', in Ibrahim Abu-Lughod (ed.), *The Transformation of Palestine: Essays on the Origin and Development of the Arab-Israeli Conflict* (Evanston, IL: Northwestern University Press, 1971), p. 98.

46 See www.un.org/Depts/dpi/palestine/ch2.pdf (accessed 01.10.10).

47 This point is routinely used by Israeli leaders to demonstrate their commitment to peace and to frame Palestinian leaders as not being committed to diplomatic efforts to resolve the situation. See Benny Morris, *1948: A History of the First Arab-Israeli War* (New Haven, CT: Yale University Press, 2008).

48 Kamrava, *The Modern Middle East*, p. 61.

49 Shlomo Sand, *The Invention of the Jewish People* (London: Verso, 2010). Sand follows this up with two books that deconstruct Zionist projects: *The Invention of the Land of Israel: From Holy Land to Homeland* (London: Verso, 2014) and *How I Stopped Being a Jew* (London: Verso, 2014).

50 Elie Kedourie, *Politics in the Middle East* (Oxford: Oxford University Press), p. 280–2.

51 Kamrava, *The Modern Middle East*, p. 70.

52 Peter Mansfield, *The British In Egypt* (London: Weidenfeld & Nicolson, 1971).

53 For a more in-depth discussion of this see Fawaz Gerges, *Making the Arab World: Nasser, Qutb and the Clash That Shaped the Middle East* (Princeton, NJ: Princeton University Press, 2018). As Gerges argues, the regime prioritised internal security and regime survival at the expense of political inclusion and the rule of law (p. 128).

54 Ayubi, *Overstating the Arab State*, p. 138.

55 Samir Amin, *The Arab Nation: Nationalism and Class Struggles* (London: Zed Books, 1978).

56 Ayubi, *Overstating the Arab State*, p. 145.

57 For a brief note outlining points to consider when studying Arab nationalism see Roger Owen, 'Arab Nationalism, Unity and Solidarity', in Talal Asad and Roger Owen (eds), *Sociology of 'Developing Societies': The Middle East* (Basingstoke, UK: Palgrave Macmillan, 1983), pp. 16–22.

58 Michael C. Hudson (ed.), *The Middle East Dilemma: The Politics and Economics of Arab Integration* (New York: Columbia University Press, 1988), p. 25.

59 Patrick Seale, 'Hafez Al Assad, Obituary' (*Guardian*, 15.06.00), available at www.theguardian.com/theguardian/2000/jun/15/guardianweekly.guardianweekly1 (accessed 16.06.15).

60 Patrick Searle, *The Struggle for Syria: A Study of Post-War Arab Politics 1945–1958* (London: I. B. Tauris, 1965).

61 For a thorough exploration of this see Salwa Ismail, *The Rule of Violence* (Cambridge, UK: Cambridge University Press, 2018).

62 Jalal Al Sayyid, *Haqiqat al-Umma al'-'Arabiyya wa 'awamil hifziha wa tamziqiha* (Beirut: Dar Al Yaqza al-'Arabiyya, 1973), pp. 40–9.

63 Antonius, *Arab Awakening*.

64 Youssef M. Choueiri, *Arab Nationalism: A History and State in the Arab World* (Oxford: Blackwell, 2000).

65 For an in-depth discussion of this see Majid Khadduri, *Political Trends in the Arab World* (Baltimore, MD; Johns Hopkins Press, 1970). Noting the influence of European ideas and a changing political climate, Khadduri explores how Sati' Al Husri argued for a separation between religion and the state as a consequence of two reasons. First, the failure of Islam to acknowledge difference amid a quest for the universal – a theme that shall be explored in later chapters – and second, the belief that in the modern age, religion was a private matter for the individual conscience. See Husri, *al-'Uruba Awwalan* [Arab Nationalism First] (Beirut: Dar al-Tali'a, 1955) , pp. 99–108.

66 Ayubi, *Overstating the Arab State*, pp. 138–51.

67 Such as that proposed by Michael Barnett.

68 Talal Asad and Roger Owen, 'The State Dimension: Introduction', in Talal Asad and Roger Owen (eds), *The Middle East* (Basingstoke, UK: Palgrave Macmillan, 1983), pp. 69–77. Such themes are explored in more detail later in the book in articles by Mark Cooper, Hugh Roberts, Lois Beck, Nikolaos van Dam, Uri Davis and Walter Lehn, who offer a case study exploration of tensions between political and economic interests and capabilities. For more on Nasser's vision see his book *The Philosophy of the Revolution*, which was the recipient of a damning review in *International Affairs* by A. J. M. Craig, who suggested that the book – a collection of three articles – was 'formless, prolix, and theatrical; full of promises of what is going to be said and of reminders of what has been said; exasperating slow to reach the point; overloaded with stale metaphors'. See *International Affairs*, 31:4 (1955), 530.

69 See Toby Matthiesen, 'Saudi Arabia and the Cold War', in Madawi Al Rasheed (ed.), *Salman's Legacy: The Dilemmas of a New Era in Saudi Arabia* (London: Hurst, 2018).

70 See Stephen Kinzer, *All the Shah's Men: An American Coup and the Roots of Middle East Terror* (Hoboken, NJ: John Wiley & Sons, 2003).

71 Searle, *Struggle for Syria*, p. 293.

72 Michael Ionides, *Divide and Lose: The Arab Revolt: 1955–58* (London: Cox & Wyman, 1960), pp. 109–97.

73 Keith Kyle, *Suez* (London: Weidenfield & Nicolson, 1991).

74 Eden, House of Commons (23 December 1929), quoted in Kyle, *Suez*, p. 1.

75 See www.nationalarchives.gov.uk/releases/2008/october/suez-14-08-1956.htm (accessed 10.11.15). See also Mark Garnett, Simon Mabon and Robert Smith, *British Foreign Policy Since 1945* (London: Routledge, 2017).

76 Michel Aflaq, *Fi Sabil al-Ba'ath* [In the Cause of the Rebirth] (Beirut: Dar al-Tali'a 1970), p. 118.

77 Ibid., p. 80.

78 Michel Aflaq, *Ma'rakat al-Masir al-Wahid* [Struggle for the Common Destiny] (Beirut: Dar al-Tali'a, 1958), pp. 18–24. For a more in-depth discussion of the work of Aflaq see Tariff Khalidi, 'A Critical Study of the Political Ideas of Michel Aflaq', *Middle East Forum*, 42 (1966), 55–68.

79 Kimche, *The Unromantics*, p. 123.

80 Ayubi, *Overstating the Arab State*, p. 150.

81 Kerr, *The Arab Cold War*.

82 Tawfiq Y. Hasou, *The Struggle for the Arab World: Egypt's Nasser and the Arab League* (London: KPI, 1985), pp. 138–9.

83 Anthony Nutting, *Nasser* (New York: E. P. Dutton, 1972), pp. 316–7. Acknowledging such an outcome, Nasser ordered the state archives to be destroyed, removing all traces of the disastrous military campaign beyond the living memory of those who served in the military at that time.

84 Marion Boulby, *The Muslim Brotherhood and the Kings of Jordan, 1945–1993* (Atlanta, GA: Scholars Press, 1999).

85 Barnett, *Dialogues in Arab Politics*, p. 158.

86 Sadik Al Azm, *Self-Criticism After The Defeat 1967* (London: Saqi, [1968] 2011), p. 37.

87 In addition to Sadik Al Azm, see also Nizar Qabbani, 'Marginal Notes in the Book of the Setback' (*Hawamish ala Daftar al-Naksa*), first published in *al-Adab* magazine, August 1967.

88 Fouad Ajami, *The Arab Predicament: Arab Politician Thought and Practice Since 1967* (New York: Cambridge University Press, 1992) pp. 32–3.

89 Ajami, *The Arab Predicament*.

90 Barnett, *Dialogues in Arab Politics*, pp. 165–74.

91 Charles Dunbar, 'The Unification of Yemen: Process, Politics, and Prospects', *Middle East Journal*, 46:3 (1992), 456–76.

92 Hudson, *The Middle East Dilemma*, pp. 10–15.

93 'United Nations Security Council Resolution 242' (United Nations, 22.11.67), available at www.un.org/Depts/dpi/palestine/ch3.pdf (accessed 12.12.15).

94 The idea of Land for Peace is based upon two clauses in the opening paragraph of UNSCR 242, which call for the withdrawal of Israeli armed forces from occupied territories, along with termination of belligerency and political recognition for a right to live in peace.

95 Walter Lacqueur and Barry Rubin, *The Israel-Arab Reader: A Documentary History of the Middle East* (New York: Penguin, 1969), p. 340.

96 'Op-Ed Contributor Declassified Documents Shed Light on a 1982 Massacre' (*New York Times*, 16.09.12), available at https://archive.nytimes.com/www.nytimes.com/interactive/2012/09/16/opinion/20120916_lebanondoc.html?action=click&contentCollection=Opinion&module=RelatedCoverage&pgtype=article&region=EndOfArticle (accessed 23.09.18); and Seth Anziska, 'Sabra and Shatila: New Revelations' (*New York Review of Books*, 17.09.18), available at www.nybooks.com/daily/2018/09/17/sabra-and-shatila-new-revelations/ (accessed 23.09.18).

97 Fred J. Khouri, *The Arab-Israeli Dilemma* (New York: Syracuse University Press, 1985), p. 414.

98 Bayat, *Revolution Without Revolutionaries*, p. 69.

99 Ira M. Lapidus, *A History of Islamic Societies* (Cambridge, UK: Cambridge University Press, 1988), p. 667.

100 Emile Nakleh, 'Op-Ed: Ian Henderson and repression in Bahrain: A Forty-Year Legacy' (Inter Press Service, 18.04.13), available at www.ipsnews.net/2013/04/op-ed-ian-henderson-and-repression-in-bahrain-a-forty-year-legacy (accessed 07.05.14).

101 Garnett et al., *British Foreign Policy Since 1945*.

102 F. Gregory Gause, *The International Relations of the Persian Gulf* (Cambridge, UK: Cambridge University Press, 2010), pp. 19–21.

103 Ayubi, *Overstating the Arab State*, p. 133.

104 Shahram Chubin and Charles Tripp, *Iran-Saudi Arabia Relations and Regional Order* (London: Oxford University Press for IISS, 1996).

105 Although not in the way commonly assumed. As we shall see, rather than Iran
     espousing support for a Shi'a agenda, it was Saudi Arabia who sought to frame events
     in Iran as a Shi'a revolution in an attempt to reduce Iran's appeal to Sunni Muslims.
106 Chubin and Tripp, *Iran-Saudi Arabia Relations*, p. 9.
107 Mabon, *Saudi Arabia and Iran*.
108 Al Rasheed, *Salman's Legacy*. See also Thomas Hegghammer and Stephane Lacroix,
     The Meccan Rebellion: The Story of Juayman al-'Utaybi Revisited (Beirut: Amal
     Press, 2011); Derek Hopwood, 'The Ideological Basis: Ibn Abd Al-Wahhab's
     Muslim Revivalism', in Tim Niblock (ed.), *State, Society and Economy in Saudi
     Arabia* (Beckenham, UK: Croom Helm, 1982), p. 32; Gwenn Okrunhlik, 'State
     Power, Religions Privilege, and Political Reform', in Mohammad Ayoob and Hasan
     Kosebalaban (eds.), *Religion and Politics in Saudi Arabia* (Boulder, CO: Lynne
     Rienner, 2009), pp. 92–3.
109 See Abdo, *The New Sectarianism*.
110 See Mabon, *Saudi Arabia and Iran*.
111 Alagha, Joseph, *Hizbullah's Documents: From the 1985 Open Letter to the 2009
     Manifesto* (Amsterdam: Amsterdam University Press, 2011).
112 James Worrall, Simon Mabon and Gordon Clubb, *Hezbollah: From Islamic Resistance
     to Government* (Santa Barbara, CA: ABC-CLIO, 2015).
113 Ann Wroe, *Lives, Lies and the Iran-Contra Affair* (London: I. B. Tauris, 1991); Chubin
     and Tripp, *Iran-Saudi Arabia Relations*, p. 10.
114 See Kanan Makiya, *Cruelty and Silence: War, Tyranny, Uprising and the Arab World*.
     (New York: W.W. Norton, 1993), p. 152.
115 'This Week in Haaretz 1996: Rabin's Assassin Gets Life in Prison' (*Haaretz*, 31.03.11),
     available at www.haaretz.com/1.5144930 (accessed 05.06.17).
116 Syrian President Bashar Al Assad used this narrative to draw international support
     in the conflict with armed groups during the Syrian uprisings. By framing events in
     such a way, atrocities committed in Aleppo and Eastern Ghouta were taken within
     the context of a war on terror and the fight against Islamist extremists, removing
     nuance from events.
117 Bruce Riedel, *Kings and Presidents* (Washington, DC: Brookings Institute, 2018).
118 Mabon, *Saudi Arabia and Iran*.
119 Dabiq 1, *The Return of Kalifah* (2014).
120 Toby Dodge, *Inventing Iraq: The Failure of Nation Building and a History Denied*
     (New York: Columbia University Press, 2005); Charles Tripp, *A History of Iraq*
     (Cambridge, UK: Cambridge University Press, 2007).
121 'Saudi Moi Says If U.S. Leaves Iraq, Saudi Arabia Will Stand With Sunnis' (WikiLeaks,
     26.12.06), available at https://wikileaks.org/plusd/cables/06RIYADH9175_a.html
     (accessed 23.12.12).
122 UN Security Council, 'Security Council Unanimously Endorses Findings of
     Investigation into Murder of Rafik Hariri, Calls for Syria's Full Unconditional
     Cooperation' (United Nations, 31.10.05), available at www.un.org/press/en/2005/
     sc8543.doc.htm (accessed 10.10.17).
123 Are Knudsen and Michael Kerr (eds), *Lebanon: After the Cedar Revolution*
     (London: Hurst, 2012).
124 There are, however, doubts as to the extent to which Iran gave a green light to
     Hizballah to go to war. For a deeper discussion see Chapter 5 of Worrall et al.,
     Hezbollah.

125 Eyal Zisser, 'Trends in Middle East Politics and their Implications for Israel', *Israel Affairs*, 12 (2006), 684–97. See also Richard N. Haass, 'The New Middle East', *Foreign Affairs*, 85 (2006), 2–12; Alexander T. J. Lennon (ed.), *The Epicenter of Crisis: The New Middle East* (Cambridge, UK: MIT Press, 2008); Robert Malley and Peter Harling, 'Beyond Moderates and Militants', *Foreign Affairs*, 89 (2010), 18–29; Marina Ottaway, Nathan J. Brown, Amr Hamzawy, Karim Sadjadpour and Paul Salem, *The New Middle East* (Washington, DC: Carnegie Endowment for International Peace, 2008); Nicolas Pelham, *A New Muslim Order: The Shia and the Middle East Sectarian Crisis* (London: I. B. Tauris, 2008).

126 Vali Nasr, *The Shia Revival: How Conflicts Within Islam Will Shape the Future* (New York: Norton, 2007).

127 Jerrold Green, 'Are Arab Politics Still Arab?', *World Politics*, 38 (1986), 611–25.

128 Morten Valbjørn and André Bank, 'The New Arab Cold War: Rediscovering the Arab Dimension of Middle East Regional Politics', *Review of International Studies*, 38:1 (2012), 3–24.

129 Christopher Phillips, 'The Arabism Debate and the Arab Uprisings', *Mediterranean Politics*, 19:1 (2013), 141–4.

130 Madawi Al Rasheed, 'The Saudi Response to the "Arab Spring": Containment and Co-Option' (openDemocracy, 10.01.12), available at www.opendemocracy.net/en/5050/saudi-response-to-arab-spring-containment-and-co-option (accessed 30.07.19); Christopher Phillips, *The Battle for Syria* (New Haven, CT and London: Yale University Press, 2016).

131 Simon Mabon, 'The Kingdom and the Glory', in Adham Saouli (ed.), *Middle Powers in the Middle East: Aspirations and Limitations* (2019, forthcoming); and Simon Mabon, 'It's a Family Affair: Religion, Geopolitics and the Rise of Mohammed bin Salman', *Insight Turkey*, 20:2 (2018), 51–66.

132 'The End of Sykes Picot' (YouTube, 28.06.2014), available at www.youtube.com/watch?v=i357G1HuFcI (accessed 29.06.14).

133 Rachel Yehuda, et al. 'Holocaust Exposure Induced Intergenerational Effects on FKBP5 Methylation', *Biological Psychiatry*, 80:5 (2016), 372–80.

3

Ink on paper

[T]he real problem, the central mystery of politics is not sovereignty, but government ... it is not the law, but the police – that is to say, the governmental machine that they form and support.

Giorgio Agamben, *The Kingdom and the Glory*

The reign of an absolute monarch is something of a rarity in the modern world. Amid the pressures of modernity, the ability to lay claim to absolute power is limited to a small number of states, a number of whom are in the Middle East. Yet such absolute power is not limited to monarchies. The prevalence of authoritarian rule across the Middle East has led to the establishment of what Nazih Ayubi has termed 'fierce states', echoing Friedrich Nietzsche's definition of the state as 'the coldest monster'.

This chapter looks at the way in which a range of political structures – formal and informal – have been created in pursuit of regime survival. Although typically viewed as the security mechanisms of a state, coercive capabilities are also embedded within the regulatory mechanisms of political systems and the ability to create bare life, underpinned by claims to legitimacy. In pursuit of this, regimes embed themselves within local contexts of tribalism, history, religion and civic myths that shape politics in an attempt to survive.

The development of political communities and the systems that regulate and order them are an essential part of closing off a community against an outside. The development of political structures is an essential part of this process, restricting the capacity of action but also giving meaning. As we have seen, amid a regional environment underpinned by shared memories and norms, the spatial exception is not restricted to one territorial area; what happens in one state can have regional implications and vice versa. The residue of history, ideology and the spread of identities across the region creates conditions that facilitate mobilisation around cross-border issues, posing serious challenges to states and structures designed to regulate life. Central to our exploration of the regulation of life and of the ban that underpins such regulation is the contingency that shapes political systems.

Acknowledgement of this position demonstrates that rulers have carefully crafted both a narrative and political infrastructure that draws upon an array of different mechanisms of control to regulate life. While religion, ideology and tribal loyalties have been moulded to meet domestic and regional needs, ruling elites have also created formal structures with the aim of ensuring the survival of the regime. Constitutions have been designed to draw upon cultural reserves to ensure that regimes are often taken to be representative of states, while opponents are often marginalised. They are imbued with a range of mechanisms to help maintain control through the capacity to strip political meaning from life, in a manifestation of the ban, and the capacity to derogate from the rule of law. Ultimately, regime survival and sovereign rule is dependent upon the combination of legitimacy, coercive capabilities, and the extent to which these aspects are embedded within territoriality.

Authoritarianism and political structures

Across the Middle East, newly established states were populated by nascent bureaucracies, with homogeneity and equality claimed to be at the heart of new political projects.[1] Security (and stability) was the primary concern of colonial overlords, yet politics was seen as a prominent mechanism of divide and rule strategies, manifesting in political structures such as in Lebanon, in tribal courts of Transjordan, or administrative separation and de facto Alawi and Druze states in Syria.[2] Within this, a number of forms of political systems have been employed with various social implications, from the Lebanese consociational model to the theocratic Islamic Republic of Iran. Each form of political organisation is unique and predicated upon context-specific contingent factors found in demographics, history, ideology and intended outcome, creating unique *nomoi* that operate within a global *nomos*.

While a cursory glance at the region sees elections in a number of states, amid various different contexts and to varying degrees of success, it is difficult to conclude that these projects meet the criteria to be considered democratic. Although elections for political positions have been an integral part of political life – understood in different ways with different restrictions – in Lebanon, Bahrain, Turkey, Israel, Iran and Kuwait, others had different experiences with democratic processes, amid allegations of corruption and malpractice. Elections have also taken place within more contested arenas such as the Kurds in Northern Iraq in 1992, Yemen in 1993, Iraq in 2005 and subsequent years and Egypt in 2012. Yet these electoral experiences do not prove the successful application of democracy, nor do they demonstrate its failure. While a number of democratic characteristics may be present, such as the *shura* meetings and tribal audiences, these have not always been replicated into the formal political structures of states, meaning authoritarian politics has dominated the region.[3] With this in mind, a number of scholars have undertaken taxonomies to articulate difference within authoritarian rule, to include strength, reformist, rentierism, fragility and failure.[4]

The dominance of authoritarianism stems from a number of reasons: first, weak civil society prohibits the emergence of a strong democratic culture, while the legacy of unions and associations have fuelled the strength of networks of patronage that cut across the region. Second, economies have historically been state run. Although in recent years a number of states have embraced liberalisation and market forces (such as Israel and the Gulf states), the legacy of statist ideologies and the power of rentierism has placed regimes centrally within the state and once again, constrained the power of society. Moreover, it has facilitated the spread of corruption through networks of patronage, where the ultimate goal was mobilising popular support, retaining authority and autonomy, but to prevent the emergence of the organised masses.[5] The potential implications of such issues are explored in depth by Hannah Arendt in *The Origins of Totalitarianism*, where she argues that the power of the mob has the capacity to dramatically reorder political characteristics of society, demonstrating the power of normative structures to reshape political life.[6]

Third, levels of education have historically been low, amid large-scale inequality. Although a recent youth bulge has co-incided with improved literacy rates and the number of people graduating with degrees, many find that there are few employment opportunities. Fourth, the region was largely absent from the third wave of democratisation that spread across the world, which Eva Bellin suggests is a consequence of geographic remoteness from the epicentre of democratisation.[7] Of course, the distinctive experiences of states across the region have created unique forms of authoritarian rule and, in the cases of Israel, Kuwait, Turkey and Lebanon, some form of democratic politics. Ultimately, difference shapes the nature of local *nomoi*, along with the intricacies of the ban.

In a number of cases, emergency powers have transitioned from exception to norm, often becoming 'coded' within legal structures of states. In Egypt, a paradigmatic example of the seemingly permanent use of emergency laws to regulate life, consecutive regimes used the law as a means of controlling populations. For the thirty years prior to the uprisings of 2011, the state existed under a de facto and *de jure* state of emergency, restricting civil liberties and political participation through the expansion of security organs of the state and blurring the *legal* and *illegal*.[8] The roots of such a strategy are found in the British military presence in the country, where Martial Law 15/1922 was used in 1914 as a mechanism of control but it was under Nasser when the blurring of law and politics, legal and illegal, became the norm. After Nasser, consecutive Egyptian presidents used emergency powers to maintain sovereign rule, embedding the exception within the fabric of the Egyptian state.[9] Similar experiences are found in Syria and Israel, where the perennial use of emergency powers creates the possibility to create bare life.

Beyond emergency powers, political systems can serve as a mechanism of overcoming societal differences through the cultivation of consociational systems of government, power-sharing agreements that give a political voice to elite representatives from societies beset by communal divisions. In Lebanon, the Taif Accords that ended a fifteen-year long civil war established a power-sharing system of government that embedded communal identities within the fabric of the political system. As Arend Lijphart advocates, the consociational approach seeks to facilitate resolution through bringing elites from key segments of society together to build coalitions, transforming a zero-sum game into a spirit of cooperation and compromise and softening communal differences.[10] Embedding communal difference into the political system provoked a great deal of criticism, but in recent years a number of scholars and analysts have softened their stance, suggesting that the power-sharing agreement has maintained peace, albeit within the context of a stagnating political climate and ongoing structural violence.[11]

We must also consider how structures have been used to integrate citizenship strip political meaning from life within the context of the camp. The reform of political structures and institutions plays a prominent role within the (re)development of the ban. The development or reform of institutions allows for the cultivation of new rules, structures and procedures, including constitutional reform, decentralisation, supervision of elections and abolition of particular ministries.[12] Of course, reform can also move away from liberalisation, as domestic challenges have often resulted in deliberalising moves. A cursory glance at political systems across the Middle East reveals that reform has been a regular characteristic of political life in the previous four decades: new constitutions, reform of existing constitutions, electoral experiments and a range of other reforms have been made in an effort to ensure regime survival.

One such example is the political liberalisation that took place in Egypt under Sadat's process of *infitah* (openness in terms of economic liberalisation). In Jordan, the first parliamentary elections were held in 1989, while in Syria, parliament was expanded to allow independents to stand in 1990. In 1992, Saudi Arabia established its Basic Law, *al hukm al-asi*, to legislate for fundamental civic rights, also adding a consultative *majlis ash-shura* the same year. Across the Gulf, new constitutions were created in 2000, which gave women the vote in Qatar, while reform in Bahrain was part of a political package to ease transition to the rule of King Hamad in 1999.

Constitutions, citizenship and 'the ban'

Political systems and their constitutions are manifestations of the formal regulation of life, adding stability and permanence to political communities. Although executives have played a dominant role within the context of Middle Eastern politics, constitutions underpin their activity and capacity to operate in a particular way. Such manifestations occur in a range of different guises and with different priorities, from monarchies to republics. Essential to our exploration is an understanding of the issue that arises when considering the interaction of *ordnung* and *ortung* and the ensuing implications for law, politics and ultimately, sovereignty.

Territorial dimensions of legal structures are often run in contradiction with broader commitments to a non-territorial community, a theme that is covered in more detail in the following chapter. This creates a dichotomy between territorial and personal laws (and obligations), both constitutionally and in customary practice. Reference to the personal does not just evoke a sense of individualism, but also to community groups often manifesting in federalism. Thus, another way of viewing this tension is between communitarian and territorial federalism, wherein legal structures shape the life of community groups.

The struggle to resolve this tension while retaining legitimacy manifests in institutional building and transnational integration, impacting upon individual loyalties.[13] Along with regional experiences, Islamic tradition contains within it rich sources of democracy and civil society. Fundamental to this is the idea that the Quran contains verses stressing that affairs must be resolved through *shura* or a process of consultation.[14] Ideas of civil society are also found within classical Islam, understood as those activities taking place beyond state control including a merchant bourgeoisie, an active judiciary and the presence of scholars all acting independently of state structures.[15] Islamist movements have traditionally capitalised upon access to such civil society, where groups have typically been able to exert influence. Ensuring that societies are run in accordance with norms is a concern for those seeking to derive legitimacy for their rule and to regulate life, from which the *nomos* offers a set of guidelines to regulate political activity; as such, a number of states have established constitutional offices to protect such norms.

It is hardly surprising that religion occupies a central role in political structures. Islam is the state religion in all but four of our states of inquiry (Israel, Turkey, Lebanon and Syria), while Islamic teachings serve as a source of law or legislation in all but three (Israel, Turkey and Lebanon). Constitutions reflect the prevalence of Islam both in the religion of the state but also through the construction of laws. In contrast, Turkey explicitly stresses its secular character. For instance, Article 2 states that, 'The Republic of Turkey is a democratic, laic and social state governed by the rule of law', while Article 174 aims to 'safeguard the laic character of the Republic'. Israel is careful to stress its democratic character, although it is also explicitly Jewish.[16] In Saudi Arabia the Basic Law of Governance of 1992 provides regulatory oversight, which is underpinned by 'the Book of God and the *Sunna* of the Prophet'.[17] Within such a context, elections were deemed inappropriate by King Fahd, the kingdom's fifth ruler.[18] In addition to such laws, norms serve as a mechanism to regulate life, seen most visibly through the importance of tribalism across the kingdom.[19]

Political projects are comprised of peoples, both citizens and non-citizens alike. An integrated notion of citizenship is created through recourse to political and legal structures, which, in turn, are shaped by culture and the interaction of identities and ideology. For Agamben, '"the people" represents a fundamental "biopolitical fracture"',[20] the totality of those integrated and sovereign citizens. This too is an exclusionary concept, referring to 'a fragmentary multiplicity of needful and excluded bodies',[21] or who were never included within the political project. As Michael Shapiro suggests, we should view citizenship in such a way, while also adding a temporal element into the discussion, which helps with the consistent process of 'renegotiation'.[22]

Citizenship occupies a central role within political projects, serving as the way in which a community closes itself off against an outside. By enshrining this difference in law, a community gains security and a temporal permanence. Yet the establishment of a number of nation states appeared at odds with traditional visions of identity, many of which transcend the sovereign state. At such points, closing the inside off against an outside that engenders loyalty among many of the inside appears increasingly difficult. Fundamentally a normative project that enshrines legal rights to people in their relationship with their polities, citizenship is seen by many to be an act that seeks to impose control on sovereign power.[23] Conversely, as Arendt argued, citizenship rights may be revoked as a mechanism of exclusion and control.[24] Historically used to regulate the *bidoon*[25] in Kuwait and Palestinians, the denial of citizenship rights continues to be powerful tool in the arsenal of regimes.[26]

Establishing states requires the closing off of an inside against an outside but even this does not necessarily entail citizenship but membership, which can be revoked through recourse to bare life. The process of state building posed a number of serious challenges to the creation of a citizenship body, requiring the delineation of territory, control of borders and identification of people to populate the new project. To identify with the nation, loyalty had to transcend traditional forms of identification that were based on looser affiliations to create loyalty to the state and, perhaps more importantly, to the interests of regimes.[27] Traditionally, those who can claim citizenship are able to trace their family lineage and territorial linkages through male parentage to the pre-independence eras.

Such concerns are particularly prominent in those states where the establishment of national projects challenged the pre-existing organisation of political life. Debate about the nature of citizenship has taken on political meaning, shaped by the context and contingency within which such considerations take place, and underpinned by nationality laws that establish stringent criteria defining who can – and cannot – be considered as belonging to the community and should be a citizen.[28] While naturalisation clauses have been added, these are underpinned by security concerns and fears about the regime survival.[29] Citizenship comes with a number of benefits. It is a mechanism to ensure loyalty amid stronger pulls towards Arab nationalism, pan-Islamism or indeed stronger nationalisms across the Gulf, facilitated by the rentier bargains that are prominent throughout the Gulf.[30] Access to such resources helped to cultivate loyalty and legitimacy among peoples, increasing regime authority in the process.[31]

The formation of states and their citizenry has been underpinned by concerns about sedition and fear about the potential to manipulate domestic events for nefarious reasons. The process of establishing control and delineating populations was shaped by the need to not only maintain security but to carve out individual identities that differentiate new political projects from what came before and from their neighbours.[32] The establishment of the United Arab Emirates out of seven distinct emirates, each with their own local identity, provides an example of such an issue. This process of establishing a federal entity posed questions about the eligibility of citizenship and passports, particularly amid the presence of a large percentage of Dubai's population who were of Persian origin.[33] Perhaps the most obvious example of this – discussed in more detail below – concerns the Kuwaiti *bidoon*, who were marginalised as a consequence of an exclusionary vision of nationality law, but one that remains pertinent today.

One response to such concerns is the revocation of citizenship – creating conditions of bare life – and in a number of cases, rendering individuals as stateless. This process gets to the very heart of ideas of belonging – *inclusion* – within political projects but also reveals the importance of context and contingency in decisions of revocation. The removal of citizenship serves as a means of excluding people from political projects, revoking their access to the benefits of citizenship with implications for their families, particularly as most of those whose citizenship has been revoked are men and nationality is traditionally passed through the father. Ultimately, it serves as a deterrent against political protest. The nature of citizenship reveals a great deal about the process through which the ban is applied and, conversely, through which life can be stripped of its political meaning. Recourse to the ban facilitates the creation of bare life, allowing for the marginalisation of peoples through the potentiality of the exception. The revocation of citizenship serves as one of the more prominent manifestations of sovereign power in operation yet potentiality means that all people *can* be reduced to the figure of *homo sacer*.

A more obvious means of understanding exclusion is revealed through consideration of the citizen–non-citizen binary. Such an approach locates citizenship both within a clearly delineated territorial space and shared cultural community, typically associated with traditional ideas about sovereignty. This vision of citizenship suggests that in search of national identities, people buy into the production of particular narratives and historiographies which supersede other identities. This position involves the development of a national myth that seeks to create a homogenous identity, derived from shared culture and tradition. Ideas that underpin such national myths and belonging require education to evoke ideas of the 'imagined community'.[34] In many cases, this has taken place within communal identities rather than at the national level, although in recent years, Gulf states have developed educational curricula that stress the importance of nationalist narratives.[35]

Amid loyalty to a range of different identities and ideologies, the construction of identity becomes incredibly complex. While the previous chapter outlined the importance of the pan ideologies of Arabism and Islamism which leave a strong residue of community spirit and belonging within contemporary political life,[36] the construction of citizenship within states often runs contrary to such sentiments. People thus retain a semblance of loyalty to both domestic and regional identities. Moreover, the formal and normative structures that emerge from history and cultural legacies typically manifest in a range of demotic experiences that are contingent upon socio-economic, cultural contexts.

Constitutions are central to these structures, which in many cases stress the importance of equality and inclusion, yet the reality of political life is somewhat different. While Article 17 of the Omani Constitution articulates that, 'All citizens are equal before the Law and share the same public rights and duties. There is no discrimination between them on the ground of gender, origin, colour, language, religion, sect, domicile, or social status', consideration of relations between indigenous Omanis and migrant workers reveals such clauses to be hollow. For those marginalised from political life, equality and inclusion are words not deeds or, as a Yemeni aphorism goes, 'ink on the paper', meaningless as few across the state care about what is written, while the central government struggles to regulate life.[37] Demands for equality and greater representation have long been a prominent feature of political opposition across the region, yet such calls have often been ignored.[38] For others, although important, citizenship and equality mean very little when people are not treated as such, reflecting deeper existential concerns about the nature of political life.[39]

Political systems serve as mechanisms of control and population management, facilitating the regulation of life while also aspiring to bring people together as an inside. In Lebanon, the Taif Accords provided major sects with permanent access to decision-making, as the key portfolios of the state are distributed between Sunni, Shi'i and Maronite. Although important in creating peace, the power-sharing system entrenched difference along communitarian lines,[40] feeding into political stagnation and exacerbating corruption along communal lines. In spite of this criticism some acknowledged that the agreement had prevented the descent into war.[41]

In Iraq, an informal system of consociational governance, the Muhasasa Ta'ifa (sectarian apportionment) was established in 2003, designed to empower representatives from Sunni, Shi'a and Kurdish communities. The implementation of this system drew upon plans made by Iraqi opposition groups at a conference in 1992 which was then imported into the country along with the exiles who became the state's new 'elite'. The Muhasasa system allocated positions according to the 'Salah al-Din principles', dividing jobs along the percentage estimates of Shi'a Sunni and Kurdish groups. These identities were placed at the heart of the agreement, which brought together a range of political parties from different communities.[42] As Toby Dodge has pertinently acknowledged, the Muhasasa Ta'ifa system has 'greatly weakened the Iraqi state', resulting in endemic corruption and widespread inefficiency. It also created conditions where the United States, Saudi Arabia and Iran could exploit Iraqi politics in pursuit of their own interests, seen in the role of Major General Qassem Soleimani playing a prominent role in government formation in 2006, 2010, 2014 and 2018.[43]

In what followed, a form of federal system was established in Iraq, creating an autonomous Kurdish zone, largely distinct from the administrative power of Baghdad, the first instance of autonomous Kurdish rule since the short lived Mahabad Republic. Of course, the implications of such structures are strongly felt in the construction of identity that replicates the community rather than the territorial. The creation of divisions – in spite of constitutional nods to inclusion – strengthen loyalty to particular identities, while conversely increasing the power of narratives of victimhood.[44] Recounting the dominance of religious identities, one senior Kurdish policy advisor suggested that 'we don't have Iraqis in Iraq'.[45]

Tribes, culture and tradition

At the heart of mass mobilisation is the power of identity and ideology. We should not view agents as the passive carriers of identity but rather as the bearers of identities, performing their roles in accordance with generally accepted practice along normative lines. Within this, identity does not operate in a primordial sense; rather, it is (re)constructed and negotiated across time and space, shaped by context and the contingency of daily life. Identity is performed, where actors behave in accordance with normative structures that clearly delineate the boundaries of acceptable action and the state. Such performances feed into the construction of the *nomos*, as each actor brings with them their own experiences and agendas that shape the regulation of political life. Within this, regimes seek to exert regulatory power and to penetrate society, but their ability to do so reveals a great deal about their own power.

The modern process of state formation was an effort to penetrate and regulate a society that was itself already regulated in accordance with previously accepted norms. New forms of political organisation contested the already existing relationship between *ordnung* and *ortung*. Different processes of tribal assimilation and contestation are seen across political projects, at various speeds and characterised by distinctive rhythms. Moreover, this did not result in the end of tribes but rather the beginning of a new set of relationships between power brokers across time and space, creating new forms and performances of regulatory power, drawing upon history, identity, solidarity and norm.[46]

Scholars including Albert Hourani, Philip S. Khoury and Joseph Kostiner have different understandings of the characteristics of a tribe, while the assimilation of tribal groups into political structures has itself become a site of contestation.[47] Efforts to assimilate tribal structures into political organisation are shaped by local and regional context, along with the particular rhythms of tribal groups, which may fall in-between different *nomoi*. The process of assimilation is a central part of state-building projects.

Khaldun's work on tribes reveals a great deal about the factors that bind such groups together, based on a shared *asabiyyah*, the principles of military-administrative slavery and religion. While these characteristics have evolved from Khaldun's initial reflections we continue to see the importance of such ideas in the contemporary state, offering a way of regulating life within contested political organisations.[48] Tribal values go alongside religion in providing a pool of reserves to legitimise political action and to help penetrate and regulate life across the modern state.

Tribal groups are malleable entities, with religious and political loyalties often transcending those of the family or the tribe. As we saw in the Battle of Jahra, members of the Al Ajmi tribe fought one another as a consequence of different political loyalties. In Jordan, much like in Iraq and Saudi Arabia, the key to domestic stability was to facilitate networks of patronage through tribal links, attracting tribal chiefs, co-opting their interests and consolidating influence.[49]

Amid this contestation and a struggle for legitimacy, regimes lay claim to whatever forms of legitimacy it may draw upon, often embodied in the ritualistic performances of tradition.[50] With such normative structures embedded within institutions and civil society, neopatrimonialism finds traction across society. As Rabi suggests, cultural heritage (*turath*) is a 'means to self-recognition', an expression of a fixed community in spite of diverse manifestations at an individual and collective level.[51] Put another way, *turath* is a means of expressing solidarity with another through the acknowledgement of a shared tradition that can be expressed and performed as law, albeit perhaps also in combination with religious and state law.[52] Much like identities, *turath* can be found at different groups, allowing for the cultivation of *asabiyyah* among different communities, including tribe, ethnicity and religion.

The importance of *turath* is also seen as a mechanism to construct legitimacy. Typically, this has been viewed through an analysis of the performance of institutions, but within the context of rentier politics, predicated upon a particular form of social contract that requires no taxation but provides little in the way of formal political expression, justice and *turath* play an important role.[53] With this in mind, Rabi speaks of the revival of *turath* in pursuit of a particular political function ¿*wazifa siyasiyya*). Islam serves as a cultural bond to tie people together within the context of political organisation, yet this was also shaped by the colonial experience, shared linguistics and culture. Although often at odds with the state, these movements are driven by leaders seeking to improve their legitimacy reserves and ensure regime survival.

Across a range of different contexts, regimes have used networks of patronage as a means of ensuring regime survival, which have, in recent years, begun to transcend state borders. This strategy of (neo)patrimonialism builds upon – and cultivates – new links across state structures, capitalising upon shared religious, tribal or ethnic identities that can be harnessed to regulate life, but conversely as a means of challenging political order. Within this melange of identities and norms, stability is achieved if its authority pattern is congruent with other authority patterns at play in society.[54]

Colonial legacies and regional forces

Further stressing contingency, global context has long provided justification and support for authoritarian regimes, first in the struggle against Communism, in some instances Arab nationalism, and more recently within the context of the War on Terror. This has provided embattled regimes with valuable international support or revenue, which can prove invaluable. As Luciani suggests, even 'limited revenue from abroad dramatically improves the state's ability to buy legitimacy through allocation and increases regime stability'.[55] One way in which this was achieved was through the tribe, which also serves as a means of demonstrating *turath* and maintaining control over space. This complex web of interrelations has embedded tribal groups within the socio-economic activities of the state, as we shall see, most notably the commercial and military arms of the state.[56]

The establishment of the territorially grounded nation state is a consequence of the collapse of imperial states that had far looser governance structures in peripheral areas, allowing tribal leaders greater autonomy. The assimilation process thus requires bringing such groups under the control of the sovereign, along with transforming tribes into citizens while retaining their tribal history. Yet in many cases, tribes retained a prominent role within state structures through their regulatory and distribution prowess. Harnessing the power of tribal norms and culture arms regimes with legitimacy and a strong regulatory arsenal, yet the inability to do so creates uncertainty and contestation, particularly in times of crisis, as the state is largely unable to develop institutions that can curtail the capacity of powerful tribal groups and lineages that offer a different way of *doing* politics and ordering space.[57]

Establishing a state over lands populated by a multitude of tribes is a difficult task. After the fall of the Ottoman Empire, the failure to address the challenges of the socio-economic landscape and the inability to assimilate rural tribal groups into the body politic of the new nation state left urban elites at the whim of powerful rural currents who were able to 'capture the state', framing its own interests and *asabiyyah* as the national interest.[58] Of course, fundamental tensions exist between states and tribes and the process of state formation sought to reconcile such differences through developing *asabiyyah* and coercion.

While the colonial era helped to establish political structures and institutions, it was most instrumental in defining the territorial aspects at play, as 'distinct states'.[59] Perhaps though, as Lisa Blaydes suggests, we should pay greater attention to earlier periods in Middle Eastern history, which help to explain the establishment of indigenous examples of civil society. For Blaydes, it was the emergence from Late Antiquity that developed – and indeed institutionalised – fiscal and bureaucratic capacities that shaped pre-Islamic societies.[60] This legacy helped the establishment of mechanisms of governance that facilitated economic life.[61]

With this in mind, a number of historians have demonstrated that the Muslim state was shaped through the interaction of the political and religious dynamics of the Middle East,[62] a position endorsed by Blaydes.[63] This argument shows how a range of factors and time periods, including the pre-Islamic, Islamic, colonial and postcolonial, shaped contemporary forms of political organisation.[64] Moreover, norms may be comprised of the residue of previous experience that remains in the historical narratives of the state or the public consciousness. Of course, some incidents had more impact than others. Indeed, the fall of the Ottoman Empire and other colonial experiences had an existential impact upon urban life across the region.[65]

Within this process of (re)construction, reform plays a prominent role in (re)shaping identity. Perhaps the most obvious example of symbolic reform is the treatment of women, wherein both legal and normative structures shape the capacity of women to act in particular ways. In Saudi Arabia, for instance, historically the role of women in the kingdom has been referred to as 'a benign apartheid' and a 'gender apartheid', reflecting the severity of legal, political and religious restrictions placed on women.[66] The severity of such expectations was felt by all living in the kingdom. One couple who worked in Saudi Arabia during the 1980s told me of a time when they had been at a party in the desert and as the man was inebriated, his female partner had driven them back to the outskirts of Riyadh. Fearing the implications of being caught driving – among a number of other convention-breaking activities – they took the decision for her inebriated partner to drive them home; the risk to their lives was seen as far less than what would happen if she had been caught driving.[67]

Of course, this has broader consequences for both the nature of society but also the construction of identity, as women are often seen as the bearers of particular identities; accepting this premise means that women can also be viewed as responsible for the construction of those identities.[68] Moreover, fears about the detrimental impact of foreign workers led to the systematic exclusion and expulsion of people who were perceived of eroding such values, a practice that continues to this day.[69]

The military and *mukhabarat*

In addition to developing (neo)patrimonial systems and reserves of legitimacy, regimes also developed coercive mechanisms to retain power. A prominent part of maintaining power was the cultivation of strong – and often parallel or competing – military and security institutions. Created more for political and symbolic purposes than in response to particular threats, they were designed to maintain power amid widespread uncertainty. In an effort to exert control, security apparatuses facilitate the destruction and reconstruction of social dynamics in support of a regime. With a focus upon both foreign and domestic threats, the establishment of institutions such as the *mukhabarat* were designed to both facilitate the regulation of life across a state but perhaps more importantly to ensure regime survival. With this in mind, the *mukhabarat* should be seen as a partisan mechanism of control, designed to regulate life.

Amid a climate of coup proofing during the 1960s and 1970s, security institutions were typically woven into the fabric of the state to facilitate regime survival. Thus, ensuring the loyalty of the security apparatus was a prominent aspect of regime survival strategies. As Eva Bellin astutely suggests, the security establishment is most likely to abandon its project amid serious financial uncertainty. When the military apparatus lacks the ability to maintain the coercive apparatus, it is compromised and disintegrates.[70] Ensuring the loyalty of military and security institutions was thus of paramount importance. Locating these institutions within (neo)patrimonial structures served two goals: providing the opportunity to reward family members, while also ensuring the loyalty of key institutions of state.

Beyond this, militaries play a prominent role within the cultivation of legitimacy and pride in nationalist projects. From vast military spending to military service, the military as an institution is central within political projects. The relationship between military and state structures has typically been close, with former military leaders becoming political leaders, while politicians across the region have served time in the armed forces as a means of improving their standing and cultivating relations with the institutional power of the state.

Militaries have also played an important role in determining political structures. In Turkey, for example, military figures have served as the self-styled protectors of democracy by maintaining the secular characteristics of the constitution. Of course, the context-specific strength of security apparatus and the prestige with which the military are held can also pose a serious threat to domestic stability, through a capacity to topple regimes. The greater that the security services are institutionalised within the state bureaucracy, the more willing it will be to disengage from politics.

Put another way, if institutionalised, an identity is developed that is separate from the state and a clear career path is opened for officers who, as Eva Bellin suggests, may not be concerned that they will be 'ruined by reform'.[71] Additionally, the military serves as a prominent facilitator of the neopatrimonial structures that have characterised regional politics. Institutions are then organised along patrimonial lines, linking members through blood, sect or patronage, blurring the distinction between public and private and linking the interests of military leadership and regime.[72]

Hafez Al Assad's rule in Syria between 1970 and 2000 was one characterised by repression and strong neopatrimonial networks, which built upon both a carefully cultivated cult of personality and a strong Ba'ath ideology.[73] The military also built upon tribal and familial networks to ensure that people loyal to both regime and leader fill key positions. These employment decisions give key security portfolios to loyal allies, feeding the construction of 'deep states', where security apparatus interests coalesce with both regime and economic interests. As such, portfolios under security apparatus control accrued vast wealth and created a vested interested in maintaining the status quo.[74]

As was common across the region at this time, the upper echelons of military and state bureaucracies were populated by close family members and other groups that benefitted strongly from patronage networks, such as the Alawi community in Syria, who comprised 11% of the population.[75] The economic interests of the Alawi community quickly became intertwined with the survival of the Assad regime.[76] This power was underpinned by a strong coercive infrastructure and an 'absolute presidency', and although elections occurred, these were largely symbolic.[77] Opposition groups such as the Muslim Brotherhood and other civil society actors were emphatically crushed to solidify such moves, resulting in the deaths of an estimated twenty-five thousand civilians.[78]

Similar experiences were found in Ba'ath Iraq, where Saddam Hussein cultivated a similar cult of personality.[79] His sons Udai and Ousai controlled key security and economic portfolios, but while Assad relied upon the Alawi community for support, Saddam drew upon the tribes and Tikritis.[80] The military played an integral role in ensuring this support, yet a sense of paranoia emerging from the spate of regional *coups d'état* prompted Saddam to create five overlapping intelligence agencies to watch the military, militias and each other.[81]

One of the most prominent examples of such an institution is the National Guard, a mechanism through which ruling elites historically distributed funds across neopatrimonial networks of tribal and Bedouin leaders. It is an institution of social control through the cultivation of strong alliances but is typically not a force to help deal with internal strife, such as urban disorder, border security or other military missions. In the Jordanian case, the interaction of such factors within the military creates a range of processes that transcend the military, carrying their production 'to the realm of national culture'.[82] In Saudi Arabia, the National Guard – established as successor to Ibn Saud's *ikhwan* – remain independent of the national military, tasked predominantly with ensuring the survival of the ruling family.

As a consequence of possessing a great deal of political influence and having accrued vast financial resources in the process, it is hardly surprising that militaries have typically been against reform that would reduce their power. Often playing the 'long game', military structures retained power and influence through a delicate balancing of political and economic interests and the continuation of (neo)patrimonial structures. Where military and security institutions were negatively affected, much like in Iraq and Yemen, the consequences have been dire as the marginalisation of individuals with military training and access to high-tech weaponry can have negative implications for regime stability.

Legitimacy and neopatrimonialism

Once constitutions and political structures have been established, political life is regulated in accordance with *turath*, which serves as a means of excluding individuals from political life. Such structures also facilitate and entrench neopatrimonialism as a tool of regime survival, through the positioning of family and tribal figures in key institutional positions, along with economic incentives. This ensures that a number of authoritarian regimes – those with strong neopatrimonial systems – were able to withstand domestic and regional pressures.[83] Neopatrimonialism not only involves the distribution of resources as a means of maintaining support, but also the allocation of prominent political positions and portfolios, serving as a means of cultivating loyalty and of circumventing political unrest.

Legitimacy plays an important role, providing some semblance of cover for the lack of democratic input, widening the support base and restricting populist movements. Such strategies are wide-ranging, employing religious, cultural, historical and economic factors. In addition to this, the importance of external influences provides support for regimes through the provision of aid or speeches supporting the regimes in international forums. When exploring neopatrimonialism, a distinction must be made as to the desired reach of such acts: Is the intention to secure the loyalty of prominent figures in key institutional positions, or is it to engender backing from across a larger support base? How one answers this question determines the strategies and narratives involved in political and security responses.

In considering the importance of bureaucratic institutions we must remember the impact of competing visions of *nomoi* that shape the construction of such institutions. While the importance of religion and Islamic law in shaping institutional development cannot be ignored,[84] we must also note that the importance of tribal values, which go some way to regulating contemporary life albeit requiring regulation within the context of the contemporary state.[85] This position is also held by Wael Hallaq, who stresses how political leaders are required to operate within the context that they inherited, which demonstrates a 'cumulative history of past action and specific manners of conduct'.[86]

The nature of political organisation prior to the establishment of contemporary states gave prominence to tribal leaders. As such, the need to assimilate tribes into political projects and networks of patronage was of paramount importance. The successful implementation of institutionalised coercive networks creates a particular form of political and economic life that can ensure loyalty to new regimes. Yet the need to restrict the power of the tribe necessitated a delicate balancing act, requiring the limitation of tribal power and influence of particular actors, while retaining the normative aspects that facilitate the construction of legitimacy particularly through tribal dress and customs.[87] The tribe serves as a means of legitimising rule through the provision of normative support for ruling elites while also eroding the coherence of the sovereign state.

The evolution of political life

Let us now consider the interaction of *nomos* and *nomoi*, formal and norm in shaping political life. The following section considers Turkey, Iran and Israel as states where the formal and normative clash to regulate life. These examples provide rich material to consider how religion shapes the interaction of *ordnung* and *ortung* and, from it, the construction of citizenship and political structures in contrasting ways. These cases although on the periphery of the region, all hold elections and explicitly articulate the role of religion within the fabric of the state.

In Turkey, after the fall of the Ottoman Empire, political life in the crumbling empire's heartland had collapsed. Under Mustafa Kemal Attatürk, a new state was established at the Treaty of Lausanne in 1923, from the embers of empire, with an explicitly secular vision at its core.[88] This almost militant form of secularism pushed religious practice to the margins of society, changing the official language from Arabic to Turkish and sought to curtail the public influence of the *ulema*. This move sought to facilitate rule 'by positivism not superstition',[89] yet in later years Ottoman traditions and cultures are said to play a more prominent role – albeit in an elusive way – ultimately leading to the emergence of the Justice and Development Party (commonly known as the AK Parti or AKP).[90]

The 'Six Arrows' of Kemalism facilitated widespread transformations across the new state, eroding the legacy of Ottoman rule.[91] It was this secularist agenda that had the most substantial impact upon Turkish public life and while religion retained influence within the private sphere, it would be removed from the public sphere.[92] In the following decades, Islamist groups gained influence, yet the secular identity of the Turkish Republic was maintained – and indeed enforced – on a number of occasions by the Turkish military in the face of rising Islamist agendas.

Following the ratification of the 1924 constitution, Article 88 stated that 'the people of Turkey regardless of their religion and race were, in terms of citizenship, to be Turkish'. A number of problems emerge from this definition, concerning belief, language, national belonging and ideology, although state practice has been different, which had a 'racist-ethnic visage' and a focus upon language.[93] The Sheikh Said rebellion of 1925 brought such issues to the fore, notably questions about Kurdish integration into the new state. State policies to such questions involved relocation and ethnic redistribution and were supported by grassroots movements such as the *Citizen Speak Turkish* campaign, resulting in political exclusion.[94]

Turkey provides an obvious example of how normative practices of citizenship, manifesting in exclusion, discrimination, relocation and marginalisation can differ – and have a serious, transformative impact upon people – from formal, legal positions. The combination of formal and normative structures helps to solidify regime and broader manifestations of hegemonic identities at the state level, resulting in deeper structural tensions within society. Such tensions then become embedded within the fabric of the state, reproducing themselves over time and manifesting in periods of intermittent violence that, in turn, have implications for the ordering of space.

In contrast to Turkey, religion occupies a more central role in post-revolutionary Iran, as state structures – both formal and normative – shaped life. The revolution in 1979 toppled the authoritarian regime of the Shah, Reza Pahlavi and imposed a new theocratic system of government, *veleyat-e faqih*, the Regency of the Jurist. This system, a theocracy with democratic traits, locates power in the hands of a supreme leader (Articles 5 and 107), whose position is given as a consequence of their Shi'i credentials.[95] Political order is conflated with theological aspects to create a system of checks and balances where democratic elements are supervised by the Guardians Council to ensure that everything is run in accordance with Khomeini's ideas.[96]

Khomeini rejected the need for government to create laws, believing that, 'If laws are needed, Islam has established them all'.[97] The Iranian constitution supports this thesis, articulating that Islamic principles and norms exemplified in the revolution 'represent an honest aspiration of the Islamic Umma'.[98] The revolution transformed all aspects of life in Iran. Women's dress also became a site of contestation, as state forces enforced the 'correct' wearing of *hijabs*.[99] Although a theocracy, elections are held for the *majlis*, the office of the president and a number of other bodies within state machinery; presidential candidates are, however, vetted by the Guardians Council.

Iranian identity is certainly not without problems. Although the state draws heavily upon a fusion of Persian nationalism and Shi'a thought, such identities are exclusionary to both ethnic and religious minorities, where around 50% of the population belong to minority groups.[100] Iran's nationality law was ratified by the *majlis* in 1929, where citizenship is 'the indisputable right of every Iranian',[101] defined initially as someone born to an Iranian father.[102] From this definition, a number of issues emerge around gender, religion, ethnicity and social origin. A direct consequence of problems with nationality has reduced both Faili Kurds and Khavari Afghans to the status of stateless peoples – essentially *homo sacer* – many of whom are living in camps and local communities, facing discrimination and restrictions to education, healthcare and employment.[103] Such tensions also manifest in structural violence over issues of language and cultural practice.[104]

Formal structures within the Iranian political system are designed to protect the vision of *veleyat-e faqih* but central to the construction of the contemporary Iranian identity is the fusion with Persian nationalism, driven by a history of conquest, expansion and a strong cultural legacy. This combination of formal with normative shapes political action and behaviour, formalising marginalisation and discrimination within the political system and the broader fabric of the state. The combination of state security mechanisms with the *basij*, the quasi-informal militia responsible for regulating opposition behaviour across the state, demonstrates the all-encompassing nature of *veleyat-e faqih* across Iran.

In contrast to both Turkey and Iran, Israel offers a much more conceptually complex discussion of citizenship, with an array of different identity groups operating across the state. The Israeli notion of citizenship is derived from an ethno-nationalist discourse, based upon Jewish descent (from the mother) and a fusion of both collectivist republicanism and individualist liberalism.[105] Amid a number of domestic challenges, particularly related to a relatively small population size, the Law of Return (1950) gives automatic citizenship to any individual with a Jewish grandparent who migrates to Israel, rather than the religious definition of a Jew. As Gershon Shafir and Yoav Peled argue, this law 'became the most important legal expression of Israel's self-definition as a Jewish state. It established ethno-nationalist citizenship that, in principle, encompassed all Jews, and only Jews, by virtue of their ethnic descent'.[106] This discourse of citizenship was fused with interpretations of the Zionist ideology – itself contested as to its vision of the state and the construction of society – and as a consequence, privileged Orthodox Jews as the 'true keepers' of the faith within Israeli society.[107]

Amid this array of identities Zionist bodies sought to homogenise Israeli society both ethnically and in terms of the urban landscape, as we shall see in Chapter 5. Even with such efforts, divisions within Jewish communities can be identified, creating classes of Jews according to diasporic roots, dividing society into *Ashkenazi* (European) and *Mizrahi* (Middle Eastern and North African) who were historically pushed to the periphery of society, although in recent years this marginalisation has been directed against Russian and Ethiopian Jews. The ensuing *kulturkampf* is predominantly found politically, ethnically and in the religious–secular struggle over political life and the character of the hegemonic narrative within the Israeli state.[108] Legal structures regulate daily life according to the Torah through observing the Sabbath, the prioritising of religious law over civil courts, state support for religious educational institutions and widespread military exemption for members from the Orthodox communities.[109] Amid concern at the perceived secularisation of Israeli society and increased prejudice towards Orthodox Jews, a number of Jewish political parties emerged that put faith at the centre of their political agendas.

After the Declaration of the State of Israel in 1948, political culture was built upon a synthesis of religious and secular ideas that were supplemented by Ben Gurion's concept of *mamlachtiyut*, understood as acting in a sovereign-like manner, concerned with the distribution of power. Supporting this project were the colonial laws of the British mandate that provided legal ground for emergency laws. The new state behaved in a pioneering manner, responding to the ideals of Zionism and expected citizens to contribute towards this broader Zionist project.[110] Somewhat counter-intuitively, this also applied to those Palestinian-Israelis who became a minority in Israel after the 1948 war and were granted citizenship, albeit with minority status. Through this combination, the nascent Israeli state took shape, yet it retained a fundamental tension between its ethnic and democratic characteristics that can be revealed in a hierarchy of citizenship, which simultaneously differentiates and incorporates. Ideas of citizenship make a distinction between those non-citizens, living under occupation in the West Bank and Gaza, which institutionalised the subjugation of Palestinian populations.

Such Palestinians thus remain distinct from Palestinian-Israelis living within Israel who are considered to be citizens, albeit with fewer rights.

When one looks at Israeli society, the ethno-nationalist discourse separates Jews from Palestinians, while the republican discourse legitimises and differentiates between the *Ashkenazi*, *Mizrahi* and other subjugated groups in Israel.[111] Such differences became embedded within political institutions and society. Along with this, the dominance of Judaism, as both formal and normative structure, plays a prominent role in the regulation of life across the state, politically and culturally. Formal and normative structures have collapsed into one another, changing the characteristics of the Israeli state, where structural violence along Jewish lines becomes a defining part of relations between Jews and non-Jewish identity groups across both Israel and the Palestinian territories.

From the cradle to the grave and everything in-between

Such issues are not limited to states with elections. The presence of vast amounts of natural resources facilitated political development in the postcolonial period, resulting in the establishment of 'rentier states', where the extraction of natural resources provides the financial resources to facilitate development, albeit not without democratic repercussions. For Rolf Schwarz, rentier states are understood as those that

> derive most or a substantial part of their revenues from the outside world and the functioning of their political system depend to a large degree on accruing external revenues that can be classified as rents. Rentier states rely on allocation and redistribution (allocation states) and hence show a remarkable different political dynamic than other states.[112]

These different dynamics reflect political, cultural, economic and religious values and regime projects are aided by vast financial resources.

Regimes in rentier states enjoy a degree of autonomy from society. The use of natural resources by regimes across the Gulf allowed leaders to create a form of social contract, where citizens paid little or no taxation but have a limited formal political voice. Rentier projects have economies that are typically state driven, with institutions that are designed to reflect local customs[113] and distributed across networks of patronage. The accumulation of finance through the sale of natural resources to external actors is central to the rentier state, which then allocates and redistributes finances across society. This reduction – or removal – of taxation within political life poses a number of challenges to those wishing to offer a taxonomy of states across the Middle East, while also resulting in a range of serious political consequences.

Vast financial resources create a workforce driven by a set of assumptions about desired job type rather than responding to demand. As a consequence, rentier states are typically home to huge numbers of migrant workers who are often caught within a zone of indistinction and the ban. In many cases, migrant workers are the most visible in public spaces: For tourists visiting the Gulf, the service industry is populated by migrant workers, whose rights and legal status are often restricted without recourse to legal and political protection.[114]

Kuwait is typically held to be one of the more democratic states within the Middle East, with a spirit of compromise at the heart of political life. Ruling elites in Kuwait have exploited vast financial resources brought about by rent from oil and gas to reorganise state institutions, maximising symbolism and loyalty, while also providing limited political space for an elected parliament and civil liberties. At this point, loyalty to the land was central to the development in Kuwait although there were no clear borders and territory was contested. Devotion to the land superseded allegiance to the tribe, seen in the battle of Al Jahra, where members of the Al Mutairi tribe were pitted against each other as Saudi-led forces went into battle against their neighbours to the east. Defence of the country was seen as tantamount to defence of the ruler and, by extension, protection of the Al Sabah meant the protection of Kuwait. Those who fought in the battle were offered citizenship, while many of those who did not became *bidoon*, those without the state.[115]

To understand how such conditions have emerged, we must consider political life before the oil boom which reveals a strategy of inclusion, designed to ensure regime survival amid tribal and geopolitical pressures. The severity of such pressures forced the dynastic Al Sabah regime to compromise instead of coercing, unlike most of its neighbours. The Al Sabah brought a range of different groups into the political realm, sacrificing resources to maintain networks of patronage and continue welfare projects[116] with tribes – who were typically attracted to the military and police[117] – merchant classes, urban workers and even Shi'a groups. In doing this, the Al Sabah embedded its legitimacy – and survival – in the stability of its society, resulting in some viewing the Al Sabah more positively than a number of the other regimes across the region. Another manifestation of such views was seen in the enfranchisement of Kuwaiti women during the 1990s, in spite of resistance from more conservative parts of society and broader regional voices.[118] Such moves were not purely altruistic, however, as the Al Sabah concentrated key ministerial portfolios in the hands of a small number of families and maintained a stronghold on the most important six ministries.[119]

Part of this process of inclusion involves engaging with Islamist parties, such as the Muslim Brotherhood, who have fed into constructions of legitimacy. Typically, the socially active side of groups like the Muslim Brotherhood develops legitimacy, but the distribution of oil wealth and provision of welfare – referred to by one US diplomat as 'cradle to the grave and everything in-between'[120] – restricted space for groups like the *ikhwan*, pushing them towards the political sphere.[121] The constitution protects the freedom of association, although the political climate has restricted the establishment of certain groups at precarious times. Such space allowed for the establishment of a local branch of the Muslim Brotherhood in 1963, which then proved useful to the Kuwaiti state in their effort to balance against the rise of Arab nationalism. Over the coming decades, the Muslim Brotherhood continued to play a prominent role in Kuwaiti politics, facilitating political reform of twenty-five districts to ten, while allying themselves with secular parties as a means to avoid discreditation.[122]

A positive form of political regulation occurs through the distribution of land in Kuwait, establishing cohesion among the family and providing close members with access to the business sector. Allocation of land would embed mercantile classes into the burgeoning bureaucratic structures, while instilling Kuwaiti citizens with the belief that one day they too may own land in their country. Similar practices occurred in the UAE, where it was alleged that each citizen would be allocated three plots of land.[123] Moreover, this also serves to depoliticise domestic communities, leaving the political arena to ruling families as other actors are moved into the economic sector, albeit with loyalty to the state.[124]

A more negative case is found when considering the *bidoon jinsiya* – stateless people – who have long been marginalised from official state structures.[125] Kuwait's national identity law defines citizens as those who had settled in the country before 1920, or who had been naturalised at a later date. *Bidoon* are those who either *refused* or were *unable* to gain Kuwaiti citizenship during the formative years of the state, many of whom are descendants of Bedouin tribes such as the Shammar and 'Aneza.[126] Fearing instability from the movement of people, the Kuwaiti government sought to strip political life from *bidoon* and to restrict access to public goods. Marginalised from state structures, they are unable to register for citizenship, access free education in state-run schools, register vehicles or purchase telephone lines and SIM cards. On their driving licences, *bidoon* are registered as 'illegal residents'.[127] In this case, they are not covered by international law as Kuwait is neither a signatory to the 1954 Convention Relating to the Status of Stateless Persons, nor the 1961 Convention on the Prevention of Statelessness. From this, it appears that the *bidoon* exist as a prime example of *hominus sacri*, existing in bare life, without recourse to political and legal structures yet bound by the very structures that abandon them. An Amnesty International report in 2016 estimated that one hundred and twenty thousand people are *bidoon* in Kuwait.[128]

In neighbouring Bahrain, a system of minority rule – of Sunni over Shi'i – historically established a form of sectarian difference into political life, stemming from long-standing fears about the other.[129] Across the history of twentieth-century Bahrain, Shi'a Bahrainis were relegated to second-class status on the island, along with urban labourers from the Asian subcontinent, as the Sunni regime sought to maintain political control by empowering the Sunni minority. Tracing relations between Shi'a groups and the regime reveals a number of crisis points: after the Iranian revolution, in the mid-1990s and more recently after the Arab Uprisings.[130] A number of political and legal structures were established that sought to regulate political life, such as the Law of Political Association Article 4 which prevents the establishment of an organisation based on sectarian, religious or ideological grounds.

In the decades after the British withdrawal, a climate of political dissatisfaction consumed the island where sectarian identity was seen as a threat to political stability.[131] Although political life is far more complex than the binary delineation of sectarian difference, Shi'a groups have historically been viewed as a source of opposition.[132] One report for a Bahraini ministry noted:

[T]here is a dangerous challenge facing Bahraini society in the increased role of the Shī'a [and] the retreat of the role of the Sunna in the Bahraini political system; namely, the problem concerns the country's [Bahrain's] national security, and the likelihood of political regime change in the long term by means of the current relationships between Bahrain's Shīʿa and all the Shīʿa in Iran, Iraq, Saudi Arabia's eastern region, and Kuwait.[133]

Much like the history of Iraq, perception of perfidious interference dominated relations between the Al Khalifa regime and its Shi'a population, coloured by beliefs about Iranian interference in domestic affairs.[134] Such perceptions have had a detrimental impact upon Shi'a politics across the island, as parties such as Al Wefaq have experienced widespread discrimination and their leaders have been jailed. Moreover, a number of Al Wefaq MPs have been arrested and stripped of their nationalities with devastating consequences for themselves and their families. In some cases, family members were detained and tortured, cast into bare life as regimes exert sovereign power in a flagrant attempt to survive whatever the cost.[135]

Creating the ban

Within the spatialised exception, different manifestations of localised *nomos* are shaped by particular contingency and subjectivity, restricting political activity and perceived challenges to regime authority and legitimacy in accordance with context-specific dynamics. In response to such challenges, regimes seek to create exclusion and legitimacy to facilitate, justify and normalise mechanisms of control. One such mechanism is to cultivate a sense of belonging to normative and ideational communities that can then be strengthened and mobilised over time,[136] fed into neopatrimonial structures and preserved through the distribution of wealth and cultural capital.[137] Supporting these approaches is the declaration of a state of exception.

For Agamben, the ban emerges as derogation from constitutional clauses is undertaken in order to protect the political project. The onset of much emergency legislation has its roots in colonial times, where the British sought to regulate life and establish order in tumultuous times. Across Israel and Palestine, recourse to British Mandate Law has provided scope for the use of emergency powers, regulating the Arab citizens of Israel between 1948 and 1966, while also regulating life in the West Bank.[138] Moving responsibility for peace and order from the police to the military was a key strategy and an indispensible means of defending imperial interests. With roots in the 1883 Act for the More Effective Suppression of Local Disturbances and Dangerous Associations, the move allowed for the use of extraordinary powers that had previously been restricted under common law. Further exploration of emergency legislation sees almost routine suspension of the law in times of crisis, reflecting a broad desire to stay in power, albeit facilitated by local context and history. Such laws are primarily used as mechanisms of control, in defiance of Article 4 of the International Bill of Human Rights' prohibition of discrimination.

We should not view political structures as neutral. As we have seen, the interaction of formal and normative structures has an undeniable impact upon the regulation of life, both letting life live and defining the type of life that is acceptable to be lived, with the ban a key part of this regulation. The ban emerges not only through potentiality found in democratic systems but also as a consequence of the development of political structures that are inherently exclusionary. Moreover, as Wael Hallaq argues, we can identify five metaphysical 'form properties' that constitute states, which reveal abstract similarities in political organisation that allow us to apply Agamben's case to the Middle East. These include a constitution from historical experience, sovereignty and ensuing metaphysics, legislative monopoly, bureaucratic machinery and a cultural hegemonic engagement with the social order.[139] Of course, such comments are deeply contested but provide an entry point into discussions of sovereignty and the ban in non-democratic states.

The application of states of emergency varies across the region, from royal decree to two-thirds majority of parliament. In Qatar, Article 69 of Chapter IV states that the Prince [sic] declares emergency law. The article then gives the Prince the power to take

> all the prompt measures needed to confront any danger threatening the State's safety, or the integrity of its territory, or its People's security and interests, or obstruct the State's institutions from performing their functions, on condition that the decree must include the nature of the exceptional circumstance for which the Martial Law was declared, and prescribe the measures taken to confront it.

In Jordan, the application of a Defence Law by Royal Decree can establish conditions of martial law, which may also 'impose a limited censorship on newspapers, publications, books and information and communication media in matters related to public safety and national defence purposes'. In Saudi Arabia, the responsibility lies with the King, as enshrined in Article 61 of the Basic Law. Article 62 states that, 'If the King feels that these measures may better be permanent, he then shall take whatever legal action he deems necessary in this regard'. As we shall see in the next chapter, this ability to define the exception – an expression of sovereign power – ultimately raises a number of questions about the *source* of that power.

Across the region we can group the reasons for derogation from the rule of law and declarations of states of emergency into three areas: war, *coups d'état* and general unrest. The establishment of the state of Israel was coeval with declaration of emergency legislation in Israel, along with martial law in Iraq in 1948, but the 1967 war created states of emergency in Egypt, Jordan and Syria. It also resulted in similar conditions in Lebanon only five years later. Amid concerns about their role in domestic politics and Israeli activity, Hizballah declared a state of emergency in 2018, asking myriad questions about sovereign power in the process. Following the Iraqi invasion of Kuwait in 1991, the later also declared martial law.

In the decades after the establishment of Israel, the interaction of parabolic pressures created a climate of uncertainty and unrest, resulting in a series of *coups d'état* across the region. Within this climate, Egypt, Saudi Arabia, Turkey, Syria, Yemen, Jordan, Lebanon and Iraq all derogated from the rule of law to maintain power. Additionally, amid conditions of domestic unrest, Saudi Arabia, Bahrain, Iraq and Egypt all declared emergency laws. Central to such moves were desires to maintain power, regulate space and retain territorial integrity amid fear about efforts to alter spatial borders and the regulation of life. In these cases, the state of exception has become the norm, where emergency legislation is taken to be a necessary part of normal politics and individuals reside in camps, both physical and metaphysical. Such a move changes the nature of political life in the region, making the exception the rule and creating the conditions wherein individuals become *hominus sacri*.

Conclusions

The space within which *ordnung* and *ortung* interact defines both *nomos* and sovereign power. Understanding the political structures that order space requires consideration of the specific context and contingency. In many cases, this is shaped by both colonial experience and broader understandings of *turath* and belonging. A range of different identities thus emerge and clash within *nomos*. Political structures try to regulate the manifestation of such identities and tensions through constitutions, institutions and regulating civil society. Returning to Migdal, regimes seek to regulate and penetrate society, while others seek to stymie such intentions.

While it is clear that biopolitical projects aim to regulate life, this chapter has shown that a spatial dimension surrounds such efforts, wherein norms and multi-layered concepts of identity clash with more formal political structures creating a zone of indistinction between *ordnung* and *ortung*. By exploring the political realm we have come to see that it serves as an arena through which layered and complex understandings of identity and citizenship merge and are regulated by norms – often in tension with formal structures – to create a particular type of spatial ordering. Here, much like the tale of Antigone, competing visions of political ordering often clash with one another.

There is little doubt that normative structures play a strong regulatory role, which goes some way to explaining the survival of the Gulf monarchies who are able to draw upon a strong sense of *asabiyyah*, which creates deep schisms in times of uncertainty. Norms and personal relationships reflect both the importance of tradition but also the instability of formal institutions, serving as a source of opposition.[140]

As Nicolas Gavrielides argues,

> What makes tribal ideology even more powerful and pervasive besides being truly Arab, is the fact that it is never formally articulated, stated, written down or even openly criticized. It is just there, permeating every action, thought or process which is of socio-political significance.[141]

Although somewhat hyperbolic and quick to ignore the importance of vast financial might, Gavrielides makes an interesting point about the power of norms in regulating life, particularly when embedded within neopatrimonial structures that facilitate the distribution of wealth in accordance with such values.

In doing this, regimes risk creating political projects that are increasingly organised along ethnic, tribal or communal lines, undermining broader political projects, while also deepening divisions between particular groups in a negative consequence of Khaldun's *asabiyyah*. The spatial repercussions of such a move risk opening up fissures within the relationship between *ordnung* and *ortung*, the spatialised *nomos*, along with the broader organisation of regional politics along the lines of a spatialised exception. While Gulf states offer perhaps the most obvious example of such practices, we should not ignore other political projects, for whom defining the spatialised exception is equally challenging, albeit in a range of different ways.

Notes

1 Roger Owen, *State, Power and Politics in the Making of the Modern Middle East* (Oxford: Routledge, 1992), p. 10.
2 Ibid., p. 13.
3 Juan J. Linz, 'An Authoritarian Regime: Spain', in Erik Allardt and Stein Rokkam (ed.), *Mass Politics: Studies in Political Sociology* (New York: Free Press, 1970), p. 255.
4 See, in particular, the work of Rolf Schwarz, 'The Political Economy of State-Formation in the Arab Middle East: Rentier States, Economic Reform and Democratization', *Review of International Political Economy*, 15 (2008), 599–621.
5 Ilkay Sunar, 'The Politics of State Interventionism in "Populist" Egypt and Turkey', research paper, Bogazici University, Istanbul (1993), 15–16, 29–31.
6 Hannah Arendt, *The Origins of Totalitarianism* (New York: Harcourt, 1968).
7 Eva Bellin, 'Coercive Institutions and Coercive Leaders', in Marsh Pripstein Posusney and Michele Penner Angrist (eds), *Authoritarianism in the Middle East: Regimes and Resistance* (Boulder, CO: Lynne Rienner, 2005), p. 23.
8 Egyptian Organization for Human Rights, 'EOHR Issues Report on Impact of Emergency Law' (IFEX, February 2003), available at www.ifex.org/egypt/2003/02/28/eohr_issues_report_on_impact_of (accessed 10.10.12).
9 See Simon Mabon and Lucia Ardovini, 'Egypt's Unbreakable Curse: Tracing the State of Exception from Ubarak to Al Sisi', *Mediterranean Politics* (2019, forthcoming).
10 Adend Lijphart, *Democracy in Plural Societies: A Comparative Exploration* (New Haven, CT: Yale University Press, 1977).
11 This view emerged from discussions with academic colleagues working on these issues.
12 Holger Albrecht and Oliver Schlumberger, '"Waiting for Godot": Regime Change Without Democratization in the Middle East', *International Political Science Review*, 25:4 (2004), 380.
13 Chibli Mallat, 'On the Specificity of Middle Eastern Constitutionalism', *Case Western Reserve Journal of International Law*, 38:1 (2006), 17.
14 Quran 42:36, 3:53. enjoining 'politics by consultation' (*al-amr shura baynakum*).
15 Ibid., p. 29.
16 Sammy Smooha, 'The Model of Ethnic Democracy: Israel as a Jewish and Democratic State', *Nations and Nationalism*, 8:4 (2002), 475–503.
17 Basic Law of Governance (*nazam al-hukm*) Royal Order A/90 (01.03.92), available at www.saudiembassy.net (accessed 10.02.18).
18 Abdulaziz H. Al Fahad 'Ornamental Constitutionalism: The Saudi Basic Law of Governance', *Yale Journal of International Law*, 30 (2005), 275.

19 Simon Mabon, 'Kingdom in Crisis: Saudi Arabia, Instability and the Arab Spring', *Contemporary Security Policy*, 33:3 (2012), 530–3.

20 Agamben, *Homo Sacer*, p. 10.

21 Ibid., p. 10.

22 Michael J. Shapiro, 'National Times and Other Times: Re-Thinking Citizenship', *Cultural Studies*, 14:1 (2000), 79–98.

23 Saskia Sassen, 'Towards Post-National and Denationalized Citizenship', in E. F. Isin and B. Turner (eds), *Handbook of Citizenship Studies* (London: Sage, 2002), pp. 227–93.

24 Arendt, *Origins of Totalitarianism*.

25 *Bidoon* are those who either refused or were unable to gain Kuwaiti citizenship during the formative years of the state.

26 For a historical discussion of this see Andrew Whitley, 'Minorities and the Stateless in Persian Gulf Politics', *Survival*, 35:4 (1993), 28–50.

27 Gianluca Paolo Parolin, *Citizenship in the Arab World: Kin, Religion and Nation-State* (Amsterdam: Amsterdam University Press, 2009); Anh Nga Longva, 'Citizenship in the Gulf States: Conceptualization and Practice', in Nils A. Butenschøn, Uri Daivs and Manuel Hassassian (eds), *Citizenship and the State in the Middle East: Approaches and Applications* (New York: Syracuse University Press, 2000), pp. 179–200.

28 Parolin, *Citizenship in the Arab World*, pp. 95–111.

29 Zahra Babar, 'Enduring "Contested" Citizenship in the Gulf Cooperation Council', in Nils A. Butenschon and Roel Meijer (eds), *The Middle East in Transition: The Centrality of Citizenship* (Cheltenham: Edward Elgar, 2018), p. 118.

30 See Mehran Kamrava, 'The Political Economy of Renterism', in Mehran Kamrava (ed.), *The Political Economy of the Persian Gulf* (London: Hurst & Company, 2012), pp. 39–68; Hazem Beblawi, 'The Rentier State in the Arab World', *Arab Studies Quarterly*, 9:4 (Fall 1987), 383–98; Abdulhadi Khalaf, 'The Politics of Migration', in Abdulhadi Khalaf, Omar Alshahabi and Adam Hanieh (eds), *Transit States: Labour, Migration and Citizenship in the Gulf* (London: Pluto Press, 2015), pp. 39–56.

31 Jane Kinninmont, 'Citizenship in the Gulf', in Ana Echague (ed.), *The Gulf States and the Arab Uprisings* (Spain: FRIDE and the Gulf Research Centre, 2013), pp. 51–2.

32 Gwenn Okruhlik and Patrick J. Conge, 'The Politics of Border Disputes: On the Arabian Peninsula', *International Journal*, 54:2 (1999), 230–48; and Claire Beaugrand, 'Nationality and Migration Control in the Gulf Countries', *INAMO*, 46 (2006), 10–14.

33 Dina Alqadi, 'The Door That Cannot Be Closed: Citizens Bidoon Citizenship in the United Arab Emirates' (Unpublished Dissertation, Duke University, 2015), p. 52.

34 See Bennedict Anderson, *Imagined Communities: Reflections on the Origin and Spread of Nationalism* (London: Verso, 1983).

35 Interview with Saudi academic, 2017.

36 Interview with female Saudi journalist, 2017.

37 Interview with Yemen analyst, 2018.

38 Interview with Bahraini Shi'a cleric, 2015.

39 Interview with Syrian analyst, 2017.

40 Theodor Hanf, *Co-Existence in Wartime Lebanon: Death of a State and Birth of a Nation* (London: I. B. Tauris, 1993); Antoine Messarra, *Théorie Générale du Système Politique Libanais* (Paris: Paris-Cariscript, Beyrouth-Librairie Orientale (avec le concours du Centre National des Lettres, 2004).

41 Interview with Lebanese policy analyst, 2017.

42 Ibrahim Nawar, 'Untying the Knot' (*Al-Ahram Weekly*, No. 625, February 2003), available at http://weekly.ahram.org.eg/archive/2003/625/sc5.htm (accessed 10.10.12).

43 Toby Dodge, 'Iraq and Muhasasa Ta'ifa; The External Imposition of Sectarian Politics', in Simon Mabon (ed.), *Saudi Arabia and Iran: The Struggle to Shape the Middle East* (London: Foreign Policy Centre, 2018), pp. 13–14.

44 Interview with Bahraini Shi'a cleric, 2018.

45 Interview with Iraqi Kurdish policy advisor, 2017.

46 For an in depth discussion of this see Khoury and Kostiner, *Tribes and State Formation in the Middle East.*

47 Khoury and Kostiner, *Tribes and State Formation in the Middle East.*

48 Ernest Gellner, 'Tribalism and the State in the Middle East', in Khoury and Kostiner, *Tribes and State Formation in the Middle East*, p. 122.

49 Ghassan Salame (ed.), *The Foundations of the Arab State* (Oxford: Routledge, 1987), pp. 159–61.

50 John G. Taylor, *From Modernization to Modes of production: A Critique of the Sociologies of Development and Underdevelopment* (London: Macmillan), 1979, p. 182.

51 Hamid A. Rabi, *Suluk al-malik fi tadbir al-mamalik: ta'lif al-'allamma shihab al-Din ibn Abi al-Rubayyi'* [Suluk al-malik fi tadbir al-mammalik: By the Scholar Shihab al-Din ibn Abi al-Rubayyi'], Vol. 1 (Cairo: Dar al-Sha'b, 1980), p. 218.

52 For example, see Frank H. Stewart, 'Customary Law Among the Bedouin of the Middle East and North Africa', in Dawn Chatty (ed.), *Nomadic Societies in the Middle East and North Africa: Entering the 21st Century* (Leiden: Brill, 2006), pp. 239–41.

53 Ayubi, *Overstating the Arab State*, p. 32.

54 Harry Eckstein, *Regarding Politics: Essays on Political Theory, Stability and Change* (Berkeley: University of California Press, 1991), p. 188.

55 Luciani, *The Arab State*, p. 78.

56 Ayubi, *Overstating the Arab State*, p. 125.

57 Bassam Tibi, 'The Simultaneity of the Unsimultaneous: Old Tribes and Imposed Nation-States in the Modern Middle East', in Khoury and Kostiner, *Tribes and State Formation in the Middle East*, pp. 127–52.

58 Ghassan Salame, *Al Mujtama' wa al-Dawla fi al-Mashriq al'Arabi* [Society and State in the Arab Levant] (Beirut: CAUS, 1987), pp. 23–4. Salame offers the example of the Alawi of Syria as an example of this.

59 Ayubi, *Overstating the Arab State*, p. 86.

60 Lisa Blaydes, 'State Building in the Middle East', *Annual Review of Political Science*, 20 (2017), 487–504.

61 Hugh Kennedy, 'The City and the Nomad', in Robert Irwin (ed.), *The New Cambridge History of Islam* (Cambridge, UK: Cambridge University Press, 2010), p. 283.

62 C. F. Robinson, 'Introduction', in C. F. Robinson (ed.), *New Cambridge History of Islam. Vol. 1: The Formation of the Islamic World, Sixth to Eleventh Centuries* (Cambridge, UK: Cambridge University Press, 2010), pp. 1–16.

63 Blaydes, 'State Building in the Middle East'.

64 This is discussed in more detail in the following chapter.

65 Khoury and Kostiner, *Tribes and State Formation in the Middle* East, p. 122; Salame, *Foundations of the Arab State*, p. 23.

66 Madawi Al Rasheed, *A Most Masculine State: Gender, Politics and Religion in Saudi Arabia* (Cambridge, UK: Cambridge University Press, 2013).

67 Interview with British expats based in Saudi Arabia in the 1980s, 2017. Their time there was spent working for a number of different companies who were supported and protected by particular royals.

68 Al Rasheed, *A Most Masculine State*.
69 Interview with British ex-pat based in Saudi Arabia in the 1980s, 2017.
70 Bellin, 'Coercive Institutions and Coercive Leaders', p. 27.
71 Ibid, p. 29.
72 Bellin, 'Reconsidering the Robustness of Authoritarianism in the Middle East', p. 133.
73 Lisa Weeden, *Ambiguities of Domination: Politics, Rhetoric and Symbols in Contemporary Syria* (Chicago: Chicago University Press, 1999).
74 See, for instance, the work of Jean-Pierre Filiu, *From Deep State to Islamic State* (London: Hurst, 2015).
75 Hanna Batatu, 'Syria's Muslim Brethren', *Middle East Research and Information Project Reports*, 110 (1982), 20.
76 Gerard Michaud, 'The Importance of Bodyguards', *Middle East Research and Information Project Reports*, 110 (1982), 30.
77 Volker Perthes, *The Political Economy of Syria under Asad* (London: I. B. Tauris, 1995), p. 139.
78 See Alasdair Drysdale, 'The Assad Regime and its Troubles', *Middle East Research and Information Project Reports*, 110 (1982), 3–11; Fred Lawson, 'Social Bases of the Hamah Revolt', *Middle East Research and Information Project Reports*, 110 (1982), 24–28; Patrick Seale, *Asad: The Struggle for the Middle East* (Berkeley: University of California Press, 1988).
79 Kanan Makiya, *Cruelty and Silence: War, Tyranny, Uprising, and the Arab World* (New York: Norton, 1993), p. 63.
80 Batatu, *The Old Social Classes*, p. 1084.
81 Isam Al Khafaji, 'State Terror and the Degradation of Politics', *Middle East Report*, 176 (1992), 19.
82 Joseph A. Massad, *Colonial Effects: The Making of National Identity in Jordan* (New York: Columbia University Press, 2001), p. 5.
83 Jason Brownlee, '… And Yet They Persist: Explaining Survival and Transition in Neopatrimonial Regimes', *Studies in Comparative International Development*, 37:3 (2002), 35–63.
84 Blaydes, 'State Building in the Middle East'.
85 P. Crone, 'The Tribe and the State', in J. A. Hall (ed.), *States in History* (Oxford: Basil Blackwood, 1986), pp. 48–77; I. M. Lapidus, *A History of Islamic Societies* (New York: Cambridge University Press, 2014).
86 Wael Hallaq, 'Islamic Law: History and Transformation', in R. Irwin, *New Cambridge History of Islam. Vol. 4: Islamic Cultures and Societies to the End of the Eighteenth Century* (Cambridge, UK: Cambridge University Press, 2010), pp. 152–3.
87 Mabon, 'Kingdom in Crisis'.
88 Andrew Mango, *Ataturk* (London: John Murray, 1999).
89 Halil Inalcik, 'Learning the Medrese, and the Ulemas', in Halil Inalcik, *Ottoman Empire: The Classical Age 1300–1600* (New York: Praeger, 1973), p. 171.
90 Interview with Turkish academic, 2017.
91 The sultan had been kept on to facilitate the smooth transition from New Turks rule to the Turkish Republic.
92 Interview with Turkish academic, 2017.
93 Kemal Kirisci, 'Disaggregating Turkish Citizenship and Immigration Practices', *Middle Eastern Studies*, 36:3 (2000), 2. See also A. Aktar, 'Cumhuriyetin Ilk Yillarinda Uygulanan Turklestirme Politikalarin', *Tarih ve Toplum*, 156 (1996), 4–18.

94 D. McDowall, *A Modern History of the Kurds* (London: I. B. Tauris, 1996), pp. 184–211.

95 Shaul Bakhash, *The Reign of the Ayatollahs: Iran and the Islamic Revolution* (New York: Basic Books, 1990).

96 For many Shi'a clerics, these ideas go against conventional Shi'a views, for whom 'the order of the clerical hierarchy is its disorder'.

97 Ayatollah Ruhollah Khomeini, 'Islamic Government', in Hamid Algar (trans.), *Islam and Revolution: Writings and Declarations of Imam Khomeini* (Berkeley, CA: Mizan, 1981), pp. 137–8.

98 Iranian Constitution, available at www.constituteproject.org/constitution/Iran_1989.pdf?lang=en (accessed 10.02.08).

99 For many Iranian women, pushing the hijab towards the back of the head and revealing hair is an act of what James C. Scott has termed 'everyday resistance'. James C. Scott, *Weapons of the Weak: Everyday Forms of Peasant Resistance* (New Haven, CT: Yale University Press, 1985).

100 Alam Saleh, *Ethnic Identity and the State in Iran* (New York: Palgrave Macmillan, 2013).

101 Iranian Nationality Law Article 41.

102 Iranian Nationality Law Article 976 (2).

103 E. Campbell, *The Faili Kurds of Iraq: Thirty Years Without Nationality* (Refugees International, 2010), https://reliefweb.int/report/iraq/faili-kurds-iraq-thirty-years-without-nationality (accessed 10.05.11); and A. Whitley, 'Minorities and the Stateless in Persian Gulf Politics', *Survival: Global Politics and Strategy*, 35:4 (1993), 28–50.

104 Iranian newspapers routinely feature cartoons that depict members of ethnic minorities as inferior.

105 Yoav Peled, 'Ethnic Democracy and the Legal Construction of Citizenship: Arab Citizens of the Jewish State', *American Political Science Review*, 86 (1992), 432–43.

106 Gershon Shafir and Yoav Peled, 'Citizenship and Stratification in an Ethnic Democracy', *Ethnic and Racial Studies*, 21:3 (1998), 412–13. It also became a source of contestation.

107 Yonathan Shapiro, *Politicians as a Hegemonic Class: The Case of Israel* (Tel Aviv: Sifriat Poalim, 1996), pp. 46–9.

108 Gideon Katz, 'The Israeli Kulturkampf', *Israeli Affairs*, 14:2 (2008), 237–54.

109 Shafir and Peled, 'Citizenship and Stratification', p. 413.

110 Peled, 'Ethnic Democracy'.

111 Shafir and Peled, 'Citizenship and Stratification'.

112 Rolf Schwarz, 'The Political Economy of State-Formation in the Arab Middle East: Rentier States, Economic Reform, and Democratization', *Review of International Political Economy*, 15:4 (2008), 604.

113 Alexander Bligh, 'The Saudi Religious Elite (*ulama*) as Participant in the Political System of the Kingdom', *International Journal of Middle East Studies*, 17:1 (1985), 37–50.

114 Ahmed Kanna, 'A Politics of Non-Recognition? Biopolitics of Arab Gulf Worker Protests in the Year of Uprisings', *Interface: A Journal For and About Social Movements*, 4:1 (2012), 146–64.

115 Interview with Kuwaiti academic, 2017.

116 K. H. Al Naqib, *Al-mujtama' wa al-dawlah fi al-khalij wa al-jazeerah al-arabiyah* [Society and the State in the Gulf and the Arabian Peninsular] (Beirut: Markaz Dirasat al-Wahdan al-Arabiyah, 1987).

117 I. Al Taher, *Kuwait: The Reality* (Pittsburg, PA: Dorrance Publishing, 1995),
     pp. 172–4.
118 Sean L. Yom, 'Oil, Coalitions, and Regime Durability: The Origins and Persistence of
     Popular Rentierism in Kuwait', *Studies in Comparative International Development*, 46
     (2011), 217–41.
119 Ayubi, *Overstating the Arab State*, p. 251.
120 'From Cradle-to-Grave: An Overview of Kuwait's Welfare Ban' (*Scoop*, WikiLeaks,
     01.05.06), available at www.scoop.co.nz/stories/WL0605/S01599/cablegate-from-
     cradle-to-grave-an-overview-of-kuwaits-welfare.htm (accessed 30.07.19).
121 Courtney Freer, 'Exclusion-Moderation in the Gulf Context: Tracing the
     Development of Pragmatic Islamism in Kuwait', *Middle East Studies*, 54:1
     (2017), 1–21.
122 P. Salem, 'Kuwait: Politics in a Participatory Emirate', *Carnegie Papers*, 3 (2007), 6. See
     also Freer, 'Exclusion-Moderation'.
123 Ayubi, *Overstating the Arab State*, p. 229.
124 Jill Chrystal, *Oil and Politics in the Gulf: Rulers and Merchants in Kuwait and Qatar*
     (Cambridge, UK: Cambridge University Press, 1990), p. 109.
125 Typically shortened to *bidoon*, meaning 'without'.
126 Interview with Kuwaiti academic, 2017.
127 Maureen Lynch and Patrick Barbieri, 'Kuwait: State of Exclusion' (Refugees
     International, 2007), available at www.refworld.org/pdfid/47a6ee9bd.pdf (accessed
     17.05.17).
128 www.amnesty.org/download/Documents/MDE1741452016ENGLISH.PDF (accessed
     17.05.17).
129 A prominent theme that emerged in conversation with Bahrainis from different
     sections of society.
130 C. Kurzman, *The Unthinkable Revolution in Iran* (Cambridge, MA: Harvard
     University Press, 2004), pp. 154–62.
131 Frederic Wehrey, 'Bahrain's Decade of Discontent', *Journal of Democracy*, 24:3
     (2013), 118.
132 'Simmering Unrest in Bahrain' (*Guardian*, 17.04.08), available at www.theguardian.
     com/world/us-embassy-cables-documents/150213 (accessed 07.05.12).
133 Salah Al Bandar, 'Al-bah rayn: al-khiyār al-dīmūqrātī wa āliyāt al-iqs a', unpublished
     report prepared by the Gulf Center for Democratic Development (September 2006),
     cited in Justin Gengler, 'Royal Factionalism, the Khawalid, and the Securitization of
     'the Shi'a Problem' in Bahrain', *Journal of Arabian Studies*, 3:1 (2013), 53–79.
134 Fawaz bin Mohammad Al Khalifa, 'The Gulf States Are Stuck Between Isil and Iran'
     (*Telegraph*, 21.01.16), available at www.telegraph.co.uk/news/worldnews/middleeast/
     bahrain/12113355/The-Gulf-states-are-stuck-between-Isil-and-Iran.html (accessed
     21.01.16).
135 Interview with former Bahraini MP, 2015.
136 Interview with Bahraini Shi'a cleric, 2018.
137 Interview with Turkish journalist, 2017.
138 Israel has no written constitution but has existed under a state of emergency since
     its inception. After forty years, the Knesset passed the Basic Law of 1992, which
     provided greater legislative oversight. Within this Basic Law, Regulation 111 allows
     for administrative detention of up to six months without trial, after which the case
     must be reviewed by a military advisory committee but detention can be renewed.

Regulation 125 empowers military commanders to define areas as 'closed', requiring military approval to enter or leave. The regulation has also been used to exclude landowners from their land.

139 Hallaq, *The Impossible State*, p. 23.
140 Lisa Anderson, 'Absolutism and the Resilience of Monarchy in the Middle East', *Political Science Quarterly*, 106 (1991), 12–13.
141 Nicolas Gavrielides, 'Tribal Democracy: the Anatomy of Parliamentary Elections in Kuwait', in Linda Layne (ed.), *Elections in the Middle East; Implications of Recent Trends* (Boulder, CO: Westview Press, 1987), p. 182.

4

The *dawla* and the *umma*

lIlmw i adwa (sa sbt eiinadstate).
[Mankind was but one nation, then it fell into variance.]

Quran 10:19

As muezzins recite calls to prayer from the minarets of mosques across the region, Muslims are reminded of the obligations of their faith. *Fajr* marks a universal start to the day before the complexities of contemporary life create countless trajectories of possibility, as life becomes shaped by the contingency of the political. Beyond this universal call, muezzins are divided by subjectivity, space, time and the complexity of everyday life. Unlike other religions, Islam is seen to be well equipped to provide guidance to its followers on circumventing the seductive trappings of this life, offering explicitly political instructions on how best to live life through adherence to the Quran and Sunna – seen to be Divine Law – yet the very interpretation of such texts by infallible human agency brings in subjectivity, couched in contingency, which leads to division, difference and ultimately, the erosion of God's sovereignty.

This chapter focuses on competing claims of authority found within religion and their political repercussions. To do this, it uses the concept of the state of exception to identify a *zone of indistinction* that is inherent within a number of political projects deriving legitimacy from religion. Much like the discussion of *turath* in the previous chapter, it is concerned with how the collapse of religion into politics and politics into religion creates a zone of indistinction, along with contesting the relationship between *ordnung* and *ortung* that transcends the traditional understanding of political organisation. In this zone, regimes are able to circumvent domestic – and regional – contestation but are simultaneously contested through recourse to such systems of belief, with serious repercussions for political life across the Middle East.

In a book entitled *Islamic Exceptionalism: How the Struggle Over Islam Is Reshaping The World*, Shadi Hamid argues that because of its inherently political nature, Islam is fundamentally different to other religions, albeit with different visions of political meaning shaping contemporary political life.[1] This identification of the political nature of Islam is not new, with a range of scholars suggesting that the religion was established alongside a political community led by the Prophet, which was inherently concerned with the ordering of people, not space. Moreover, such scholars also argue that the Quran offers guidance on all facets of life, which makes it political. Of course, these views are contested. Nazih Ayubi argues that this approach is Orientalist and that the Quran offers no explicit guidance on political life and community, albeit using a narrow definition of politics.[2] This view supports the position of Sheikh Ali Abd Al Raziq, an Egyptian jurist whose framing of Islam as *apolitical* helped support the development of sovereign entities after the First World War, while also permitting Muslim heads of state to have relations with non-Muslim states.[3]

Yet this too is not without problems. One approach is to reject Abd Al Raziq's thesis that political authority is not part of Islam, suggesting that Sharia can be applied to the contemporary world.[4] A second approach stems from a discussion of Islamic conceptions of society initially identified by Khaldun but developed by other Muslim thinkers who stressed the importance of adding the seemingly coeval conception of the state to society as a means of safeguarding the latter.[5]

Fundamental to discussion about the relationship between religion and politics is the source of sovereignty. For Muslims, God is the source of sovereignty and as the Quran proclaims, 'It is God unto whom belongeth the sovereignty of the heavens and earth'.[6] But while sovereignty is found in God, questions arise as to who should rule on earth after the death of the Prophet. Andrew F. March suggests that different interpretations of authority offer a range of ways to resolve such questions. First, political authority is seen as a form of contract between rulers and ruled, when a council of representatives selected a leader to guide the community in accordance with his message. A second view is that God's will is embodied in the corpus of the divine law itself and so divine sovereignty is derived from the extent to which God's law is applied, albeit opening up a raft of new questions in the process.[7]

Religion and politics

On 1 April 1979, less than three months after the abdication of the Shah of Shahs, Iranians voted to establish an Islamic Republic on the basis of principles espoused by Grand Ayatollah Ruhollah Khomeini who was later installed as Supreme Leader of the new state. Khomeini had returned to Iran on 1 February where he was greeted by an estimated crowd of five million who had grown angry at the Shah's regime. Over the course of the protests, political opposition to the Shah coalesced around Khomeini's vision, some more willing than others amid allegations that the revolution was hijacked by Khomenei, but in the months that followed, Islam played a prominent role in regulating life across the new republic.[8]

The new republic placed Shi'a values at the centre of its approach to politics, both domestic and foreign and, as such, dramatically altered the nature of Middle Eastern politics. Values of resistance and counter-hegemony became integral to understanding Tehran's foreign policy, extrapolating from the Karbala Narrative in Shi'a history.[9] Revolutionary fervour dramatically altered the regional order, fusing geopolitical concerns with sectarian schisms seen in the establishment of Hizballah[10] and provision of support for other Shi'a groups across the region. Following such support, in the years that followed, the blame for domestic unrest in states with sectarian tensions was firmly placed on Iran.

Later the same year, a group of Saudi tribesmen led by Juhayman Al Utaybi entered the Grand Mosque in Mecca and seized control of it by force. The group held the belief that modernisation strategies deployed by the Al Saud – coupled with their 'un-Islamic' behaviour – were contrary to Islam. Al Utaybi garnered support from disaffected groups across the kingdom and gained credibility through his family lineage; his ancestors had been part of the *ikhwan* rebellion of the 1920s, which rose up against Ibn Saud's state-building project for its departure from the rightful path of Islam. Events in Mecca shook the kingdom, revealing the fragility of the Al Saud's relationship with their Islamic backers and stressing the complexity of the dual path of political rule and adherence to Wahhabist doctrine.

Amid the rapid transformations of the previous decades across the region, such unrest was hardly surprising. Transformation from empire to colonial rule fashioned a range of different experiences and interpretations of Islam, demonstrating the contingency of relationship between state, regime and society. Within anti-colonial and nationalist movements, religion took on an important role beyond faith as a means through which collective identities could be mobilised and alternative visions of political organisation could be established. Islam also initially served as a source of culture and tradition for the nascent Arab nationalist movement, along with providing the means through which the movement could spread, but while it initially lost ground to projects espousing Arab unity, the importance of Islam as a means of ordering politics and space remained.

There is little doubt that Islam has had a dramatic impact on the political arena, existing in numerous forms: from the puritanical Wahhabism in Saudi Arabia to the quietist Ibadism in Oman, via competing visions of the role of clerics in Shi'a thought. This plurality of interpretations has implications for the ordering of life for individual believers, communities and states even before they are placed in the context of political life and parabolic regional currents. Yet much like *nomos*, Islamic unity proved to be an illusion. Instead, competing interpretations of faith and the ordering of life in accordance with Islamic traditions quickly emerged, in some cases, operating in tension with state projects. One of the most devastating points of tension concerns sectarian difference.

Few terms possess such vitriolic connotations as sectarianism which, in recent years, has become imbued with all manner of issues pertaining to identity politics and violence. Although there is a complex history of relations between the different sects of Islam, there is nothing inherently violent about this difference. In recent times it has become imbued with negative connotations, amid the perception of deviating from the norm, while also being extended to include political and ethnic minorities.[11] As a consequence, as Fanar Haddad acknowledges, the concept of sectarianism has become almost meaningless. Deeply politicised and emotionally charged, the concept has become a 'catch-all' term, an elastic concept applied to a range of issues that can often be understood as everything from the perfectly legitimate expressions of sect-centric behaviour to inter-sect violence.[12] Consideration of the concept reveals tensions about the construction of identity and debate between primordialists and constructivists.[13] Putting this debate aside, we can identify three distinct periods where inter-sect violence escalated to play a prominent role in regional politics in 1979, 2003 and 2011; unsurprisingly, regional politics also shape the relationship between sects and broader political communities. These periods correspond with crises in regional politics: the Iranian Revolution, the Iraq War and the Arab Uprisings.

The mobilisation and manipulation of sect-based identities for political reasons has been a common feature of political life. After the fall of the Ottoman Empire, sect-based identities were mobilised for political purposes, both domestic and regional, as regimes attempt to exert control and influence and, ultimately seek to ensure their survival. Speaking to constituents is one means through which this can be achieved, while also strengthening claims to unity through fear of *the other*. Efforts to regulate the territorially bounded *polis* often involve recourse to religion, which transcends territoriality. As such, given recourse to a shared normative environment we can see how internal actions can have regional repercussions.

Contemporary debates on the role of religion across the Middle East are characterised by tension over the extent to which religion shapes politics or politics shapes religion. Yet the role of religion is far more complex that being reduced to two opposing positions. Indeed, a religious community should not be viewed as a monolithic, homogenous bloc; instead, in addition to doctrinal differences, we must also consider movements on the left and right, economical disparities, the conservative, the peaceful and violent, allowing for context-specific contingencies to shape analysis. Religion is also a site of tension between tradition and modernity, best seen in the anachronistic demands of fundamentalist movements to return to the golden ages of their faith. At its heart is a desire to ensure that religion retains a 'authoritative' position within contemporary life; although what this authoritative position looks like is open to interpretation.

The emergence of an 'Islamist revival' during the 1970s sought to challenge the status quo across the region, arguing that political trajectories had failed and that only Islam could correct this failure. Across the region, Islam occupied a seemingly contradictory place within states, acting as a legitimising tool yet also posing a serious threat to regime stability and sovereign power.[14] As a result, regimes faced a delicate balancing act to ensure that Islamic legitimacy was maintained while also restricting the capacity for groups to charge regimes with impropriety or to use the mosque as a means through which to challenge political elites and also regulate life; religion itself became a zone of indistinction and a site of possibility for political empowerment, repression and everything in-between. A range of methods were used to regulate and control the role of Islam within state structures including constitutional reform and the marginalisation of particular individuals and groups. Ultimately, however, religious groups were largely unable to seize power, leading Olivier Roy's famous claim about 'the failure of political Islam'[15] and, later, a move towards post-Islamism amid debate about the role of religion in society, politics and the public sphere.

The importance of contingent factors that shape the place of religion in society means that we cannot understand such groups and their place within societies – or across the region more broadly – without putting them into political, social and legal contexts. In support of this, Asef Bayat stresses the importance of social agents and the context in which they operate in order to understand group behaviour and the characteristics of faith.[16] As Shahab Ahmed suggests, current 'analytical conceptualisations' of Islam fall short of 'identifying the coherent dynamic of internal contradiction which lies at the crux of any successful conceptualisation of Islam as a human and historical phenomenon'.[17] From this position we can see the emergence of a number of 'Islams' contingent upon context. This leads to inherent diversity, difference and disagreement, a point stressed by Ahmed who argues that 'Muslims have long been well aware that they are not all the same ... that their identity as components of universal Islam includes diverse experiences, agreement, disagreement ... that they mostly agree to disagree and be different.'[18]

The logical conclusion of such an argument is the idea that each Muslim is simultaneously an instance of 'local imam' and a member of the *universal* community of Muslims.[19] This distance in positions is also populated by membership of different communities, from family, tribe, sect or state. Running Ahmed's argument to its conclusion, with competition over symbolic forms and manifestations of Islam, 'there can be only one true Islam, and that is usually the believer's own'.[20] Such a position leads to serious tensions between competing visions of unity, from local community to broader claims to the *umma*, along with disparate views of the ordering of life. Moreover, it also opens up debate about the relationship of religion and territory with discussions about *dar al Islam*, the land of Islam and *dar al harb*, literally the 'land of war' but better understood as any contested territory not under Islamic rule.[21] Parallels also emerge with the concept of the *nomos*, which draws people together amid shared belief in a particular vision but implodes after a fleeting instance of unity. Managing such difference is fundamentally a political task, albeit couched in theological dissonance.

From this, faith serves simultaneously as a source of legitimacy and an existential threat to political stability and the future of the territorially grounded sovereign state. Religion is a means through which opposition can emerge through the existence of competing sovereignties, yet it retains an integral position within mechanisms of control. One of the mechanisms through which regimes create bare life is through the manipulation of religious structures and the cultivation of sectarian difference. To understand such processes we must explore the means through which regimes have 'played' with both religion and the law, co-opting both formal and normative structures within the framework of political organisation.[22]

Although Islam is seen to be all encompassing with God the source of all laws, we cannot isolate it from context and socio-economic facts, for it is through engagement with such a reality that region exists and evolves. As James Piscatori suggests, 'even a religious code such as Islam must be accepted as variable and evolving with changing circumstances'.[23] From this, it is easily apparent that when placed within political, social, economic and historical context, religion has a prominent role in ordering and regulating life. Joseph Schacht, one of the foremost scholars on Islam notes how Islam is biopolitical in nature: '[T]he central feature that makes Islamic religious law what it is, that guarantees its unity in all its diversity, is the assessing of all human acts and relationship, including those which we call legal, from the point of view of the concepts.'[24] At the heart of the biopolitical project is the regulation of life, which serves as a means of exerting control across populations and defining the spatial borders of political organisation in the process.

As Dale Eikelman and James Piscatori suggest, politics takes on an Islamic dimension through 'the invocation of ideas and symbols, which Muslims in different contexts identify as "Islamic", in support of … organized claims and counterclaims'. Given that a plurality of ideas and symbols can be used amid a range of different interpretations of such symbols, it appears obvious that there can then be myriad definitions of political Islam.[25] It is generally accepted that most Muslims hold the law to be 'divine and sacred', revealed through the Quran and the Sunna. Yet in application and interpretation, law is not monolithic or without critical reflection as it is interpreted by 'infallible' actors who are products of the contingency of time and space. Comprised of both formal and normative aspects – where rules and rituals merge – the establishment of the rule of law and its meaning within Islam is contingent upon the relationship between religion, law and the nature of political organisation. Thus, local histories and cultural narratives shape such contingency, feeding into the construction of what a person is refrained from doing and with it, spatial boundaries.[26]

Put another way by Joseph Schacht:

> The central feature that makes Islamic religious law what it is, that guarantees its unity in all its diversity, is the assessing of all human acts and relationship, including those which we call legal, from the point of view of the concepts 'obligatory/recommended/indifferent/reprehensible/forbidden'.[27]

Yet with the societal, political and technological developments since the establishment of Sharia, the regulation of conduct is 'unsettled'[28] leading to different interpretations shaped by local contingency. This, in itself, is a source of consternation for many such as Mawdudi, who hold that God's law must govern over the infallible contingency of human-made laws.[29]

Debate over ideas and their application in political contexts has long been a source of contention. Efforts to circumvent such issues and to appease disparate groups of people have required developing reserves of legitimacy. Demonstrating the importance of retaining Islamic legitimacy, a number of states sought to demonstrate legitimacy and compliance with Sharia by establishing Sharia guarantee clauses, designed to offer guidance on 'what Islamic states were permitted to do'.[30] Such clauses have to be applied constitutionally, requiring a particular set of clauses to ensure compliance and ratification of theological requirements in both public and private realms. Of course, the development of these clauses led to doubt concerning elements of historical Islamic legal thought while also resulting in factionalism within *dar al Islam*.[31]

Amid efforts to create unity among such difference, there is often recourse to an 'ideal' time of Islam. Although the 'golden age' of Islam is often heralded as the most ideal period, leading many Salafists to desire the somewhat anachronistic return to such a time, this was a highly idealised period that bore little resemblance to contemporary narratives of the time.[32] With this in mind, it is important to remember that religion exists within contingent factors in order to provide a more holistic picture of events. Moreover, we must also recognise the tension between public and private, which becomes particularly important during the apparent rise of post-Islamism and the move away from formal structures of Islamic teaching.

Such issues are not limited to Islam but emerge when considering the relationship between other faiths and politics. In Israel, the complex relationship between state and synagogue has been equally contested. The interaction of faith with different interpretations of Zionist ideology – themselves shaped by different socio-economic, cultural and historical experiences – has resulted in a melange of different groups operating both inside and outside the recognised borders of the state of Israel. Moreover, in the case of groups such as the Hilltop Youth and Gush Emunim (along with a number of others) there is a rejection of the legitimacy of the state and its borders, with the groups' members seeking to alter the geographical parameters of the state.

Religion, authority and interpretive dissonance

Facing challenges to their sovereignty, Middle Eastern rulers have long sought to circumvent contestation through the construction of exclusionary projects that fuse faith, tradition and culture.[33] Yet recourse to religion or culture does not necessarily preclude others from subscribing to particular communities and, perhaps, such constructions create scope for further contestation across state boundaries. The establishment of mandate-era territorially grounded forms of political organisation created colonial forms of statehood, clashing with the prominence of Islam in political structures.[34] Although not theological concepts, *dar al Islam* and *dar al harb* are classical legal doctrines treated in the Sharia that help to regulate interactions between Muslims and non-Muslims that are not necessarily separated territorially. The establishment of territorially defined forms of political organisation in the mandate period were thus directly at odds with a religion that recognised 'no boundaries for its kingdom'.[35]

In addition to this clash of territorial principles, the evolution of political organisation during the state-building process required the transition of social dynamics from largely rural, tribal and Bedouin communities to more sedentarised and urban communities. Regulating life in these new communities was of paramount importance and constitutions provided scope through which to achieve this goal, yet most of the newly urban population were not familiar with the workings of constitutional documents and, amid the uncertainty of their new life, found certainty in religion. Most states across the region positioned Islam centrally, with the Sharia serving as a source of laws within constitutions, yet religion also plays an important role in regulating behaviour through the establishment of a normative code that believers subscribe to.

To understand how religion is used within contemporary politics we must begin by engaging with a dichotomy that shaped interactions between Islam and politics in the formative stages of state-building processes. Islam as a religion occupies a space within both theological and political realms as the Prophet Mohammad served both as a head of faith and also as the leader of a political community and this tension remains. The Madinah Constitution that governed political life under Mohammad is widely believed to be the first written constitution. Theories of politics and the state within Islam and Islamic law are shaped by the interaction of these two difference concepts but it is debate about the ultimate source of sovereignty that are of paramount importance. Within Islam, God is sovereign, the ultimate source of law and authority. The Quran supports such a position: 'Allah is the One who has sent the Messenger with guidance and the religion of truth to prevail over all religions.'[36]

It also provides guidance as to how to live: 'verily those decrees guide you to my straight path, so follow the way and do not follow other paths.'[37] Given its holistic nature, Islam is a public faith, seeking to regulate political activity to maintain well-being and as such, it provides guidance on all facets of life. It follows that the Sharia is the basic constitution for Muslims and written political constitutions across the region pay heed to this, acknowledging the Quran and Sharia as providing guidance in how to live. From such a position it is easy to see how Islam can be seen as a *political* religion, although issues of interpretation arise amid efforts to regulate the complexities of modern life.

The history of Islam is one replete with difference, from the Khawarij to the Shi'a manifesting not only in theological and political schisms, but also within sects.[38] The spread of Islam across the Middle East means that different sects and interpretations within sects have created allegiances within and across states and challenged the spatial regulation of life in the process.

In engaging in debate about sovereignty, one must consider its roots, limitations and the right of rebellion, representation and relationship between Sharia, democracy and policy enactments.[39] How one answers such questions is contingent upon context, both within and between states, where history and interpretation are important in shaping the relationship between Islam and political structures and ultimately, political life. With its focus on the regulation of life, Islam has long possessed a political dimension. As we have seen, however, with the plurality of views and interpretations, political decisions require legitimisation – often by the *ulema* – who justify rule by stressing that their authority is a consequence of either the sovereignty of Divine Law, or the contract between ruler and ruled.[40] The relationship between ruling elites and prominent clerics is then of paramount importance when considering stability within a territory, where human order is to conform to 'the Divine norm'.[41]

Here lies a fundamental tension within debate about religious sovereignty. While some argue that Divine Law is the source of sovereignty, others suggest that the very interpretation of Divine Law brings subjectivity and human infallibility into the theological realm, diluting God's message. Such a conclusion results in numerous challenges to the sovereign order, particularly among efforts to derive legitimacy and authority from theological sources.

During the fragmentation of empire, political figures sought to codify aspects of Islamic law within constitutions as a means of ensuring regime survival in the face of burgeoning nationalist movements. Around this time, Egyptian scholars at Al Azhar sought to repudiate claims made by Alī ʿAbd Al Rāziq that the Prophet Mohammad was a religious messenger, without political doctrine.[42] In response, Muḥammad Rashīd Riḍā argued that justice, equality and accountability are found within Islam and are regulated by following the correct path:

> As far as civil and social governance is concerned, Islam laid down its foundation and principles, and prescribed for the umma that it employ judgment and discretion in this area, because it changes along with time and place and it advances along with civilization and knowledge. Among its basic principles is that authority over and command of the umma belongs to it itself [*sulṭat al-umma laha*] and that its affairs are a matter of consultation within it.[43]

Rida's views were influential on the ideas of Hassan Al Banna, the founder of the Muslim Brotherhood, for whom Islam served as a political response to colonial projects, bringing the political into the theological and the theological into the political. The colonial legacy, Al Banna suggests, can be found in the very establishment of nations and nationalities across the Arab world.[44] Yet all too aware of the need to tailor comments to particular audiences, prima facie consideration of Al Banna's speeches suggest that they are rife with contradiction, particularly over the idea of a nation. In a letter to Egypt's King Faruq in 1948, Al Banna wrote that 'Islam is guaranteed to supply the renascent nation with its needs'.[45] For Al Banna, one of the main objectives of the Brotherhood was to 'establish Allah's sovereignty over the world. To guide all of humanity to the precepts of Islam and its teachings (without which mankind cannot attain happiness)'.[46]

The formation of the Muslim Brotherhood as a political movement marks the establishment of an *Islamist* group, an organised collective believing that Islam should play a prominent role in the organisation of public life. The creation of the group was a conscious act of political agency, simultaneously a response to modernity and a product of it.[47] Yet the group was not homogenous, reflecting the importance of contingency and interpretation. As the Brotherhood's ideological canon developed, it also began to fragment.

In contrast to Al Banna, Sayyid Qutb argued that the world is steeped in *jāhiliyya*, stemming from 'rebellion against the sovereignty of God on earth'. Supporting this, Qutb argued that rebellion emerged from

> attempts to transfer to man one of the greatest attributes of God, namely sovereignty, by making some men lords over others … in the more subtle form of claiming that the right to create values, to legislate rules of collective behavior, and to choose a way of life rests with men, without regard to what God has prescribed.[48]

Intellectual tensions between Qutb and Al Banna reflect fissures within Islamist movements themselves, concerning activity and spatial arena, but shaped by different contexts that give old ideas new meanings. Since the 1970s, a more nuanced form of engagement with debates about their role in politics has emerged, which sees some Islamist groups taking a more active role in civil society, in addition to those more radical groups for whom violence is viewed as the means to achieve their goals. This view reflects the contingency of modernity and local factors in shaping the relationship between religion, law and politics. A secondary dimension emerges, concerning the relationship between Islamist groups across state borders and the extent to which groups should operate at a transnational or national level.[49]

How one understands Islam and the contingent factors that determine its position in – and beyond – the state defines the relationship between religious and political realms. In accordance with the emergence of the modern state, religious belief and practice is subordinate to state structures. Yet for most Muslims, the law is *divine* and *sacred* and for many, legal doctrine – as revealed in the Quran and Sunna – must be immune from critical discourse. God is seen to be the ultimate sovereign, the final arbiter of power and the source of all laws. Yet questions still remain over territorial control. Following this, for Michelle Burgis, authority is derived from God's authority – from application of Sharia to *umma* – and not through the regulation of territory.[50]

Religious revivalism: engagement, opposition and failure?

Today the Jurists of Islam are proofs (of God) to the people, proofs of the Imam. Total obedience is owed to them, since they are specially appointed by the Prophet to be his successors and to rule. The Jurists' authority in government affairs is equal to that of the Prophet and of the Imams, since they all share in common the burden of executive power to apply the divine law.[51]

As we saw in the previous chapter, the prevalence of authoritarianism stems from regime efforts to ensure the survival of their rule. Supporting this, Mounia Bennani-Chraibi suggests that the main reason for authoritarian persistence was 'to remain in power and protect their personal interests ... [and as a result they often have] to defend themselves against their own people'.[52] Within this context, access to political space became restricted. One way in which groups could gain access was through religion, as a consequence of state reliance upon religious views to maintain legitimacy and authority. As we shall see, the notion of political community is a source of much contestation within Islamic thought, with the repercussions of such debates having serious implications for state sovereignty and security. This type of debate raises a number of questions about the spatial ordering of society and the means through which society is regulated. The resolution of debates over the role of Islam within political community can provide the means through which ruling elites can strengthen their claims over political leadership, both ideologically and materially.

When state structures begin to fragment, people are forced to find alternative sources of support to meet their basic needs.[53] From this vacuum, opportunities emerged for groups such as the Muslim Brotherhood, Hizballah and Badr Brigades to gain prominence through the provision of social goods and services. A number of these groups desired a political role, yet beyond Iran, they were largely unsuccessful, prompting a move towards 'post-Islamism', which saw the relocation of religion from public to private realms. Before we reach this point, however, let us briefly trace the role of religion within political life.

After the fall of the Ottoman Empire and establishment of the mandate system, questions about the role of religion within the fabric of newly established states were central to the construction of political organisation. The struggle over the place of religion in the public realm is perhaps best seen across twentieth-century Turkey, as the struggle to locate religion was integral in shaping the political nature of the state. In Iraq, mandate forces sought to restrict the influence of the clerics of the south by allying with the Sunni minority and establishing a monarchical system that restricted the political influence of the Shi'a clerics. In Mandatory Palestine, Jews continued to make *aliyah*, establishing settlements and kibbutzim as a mechanism of transforming land, coordinated by the Jewish Agency and, while religion was important, Marxist-inspired material factors played a prominent role in activity at this time.

From the 1940s to the 1960s regimes and religious groups typically worked in unison, in battle against secular, leftist and pan-Arab ideologies that threatened the political status quo.[54] Nowhere was this more apparent than in Jordan, where the influx of Palestinian refugees after the *nakba* created fertile ground for populist ideologies to spread. In this context, the Muslim Brotherhood established a political wing, the Islamic Action Front. Of course, relations between the Brotherhood and the regime would fluctuate, based upon the interaction of domestic and regional dynamics. While religion operates as a means of legitimising political rule, it also serves as a double-edged sword, providing scope for groups to challenge the status quo within this zone of indistinction.[55] A number of groups have challenged regimes in this zone, accusing them of not upholding religious values, doing so from both inside and outside political systems; both legally and illegally.

With the discovery of oil, the role of religion within society became more prominent as regimes sought to ensure their legitimacy amid widespread economic and social development. With the rapid and in many cases existential transformation of societies that took people from rural to urban settings and challenged their traditions, faith provided a sense of certainty. While some rulers such as Faisal Al Saud were able – and willing – to demonstrate their piety, others such as Anwar Sadat, the 'Believer President', sought to position themselves in a way to harness the power of religion.[56] This revivalism has resulted in even greater diversity within the concept of political Islam, between and within sects, over the use of violence and, once again, as to the final vision.

The discovery of oil also shaped the trajectory of a state's foreign policy, as the proliferation of Islamist narratives and visions began to be used as a mechanism to challenge the pan-Arab vision. The financing of a range of different actors in several contexts was fuelled by the exponentially increasing Saudi petro-dollars during the 1970s. This financial clout allowed Wahhabist thought to attain a 'preeminent position of strength' across global manifestations and expressions of Islam, achieved in no small part through the establishment of the Islamic University of Medina.[57]

The 'crisis of Arab nationalism' in the aftermath of the 1967 war provided the kingdom with the opportunity to challenge Egypt as the dominant regional actor through the mobilisation of pan-Islamist narratives. Poor socio-economic conditions left the region ripe for Islamic narratives to challenge the bulbous Arab nationalist regimes, and these Islamic narratives spread across increasingly disaffected urban populations, along with those marginalised from elite politics. The flows of workers, ideas and capital that began in the 1970s only served to facilitate the *dawa* (call to Islam) through the spread of Wahhabist ideas,[58] supported by seemingly inexhaustible financial resources, much like in Qatar that also follows Wahhabi thought. While Saudi funding for groups across the world began in earnest in the 1970s, Qatari support became more prominent in the years after the Arab Uprisings as the state embarked on a more proactive foreign policy. Yet Wahhabism would not be accepted by all, given their fundamentalist approach to faith and association with the Al Saud dynasty,[59] whose behaviour was viewed by some as incompatible with strict Islamic doctrine.[60]

Islamist parties often referred to religion as a means of eroding the political credentials of ruling elites, seeking to demonstrate the impropriety of rulers, ultimately arguing that they were unfit to rule. All too aware of the challenges posed by mosques and their capacity for mobilisation, regime observation and restriction of Friday prayers was hardly surprising. In spite of this, those leading the prayers were able to frame sermons within the word of God, leaving criticism implicit and avoiding direct incitement. Yet by not performing within the accepted limits of Islam, one is then trapped by the mobilisation of such narratives, wherein the double-edged sword served simultaneously as a means to legitimise and criticise.

The prominence of Islam within state building is perhaps best seen in the establishment of Saudi Arabia and the ongoing efforts to ensure the legitimacy of the Al Saud. With less than favorable tribal and nationalist credentials, the alliance with Wahhabist *ulema* was essential in the establishment of the state. Due to a centuries-old alliance between the Al Saud and Wahhabi clerics, religion has served a dual role in the kingdom, providing the means for the Al Saud to gain legitimacy and also to develop a national identity. Contingent factors of time, place and economic context stress the importance of a strong communal identity, amid disparate historical, tribal and religious experiences, which mean that identity has been built around the power of the Al Saud family and its Islamic values. Nationalist narratives evoke collective memory of history, territory and societal love; the Saudi nationalism revolves around faith and loyalty to the Al Saud, the Protectors of the Two Holy Places of Islam. The need to maintain this social contract in spite of evolving socio-economic conditions has thus proved central in the very survival of the Saudi state.

Islam occupies a central role within the Saudi legal system, with the Sharia as the source of its laws – underpinning the Basic Law of 1992 – while concepts such as *qanun* (law) and *musharr'i* (legislator) were peripheral in political discourse to prevent the emergence of challenges to Sharia.[61] The prominence of Islam in legal and political structures is not without issues, however, as it raises questions as to the source of sovereign power. As we have seen, sovereignty is exercised through the declaration of an emergency and the sovereign decision, yet a zone of indistinction emerges here when considering clauses within the Basic Law.

Article 61 states that, 'The King declares a state of emergency, general mobilisation and war, and the law defines the rules for this', while Article 62 offers more guidance on this. From our earlier discussion about the sovereign decision this is hardly surprising. However, consideration of earlier articles and principles appears to challenge this. Article 1, for example, states that: 'The Kingdom of Saudi Arabia is a sovereign Arab Islamic state with Islam as its religion; God's Book and the Sunnah of His Prophet, God's prayers and peace be upon him, are its constitution, Arabic is its language and Riyadh is its capital.' Building on this, Article 7 states that, 'Government in Saudi Arabi derives power from the Holy Quran and the Prophet's tradition', while Article 11 begins, 'Saudi society will be based on the principle of adherence to God's command'. It is quickly apparent that a fundamental tension emerges as to the source of sovereignty; while the monarch takes the decision, the roots of sovereignty appear to lie elsewhere.[62]

The alliance between Wahhabism and Al Saud is mutually beneficial, ensuring the survival – and ultimately predominance – of both clerics and statesmen. The coercive apparatus of the state protects religion while the Sharia legitimises the state, preventing it from descent into tyranny.[63] It is, of course, a relationship not without tension, as seen with the *ikhwan* rebellion against Ibn Saud's forces in the 1920s out of concern at modernisation processes going against Islamic values and the seizure of the Grand Mosque in 1979.[64] In response to criticism about Islamic practice, the state supported *ulema* issued fatwas legitimising regime actions when necessary[65] and in the years after the seizure of the Grand Mosque, the importance of the *ulema* for political survival was increasingly apparent.[66]

In addition to the fatwa justifying action in the Grand Mosque, a similar fatwa was issued to restrict Shi'a political activity:

> The Rafidah of the Hasa [al-Ahsa'] be obliged to surrender to true Islam and should abandon all their defective religious rites. We asked the Imam, Ibn Saud, to order his viceroy in al- Hasa, Ibn Jiluwi, to summon the Shi'is to Shaikh ibn Bishr, before whom they should undertake to follow the religion of God and his Prophet and to cease the invocation of the saintly members of Ahl al-Bayt, and to abandon other innovations in their public assemblies, and to conform to the rule of prayer five times daily in the mosque. Prayer callers (muaddhin) are to be sent. The people are also to study the three principles of the Wahhabi tenets; their houses of worship are to be destroyed and those that object to this will be exiled.
>
> With regard to the Shi'is of Qatif, we have advised the Imam to send missionaries and preachers to certain districts and villagers, which have come under the control of the true Muslims and in which Shari'ah laws should be put in effect.[67]

The fatwa reveals the Wahhabi suspicion and rejection of Shi'a beliefs and, given the prominence of the *ulema* within the fabric of the Saudi state, the kingdom's Shi'a population were subjected to widespread discrimination and marginalisation.[68]

Much like in Saudi Arabia, consecutive regimes in Egypt sought to facilitate the bureaucratic co-option of the *ulema* of Al Azhar. Having witnessed the influence of the clerics of the *ulema* across the previous decades,[69] Nasser sought to solidify his rule by bringing the clerics 'to heel', in what was described as the 'capitulation of the *ulema* to the state'.[70] Yet the clerics quickly ascertained their importance and sought to improve their position within bureaucratic structures as they recognised their value in countering challenges posed by the Muslim Brotherhood and their Saudi neighbours. The reforms also had the unintended by-product of political empowerment as expansion created new forms of expertise, negatively seen by some as *bricolage* – the fragmented intellectual constructions of Islamist protest[71] – but later serving as a means of political empowerment.[72]

The struggle to regulate society was far greater than the struggle to regulate the *ulema*, as the Brotherhood occupied a prominent role within civil society, providing much needed social goods and services. The Brotherhood itself had spent a great deal of time reflecting on the desired place of the organisation within Egyptian society, as a public, political actor, noted by its founder Hassan Al Banna, who recounted that 'No one but God knows how many nights we spent reviewing the state of the nation ... analysing the sickness, and thinking of the possible remedies. So disturbed were we, that we reached the point of tears.'

Under Anwar Sadat, the 'Believer President', the political constraints placed on Al Azhar were loosened as he sought to use religion as a mechanism of legitimacy and to achieve political goals just as his predecessor had done. While Nasser had used the clerics of Al Azhar to legitimise arrests of the Muslim Brothers, Sadat provided greater space for Islamic expression as he sought to limit the power of the Nasserist cabal although it was here that prominent members of the *ulema* demanded greater influence. The rise of *jamaa Takfir wa Hijra*, a group that capitalised on tensions between regime and *ulema*, led to the clerics taking a stronger line against more militant forms of Islamist action and moving towards the centre of the political arena. Following the assassination of Sadat, his successor Hosni Mubarak sought to crush the threat posed by radical Islam while also co-opting the *ulema* and increasing the regime's Islamic legitimacy by giving them administrative responsibility and control over a number of areas.[73]

In Jordan, Islamist movements provided the means to challenge the burgeoning Arabist, leftist and Palestinian movements. These opportunities secured the Hashemite monarchy in the face of a number of threats, while also building upon one pillar of their domestic legitimacy, namely descent from the Prophet. In the first fifty years of the state, an implicit alliance between the Hashemites and the Muslim Brotherhood increased monarchical claims to legitimacy by using the Brotherhood's networks to speak to populations through informal channels. At this time, the *ikhwan* in Jordan was dominated by Palestinians and thus working with the Muslim Brotherhood provided another means for the Hashemite regime to secure its rule. Much like in Saudi Arabia and Egypt, over time Islamist groups would utilise their role in society to challenge the regime, resulting in a clamp down on Islamist groups between 1989 and 1993. It also prompted constitutional changes to monitor and regulate Friday sermons, bringing mosques under the control of the Ministry of Awqaf Islamic Affairs and Holy Places. Constitutional placed religious institutions – including mosques – under supervision and provided training to those wishing to preach or offer Islamic guidance.[74] Later reforms would also require written ministerial approval in order to give sermons and offer Islamic guidance, punished by a ban, jail sentence or fine.

As we have seen, Kuwait's political history of compromise created space for groups such as the Muslim Brotherhood to operate, yet unlike their counterparts in Egypt and Jordan, this action was driven by the *harakat* (movement) rather than the *hizb* (party). As one prominent Islamic figure noted, the Kuwaiti branch of the Muslim Brotherhood was formed in 1951 in response to burgeoning Western influence and amid the secular movements of Arab nationalism:

> Our Islamic movement started in the early fifties, during the period in which Kuwait was under the fierce assault from Western concepts and values of secularism and nationalism, the most noticeable of which were the pan-Arab Nationalism, Ba'athism, and Socialism. Such an assault was meant to distract the Kuwaiti Muslims from their faith. That was the main reason for the establishment of political Islamic activities.[75]

Members of the newly formed *ikhwan* ran in local elections but as individuals rather than as members of the political party.[76] Across Kuwaiti politics, the Constitutional Court occupies a central role, serving an intermediary role between different groups across the state and on some occasions ruling against the Al Sabah.[77] Although often viewed with a sense of pride because of its spirit of dialogue and compromise, there are growing demands for reform of the social contract, which was initially due to be reformed in 1966 to reflect changing social and religious dynamics.[78]

In Lebanon, political parties have been mapped on to the sectarian construction of the state.[79] After the civil war, the establishment of the consociational power-sharing system of government gave each sect a share in the running of the country as a means of providing each group with access to political space. While serving as a means of ensuring that all groups can express their views and grievances amid historical conditions of extreme poverty, marginalisation and violence,[80] the system is flawed in the sense that it constitutionalises and enshrines sectarian difference in the political realm, creating a system that is easily deadlocked by veto powers.[81]

Although religious values have provided some actors with the ability to shape regional affairs, context remains central to such capacity. Some Shi'a Muslims in Lebanon, aware of the need to operate within a confessional system and fearing a return to the darker days of the civil war, express solidarity with their Christian kin by putting up Christmas decorations in a visible manifestation of the negotiation between the transnational – *Twelver Shi'ism* – and the national – *Lebanese identity*.[82] For others, their faith shapes political behaviour in different ways. While faith may be abstract, we must not remove it from the context within which it operates, for it is the political, social and economic contexts that are given direction by religious beliefs and conversely, context shapes the capacity to act in a particular way.

In Iraq, from the establishment of the state until 2003, sectarian difference was propagated as a mechanism of survival, seeking to limit the power of the Shi'a clerics – and by (perceived) extension, Iran – and ensuring the survival of successive regimes.[83] In response to historical discrimination, a number of Islamic parties – predominantly Shi'a – provided a political voice for those marginalised by the erstwhile regime.[84] The most prominent of these parties, Al Da'awa Islamiyah, emerged in the late 1950s as a consequence of the impact of modernisation and marginalisation on communities.[85] Al Da'wa drew support from clerics across the south and was inspired by the theological ideas of the Iraqi Shi'a cleric Muhammad Baqir Al Sadr. Although most of its members were exiled to Iran, the party retained influence as a prominent opposition movement and played an important role in the post-2003 landscape. While based in Iran, Da'awa was supported by the creation of the Supreme Council of the Islamic Republic in Iraq, which was more vocal in its support of *veleyat-e faqih*. Despite possessing a sectarian dimension, Al Da'awa initially found support from a number of Sunni Muslims as a consequence of drawing on the writing of Sayyid Qutb. Some Shi'a clerics stressed unity, in spite of the conditions inside Iraq, perhaps most notably Al Sadr.[86]

In spite of such sentiments, when political contexts changed post 2003, relations between Sunni and Shi'a took on increasingly violent dimensions in their relations. While countless factors had shaped political life in the previous eighty years, the new political climate brought sectarian tensions to the fore, albeit shaped by a range of social, economic and tribal contingent factors.

Religion also found space in political structures in Bahrain. While also historically populated by secular, leftist and Arab nationalist parties, Shi'a opposition groups gained a great deal of support in Bahraini politics following the Iranian revolution. Relations between regime and opposition groups ebbed and flowed in the subsequent years, culminating in a 'decade of discontent' in the 1990s.[87] Amid socio-economic difference, religious symbolism played a prominent role in the construction of political opposition, drawing people together under a shared banner of Shi'a Islam. This symbolism played an important role in constructing unity and a Shi'a identity, within which religious figures such as Sheikh Isa Qassim serve as the spiritual leadership of parties like Al Wefaq.[88] Religious denomination resulted in political, social and economic discrimination but grievances stemmed from such discrimination, where unemployment has disproportionately impacted upon Shi'a communities.[89] Ultimately, the relationship between Shi'a parties and the regime is shaped by security calculations, which determines the nature of interactions.

The inability of groups across the region to capture and consolidate political power after the Iranian revolution led Olivier Roy to argue that political Islam 'failed'.[90] Following the work of scholars such as Asef Bayat, in later works, Roy suggested that after its failure, Islam took on a more private dimension in what became known as post-Islamism. In this sense, Islamic commitment moves from the public realm into the private. The argument suggests that Muslims lost interest in transforming faith into a political ideology and social movement. Instead, moving away from state-led efforts to transform society, post-Islamism is a search for a form of Islamic 'good life' amid the fragmentation and transformation of traditional forms of religious authority and their relationships with state structures. To this end, 'contemporary re-Islamisation is a cluster of individual practices that are used as a means of finding jobs, money, respect and self-esteem, and bargaining with a marginalised state that has played on conservative re-Islamisation but been unable to control it'.[91]

Amid the uncertainty of the modern world, faith provides a degree of certainty.[92] In this case, the move to a more private Islam occurs with a new form of knowledge production and new application of Islam to the modern world. This also results in the emergence of a new type of preacher, able to speak to the urban youth while also demonstrating Quranic excellence in a single thought.[93] Although suggesting a move towards the individualisation of religion, some such as Bayat demonstrate that in spite of such individualistic practice, Muslims also embody forms of the good life.[94] Here we see the fusion of modernity with tradition and public with private in numerous discourses about human dignity and the good life. Such a move becomes increasingly important in the years leading up to the Arab Uprisings as previous failures of political aspirations created different forms of political expression and belonging, within both national and discursive collectives.

Dar al Islam, dawla and umma

Central to discussions about the relationship between Islam and sovereignty are questions about territory and jurisdiction, the ordering of life and the spatial limitations that emerge from such ordering.[95] For some such as Majid Khadduri, Muslims are bound by the 'law' of their faith regardless of territory or place of residence. Yet such a position fails to accommodate the realities and contexts of individual Muslims and their communities, which shape their action and identity.

As Khadduri notes,

> A distinction ... must be made between an authority which is directly derived from and exercised by God, and an authority which is derived from a divine code endowed by God but enforced by His viceregent (or by a secular ruler) which is equally binding upon the latter and the people.[96]

Tension over sources of authority is a prominent feature of debate over the role of religion in political organisation. The dawla and umma are fundamentally two discordant bedrocks for the contemporary state, revealing tensions between and within theological circles about the nature and trajectory of political organisation.[97] Historical understandings are associated with the efforts of Jamal Al Din Al Afghani whose writings sought to mobilise Muslims across the world around the concept of Islamic unity. Afghani's work framed Islamic unity as a response to colonial oppression, where injustice provoked the need for collective response. Yet this was not a call for the rejection of the nation state, but rather a 'civilisational discourse' in response to colonialism.[98]

The inability of Muslims across the world to identify with this 'imagined community' meant that Afghani's project ultimately failed in practice, but the legacy of his work continued. Rashid Rida's work in the aftermath of fall of the Ottoman Empire called for states to adopt the normative values of Islam – as found in the Sharia – which resulted in the establishment of groups such as the Muslim Brotherhood, working within the confines of territorial borders.[99] In the following years, the concept of a broader pan-Islamic movement became associated with a more militant form of violent extremism who espoused membership of an *umma* as an imagined community akin to *dar al Islam*.[100]

The concepts of *dar al Islam* and *dar al harb* provide insight into the relationship between faith, law and territory. *Dar al Islam* is generally understood as 'the whole territory in which the law of Islam prevails', while *dar al harb* refers to land not encompassed by *dar al Islam*.[101] Although Ibn Al Arabi depicted Islam as a single person, the concept of *dar al Islam* was binding to communities that, by their very nature had become territorial.[102] For Parvin and Sommer, *dar al Islam* is 'a legal construct that has a territorial dimension: a territorial expression of the *umma* … which itself has a political component'.[103]

It is helpful at this point to return to the concept of the *nomos* to consider the roots of political organisation across the Islamic world. The concept provides insight into the relationship between law and territory, along with interpretations of 'how to live'. While early understandings of the *nomos* suggest an attachment to soil, consideration of pre-Islamic history across the Arabian Peninsula, reveals how the nomadic way of life left little attachment to land. The words of incitement used by Umar to aid the conquest of Iraq reveal a great deal in this regard: 'The Hijaz is your home only in as far as it is a pasturage. Those who dwell there have no power over it except in this respect. Where do newcomers who emigrated stand with regard to God's promise, "Roam the earth?"'[104]

Similar views are also found in the work of Khaldun, whose reflections of the nature of tribal life we have encountered previously. Speaking about the nomadic characteristics of the tribe, Khaldun notes that such groups

> have no homelands they might use as a fertile (pasture), and no fixed place to which they might repair. All regions and places are the same to them. Therefore, they do not restrict themselves to possession of their own and neighboring regions. They do not stop at the borders of their horizon. They swarm across distant zones to achieve superiority over faraway nations.[105]

These remarks share similarities with Parvin and Sommer, who suggest that territoriality at this point was 'a function of time more than space', as territorial boundaries were defined through a tribe's movements.[106] Such movements were later harnessed in an effort to facilitate the expansion of Islam, which became fixed with the development of communities. As the expansion of sovereignty began to wane, a more static, permanent sense of politics began to emerge, supplanting the personal, sociological character of Islamic sovereignty with an identity that was shaped by spatial and territorial factors.[107]

The emergence of divisions within the community was hardly surprising, in spite of widespread criticism from jurists at the time, who suggested that Islamic law 'recognises neither division in Moslem authority nor differentiation among Moslems on racial or cultural background'.[108] Amid these internal visions, the idea of the *universal* form of *dar al Islam* began to wane, ceasing to be able to shape the reality of its members. In spite of such concerns, the appearance of different groups was acknowledged in the Quran: 'We made you into nations and tribes so that you may know each other'.[109]

The emergence of divisions began to be categorised by cultural and political differences, while affinity with soil developed over time grounding communities in space. With the spread of Western ideas, first through the crusades and much later, the mandate system, territorial segregation became the primary form of political definition.[110] Although some have suggested that Islam is incompatible with the concept of the territorially grounded nation state,[111] Piscatori suggests that there is nothing about Islam that makes it incongruent with such ideas.[112] While this position is certainly more accurate than others, there are tensions that emerge when we look at the political manifestations of Islam and its relationship with territory.

The German historian Reinhard Schulz argued that the *umma* served to reinforce the territorially grounded national state,[113] as a range of different definitions of *umma* are given in the Quran. As a consequence, this plurality of meanings provides scope for actors to use it in particular contexts and for political reasons, creating a form of contingency. Of course, context is key in understanding the concept, as it is shaped by nationalism, states, movements and socio-economic forces.

As Fred Halliday suggests, the term *umma*

> was available, in a range of meanings ... It is not surprising, therefore, that, on the one hand, the term, *umma*, should have become a common one in the political discourses of the Arab world in the twentieth century and that it should have a variety of distinct, equally licensed, meanings within both the discursive legacy of the substratum and the contemporary, world-historical, context of the Arab world.[114]

Halliday notes how the concept is contingent upon the complexities of contemporary political life. Supporting this thesis, Schulze argues that local and national interest far outweighed broader Islamic sentiments, particularly within moments of crisis, even in the burgeoning moments of the sovereign state.[115]

Discourses that mobilise the concept of the *umma* are based on such contingency; after all, ideas and discourse alone cannot transcend difference or indeed shape political activity. Instead, they rely on actors who are themselves shaped by context.[116] As a consequence, we must consider the broader context that shapes contingency, as social, cultural, economic and historical factors shape group intentions, capabilities and the type of relationships that they have with society. Put another way, we must locate groups not only within ideological streams and socio-economic factors, but also geopolitical conditions.[117] It is through this that we are able to understand the emergence of ideas and groups that reject the state in favour of broader transnational projects.[118]

Geo-sectarian politics

In addition to different spatial and temporal differences, faith is also characterised by distinct theological interpretations, resulting in the emergence of different sects.[119] The roots of sectarian difference are initially political, stemming from dispute over who was to lead the caliphate after the death of Muhammad. This dispute reached its zenith on 10 October 680 AD where Hussein, the grandson of the Prophet, and his followers were ambushed by a larger Ummayad force. In the ensuing battle at Karbala, Hussein and his young son were killed, along with all of his male companions. The Battle of Karbala is a central point within the history of Shi'a Islam, routinely marked in the festival of Ashura. Hussein had spent a great deal of his life challenging the perceived corruption of the Ummayad court, ultimately leading to his death at Karbala. The narrative of the battle creates ideas of guilt and martyrdom among Shi'a Muslims, as a consequence of ancestral failures to help Hussein and his followers.[120]

Historical developments at this time also document the emergence of the Kharijite movement – taken literally to mean those who rebel against religion – who rejected submission to human authority. After the Battle of Siffin ended in a truce, the Kharijites criticised Ali for ending the battle, rejecting his position as leader and the role of arbitrators in ending the war. The Kharijites took a literal reading of the Quran and the phrase *la hukma ila lillah* – there is no rule but God's – as a literal manifesto, rejecting all forms of human authority, even if this was God's representative on earth.[121] The challenge of this idea also raised fundamental questions over authority, such as who determined the law and, in keeping with our discussion of sovereignty, who determines the exception?

While all Muslim states in the region refer to the Sharia within either constitutions or Basic Laws, the Islamic Republic of Iran explicitly uses it as the source of all of its laws. In the aftermath of revolution, the system of *veleyat-e faqih* enshrined the values of Twelver Shi'a thought within the fabric of the newly established Islamic Republic, which provided the state with much needed legitimacy. Moreover, the structure of *veleyat-e faqih* facilitated the regulation of both formal and informal space, thus harnessing the power of religion, something that the Shah had previously been unable to do.

While Khomeini's vision established the Islamic Republic, earlier in his life he had followed a more quietist trend within Shi'a thought, arguing that clerics should remain removed from politics. This view, as currently espoused by the likes of Grand Ayatollah Ali Sistani remains the predominant difference between the two great schools of Shi'a thought, in Qom and Najaf. In spite of such tensions, Khomeini articulated the compliance of *veleyat-e faqih* with Islam in a constitution that

> advances the cultural, social, political, and economic institutions of Iranian society based on Islamic principles and norms, which represent an honest aspiration of the Islamic Ummah. This aspiration was exemplified by the nature of the great Islamic Revolution of Iran, and by the course of the Muslim people's struggle, from its beginning until victory, as reflected in the decisive and forceful calls raised by all segments of the population.[122]

Amid such comments, in its aftermath, the revolution was greeted with superficial optimism by some in Riyadh. Shortly after the establishment of the Islamic Republic, King Khalid proclaimed:

> It gives me great pleasure that the new republic is based on Islamic principles which are a powerful bulwark for Islam and Muslim peoples who aspire to prosperity, dignity, and well-being. I pray the Almighty to guide you to the forefront of those who strive for the upholding of Islam and Muslims, and I wish the Iranian people progress, prosperity, and stability.[123]

Yet relations between the two quickly soured, as geopolitical and political concerns began to play an important role. It was here that sectarian difference also took on a security dimension, as the two sides expressed their intent and concerns. For Khomeini, Iran sought to 'export our experiences to the whole world and present the outcome of our struggles against tyrants to those who are struggling along the path of God'.[124] Khomeini's comments were a source of great consternation for Sunni Arab states, not only through an apparent desire to spread the revolutionary goals of Shi'a Islam, but also to challenge the regional status quo.[125]

In response, a cycle of rhetoric emerged between the leaders of Saudi Arabia and Iran in an effort to demonstrate Islamic legitimacy.[126] In pursuit of this, Khomeini sought to stress unity across the Muslim world:

> There is no difference between Muslims who speak different languages, for instance the Arabs and the Persians. It is very probable that such problems have been created by those who do not wish the Muslim countries to be united … They create the issues of nationalism, of pan-Iranianism, pan-Turkism, and such isms, which are contrary to Islamic doctrines.[127]

In spite of his efforts to foster unity, Khomeini was vociferously critical of the Al Saud who were seen as 'corrupt and unworthy to be the guardians of Mecca and Medina'[128] and later referred to as 'traitors to the two holy shrines'.[129] In a damning indictment, Khomeini claimed that:

> If we wanted to prove to the world that the Saudi Government, these vile and ungodly Saudis, are like daggers that have always pierced the heart of the Moslems from the back, we would not have been able to do it as well as has been demonstrated by these inept and spineless leaders of the Saudi Government.[130]

In response, King Fahd condemned the 'hypocrites and pretenders who are using Islam to undermine and destabilise other countries'.[131] Tensions erupted in violence on the 1987 *hajj* where an estimated 450 pilgrims died, of whom 275 were Iranian,[132] which later resulted in the politicisation of *hajj* licenses and the Iranian boycott of the *hajj*. There was also an explicit attempt by Saudi leaders to frame the revolution as a Shi'a – Persian – event, seeking to reduce Tehran's appeal to Sunni communities.

Although Khomeini spoke of providing support to the *mustazefin* (downtrodden), this was then to be placed within the context of long-standing Sunni–Shi'a tensions alongside suspicions about Persian expansionism. In the following years, the two states began to engage in ideological and political competition to increase their influence across the Middle East and wider Islamic community.

Perhaps the most visible manifestation of this was in the Organisation of Islamic Cooperation (OIC), the forum to resolve issues across the Islamic world.[133] As Jeffrey Haynes notes, the OIC was plagued by contending visions of an 'appropriate' Islamic society, politicising belief and challenging the spirit of the organisation.[134] Saudi dominance of the organisation is hardly surprising. The headquarters of the OIC are in Jedda, while the kingdom has donated large sums of money to the organisation and its various institutions. In return, Saudi Arabia possesses de facto veto power, while also seemingly uses the organisation as a platform to support its political agenda. In 2012, Saudi Arabia called for the suspension of Syria's membership of the OIC as a consequence of the Assad regime's violence against citizens. As tensions between the two major Gulf powers escalated, it was hardly surprising that the OIC became an arena for tensions to play out, resulting in the vocal condemnation of Iran for 'its continued support for terrorism' and for interfering in the domestic affairs of states across the Middle East.[135]

Beyond the OIC, both Saudi Arabia and Iran have capitalised on shared religious networks to exert influence across the Middle East, attempting to reduce the political influence of the other by funding religious groups. While Iraq offers an obvious example of such mobilisation, similar links can be drawn in Lebanon, Bahrain, Syria, Yemen, India, Pakistan, Indonesia and the Horn of Africa. It is widely acknowledged that Saudi Arabia has provided vast sums of money to clerics for spreading the Wahhabi message.[136] One Shi'a cleric recounted a flight from Medinah that he shared with Imams returning home from receiving religious schooling in Saudi Arabia. In return for undertaking this training, the clerics received a monthly stipend along with support for their families.[137] Yet in spite of this funding, their actions were shaped by local context. While Salafis have gained prominence in Lebanon, this is not the strict Wahhabist form of Salafism. A Lebanese journalist recalled visiting the home of a Salafi cleric, where he met the cleric's daughter who, much to his surprise, was 'wearing jeans and a T-shirt'.[138] Such a story demonstrates how transnational forces interact with local contexts to shape space in a particular way.

In times of uncertainty, shared religious values – transcending territorial borders – provide the capacity to shape relations with groups beyond state borders. In post-invasion Iraq, US diplomatic cables released by WikiLeaks document the perceived role of Shi'a actors and, by extension, Iranian influence, including the funding of groups such as the Supreme Council for Islamic Revolution in Iraq (SCIRI) and Badr, in the region of $100 million and $45 million respectively.[139] This campaign also involved engagement with Iraqi politics, where Iran was accused of pushing Maliki into a confrontation with the Sadrist movement to ensure the *political* dominance of its Iraqi allies and the *spiritual* dominance of the Persian *marja'iyya*.[140]

The implications of this for the ordering of space – and the territorial borders of such a project – are clear, with serious implications for sovereign power and space, as regional currents interact with the intricacies of life, across southern Iraq and also in Yemen where conflict took on an increasingly sectarian nature amid the conflation of domestic politics into geopolitical currents shaping the Middle East.[141]

A zone of indistinction

As we have seen, religion exists simultaneously as a zone of possibility and restriction. Within this zone, believers find guidance on how to live, regimes find the means to legitimise their rule, and dissidents find the tools through which to challenge political order. Interpretation of text and tradition thus serves as a source of possibility, shaped by the interaction of context-specific contingency. Ultimately, what we have seen across the Middle East is that religion has become the arena through which states and their opponents can play out their political struggles amid competing visions of how to live. With its role in public life, religion becomes the means through which dissent – in a range of different guises – can emerge. Even when religious space is restricted, narratives and norms can be used as a means to challenge the status quo and to shape life both formally and informally.

Moreover, Islam serves as a means through which ruling elites can increase legitimacy by stressing conformity with Islamic norms and practices. This then opens up scope for criticism as regimes may not be seen as Islamic enough, leading to challenges from opposition movements on religious grounds. Thus, religion exists as a double-edged sword, simultaneously serving to legitimise and delegitimise, depending upon the particular contexts in operation. If this is so, there is more to religion than faith and a discussion about the organisation of society. Instead, there appears to be a greater existential dimension to the role played by religion within political community: as a zone of indistinction, contingent upon interpretation that shapes the spatial ordering of life.

We can see how Islam becomes the vehicle through which opposition emerges, requiring regulation from regimes in an attempt to maintain control. Such regulation ranges from fatwas justifying behaviour, to the banning of groups from particular backgrounds. Historically, political opposition has also been marginalised by regimes that have cultivated sectarian master narratives, wherein the grievances of political agents have been subsumed by broader debate around legitimacy of belief. Yet within conditions of regulation and control, religion also serves as an ideological framework to challenge the status quo and to mobilise networks against state structures, opening tension between *ordnung* and *ortung*. Inherent within Islam are structures that help spread ideas and mobilise people, which has long been a source of concern, leading to the regulation and monitoring of Friday prayers. Here, the mosque becomes a battleground of ideas to shape the attitudes of the public.

Such issues are not unique to Islam; instead, they can be found whenever there is certainty of belief.[142] For example, Israel is often referred to as a 'Jewish and democratic' state yet as a number of Israeli scholars have acknowledged, this political system is better suited by the concept of 'ethnocracy'.[143] As Oren Yiftachel argues, ethnocratic regimes 'promote the expansion of the dominant group in contested territory and its domination of power structures while maintaining a democratic façade'. In the Israeli case, this form of ethnocracy reflects the broader Zionist strategy of 'Judaizing the homeland'[144] and the physical transformation of the land.[145]

In the Israeli case, the expansion of the dominant group is at the cost of Palestinians in the West Bank and Gaza, along with other ethnic groups in Israel proper. Essentially, Yiftachel suggests that the process of Judaising the 'Land of Israel' creates a set of power relations that shape interactions between Israelis and Palestinians, between *Ashkenazi* and *Mizrahi* Jews, Orthodox and secular Jews and many other groups. It is a holistic approach that facilitates existential transformation of life across Israel and Palestine in the quest to Judaise territory, as a form of 'creeping apartheid'.[146] Moreover, it is an attempt to order space, defining spatial borders in the process, albeit with competing visions of how to live. Here, *nomos* is itself a zone of indistinction, serving to legitimise a range of different positions.

Although there is little doubting the impact of Judaism upon life across Israel, symbolically, politically and socially, an important impact concerns settlement policies. Religious views of the so-called 'Land of Israel' vary depending upon interpretation and the fusion of Torah and political factors on the ground. Beyond Israel proper, ideological views found in the religious Zionism trend – itself not a homogenous bloc – have shaped political action across the West Bank. Such action has taken place by both state and non-state actors, using land transformation as a mechanism for political expansion.[147] Settler movements have long been used as a means to define the nation and its citizens, but across the West Bank this has an impact on both Israel and Palestine. As we shall see in the next chapter, the transformation of urban landscapes plays a prominent role in the regulation of political life but before reaching this point we must consider the religious views that have shaped settlement behaviour beyond the formal practices of the state.

Although initially resistant to the civilian presence in the West Bank, which had previously been designated as a military zone to abide by international law, resettlement efforts driven by civilians – led by the group *Gush Emunim* – were given approval by Prime Minister Levi Eshkol who famously pronounced, 'Well kids, if you want to – ascend'. Demonstrating the importance of territory, an alternative transliteration of this quote reads, 'Children, you may return home'.[148] In the aftermath of this proclamation, the ascent into the hills of the West Bank was undertaken by some 20 trucks and cars carrying around 100 settlers along with Rabbi Zvi Yehuda Kook, the settlers' spiritual guide.[149]

Following this effort, the settlers published a pamphlet detailing the importance of civilian settlement. In it, the pamphlet proclaimed that the group 'set out today to found a city in the heart of Eretz-Israel near Nablus'.[150] The settlers and military apparatus of the state agreed upon the terms of the civilian presence in the West Bank, building settlement housing and services. The Secretary of Gush Emuni, Zvi Slonim, later reported that

in 'basement' conditions yet 'penthouse' morale … the settlement gradually constructed itself as a separate entity … Supporters who came here saw the making of a new form of pioneer life … [and] were sparked with the seed that fruited with more and more Elon Moreh [settlements] in Judea and Samaria.[151]

Such efforts sought to transform the West Bank from 'enemy territory' to Jewish homeland.

Later plans outlined far more ambitious projects seeking to transform life in the West Bank and Gaza. Negotiating a difficult relationship with political elites in Israel, large aspects of the settlement project were consumed by state apparatus wherein the transformative aspect was used for political and security purposes. The success of such transformative processes is revealed when we consider that Avigdor Lieberman, the Israeli Defence Minister (who made *aliyah* from the former Soviet Union) is a West Bank settler, embodying the breach of international law and conventions while serving as a high-ranking official in the Israeli government.[152]

Political disengagement from the West Bank and Gaza proved incendiary, moving away from a theological imaginary and a political vision. This goes some way to explaining the violence that erupted amid the disengagement from Gaza and the destruction of 'illegal' settlements.[153] Such illegal settlements push the sovereignty of the Israeli state beyond the territorial borders in search of a broader vision of Eretz Israel. A secondary point of tension stemming from the relationship between Judaism and the state concerns the role of the ultra-Orthodox in the military. Competing views on the source of sovereignty emerge when considering military action in the West Bank and Gaza. Disengagement policies were deeply contested by a range of religious sources who rejected the political decision to withdraw, leading to widespread protests.

Although previously exempt from the military service that is compulsory for all other Israelis, a long-running legal battle was ended when the Supreme Court declared the exemption to be 'discriminatory' and 'unconstitutional'.[154] With concerns that the IDF was becoming more religious, fears about disobeying military orders increased amid calls for disobedience from individuals such as Rabbi Avraham Shapira, a former Chief Rabbi of Israel, and leader of Merkaz HaRav Kook.[155] Following acts of disobedience, *Haaretz*, a leading Israeli newspaper, published an opinion piece entitled 'Drafting Ultra-Orthodox Jews into the Israeli Army Is Dangerous'.[156] When faced with such decisions, soldiers face a test of their loyalty: to their state or their Rabbi. As the political situation becomes increasingly complex, such tensions will strike at the very heart of the Israeli state amid efforts to exert sovereign power.

Conclusions

When placed in political and economic context, religion is a means through which individuals can be included/excluded from state structures, while also serving to shape political activity through intellectual curiosity, ethical values and normative behaviour. Amid the uncertainty of modernity and a fragmenting regional system, the certainty provided by faith has proved attractive to many. Within the Middle East, the existence of groups who run welfare programmes and offer moral certainty prove attractive and those who are able to offer protection amid uncertainty can develop widespread support.

Although often overlooked by scholars of politics and other disciplines, we should remember to acknowledge that faith is a means for action in and of itself. While scholars are quick to consider how faith is populated with political meaning, we should not disregard belief. That being said, we can also explore the political dimensions that are taken alongside belief as a consequence of tensions between different ideas about the role of religion within society that are ultimately grounded in contingency. Discussion about membership of communities of faith leads to division, contingent on a range of factors. Much like the *nomos*, unity is a fleeting instance that fragments into countless different visions with their own regulatory capacity. As a consequence, we should not seek to reify religion as a homogenous force; rather, we must remember that it is shaped by particular experiences of economic, social, ideological, historical and geopolitical interactions.

While simultaneously creating a *nomos* by seeking to regulate behaviour, it is shaped by particular contexts. Historically, debate about the relationship between religion and politics shaped society, whereas at present, the debate serves as a means of ensuring control and regulation over society. Within this position, the range of normative, structural, cultural and multifarious positions within religion broadly serves as a mechanism through which governance – and biopolitical control – can be exerted. Religion is then central to political struggles but also broader efforts to regulate life and define spatial borders.

Within political projects are countless interpretations and narratives that reflect regime, opposition and populist views that quickly spread within and between states. With the spread of TV, radio, print media and the Internet, individuals are also able to access the views of figures in neighbouring states, speaking to local populations, but also across a region as a whole. Complicating matters is the fact that each position is then interpreted by individuals who are shaped by history, culture, society, economic and political factors, leading to a plurality of views before ascertaining the nature of one's faith. Fundamentally, this discussion relates to the regulation of life within particular territories, shaped and defined by both time and space. But it also provides scope for challenges to the manner in which life is regulated, a means through which legitimate challenge to the status quo can emerge. As such, Islam simultaneously serves as a source of authority and of opposition, a zone of indistinction that is necessarily – and simultaneously – a zone of possibility and repression.

Within these conditions, regimes often constructed and referred to sectarian master narratives in an attempt to ensure their survival, deepening divisions within already fractious societies. Sectarian difference served as a mechanism of control, with explicit support for particular sects over others who were often then politicised and securitised, showing the power of norms to shape formal structures. The construction of narratives of belonging can transcend state borders to easily result in theological debate possessing both political and geopolitical ramifications. This also provides the mechanisms through which foreign policy goals can be reached, when theological narratives cross borders and become shaped by the contingency of local context.

Notes

1 Shadi Hamid, *Islamic Exceptionalism: How the Struggle Over Islam Is Reshaping the World* (New York: St Martin's Press. 2016).
2 Nazih Ayubi, *Political Islam: Religion and Politics in the Arab World* (London: Routledge, 1991).
3 Ali Abd Al Raziq, *Al-Islam wa Usul al-Hukm* (Cairo: n.p., 1925).
4 A. Sanhoury, *Le Califat: Son Evolution vers une Societe des Nations Orientale* [The Caliphate: Its Evolution Towards a Society of Oriental Nations] (Paris: Libraire Orientaliste Paul Geuthner, 1926), cited in Majjid Khadduri, 'Islam and the Modern Law of Nations', *American Journal of International Law*, 50:2 (1956) 358–72.
5 Majjid Khadduri, *War and Peace in the Law of Islam* (Baltimore, MD: Johns Hopkins Press, 1955), pp. 3–18.
6 Quran 5:40.
7 Andrew F. March, 'Genealogies of Sovereignty in Islamic Political Theology'.
8 See Charles Kurzman, *The Unthinkable Revolution in Iran* (Cambridge, MA: Harvard University Press, 2004); Nikki Keddie, *Modern Iran: Roots and Results of Revolution* (New Haven, CT: Yale University Press); Baqer Moin, *Khomeini: Life of the Ayatollah* (New York: Thomas Dunne Books, 2000). See also Robert Fisk, *The Great War for Civilization: The Conquest of the Middle East* (London: Harper Perennial, 2006).
9 See Simon Mabon, 'The Circle of Bare Life: Hizballah, Muqawamah and Rejecting "Being Thus"', *Politics, Religion and Ideology*, 18:1 (2017), 1–22; Rola El-Husseini, 'Hezbollah and the Axis of Refusal: Hamas, Iran and Syria', *Third World Quarterly*, 31:5 (2010), 803–15; Edith Szanto, 'Beyond the Karbala Paradigm: Rethinking Revolution and Redemption in Twelver Shi'a Mourning Rituals', *Journal of Shi'a Islamic Studies*, 6:1 (2013), 75–91.
10 A vast literature on Hizballah exists, including Augustus Richard Norton, *Hezbollah: A Short History* (Princeton, NJ: Princeton University Press, 2007); Nicolas Blanford, *Warriors of God: Inside Hezbollah's Thirty-Year Struggle Against Israel* (New York: Random House, 2011); Worrall et al., *Hezbollah*; Judith Palmer Harik, *Hezbollah: The Changing Face of Terrorism* (London: I. B. Tauris, 2005); Adham Saouli, *Hezbollah: Socialisation and Its Tragic Ironies* (Edinburgh: Edinburgh University Press, 2018).
11 See Roy Wallis, *Sectarianism: Analyses of Religious and Non-Religious Sects* (London: Peter Owen, 1975); Lawrence Potter, *Sectarian Politics in the Persian Gulf* (London: C. Hurst & Co., 2013); Jacqueline Ismael and Tareq Ismael, 'The Sectarian State in Iraq and the New Political Class', *International Journal of Contemporary Iraqi Studies*, 4:3 (2010); Simon Mabon and Lucia Ardovini (eds), *Sectarianism in the Middle East* (Oxford: Routledge, 2017), among many others.
12 Haddad, '"Sectarianism" and Its Discontents'.
13 For the primordialist, identities exist in a fixed manner, reinforced through biological factors and through association with territory. Culture and tradition reinforce such identities. In contrast, the constructivist holds that identities are imagined and

fabricated around a particular theme, suggesting that the political community is an imagined concept.

14 See the work of Joseph Nevo, 'Religion and National Identity in Saudi Arabia', *Middle Eastern Studies*, 34:3 (1998), 34–53.

15 Olivier Roy, *The Failure of Political Islam* (London: I. B. Tauris, 1994).

16 Asef Bayat, *Islam and Democracy: What Is the Real Question?* ISIM Paper 8 (Amsterdam: Amsterdam University Press, 2007), p. 10.

17 Shahab Ahmed, *What Is Islam? The Importance of Being Islamic* (Princeton, NJ: Princeton University Press, 2016), p. 114.

18 Ibid., p. 147.

19 Ibid., p. 141.

20 Ibid., p. 275.

21 Manoucher Parvin and Maurie Sommer, 'Dar al-Islam: The Evolution of Muslim Territoriality and Its implications for Conflict Resolution in the Middle East', *International Journal of Middle East Studies*, 11(1980), 3.

22 Agamben talks about playing with the law; the idea of playing with religion is mine.

23 James Piscatori, 'Order, Justice, and Global Islam', in R. Foot, J. Gaddis and A. Hurrell (eds), *Order and Justice in International Relations* (Oxford: Oxford University Press, 2003), pp. 262–92, at p. 267.

24 Joseph Schacht, *An Introduction to Islamic Law* (Oxford: Clarendon Press, 1964), p. 200.

25 Dale F. Eickleman and James Piscatori, *Muslim Politics* (Princeton, NJ: Princeton University Press, 1996), p. 4.

26 Duncan B. Macdonald, *Development of Muslim Theology, Jurisprudence and Constitutional Theory* (New York: Russell & Russell, [1903] 1965), p. 66.

27 Schacht, *An Introduction to Islamic Law*, p. 200.

28 Hossein Esmaeili, 'The Nature and Development of Law in Islam and the Rule of Law Challenge in the Middle East and the Muslim World', *Connecticut Journal of International Law*, 26:329 (2010), 344.

29 Sayyid Abul A'la Maududi, *The Islamic Law and Constitution* (Khurshid Amhad ed. and trans.), 7th ed. (Lahore, Pakistan: Islamic Publications, [1955] 1980).

30 Clark B. Lombardi, 'Designing Islamic Constitutions: Past Trends and Options for a Democratic Future', *International Journal of Constitutional Law*, 11:3 (2013), 619.

31 Sami Zubaida, 'Contemporary Trends in Muslim Legal Thought and Ideology', in Robert W. Hefner (ed.), *The New Cambridge History of Islam: Muslims and Modernity: Culture and Society Since 1800* (Cambridge, UK: Cambridge University Press, 2010), p. 270. See also Robert W. Heffner, 'Introduction', in Robert. W. Heffner (ed.), *Shar'ia Politics: Islamic Law and Society in the Modern World* (Bloomington: Indiana University Press, 2011).

32 Nathan J. Brown, 'Shari'a and State in the Modern Muslim Middle East', *International Journal of Middle Eastern Studies*, 29 (1997), 359–76.

33 Ajami, *The Arab Predicament*; and Ayubi, *Overstating the Arab State*.

34 For a greater discussion of this see Parvin and Sommer, 'Dar al-Islam'.

35 Khadduri, *War and Peace in the Law of Islam*, p. 46.

36 Quran 48:28.

37 Quran 6:153.

38 See Julius Wellhausen, *The Religio-Political Factions in Early Islam* (Oxford: North-Holland Publishing, 1975).

39 Andrew F. March, 'Genealogies of Sovereignty in Islamic Political Theology', *Social Research* (Special Issue on Political Theology), 80:2 (Spring 2013), 293–320.

40 Ibid.

41 Seyyed Hossein Nasr, *The Heart of Islam: Enduring Values for Humanity* (New York: HarperCollins, 2002), pp. 117–18.

42 Alī ʿAbd Al Rāziq, *al-Islām wa uṣūl al-ḥukm: baḥth fiʾl-khilāfa waʾl-ḥukūma fiʾl-Islām* (Cairo: Maṭbaʿat Miṣr, 1925). English translation: Ali Abdel Razek, *Islam and the Foundations of Political Power* (Maryam Loutfi trans. and Abdou Filali-Ansary, ed.) (Edinburgh: Edinburgh University Press, 2012).

43 Muḥammad Rashīd Riḍā, *Al- Khilāfa aw al-Imāma al- ʿUẓma* (Cairo: al-Zahrāʾ liʾl-iʿlām al-ʿarabī, [1922] 1988).

44 Paul Brykczynski, 'Radical Islam and the Nation: The Relationship Between Religion and Nationalism in the Political Thought of Hassan al-Banna and Sayyid Qutb', *History of Intellectual Culture*, 5:1 (2005), 7.

45 Hassan Al Banna, 'Towards the Light', in Charles Wendell (ed.), *The Five Tracts of Hassan al-Banna* (Berkeley: University of California Press, 1975), p. 107.

46 Hassan Al Banna, *To What Do We Invite Humanity?* (Cairo: n.p., 1934). This was also published as a pamphlet in 1936, available at http://thequranblog.files.wordpress.com/2008/06/_2_to-what-do-we-invite-humanity.pdf (accessed 10.10.12).

47 Hamid, *Islamic Exceptionalism*. Countless Islamist groups exist, shaped by context and interpretation. Some locate themselves within political structures while others call for revolution.

48 Sayyid Qutb, *Maʿālim fiʾl-Ṭarīq* [Milestones] (Cairo: Dār al-Shurūq, 1964), p. 8.

49 For discussion of the transnational, see Fawaz A. Gerges, *The Far Enemy: Why Jihad Went Global* (Cambridge, UK: Cambridge University Press, 2005); and Olivier Roy, *Globalized Islam-Fundamentalism, Deterritorialization and the Search for a New Ummah* (London: Hurst, 2004), among others. For a discussion of the national, see Gilles Kepel, *Jihad: The Trail of Political Islam* (London: I. B. Tauris, 2002); and Roy, *The Failure of Political Islam*, among others.

50 Michelle Burgis, 'Faith in the State? Traditions of Territoriality and the Emergence of Modern Arab Statehood', *Journal of the History of International Law*, 11 (2009), 53.

51 Ayatollah Ruhallah Khomeini, *Hukumat-iIslami* (Najaf: n.p., 1971), pp. 62–3.

52 Mounia Bennani-Chraibi, *Soumis et rebelles: les jeunes au Maroc.* (Paris: CNRS Editions, 1994), p. 243.

53 See Simon Mabon, 'Sovereignty, Bare Life and the Arab Uprisings', *Third World Quarterly*, 38:8 (2017) 1782–99.

54 Gerges, *Makings the Arab World*; and Ayubi, *Overstating the Arab State*, p. 1.

55 Nevo, 'Religion and National Identity in Saudi Arabia'.

56 For a biography of Faisal see Joseph A. Kechichian, *Faysal: Saudi Arabia's King For All Seasons* (Gainesville, FL: University Press of Florida, 2008). For Sadat, see his autobiography, *In Search of Identity* (New York: Harper Collins, 1978).

57 Kepel, *Jihad*, p. 61. For a detailed discussion of the establishment of the Islamic University of Medina, see Farquar, *Circuits of Faith*.

58 Hamid Algar, *Wahhabism: Acritical Essay* (New York: Islamic Publications International, 2002); Madawi Al Rasheed, *A History of Saudi Arabia* (Cambridge, UK: Cambridge University Press, 2002), p. 164.

59 David D. Commins, *The Wahhabi Mission and Saudi Arabia* (London: I. B. Tauris, 2006).

60 Said K. Aburish, *The Rise, Corruption and Coming Fall of The House of Saud* (London: Bloomsbury, 1994).

61 Nevo, 'Religion and National Identity in Saudi Arabia', p. 35.

62 Saudi Constitution, available at www.constituteproject.org/constitution/Saudi_Arabia_2013.pdf?lang=en (accessed 10.02.08).

63 Aharon Layish, 'Ulama and Politics in Saudi Arabia', in Metin Heper and Raphael Israeli (eds), *Islam and Politics in the Modern Middle East* (London: Croom Helm, 1984), p. 56.

64 Rif'at Sayid Ahmad (ed.), *Ras'il Juhayman al-'Utaybi: Qa'id al-Muqtahiminlil-Masjid al-Haram bi-Makka* (Cairo: n.p., 1988).

65 Amin Al Sa'ati, *Al-Shura fi al-Mamlaka al-'Arabiya al-Sa'udiya* (Cairo, 1992), pp. 109–15.

66 Joseph A. Kechichian, 'The Role of the Ulama in the Politics of an Islamic State: The Case of Saudi Arabia', *International Journal of Middle Eastern Studies*, 18, 53–71.

67 Fouad Ibrahim, *The Shi'is of Saudi Arabia* (London: Saqi Books, 2006), p. 26.

68 For a detailed discussion of this see Toby Matthiesen, *The Other Saudis: Shiism, Dissent and Sectarianism* (Cambridge, UK: Cambridge University Press, 2014).

69 Meir Hatina, 'Historical Legacy and the Challenge of Modernity in the Middle East: the Case of al-Azhar in Egypt', *The Muslim World*, 93 (2003), 51–68.

70 Daniel Crecelius, 'Non Ideological Responses of the Egyptian Ulama to Modernazation', in Nikki R. Keddie (ed.), *Scholars, Saints and Sufis. Muslim Religious Institutions in the Middle East since 1500* (Berkeley: University of California Press, 1972), p. 208.

71 See Olivier Roy, 'Les Nouveaux Intellectuals islamistes: Essai d'approach philosophique', in Giles Kepel and Yann Richard (eds), *Intellectuals et Militants de l'Islam Contemporain* (Paris: Seuil, 1991).

72 Malika Zeghal, 'Religion and Politics in Egypt: The Ulema of Al-Azhar, Radical Islam and the State (1952–94)', *International Journal of Middle East Studies* 31(1999), 371–99.

73 Steven Barraclough, 'Al-Azhar: Between the Government and the Islamists', *Middle East Journal*, 52:2 (1998), 236–49.

74 See http://lob.gov.jo/ui/laws (accessed 15.05.2010).

75 Abdullah al'Ali al-Mutawa, quoted in Sami Awadh, 'Islamic Political Groups in Kuwait: Roots and Influence' (PhD dissertation, University of Exeter, 1988), p. 179.

76 S. N. Al Khalidi, *Al-Ahzab Al-Islamia fil-Kuwait: Al-Shi'a, Al-Ikhwan, Al-Salaf* [Islamic Parties in Kuwait: The Shi'a, The Brotherhood, The Salafis] (Kuwait: Dar Al-Naba' Lil-Nashar wa-I-Tawzi' (1999), p. 175.

77 Interview with Kuwaiti academic, 2018.

78 Ibid.

79 Knudsen and Kerr, *Lebanon.*

80 Augustus R. Norton, *Amal and the Shi'a: Struggle for the Soul of Lebanon* (Austin: University of Texas Press, 1987).

81 Knudsen and Kerr, *Lebanon.*

82 Interview with Lebanese journalist, 2017.

83 Simon Mabon and Stephen Royle, *The Origins of ISIS: The Collapse of Nations and Revolution in the Middle East* (London: I. B. Tauris, 2017).

84 Hanna Batatu, 'Iraq's Underground Shi'I Movements' (MERIP, 1981), available at www.merip.org/mer/mer102/iraqs-underground-shii-movements (accessed 13.12.15).

85 Soren Schmidt, 'The Role of Religion in Politics. The Case of Shia-Islamism in Iraq', *Nordic Journal of Religion and Society*, 22:2 (2009), 129.

86 Amatzia Baram, 'The Radical Shi'ite Opposition Movements in Iraq', in Emmanuel Sivan and Menachem Friedman (eds), *Religious Radicalism and Politics in the Middle East* (Albany: State University of New York Press, 1990), pp. 108–9.

87 Frederic Wehrey, 'Bahrain's Decade of Discontent', *Journal of Democracy*, 24:3 (2013), 116–26.

88 Steven Wright, *Fixing the Kingdom: Political Evolution and Socio-Economic Challenges in Bahrain* (Doha: Center for International and Regional Studies, Georgetown University, Qatar, 2008).

89 Luayy Bahri, 'The Socioeconomic Foundations of the Shiite Opposition in Bahrain', *Mediterranean Quarterly*, 11:3 (2000), 129–43.

90 Roy, *The Failure of Political Islam*.

91 Oliver Roy, *Globalized Islam: The Search for a New Umma* (New York: Columbia University Press, 2004), p. 99.

92 Simon Mabon, 'ISIS: Sectarianism, Geopolitics and Strong/Weak Horses' (*e-International Relations*, 10.04.15), available at www.e-ir.info/2015/04/10/isis-sectarianism-geopolitics-and-strongweak-horses (accessed 10.04.15).

93 Peter Mandaville, 'Transnational Muslim Solidarities and Everyday Life', *Nations and Nationalism*, 17:1 (2011), 7–24.

94 Asaf Bayat, 'Islamism and Social Movement Theory', *Third World Quarterly*, 26:6 (2005), 904.

95 See Matthew Derrick, 'Containing the *Umma?* Islam and the Territorial Question', *Interdisciplinary Journal of Research on Religion*, 9 (2013), 1–30.

96 Khadduri, *War and Peace in the Law of Islam*, p. 14.

97 See Tamim Al Barghouti, *The Umma and the Dawla: The Nation State and the Arab Middle East* (London: Pluto Press, 2008).

98 Mandaville, 'Transnational Muslim Solidarities and Everyday Life', p. 9.

99 Ibid., p. 10.

100 See Thomas Hegghammer, *Jihad in Saudi Arabia: Violence and Pan Islamism Since 1979* (Cambridge, UK: Cambridge University Press, 2010).

101 *Encyclopedia of Islam*, 2nd ed. (London: Luzac & Co., 1960), s.v. *dar al-Islam*, p. 127.

102 See G. E. von Grunebaum, 'Islam: Its Inherent Power of Expansion and Adaptation', in G. E. von Grunebaum, *Modern Islam: The Search for Cultural Identity* (New York: Vintage Books, 1964), p. 1. See also Khadduri, *War and Peace in the Law of Islam*, p. 43.

103 Parvin and Sommer, 'Dar al-Islam', pp. 4–5.

104 Ibid., p. 7. In the Quran this sentiment is shared at: 6:11, 27:69, 29:20, 30:42.

105 Khaldun, *The Muqaddimah*, p. 295.

106 Parvin and Sommer, 'Dar al-Islam', p. 7.

107 Ibid., p. 11.

108 Khadduri, *War and Peace in the Law of Islam*, p. 157.

109 Quran 49:13.

110 Majid Khadduri (trans.), *The Islamic Law of Nations: Shaybani's Syiar* (Baltimore, MD: Johns Hopkins Press, 1966), p. 65.

111 Authors such as Huntington and Lewis are thus guilty of denying local agency.

112 James Piscatori, *Islam in a World of Nation-States* (Cambridge, UK: Cambridge University Press, 1986), p. vii.

113 Reinhard Schulze, *A Modern History of the Islamic World* (London: I. B. Tauris, 2000), p. 303.
114 Fred Halliday, 'The Politics of the *Umma*: States and Community in Islamic Movements', *Mediterranean Politics*, 7:3 (2002), 27–8.
115 Schulze, *A Modern History of the Islamic World*, p. 41.
116 Halliday, 'The Politics of the *Umma*'.
117 Eickleman and Piscatori, *Muslim Politics*.
118 Interview with Lebanese journalist, 2017.
119 Peter Berger, 'The Sociological Study of Sectarianism', *Social Research*, 51:1/2 (1984), 367–85.
120 Mabon, 'The Circle of Bare Life'.
121 March, 'Genealogies of Sovereignty in Islamic Political Theology'.
122 Iranian Constitution, available at www.constituteproject.org/constitution/Iran_1989.pdf?lang=en (accessed 10.02.08).
123 Lawrence Rubin, *Islam in the Balance: Ideational Threats in Arab Politics* (Palo Alto, CA: Stanford Security Studies, 2014), p. 52.
124 Ibid., p. 7.
125 Chubin and Tripp, *Iran-Saudi Arabia Relations and Regional Order*.
126 Mabon, *Saudi Arabia and Iran*.
127 Amirahmadi Hooshang, and Nader Entessar (eds), *Iran and the Arab World* (Basingstoke, UK: Palgrave Macmillan, 1993), p. 3.
128 Con Coughlin, *Khomeini's Ghost* (London: Macmillan, 2009), p. 274.
129 'Excerpts from Khomeini's Speeches' (*New York Times*, 04.08.87), available at www.nytimes.com/1987/08/04/world/excerpts-from- khomeini-speeches.html?pagewanted=all&src=pm (accessed 11.02.08).
130 Ibid.
131 See Jacob Goldberg, 'The Saudi Arabian Kingdom', in Itovar Rabinovich and Haim Shaked (eds), *Middle East Contemporary Survey Volume XI: 1987* (Boulder, CO: Westview Press, 1987), p. 589.
132 Widespread allegations exist that such events were orchestrated by the Iranian Revolutionary Guards. See Goldberg, 'The Saudi Arabian Kingdom', p. 590.
133 Turan Kayaoglu, *The Organization of Islamic Cooperation: Politics, Problems, and Potential* (New York: Routledge, 2015).
134 Jeffrey Haynes, *Religion and Development: Conflict or Cooperation* (Basingstoke, UK: Palgrave Macmillan, 2007), p. 95.
135 Yesim Dikmen and Melih Aslan, 'Muslim Nations Accuse Iran of Supporting Terrorism: Summit Communique' (Reuters, 15.04.2016), available at www.reuters.com/article/us-turkey-summit/muslim-nations-accuse-iran-of-supporting-terrorism-summit-communique-idUSKCN0XC1LQ (accessed 15.04.06). See also Bassel F. Salloukh, 'The Arab Uprisings and the Geopolitics of the Middle East', *International Spectator*, 48:2 (2013), 32–46.
136 Hussein Kalout, 'The Struggle for Islamic Supremacy', *Global Discourse*, 7:2–3 (2017), 357–70.
137 Interview with Iraqi Shi'a cleric, 2015.
138 Interview with Lebanese journalist, 2017.
139 'Building a House on Shifting Sands: Iran's Influence in Iraq's Center-South, (WikiLeaks, 20.07.05), available at www.wikileaks.org/plusd/cables/05BAGHDAD3015_a.html (accessed 12.12.05).

140 'Sadrist Confidante Warns of Bad Pressure Building Within Sadrist Movement' (WikiLeaks, 09.04.08), available at https://wikileaks.org/plusd/cables/ 08BAGHDAD1105_a.html (accessed 12.12.15).

141 See Stacey Philbrick Yadav, 'Sectarianization, Islamist Republicanism, and International Misrecognition in Yemen', in Hashemi and Postel (eds), *Sectarianization*, p. 188.

142 Matthew T. Johnson and Simon Mabon, 'Fundamentalism: Explaining the "Non-Liberal" Approaches to "Unreasonable" Doctrines', *Australian Journal of Political Science*, 53:2 (2018), 1–16.

143 See the work of Oren Yiftachel, in particular *Ethnocracy: Land and Identity Politics in Israel/Palestine* (Philadelphia: University of Pennsylvania Press, 2006).

144 Ibid, p. 3.

145 A prerequisite for Carl Schmitt.

146 Yiftachel, *Ethnocracy*, p. 7.

147 In a manner reminiscent of Schmitt's idea of the *nomos*, yet as laws and norms took form, we see mechanisms for regulating life emerge.

148 See Ariyeh Ruttenburg and Sandy Amichai, *The Etzion Bloc in the Hills of Judea* (Kfar Etzion: Kfar Etzion Field School, 1997).

149 Yael Allweil, 'West Bank Settlement and the Transformation of the Zionist Housing Ethos from Shelter to Act of Violence', *Footprint: Spaces of Conflict*, 19 (2016), 13–36.

150 Ibid.

151 Zvika Slonim, '*Daf Lamityashev*' (Gush Emunim, 1980), pp. 1–2, cited in Allweil, 'West Bank Settlement', pp. 13–36.

152 Yiftachel, *Ethnocracy*, p. 5.

153 All settlements are deemed illegal by international law but in this case, I refer to those deemed illegal by Israeli law, the unofficial processes that challenge the sovereignty of the state and provoked widespread opposition.

154 'Israel's Military Exemption for Ultra-Orthodox is Ruled Unconstitutional' (*New York Times*, 09.12.17), available at www.nytimes.com/2017/09/12/world/middleeast/israel-ultra-orthodox-military.html (accessed 15.09.17).

155 Stuart A. Cohen, 'Tensions Between Military Service and Jewish Orthodoxy in Israel: Imagined and Real', *Israel Studies*, 12:1 (2007), 103–26.

156 Carolina Landsmann, 'Drafting Ultra-Orthodox Jews into the Israeli Army is Dangerous' (*Ha'aretz*, 15.09.17), available at www.haaretz.com/opinion/.premium-drafting-ultra-orthodox-jews-into-the-israeli-army-is-dangerous-1.5451098 (accessed 15.09.17).

5

Building Beirut, transforming Jerusalem and breaking Basra

Empires collapse. Gang leaders
are strutting about like statesmen. The peoples
Can no longer be seen under all those armaments.
So the future lies in darkness and the forces of right
Are weak. All this was plain to you.

Walter Benjamin, *On the Suicide of the Refugee*

Cities of Salt, a novel by Abdelrahman Munif set in an unnamed Gulf kingdom tells the story of the transformation of Wadi Al Uyan by Americans after the discovery of oil.[1] The wadi, initially described as a 'salvation from death' amid the treacherous desert heat, played an important role in the lives of the Bedouin community of the unnamed kingdom – although the reader quickly draws parallels with Saudi Arabia – and its ensuing destruction has a devastating impact upon the people who lived there. The novel explores tensions between tradition and modernity that became increasingly pertinent after the discovery of oil, outlining the transformation of local society amid the socio-economic development of the state. The narrative reveals how these developments ride roughshod over tribal norms that had long regulated life, transforming the regulation and ordering of space, grounding the exception within a territorially bounded area. It was later banned by a number of Gulf states.

Although fictional, the novel offers a fascinating account of the evolution of life across the Gulf. World Bank data suggests that 65% of the Middle East's population live in cities, although in Kuwait this is 98%, in Qatar it is 99%, but in Yemen it is only 35%.[2] Legislation designed to regulate life finds most traction within urban areas, where jobs and welfare projects offer a degree of protection. The city is a fluid entity, often viewed through the lens of networks that go some way into ordering life.[3] Beyond this, the aesthetics of a city can be used to develop a national identity, which also brings about exclusion. Decisions over infrastructural and development projects are taken for political reasons, driven by domestic and regional concerns, yet impacting on the lives of citizens and non-citizens within states and across space. This chapter explores the role of urban environments as sites of sovereign power and contestation. It considers the way in which urban environments simultaneously shape – and are shaped by – political projects across the twentieth and twenty-first centuries.

Understanding the concept of sovereignty entails exploration of relations between peoples and their leaders within space. A range of factors shape the essence of these interactions, from identity and ideology to the nature of the political system. The environment within which interactions occur can also shape relations between rulers and ruled. As Henri Lefebvre argues, space is 'a social project ... the space thus produced also serves as a tool of thought and action ... in addition to being a means of production it is also a means of control, and hence of domination, of power'.[4]

Urban space is the physical representation of aspects of the *nomos*, as an arena through which life clashes with an array of identities and values that may impact upon the capacity of the life to live. A range of factors shape the (re)construction of space – both urban and rural – and the movement of people within and across spatial borders. Existential challenges emerging from environmental issues coupled with the nature of state building has left a large percentage of the region's population living in urban environments. This relocation positions the city as the main arena of contemporary politics, the dominant space where life is regulated.

Migration from rural to urban environments was an integral part of the transformation of political organisation. A range of strategies were then deployed in an effort to regulate this space, but amid contestation, alternative sources of governance have emerged, providing legitimacy to those groups well placed to develop social welfare programmes. Reflecting the growing penetration of neoliberal ideas, as the century progressed state institutions took less of a role in urban planning, creating space for private entrepreneurs to act. This type of strategy serves to reinforce neopatrimonial networks that support sovereign power and often occur along sectarian lines, regulating life in the process.

Within the urban environment, identities, groups and networks interact and collide, simultaneously reinforcing and challenging national projects. Amid an array of tribal, ethnic, religious, political and ideological loyalties, regulating life within the city is of paramount importance for regime survival. As such, the city is the arena through which networks of patronage – family, tribal, religious or bureaucratic – can be mobilised to retain power. While legal structures go some way to restricting agency, norms have also been used to reduce the capacity of civil society to challenge regime stability.

The governance of a city goes beyond enforcing the laws of a state as it also aims at *letting life live*. But the city is also a site and perpetrator of urban violence, encapsulating both direct and indirect forms of violence and repression, regulating life in the process. This violence takes a range of different forms, from that enforced by security personnel, to imagery and structural violence, while also possessing a spatial aspect. Thus we should not view the city as a neutral zone; in turn, the city plays both a regulatory role and also a performative role, wherein the buildings and streets take on additional meaning, becoming the bearers of identities and ideologies. Yet neither are cities solely the zones of performance, stages wherein political dynamics are played out; they are also landscapes of the mundane, where the routine of daily life is a product of regulatory structures.

A great deal of work has been written on spaces of exclusion within and beyond the contemporary city that are typically populated by refugees and displaced peoples[5] and also the militarisation of the city,[6] but very little has explored broader understandings of violence and its impact upon agency. It is through this that we can see how daily life is regulated across the Middle East, combining both the laws of a state and the normative structures of ideology, imagery, rhetoric and narratives in the manifestation of a clash between *ordnung* and *ortung*, the regulatory aspects of sovereign power interacting with the spatial characteristics.

The evolution of the urban

Territory is no doubt a geographical notion, but it's first of all a jurido-political one: the area controlled by a certain type of power.[7]

Urban planning and development are not a neutral process; development will, almost certainly, have implications for people affected areas. The city is the space in which contemporary politics occurs, with the interaction of people with institutions, infrastructure, ideas, capital and the regulatory mechanisms of a state.[8] The city landscape is routinely structurally – and symbolically – violent. With this in mind, the urban landscape becomes a canvas for regime and nationalist narratives. Amid times of crisis, where the legitimacy of regimes is challenged, the canvas of the cityscape evolves to take on additional forms of representative violence.

Given the rapid urbanisation across the twentieth century, the city quickly became the arena within which life is regulated and contested.[9] Population density meant that politics was increasingly played out within urban environments, bringing together laws, religion, ethnicity, sex and class into a melting pot of identities, issues and agendas. Development projects transform the social dynamics of a city, not only through the need to house workers responsible for undertaking the changes – often in deplorable conditions – but also through the changing social fabric of the state, wherein indigenous populations within a number of Gulf states are often in the minority.

Urban violence can be seen in two ways: the first is the structural violence of the architecture and depiction of civic loyalty within the city, which supports regime interest and nationalist projects. This may occur in the guise of latent structural and symbolic violence along political, ethnic, sectarian, tribal or national lines. The second is the regulation of life within the city, or the means through which security is enforced and regime stability is maintained, often through the guise of direct violence. These two concepts of violence often intertwine, feeding into one another and contributing to marginalisation and discrimination. Of course, this landscape reflects broader political trends within and between states. Moreover, the means through which life is regulated within the city can also be used as a mechanism of political control. Enforced by the security apparatus of the state, access to public space in lieu of civil society or political space can be restricted in times of crisis. The interaction of these instances of violence can result in the emergence of a transformative space, a site of becoming or, put another way, a zone of indistinction, both possibility and repression.

An additional point of tension that manifests in the urban environment is the clash between the public and the private. Understanding the interaction between such concepts within particular contexts is at the heart of exploring the role of the city in shaping political life. Ultimately, as Mark Wigley explains,

> What binds violence and space together is not the discrete events which appear to disturb the spaces we occupy but the more subterranean rhythms that already organize those very spaces ... In the end there is no space without violence, and no violence that is not spatial. Violence is the very structure of space. Each discourse maintains a strategic silence about the particular forms of violence which makes both it and what it appears to address possible.[10]

As such, to understand urban violence we must combine the analysis of terrain with both legal and pragmatic structures that regulate life and those contextual 'rhythms', currents or norms that shape political action. This interaction helps to reveal the nature of sovereignty and the extent to which rulers can regulate life or strip it of political meaning. Ultimately, the interactions of such structures and rhythms feed back into ordering of space and the demarcation of borders.

Transformations occurred as local actors sought to secure their rule and to engage with processes of globalisation. The transformation of society exposed a tension between old and new, traditional and modern forms of public space. The evolution from mandate to independence fuelled such dichotomies. Those able to facilitate urban development projects were immediately positioned as those with power and influence and, as a consequence, the transformation of urban landscapes secured political power. Gaps in marginal regions result in a vacuum, filled by a range of documentary practices, including the face of martyrs on billboards, lamp posts, walls, commemorative structures and across public spaces.[11] Such zones of indistinction thus become zones of possibility wherein agency can be exerted amid efforts to regulate life.

Urban development and the transformation of life from rural to urban brought with it serious changes to the organisation of life, a great deal of which went against indigenous values. Ensuring that such networks and traditions continued albeit within a territorially defined space was a key part of the state-building process.[12] Maintaining control over fluid networks was an essential feature of laying claim to power but with the onset of urbanisation, which dramatically altered the organisation of life, bringing in territorial rights and with it, private property, this became increasingly difficult.

The legacy of empire and mandate rule played a prominent role in the transformation of Middle Eastern cities. Those cities that had played important roles during the Ottoman Empire, facilitating trade links with Europe such as Beirut, Alexandria and Izmir, experienced rapid transformation,[13] while new mandate capitals also experienced rapid developments as they took on burgeoning importance. The establishment of political institutions and bureaucracies in new states also facilitated transformation of both formal and normative structures, as people moved from the countryside to the cities in search of work.

As Charles Tripp suggests,

> For those who inherited the colonial state and then proceeded to claim the exclusive right to rule it, the very languages and practices of power that gave them dominion were eventually turned against them. Idioms that had been used to buttress the power of a restrictive elite were taken up by their opponents and given a very different significance, while retaining their potency.[14]

Idioms, language and practices differ within and between states and, as a consequence, the nature of political life within cities differs, once again shaped by contingent factors. For instance, the cities of the Persian Gulf range from company towns, secondary port cities and aspiring global metropolises,[15] which differ from the more historic seats of regional power in Baghdad, Beirut and Cairo. It is then important to make distinctions between cities across the region, not only by considering their expressions of political power, but also by considering their engagement with the global *nomos*. The discovery of oil in the 1920s and 1930s facilitated the development of so-called 'company towns', where the city dominated all forms of life, political, cultural and social, creating hierarchical structures of control.[16] Dammam, Al Khobar, Dharan, Abadan, Ahmadi and Awali were all formed as company towns by the activity of external oil companies, who brought with them Western architects and ideas, seemingly with little regard for the impact on people who had been living there, for whom this was yet another damning criticism of modernity.[17]

This transformation of life across the Gulf states required large-scale investment and with it a workforce that had its own impact upon life in the Gulf; an influx of non-indigenous workers meant that by the 1950s around 40% of employees in the oil and gas sector were from abroad.[18] Even states without oil reserves profited as they sent off workers to oil states and received vast remittances in return, facilitating the transformation of the homeland, enabling the purchase of land and rapid commercial ventures.[19] Some, such as the Lebanese businessman Rafik Hariri, earned a great deal in the Gulf, which funded his involvement in political life before his assassination in 2005.[20] The legacy of such transformations remains evident in the commercial districts of cities and the high-rise structures that dominate skylines. To their critics, such structures 'often ignore the living tissue of their surroundings in their physical outlook and in catering to new, exclusive sections of the local economy. High-rise dwellings, often located in the midst of less-affluent city spaces, further exemplify this novel, decontextualised urban reality'.[21]

Of course, this position within the networks of a global economy came at a social – and indeed political – cost. As Fuad Malkawi suggests, traditional forms of urban organisation, cityscape and construction have been transformed in the quest for new spaces of global consumption, materialism and communication.[22] These new urban spaces were carefully planned to restrict and monitor life, tailoring it to the needs of the company and contemporary visions of the state.[23] In Turkey, Ottoman architecture was removed to prevent recourse to erstwhile normative structures.[24] Moreover, there was, as Kaveh Ehsani articulates, an increased obsession with the idea of using the urban environment as an instrument of coercion over the population.[25] Such processes were driven by Western experience, where once again, architecture, necessity and political calculations trumped local contexts and values and were designed in accordance with an imaginary construction of 'Arabia'.[26]

In the first half of the twentieth century, a burgeoning scholarship on cities in the region – underpinned by Orientalist tropes – was concerned with the defining characteristics of an 'Islamic city'. From this scholarship, a mosque, suq and public bathhouse were deemed necessary criteria to become a city in the Middle East in spite conclusions being derived from North Africa alone.[27] While cities undoubtedly share similar characteristics, contingent factors create difference as a consequence of climate, technologies of production and distribution, social dynamics and political systems. The interaction of these factors produced urban forms of organisation that differed across the region amid competing visions of political organisation. Cities became spaces of contestation as tradition and modernity collapse into zones of indistinction and possibility, simultaneously drawing on the past and future, underpinned by Orientalist interpretations of the 'Islamic city' in the process.[28] Yet one Emirati woman told me that Emirati traditions such as pearl diving had largely been discarded unlike in neighbouring Qatar, where the *dhows* (boats commonly found in the Persian Gulf, Indian Ocean and East Africa) were turned into tourist attractions.[29]

This contemporary construction of an imaginary 'Arabia' is perhaps best seen amid recent developments in Kuwait, where an architectural firm involved in designing Madinat Al-Hareer, the City of Silk, plays upon such concepts while also serving as a beacon of Kuwaiti power. The new city will be home to the 'Tower of a Thousand and One Nights', and upon completion, it will be the largest tower in the world, dwarfing both the Freedom Tower in Saudi Arabia and the Burj Khalifa in Dubai. For Kuwait, the Madinat Al-Hareer is supposed to represent life on the Arabian Peninsula inspired by 'the defiant flora of the desert as much as the rich folklore of Arabic heritage described in Kitab'Alf Layla wa-Layla'.[30]

The means and extent to which urban landscapes have transformed has serious implications for the political environment of a state. In Abu Dhabi, after Sheikh Zayed's decision to embark on an ambitious development programme, 40% of the workforce was dedicated to construction projects.[31] Similar stories are found across the Gulf. Doha's journey from Bedouin rule to global hub occurred at vast speed amid independence movements and the British withdrawal.[32] In Kuwait, Abu Dhabi, Dubai, Saudi Arabia and Bahrain, the speed of transformation created contradictions within society between traditional values and modernity, many of which were reflected within architecture and the incongruence of suq and skyscraper.

Urban landscapes, public space and symbolic architecture

Attempts to rewrite the social contract impact on cities first. Furthermore, when state-run bureaucracies retreat from public service amid an array of socio-economic challenges, citizens are forced to find other sources of employment, welfare and support. Inhabitants of the major cities of the developing world live in challenging conditions, where many survive on the few resources they can access. The move to informal networks of support creates space for groups such as the Muslim Brotherhood, Hizballah, Hamas and Fatah to gain large-scale support. Open space within urban environments provided scope for contestation, transformation and expressions of political dissent, where urban landscapes become canvases for counter-hegemonic narratives of martyrdom and resistance. Of course, this resulted in the increased policing and regulation of urban space through coercion and violence.

Religion, tradition and culture provide guidance for the structuring of space in accordance with regulatory goals. The type of mosque – or temple or church – helps to shape the identity of the area yet this must also be placed within economic contexts.[33] Although people are seen to reside within homogenous areas, such a reductive argument serves to reify sectarian identities, at the expense of class and economic factors.[34]

Endogenous and exogenous forces – both with and without consent – shape the spatial dimensions of the urban space, with implications for the capacity of people to live their lives.[35] Cities themselves are exclusionary projects in their governance and their architecture, which has violent spatial properties. Within cities, political, social, ethnic or religious differences can have spatial implications, which are then amplified by national and regional aspirations. One such way in which power and aspiration can be demonstrated is through architecture and imagery. In addition to security mechanisms such as armed police, barbed wire and security cameras, violence also possesses a symbolic side, playing a political role and bearing an identity.

Urban environments provide an array of opportunities for such domination and violence to be displayed and for latent structures to manifest. The rising importance of urban environments also provides scope for authority to be challenged, often in visual form using the urban landscape as a canvas. The power of the image across the Middle East should not be ignored. From the martyrdom posters in Lebanon and Palestine, to the posters of Khomeini and Khamenei in Iran and Iraq, taking in the images of Gulf leaders, it is hard to ignore the presence of political narratives that remind people of their *nomos*, of the context and contingency that regulates their life.

Regulating and transforming life in rural and urban contexts is thus a demonstration of sovereign power:

> The reorganisation of towns and the laying out of new colonial quarters, every regulation of economic or social practice, the construction of the country's new system of irrigation canals … the building of barracks, police stations and classrooms, the completion of a system of railways – this pervasive process of 'order' must be understood as more than mere improvement or 'reform'. Such projects were all undertaken as enframing, and hence had the effect of representing a realm of the conceptual, conjuring up for the first time the prior abstraction of progress, reason, law, discipline, history, colonial authority and order.[36]

Transformation also occurs through expropriation, gentrification, occupation and ethnic redistribution as a range of strategies facilitate demonstrations of sovereign power, brought about by formal and normative structures but contingent upon context-specific factors.[37] Such actions shape political landscapes, creating a metaphysical environment wherein people resort to extralegal strategies as mechanisms of exerting agency.[38]

Amid such challenges, public space became monopolised by regimes. For many Egyptians, public space was synonymous with space that is 'owned by the government'.[39] In spite of this, Tahrir Square had long been a place in which dissent was expressed, such as Evacuation Day in 1946, which called for the British withdrawal from Egypt. This was later followed by an occupation by a student movement in 1972; sympathisers of the second *intifada* in 2001; people protesting against Hosni Mubarak's support for the US-led Iraq War; and political reform movements in 2005 and 2006.[40] In the following years, the area around Tahrir Square underwent what was ostensibly the development of the Cairo metro and a parking garage, but as crowds entered the square in early 2011, it became evident that the work had instead been a move to prevent symbolic protest, albeit unsuccessfully.

Myriad efforts were undertaken to regulate life across cities in the region. As Stephen Graham notes, the city is the arena within which tracking, surveillance and targeting have all begun to play an integral role in daily life.[41] Of course, this demonstrates the power of formal security structures – supported by security agencies, the police and military – along with the speed at which such techniques can evolve. Yet we must also consider the architecture and the symbolism deployed across the city, which acts as a daily reminder of sovereign power.

While state mechanisms routinely used violence as a mechanism of control, urban violence occurs in a number of other guises. The careful development of nationalist iconography was a prominent part of the urban environment in the formative stages of nationalist projects, which often revolved around a leader's cult of personality and benevolence. In a nod towards aspects of totalitarianism, roads and buildings were often adorned with images of rulers and their families, in explicit displays of power. This imagery is representative of the social contract in operation across many Gulf societies where ruling families have become almost synonymous with political projects in states.

Gentrification and transformative violence

The evolution of the city, much like the city itself, should not be viewed as a neutral process. Investment, change and urban planning all reflect political decisions and aspirations with regard to regulating political life and the urban environment. While this contains aspects of improving life for people living within the city, such decisions are loaded with political meaning. Transformation is often a violent process, uprooting people from homes and radically altering daily life. In addition, the ongoing gentrification of a number of areas simultaneously erases history and creates a more precarious life. Gentrification offers a process through which dilapidated areas are renovated. In a number of contexts, these areas are also home to dissident groups and thus, while there is an economic dimension at play, there is a clear political dimension to processes of gentrification.

Gentrification serves both to facilitate further transformation away from prior incarnations of the urban environment and to reinforce new identities. With the increased ease of access to knowledge and imagery, this has taken on paramount importance, particularly in areas that have large numbers of tourists. With lower land prices on the peripheries of cities, the desire for property is higher than in the historic centres. This is exacerbated by economic developments within the global economy that have had an impact in local areas. Take the suq in Manama, previously occupying a central role in daily life, it has now become almost peripheral to economic developments such as the Financial Harbour, built upon land reclaimed from the sea. Moreover, the historic suq has begun to play a lesser role to the malls that have emerged across the island and even to the shops close to the nearby Bab al Bahrain, which was itself part of a land reclamation process. Within the suq, traditional shops have been occupied by migrants from the Asian subcontinent, reflecting both the changes in identity and urban life across Bahrain, along with the emergence of new hierarchies.

The city of Jaffa, once an Arab city overlooking the Mediterranean Sea, is another example of the extent to which cities can play a transformative role. In the British mandate era, Jaffa became a site of protest between Arabs and Jews, which resulted in the establishment of Tel Aviv to the north. During the struggle to establish the state of Israel, Jaffa was defended by a group identified as the Muslim Brotherhood who surrendered to the Zionist forces after five months of intense fighting.[42] The regulation of life in Jaffa under the British was done in accordance with martial law established by mandatory rule. Under martial law, house demolitions were a common part of daily life along with the militarisation of the city. Such experiences were later adopted by the Israeli security services as a means of maintaining control of life in the West Bank and Gaza. In recent years, the gentrification of Jaffa has seen the restoration of traditional Arab monuments, such as the Mosque of the Sea and the Hassan Bek Mosque, turning the Old City of Jaffa into a tourist area.[43] Additionally, other reports have noted efforts to 'Judaise' the area by building Jewish only complexes.[44] As a consequence, retail and rent prices have been driven up, disproportionately affecting Palestinian-Israelis, referred to by a legal defence coordinator as 'ethnic cleansing'.[45]

Efforts to improve the infrastructure of cities can also have negative social implications. Across Beirut, urban planning has detrimentally impacted upon local communities[46] and their engagement with life across the city. Massive investment from Saudi nationals transformed the area between Ras Beirut and Ain al Mraiseh, which is now largely empty. The construction of bridges and highways such as the Yerevan Bridge in Bourj Hammoud, the Hawd Al Wilaya Bridge in Basta and the Charles Helou Avenue have all divided neighbourhoods, resulting in economic and social repercussions.[47] After all, the fundamental point of a city is to provide a home and welfare to people and as an urban environment experiences transformation, there will be consequences for people.

While urban planning is undertaken by regimes and actors empowered by regimes through networks of patronage or cronyism, there are a number of examples of societal actors driving the transformation of political terrain. Perhaps the most obvious example of this is found in the settler movements in the West Bank who seek to use architecture and building projects as a means through which the borders of the state of Israel can be pushed. The establishment of such settlements, deemed illegal under international law yet both legal and illegal under Israeli law, brings with it infrastructural programmes that facilitate such transformations, including the development of roads and water supplies. Such projects have symbolic importance, along with a transformative sense of permanence, impacting on facts on the ground.

In addition to transformation of land for settlement, land has also been renovated for tourist purposes. Much like in Jaffa, the process of gentrification was designed to increase the flow of tourists to the Old City and the development of the old harbour and transformation into a market area with bars and restaurants was a prominent part of this goal. Yet perhaps the best example of such forced exclusion is the case of the Jordanian Bedouin living in Petra, who were evicted to provide the Jordanian state with access to a vast revenue stream from tourism.

Of course, other cities have experienced similar transformations, as the rhythms of state politics clash with hegemonic globalising forces. In Mecca, the need to accommodate large numbers of pilgrims resulted in dramatic change to the city.[48] In the Grand Mosque, a seventeenth-century portico was removed, meaning that around 95% of Mecca's old buildings had been destroyed in the past two decades, later described as 'cultural vandalism' by the head of the Islamic Heritage Research Foundation, Irfan Al Alawi.[49] The development of the Mecca Royal Clock Tower was erected on the graves of around four hundred culturally significant sites, while the house of Khadijah, the Prophet's first wife, has been transformed into a block of toilets.[50] Earlier renovations at the Grand Mosque resulted in the destruction of the Ottoman Al Ajyad Fortress and claims from Ankara that such developments were an 'act of barbarism' and the destruction of shared Islamic heritage.[51] The politicisation of Mecca continued as developments cost the lives of thousands of pilgrims, when in 2006 the Al Ghaza hotel collapsed and in 2015, a crane collapsed into the Grand Mosque, killing 118 people. The same year, between 2,000 and 4,000 pilgrims were crushed close to the Jamaraat Bridge.

As a number of scholars have shown, violence maintains a regulatory capability, in some cases restricting the capacity of people to travel within certain areas. The case of Palestine provides a harrowing example of how the Israeli state has used architecture as a means of exerting control.[52] In Khuzestan, the south-western province of Iran, political aspirations of Arabs residing in towns such as Abadan were a source of existential concern to the Iranian regime. In addition to concerns about the territorial integrity of the state,[53] the province was home to around 80% of Iran's oil reserves yet lacked substantial economic investment and infrastructural development, resulting in large-scale political and social grievances including suggestions of widespread drug addiction.[54] In response to perceived irredentist agendas, Tehran embarked on a process of ethnic redistribution, moving ethnic Persians into Arab-Iranian areas in an attempt to erode unrest and ensure stability.[55] This strategy would later be used by Bashar Al Assad in an attempt to create order and maintain power in post-uprisings Syria.[56]

Existential transformation and becoming

The transformation of Jerusalem provides scope to explore how urban landscapes take on political meaning, while the regulation of the urban environment feeds into broader, existential political projects. Jerusalem offers an example of how cities serve both as a means through which life is regulated but also how identity and ideology is performed. Jerusalem has long occupied a central role in the conflict between Israelis and Palestinians, with both claiming the city as capital of their states. Consideration of architecture and symbolism across the city reveal mechanisms of control and the way in which life has been regulated reveals a great deal about the nature of sovereignty within Jerusalem and Israel more broadly.

In the summer of 1943, the Zionist Planning Committee was established to develop a plan to transform the urban landscape of Jerusalem, five years before the formal establishment of the state of Israel. The aim of the group was 'the economic recovery of Jerusalem to enable the city to attract large numbers of residents', which was central to the broader Zionist project.[57] In support of this, a subcommittee was established, focusing entirely upon industry in Jerusalem to facilitate its rebirth. For David Ben Gurion, the subcommittee was to facilitate a rise in 'Jewish settlement in Jerusalem and its environs, to rehabilitate and strengthen its economic basis, and to ensure that the capital of our country will have a Jewish majority in population and building'.[58]

In spite of such demands, before the establishment of Israel in 1948 Jerusalem became peripheral to the transformation of other areas of Palestine, notably Jaffa and Tel Aviv, amid concerns that mistakes in Jerusalem could prevent the establishment of the state. It was only by 30 July 1980 that the Jerusalem Law was passed by the Israeli Knesset, which formalised the regulation of eastern parts of Jerusalem. Facts on the ground, however, reflected de facto control of Jerusalem, which had been declared as the capital of the Israeli state on 13 December 1949.[59]

In the aftermath of the seizure of East Jerusalem in 1967 with the historic Old City as its symbolic prize, Israeli strategists sought to solidify their state-building efforts. Ensuring the retention of a unified Jerusalem under Israeli control was the main goal.[60] The importance of this was stressed by Moshe Dayan, who on entering the city stated that 'we have reunited divided Jerusalem, the dismembered capital of Israel. We have returned to our most holy places; we have returned and we shall never leave them'.[61] In his memoirs, Abba Eban, the Israeli Foreign Minister, wrote how 'we had come back to the cradle of our nationhood to stay there forever'.[62] Reflecting this existential transformation, shortly after the capture of East Jerusalem and the West Bank, Israeli maps were ordered to stop using to the 1947 'Green Line' as the border of Israel.[63]

In a speech at the UN headquarters in New York, Abba Eban described Israel's emergence 'from grave danger to successful resistance', attempting to shape public sentiment in what was described by the *Chicago Tribune* as 'one of the greatest speeches of modern times'.[64] Yet the aftermath of the 1967 war would have serious territorial repercussions for both Israel and Palestine. On 22 September 1967, Israeli newspapers published a 160-word statement by a group calling itself the Movement for a Greater Israel:

> The victory of the Israeli defense forces in the Six Day War has brought the nation and the state into a new and fateful era. Undivided Israel is now in the hands of the Jewish people, and just as we had no right to renounce the State of Israel, so are we commanded gratefully to receive what this era has granted us: namely, the entire Land of Israel.
>
> We owe allegiance to the integrity of our land; to its past and its future. And no government in Israel has the right to give up this wholeness.[65]

With this statement, the political landscape of Israel was dramatically transformed, resulting in Palestinian territory becoming the site of decades-long contestation between Israelis, Palestinians and settler movements.

Within this context, the regulation and retention of land took on existential importance. Urban planning became a central aspect of an existential strategy designed to normalise the occupation and create cohesion among territories held by the Israeli state. In doing so, the city became a site of contestation deployed by the Israeli state against Palestinians in the name of sovereignty. A ring of settlements was built around East Jerusalem, cutting off the city's Palestinian population from other Palestinians in the West Bank. In the city itself, the Maghriba Quarter located in front of the Western Wall was destroyed immediately after military victory to facilitate access to the wall. Further architectural moves were undertaken, demonstrating the power of the new Israeli state. Architectural and archeological efforts were reflective of the broader Zionist project, which David Ben Gurion suggested required 'digging the soil with our own hands'[66] as a necessary part of transformation. This process of transubstantiation serves as a form of creative destruction, an opportunity for *becoming*, where destruction is a form of regulation, an attempt to shape the future by destroying the past.

The transformation of the city of Jerusalem quickly took shape, combining old British colonial laws with the establishment of new urban planning institutions. Policy briefings such as *Israel Builds* became a prominent feature of Israeli political and security discourse. In this volume, Ram Karmi, wrote that, 'Home means more than just the narrow confines of one's apartment; it also implies a sense of belonging to the immediate surroundings.'[67] Transformation took on both personal and nationalist characteristics where the two feed into one another and, as a first order of business, the barriers separating the two sides of the city were removed. Of course, sovereign power also regulates space through placing restrictions on land ownership. In accordance with Israeli law, 80% of the land comprising the territorial area of Israel can only be purchased by Jews.[68] Such regulation has changed the demographic status of the Old City, as previous Arab inhabitants have given way to Jewish owners, many of whom are bankrolled by Zionist organisations.

Such symbolic violence is also seen in rural areas of the West Bank under military control. When travelling towards Nablus from the south of Israel at night, one is struck by the bright lights of a Star of David on the Palestinian hills, while Stars of David are also found within the Old City of Jerusalem, in the Christian and Muslim Quarters, once again demonstrating the extent of structural violence within the urban environment. Life for Palestinians living in Jerusalem is increasingly difficult, regulated by police and security apparatus and subjected to structural violence across the city. Checkpoints are routinely used across the Old City to regulate movement, most recently seen in the installation of metal detectors at the entrance of the Al Aqsa mosque, which resulted in widespread demonstrations in the summer of 2017.

Since 1967, East Jerusalem and the West Bank have themselves undergone existential transformation, not only in the structure of urban life but also in the capacity of agency to live within these structures. The development of infrastructure within territorial borders was politically contested but integral to the development of Israel. In ensuring that Jerusalem remained united, successive governments supported settlement building in the east of the city in predominantly Arab neighbourhoods. Such moves were not without consequence and seemingly little thought was given to the implications for Palestinians. Prime Minister Levi Eshkol reflected, 'What are we going to do with a million Arabs?' Eshkol paused for a moment and then responded, 'I get it. You want the dowry, but you don't like the bride!'[69] Addressing this question brought security officials and urban planners together to develop an urban landscape that served as a symbol of a sovereign Jewish state while also protecting its territorial borders, citizens and identity.

Gentrification and urban development processes have facilitated the transformation of East Jerusalem from Arab to Jewish, as part of broader political projects. Speaking on a tour of East Jerusalem in September 2017, Israeli Public Security Minister Gilad Erdan articulated his excitement to see Jewish families in East Jerusalem, along with the claim that, 'Our sovereignty in the State of Israel and the Land of Israel begins here.'[70] Governance of East Jerusalem reveals a great deal about political dynamics. Since 1967 one can see power disparities between Arab and Israeli communities, reflected in access to land, education, electricity and mobility.

Amid rising violence stemming from two *intifadas*, a separation wall 422 miles long was built east of the so-called Green Line[71] with the declared objective of 'regulating the entry of Palestinians from the West Bank into Israel'.[72] Regulating access are twenty-seven permanently manned checkpoints that punctuate the wall while access into and out of Gaza is subject to approval from Israeli security officials. Within the West Bank itself, Palestinian life is also restricted, as the development of settlements means that there are around forty roads in the West Bank that Palestinians are not able to use.

Since then, those on the east of the wall have restricted access to Jerusalem. Although initially designed as a mechanism to reduce the threat of terrorism, what has developed is a formal security structure that also serves to regulate life and embed the occupation within the fabric of Palestinian daily life, referred to by many as apartheid.[73] Checkpoints are spaces of exception where life is be reduced to its barest form as people are caught in a zone of indistinction, routinely subjected to violence, humiliation and harassment.[74] While checkpoints restrict access from the West Bank into Israel, they also have a broader impact in terms of Palestinian efforts to situate any future capital in Jerusalem, restricting connectivity – emotional and logistical – through limiting access to and communication with Palestinian East Jerusalemites. Similar restrictions are also found across the West Bank. Checkpoints in Hebron regulate movement across the city as a consequence of the presence of a large number of Palestinians and a small settler population that is protected by soldiers from the IDF. The Abed checkpoint, which is permanently staffed, is situated fifty metres away from the Ibrahimi Mosque, requires passage through cages and under the watchful eye of heavily armed soldiers.

Transformation of the urban architecture can also be used in a punitive manner: Those deemed guilty of violence against the Israeli state may have their houses demolished, creating more space for future settlement building, while such measures are justified by emergency legislation from the British mandate that legalised the transformation and militarisation of Jaffa. Such moves show the transformative power of the city, while also demonstrating how urban environments can themselves be violent towards inhabitants. While initially latent, this structural violence often manifests in direct acts of violence against individuals or representatives of the state as marginalised individuals seek to assert their agency. As we shall see, similar practices took place across the region, as space and architecture took on political meaning.

Camps and enclaves

The 'national state', having lost its very foundations, leads a life of a walking corpse, whose spurious existence is artificially prolonged by repeated injections of imperialist expansion.[75]

The urban environment possesses a strong, restrictive element that is inherently violent. The sovereign order has restricted political life across the Middle East, resulting in all people *having the potential* to become *homo sacer*. For Agamben, *the camp* is the hidden paradigm of modernity, the means through which all of life is captured, comprised of particular zones where life is stripped of meaning and also a broader site of potentiality. Urban environments contain both of these aspects, but the centrality of the city within daily life means that governance of urban environments is an attempt to regulate this potential. Urban planning requires taking decisions about the manner in which life is regulated, through the design of the city, the installation of fences, traffic management, surveillance and access to welfare systems. Yet it can also contribute to marginalisation and political evisceration through structural violence and the perpetuation of normative structures of control.

Exclusionary narratives in support of regime and nationalist interest manifest in the architecture of the city and the imagery that adorns it, creating norms that are violent towards those not included within such projects. Of course, amid urban transformation and the ensuing repercussions, such moves may, in turn, provoke people to resort to violence, shaped by context-specific contingent factors.[76] Here, not only do we see the emergence of a logic of necropolitics but also the emergence of war machines as groups seek to contest sovereign power.

Although Agamben argues that in bare life one has to accept this position of 'being thus', the denial of agency is not reflected in events on the ground.[77] Amid challenges to regime monopolies on violence, the urban environment becomes an arena for actors from a range of backgrounds to exert agency. While urban landscapes impact upon people in different ways, it is obvious that life in a camp has similar consequences for people, albeit shaped by the intricacies of local context and contingency. The widespread reduction of political agency, restrictions on movement and labour and general structural violence serves to reinforce the idea of life being stripped of political meaning, abandoned by the law yet bound by it. In some cases, camps themselves are subjected to raids from security forces as a means of preventing the emergence of agency, yet in others, camps are left to self-regulate.[78]

Widespread restrictions have eviscerated political life, creating zones where individuals and communities are cast aside by legal and normative structures, receiving no protection yet bound by law. Within this zone, individuals seek to assert agency, adorning the streets with new meaning through graffiti, martyrdom posters and other ideological motifs.[79] Yet in some cases, the city serves as a zone of possibility. The power of imagery, narratives and community gains traction in urban environments, as such factors can transcend economic, class, gender and political divides, serving to empower groups. In Lebanon, Palestinian groups such as Fatah al Islam and Shi'a groups such as Amal and Hizballah all sought to improve their socio-economic positions through engaging with the urban environment. In Iraq, parts of Baghdad took on new meaning amid the empowerment of Shi'a groups, with repercussions for Sunni minorities and the stability of the city. Spaces with sectarian divisions became zones of indistinction, brought about by suspension of the rule of law. Underpinning this was the political climate of the state, which revealed the influence of formal and normative structures and the power of a range of groups to capitalise on urban disenfranchisement.[80]

While the city is a space of exception where formal structures operate to remove political meaning from life and create bare life, it is also the space where norms are (re)created and facilitate the process of stripping meaning from life. The camp is the example of bare life par excellence, seen in both forms routinely across the Middle East. As a consequence of exclusionary policies across the region, large-scale displacement of peoples has resulted in the establishment of physical camps to provide refuge to those affected. Although initially deemed temporary, the Belata camp outside Nablus has existed since 1948. Following large-scale displacement of peoples as a consequence of conflict, organisations such as the United Nations Relief and Works Agency (UNRWA) have taken on responsibility for refugees. In Lebanon, UNRWA has been tasked with protecting around four hundred and fifty thousand Palestinian refugees.[81] As crises across the region continue, this number increases; estimates put the number of Syrian refugees living in Lebanon at around 1.5 million.[82]

Across the first decade of Palestinian camps in Lebanon, the Lebanese security forces remained outside of the refugee camps, resulting in the creation of internal mechanisms of control. The intelligence wing of the Lebanese army – the Deuxième

Bureau – maintained a presence in the camps and the state began to play a more repressive role in both political life and the architecture of the camps, where roofs were banned, cement was prohibited and cartographical boundaries were stringently enforced.[83] Life in the camps became increasingly violent, particularly during the PLO clashes with Israel and the civil war, as Palestinians sought to assert a form of political agency, yet urban planning meant that access to the camps was restricted, subject to checkpoints and monitoring.[84]

The case of Nahr el-Bared is one that provides an example of clashes between competing forces within the spatial borders of the camp. In the summer of 2007 the camp was the site of a fierce battle between the Lebanese military and Fateh al Islam, a militant Islamist group. Over the course of the summer, large swathes of the camp were destroyed and Palestinian residents were forced out. This is, as Adam Ramadan suggests, a case of urbicide within a spatialised exception[85] as violence transcended necessity and became

> the deliberate and systematic erasure of the camp ... made more possible by the very nature of the political spaces of the camp, which are in Lebanon but not of Lebanon, in which Lebanese sovereignty and law are not fully enforced, in which a whole range of non-Lebanese actors exercise political power outside the control of the Lebanese state.[86]

Here, the rule of law was suspended allowing for the Lebanese armed forces to undertake vandalism, looting and destruction without sanction as a consequence of the declaration of the exception. The fighting resulted in a large number of deaths and worsened the conditions facing Palestinians in the camps. Across present-day Beirut, Syrians fleeing conflict endure similar challenges. Similar experiences and stories can be told of camps across the Middle East, in Gaza, the West Bank, Jordan, Turkey, Iraq, Iran and Syria, where processes of self-regulation emerge amid the suspension of the rule of law.

Historical examples of Palestinian resistance show how agency can be expressed within the context of bare life. Both Jordanian and Lebanese camps for Palestinians were sites of resistance – in Al-Wihdat and Shatila respectively – and symbolic of the burgeoning Palestinian nationalism. The failure of assimilation and legacy of both *nakba* and *naksa* (the day of the setback, commemorating the displacement of Palestinians after the 1967 Six Day War) facilitated this mass mobilisation of Palestinians in refugee camps – known as *al thawra* (the revolution) – across the region, creating narratives of heroism and resilience. Camps were seen to be liberated areas, furnaces in which *Fedayeen* (guerilla fighters) were forged, while Palestinian symbolism fuelled this nationalist sentiment.[87] Such symbolism remains an integral part of the Palestinian camps, resulting in the perception that such spaces remain militant zones. These tensions have longer-term ramifications for assimilation within host countries and their own state-building projects, yet their expression demonstrates the capacity for political agency.

Amid the fragmentation of urban environments, typically along communitarian lines, there has typically been an increase in the development of infrastructure and welfare programmes by non-state actors as a means of expressing agency and rejecting being thus. When state sovereignty fragments and regimes either choose not to – or are unable to – provide welfare and governance strategies that help people meet basic needs then other actors are required to care for peoples, reinforcing socio-political divisions. Filling this space provides opportunities for other actors to gain legitimacy by playing the role of a state and fulfilling its responsibilities under a social contract.

The nature of political life across the region has meant that such conditions are rife. From the Muslim Brotherhood to Hizballah, a range of groups have gained prominence through offering social care and physical protection to those in urban environments who have been excluded or marginalised by state structures. In Lebanon, Shi'a Muslims have long been marginalised, while poverty, disenfranchisement and marginalisation has been a prominent part of daily life dating back to the nineteenth century.[88] A century later, similar conditions remained. By 1974, Shi'a Muslims comprised somewhere in the region of 30% of the Lebanese population but received less than 1% of the state budget.[89]

The combination of these factors contributed to creating conditions of bare life in Lebanon.[90] Furthermore, election laws required those wishing to vote to return to the villages of their birth in an attempt to provide an accurate demographic snapshot of life across Lebanon.[91] Such a law failed to recognise the large-scale migration to urban centres, further adding to the disenfranchisement facing Shi'a groups. Within this context, it is hardly surprising that a group such as Hizballah, supported by the financial and logistical might of Iran, would garner support through the provision of welfare services.

In contemporary Beirut, the situation is much improved, but Hizballah remains the most influential actor in the city, if not the whole of Lebanon. The Party of God regulates life across Shi'a areas such as Dahiyya, where the group's ideology is visible across the fabric of the streets as flags, images of Nasrallah and Khomeini and martyrdom posters adorn buildings around the area. Even the road names reveal key figures and ideologues. The governance of Dahiyya, with its own particular security concerns, combines the old and the new; with video cameras on every corner and armed guards on prominent crossroads, relying on a delicate relationship with the formal mechanisms of power in the Lebanese to retain control, evoking questions about the ordering of space within Beirut, a veritable state within a state.

In post-2003 Iraq, which experienced an Al Qa'ida insurgency, increasingly sectarian violence taking place between a range of militias, a counter-insurgency campaign and serious economic challenges, US forces established the so-called Green Zone to facilitate governance efforts. The influx of political figures who had been ostracised by the Ba'ath regime, along with Iranian officials such as the senior Revolutionary Guards General Qassem Soleimani created a new form of political life in Baghdad. The Green Zone is secured by a range of different security structures, including military, police, members of the Ministry of Interior and the Prime Minister's regiment. Life within the Green Zone is heavily securitised and regulated, wherein individuals are unable to walk around the streets without the correct credentials.[92] Yet it is situated in an area that is socially and economically impoverished. If one walks out of the Green Zone and crosses the road, there is a dramatically different form of life. Post 2003, the influx of Iraqis from the diaspora has established a new, hierarchical form of Iraqi politics – and disenchantment – and additionally, a form of class politics that is tangible at the very heart of governance.[93]

In the south of the country, a range of obstacles challenge both state sovereignty and the capacity of people to live their lives. The city of Basra has long been a source of political unrest, from the establishment of the state to the present day. In the aftermath of the Gulf War, dissent against Saddam's rule began in Basra before spreading across the south, revealing the failure to assimilate into political projects. Post 2003, sectarian divisions were exacerbated by financial support for groups such as Thra'rallah, who were implicated in efforts to incite sectarian tensions and to penetrate the local police force amid support from Iran.[94] This Iranian support is perhaps best acknowledged in a comment from a senior advisor to the Ministry of Interior, who referred to the city as 'the Iranian city of Basra'.[95]

Although shared religious ties helped facilitate an Iranian presence, revealed through posters and banners of Khomeini and Khamenei, such a presence was not always popular, particularly in light of excessive violence against protesters.[96] More important are socio-economic challenges that often escalate amid tensions between tribes and Shi'a militias such as the Asaib al-Haq.[97] Tribal tensions manifest in regulatory struggles, creating conditions of uncertainty for people who are trapped in an increasingly precarious position. Amid a range of economic challenges, drug dealing is prevalent as a means of raising money, with crystal meth a popular choice. One Iraqi analyst referred to the problem as *Breaking Basra* after the popular TV series *Breaking Bad*.[98] Such problems are not limited to Iraq, as people in Syria, Lebanon and Yemen will attest. As conditions deteriorate, black economies emerge as actors seek to fund their actions. In spite of proclamations of Islamic purity, drug dealing is rife as a means of raising funds quickly and easily.

Conclusions

As the majority of the region live in urban environments, cities are the arenas within which politics occurs. They are camps in both forms, the space in which *ordnung* and *ortung* clash, with devastating consequences. The structure and organisation of cities and their architecture and symbolism all serve as a means of *doing* politics. The symbolism found within cities across the Middle East displays a legacy of political activity and with it makes visible the colonial legacy of external penetration. The evolution of political organisation is a direct consequence of securing territory and the evolution of a state-building project. The delineation of territorial borders and efforts to exert sovereignty over this territory results in the establishment of governance structures within particular territories, but with this comes a serious change.

There remains little doubt that cities in the Middle East have been simultaneously the arenas and perpetrators of violence. The urban landscape provides a means through which life can be regulated but also the mechanism to demonstrate power and structural violence through the use of force, governance and architecture itself. For scholars of urban geopolitics, the city is increasingly the site of political violence: of terrorism, war and protest; direct and indirect; latent and manifest. Planners and strategists seek to design cities that can respond to such challenges, yet the design of cities also serves to reflect both formal and normative structures within political environments. In spite of the literature focusing upon the militarisation of urban landscapes, we must not solely consider cities as battlegrounds of insurgent struggles; they are much more.

While the camp can be both the physical and metaphysical sites of exception, the suspension of the rule of law creates zones of indistinction and conditions of potentiality where individuals can easily be reduced to bare life.[99] Beyond this, life is all too often subjugated to death, seen in the manifestation of urbicide across the region. Beyond these examples, we can also see the emergence of migrant compounds across the Gulf, where workers reside in squalor, abandoned by the law yet bound by it. Within such spaces, they are reduced to bare life.

Sovereign structures are imposed on to pre-existing socio-economic experiences, on communities that have a history of political interaction and organisation. With this in mind, we should not ignore the role of norms within the development of the sovereign state. Other scholars have argued for the existence of 'informal sovereignty' within political projects, but this approach is problematic when considering the already contested – and from this, hierarchical – nature of sovereignty. Instead, history, norms and cultural practices all shape the capacity of people to act, with groups often filling the role of the state when regimes are either unwilling or unable to regulate activity within a particular area. This type of regulation ranges from security, as seen in Hizballah-controlled southern Beirut, to the provision of hospitals by the Muslim Brotherhood across Cairo. As suggested in Chapter 3, Islam provides space through which civil society actors can engage in informal politics and, in doing so, providing much needed infrastructural support to those within society who did not have access to state-run institutions.

Notes

1 Abdelrahman Munif, *Cities of Salt* (New York: Random House, 1984). Originally published in Arabic in 1984 by the Arab Institute for Research and Publishing in Beirut.

2 See https://data.worldbank.org/indicator/SP.URB.TOTL.IN.ZS?locations=ZQ&view=map (accessed 12.02.18).

3 Manuel Castells, *The Rise of the Network Society: Economy, Society and Culture* (Malden, MA: Blackwell, 1996).

4 Henri Lefebvre, *The Production of Space* (Oxford: Blackwell, 1991), p. 26.

5 Adam Ramadan, 'From Tahir to the World: The Camp as a Political Public Space',
   European Urban and Regional Studies, 20:1 (2013), 145–9; Adam Ramadan,
   'Spatialising the Refugee Camp', *Transactions of the Institute of British Geographers*,
   38:1 (2013), 65–77; Adam Ramadan and Sara Fregonese, 'Hybrid Sovereignty and
   the State of Exception in the Palestinian Refugee Camps in Lebanon', *Annals of the
   American Association of Geographers*, 107:4 (2017), 949–63.
6 See Stephen Graham, *Cities Under Siege: The New Military Urbanism* (London: Verso,
   2011); and Derek Gregory, 'Seeing Red: Baghdad and the Event-Ful City', *Political
   Geography*, 29 (2010), 266–79.
7 Michel Foucault, *Power/Knowledge: Selected Interviews and Other Writings 1972–1977*
   (New York: Pantheon Books, 1980), p. 68.
8 Henri Lefebvre, *The Urban Revolution* (Minneapolis: University of Minnesota
   Press, 2003).
9 Mustapha Ben Hamouche, 'The Changing Morphology of the Gulf Cities in the Age
   Of Globalization: The Case of Bahrain', *Habitat International*, 28 (2004), 521–40; I.
   M. Al Shaheen, *Dirasat fi attakhit wa al imara* (Kuwait: Al-Salam, 1987); Saheen Al-
   Hathloul and Narayanan Edadan (eds), *Urban Development in Saudi Arabia Challenges
   and Opportunities* (Riyadh: Dar Al-Sahan, 1998).
10 Mark Wigley, 'Editorial', *Assemblage (Violence Space)*, 20 (1993), 7.
11 Lucia Volk, 'Martyrs at the Margins: The Politics of Neglect in Lebanon's Borderlands',
   Middle Eastern Studies, 45:2 (2009), 266.
12 John C. Wilkinson, 'Britain's Role in Boundary Drawing in Arabia: A Synopsis', in
   Richard Schofield (ed.), *Territorial Foundations of the Gulf* (New York: St Mark's Press,
   1994), p. 97.
13 Haim Yacobi and Relli Shechter, 'Rethinking Cities in the Middle East: Political
   Economy, Planning, and the Lived Space', *Journal of Architecture*, 10:5 (2005), 499–515.
14 Charles Tripp, *The Power and the People: Paths of Resistance in the Middle East*
   (Cambridge, UK: Cambridge University Press, 2013), p. 311.
15 Kamrava, 'The Political Economy of Renterism', pp. 43–78.
16 J. D. Porteous, 'The Nature of the Company Town', *Transactions of the Institute of
   British Geographers*, 51 (1970), 133.
17 Munif, *Cities of Salt*.
18 Richard Lawless and Ian Seccombe, 'Impact of the Oil Industry on Urbanization in the
   Persian Gulf Region', in Hooshang Amirahmadi and Salah S. El Shakhs (eds), *Urban
   Development in the Muslim World* (New Brunswick, NJ: Transaction Publishers, 1993),
   pp. 189–90.
19 Yacobi and Shechter, 'Rethinking Cities in the Middle East'.
20 See Hannes Baumann, *Citizen Hariri: Lebanon's Neo-Liberal Reconstruction*
   (London: Hurst, 2017).
21 Relli Shechter and Haim Yacobi, 'Cities in the Middle East: Policies, Representation
   and History', *Cities* 22:3 (2005), 186.
22 Fuad K. Malkawi, 'The New Arab Metropolis', in Y. Elsheshtawy (ed.), *The Evolving
   Arab City* (Oxford: Routledge, 2008), p. 35.
23 Kaveh Ehsani, 'Social Engineering and the Contradictions of Modernization in
   Khuzestan's Company Towns: A Look at Abadan and Masjed-Soleyman', *International
   Review of Social History*, 48:3 (2003), 362.
24 Interview with Turkish academic, 2017.
25 Ehsani, 'Social Engineering', p. 389.

26 Mehran Kamrava, 'Contemporary Port Cities in the Persian Gulf: Local Gateways and Global Networks', in Mehran Kamrava (ed.), *Gateways to the World: Port Cities in the Persian Gulf* (Oxford: Oxford University Press, 2016), p. 69.

27 Albert Hourani and S. M. Stern (eds), *Islamic City: A Colloquium* (Oxford: Bruno Cassirer, 1970).

28 Janet L. Abu-Lughod, 'The Islamic City: Historic Myth, Islamic Essence, and Contemporary Relevance', *International Journal of Middle East Studies*, 19 (1987), 155–76.

29 Interview with Yemeni-Emirati student, 2018.

30 See www.civicarts.com/madinat-al-hareer (accessed 05.06.16), cited in Kamrava, *Port Cities*, p. 73.

31 Jane Bristol Rys, 'Socio-Spatial Boundaries in Abu Dhabi', in Mehran Kamrava and Zahra Babar (eds), *Migrant Labour in the Persian Gulf* (New York: Columbia University Press, 2011), p. 65.

32 Kamrava, 'Contemporary Port Cities', pp. 60–5.

33 This may not always be apparent to visitors, but names provide context.

34 Hamouche, 'The Changing Morphology of the Gulf Cities'.

35 Ibid., p. 522.

36 Timothy Mitchell, *Colonising Egypt* (Cambridge, UK: Cambridge University Press, 1988).

37 'Demolition Watch' (United Nations Relief and Works Agency for Palestine Refugees in the Near East), available at www.unrwa.org/demolition-watch (accessed 10.04.16).

38 'The Planning Crisis in East Jerusalem' (UN Office for the Coordination of Humanitarian Affairs, 2009), available at https://reliefweb.int/sites/reliefweb.int/files/resources/63BFD8D187E28D0CC12575A9002A5724-Full_Report.pdf (accessed 10.04.16).

39 Hussam Hussein Salama, 'Tahrir Square: A Narrative of Public Space', *Archnet-IJAR*, 7:1 (2013), 128.

40 Derek Gregory, 'Tahrir: Politics, Publics and Performances of Space', *Middle East Critique*, 22:3 (2013), 235–46.

41 Stephen Graham, 'Cities as Battlespace: The New Military Urbanism', *City: Analysis of Urban Trends, Culture, Theory, Policy, Action*, 13:4 (2009), 397–8.

42 Yoav Gelber, *Independence Versus Nakba* (Tel-Aviv, Israel: Kinneret–Zmora-Bitan–Dvir Publishing, 2004), p. 104.

43 Mairav Zonszein, 'Israel's "Ethnic Cleansing" of Jaffa City' (*Al Jazeera*, 16.04.14), available at www.aljazeera.com/news/middleeast/2014/03/gentrification-jaffa-israel-palestine-20143692621437677.html (accessed 10.11.17).

44 Chaim Levinson, 'Israeli Contractor Plans Jewish-Only Residential Project in Jaffa' (*Ha'aretz*, 28.01.14), available at www.haaretz.com/israel-news/.premium-1.571018 (accessed 10.11.17).

45 Zonszein, 'Israel's "Ethnic Cleansing" of Jaffa City'.

46 Belen Fernandez, 'From Paris of the Middle East to a Depressing Hollywood Film Set: How Gentrification Changed Beirut' (*Middle East Eye*, 12.10.17), available at www.middleeasteye.net/columns/paris-middle-east-depressing-hollywood-film-set-how-gentrification-changed-beirut-968875750 (accessed 10.11.17).

47 Khalil Hariri, 'The Other Side: How Highways Divided Beirut's Neighbourhoods' (*Executive*, 11.10.17) www.executive-magazine.com/special-report/the-other-side (accessed 10.11.17).

48 Maureen Ahmed, 'The Center of the Muslim World Is Being Gentrified: Here's Why
    We Should Be Upset' (*Your Middle East*, 13.03.14), available at www.yourmiddleeast.
    com/features/the-center-of-the-muslim-world-is-being-gentrified-heres-why-we-
    should-be-upset_22173 (accessed 10.11.17).
49 Hanan Chehata, 'Saudi "Cultural Vandalism" of Muslim Heritage Continues' (*Middle
    East Eye*, 14.04.14), available at www.middleeasteye.net/culture/saudi-cultural-
    vandalism-muslim-heritage-continues-1605359828 (accessed 10.11.17).
50 Ziauddin Sardar, 'The Destruction of Mecca' (*New York Times*, 30.09.14), available
    at www.nytimes.com/2014/10/01/opinion/the-destruction-of-mecca.html (accessed
    10.11.17).
51 Ibid.
52 Eyal Weizman, *Hollow Lands: Israel's Architecture of Occupation* (London: Verso,
    2007); and Mbembe 'Necropolitics'.
53 Mabon, *Saudi Arabia and Iran*.
54 John Bradley, 'Iran's Ethnic Tinderbox', *Washington Quarterly*, 39:1 (2007), 181–90.
55 'Iran Parliamentary Think Tank Warns of Ethnic Unrest' (UNPO, 05.01.06), available
    at www.unpo.org/article/3460 (accessed 17.06.09).
56 Aron Lund, 'Dispossession or Development? The Tug of War Over Syria's Ruined
    Slum Dwelling' (IRIN, 04.07.18), available at www.irinnews.org/analysis/2018/07/04/
    dispossession-or-development-tug-war-over-syria-s-ruined-slum-dwellings (accessed
    04.04.18).
57 Yossi Katz, 'The Marginal Role of Jerusalem in Zionist Settlement Activity Prior to the
    Founding of the State of Israel', *Middle Eastern Studies*, 34:3 (1998), 122.
58 Central Zionist Archive File J1/6768, Letter from Ben Gurion to Ben-Zvi, 7 August
    1944, in Yossi Katz, 'The Marginal Role of Jerusalem in Zionist Settlement Activity
    Prior to the Founding of the State of Israel', *Middle East Studies*, 34:3 (1998), 121–45.
59 Yael Yishai, 'Israeli Annexation of East Jerusalem and the Golan Heights: Factors and
    Processes', *Middle East Studies*, 21:1 (1985), 45–60.
60 Andreas Faludi, 'A Planning Doctrine for Jerusalem?', *International Planning Studies*,
    2:1 (1997), 83–102.
61 Mero Benvenisti, *Jerusalem: The Torn City* (Jerusalem: Isratypset, 1976), p. 84.
62 Abba Eban, *Personal Witness: Israel Through My Eyes* (London: Jonathan Cape, 1992),
    p. 427.
63 Faludi, 'A Planning Doctrine for Jerusalem?'; and Elisha Efrat and Allen G. Noble,
    'Planning Jerusalem', *American Geographical Society*, 78:4 (1988), 387–404.
64 Eban, *Personal Witness*, p. 418.
65 Ibid., p. 460.
66 David Ben Gurion, *Recollections* (New York: Macdonald & Co, 1970), p. 70.
67 Ram Karmi, 'Human Value in Urban Architecture', in Amiram Harlap, Frank Hari and
    Misrad ha-shikun Israel, *Israel Builds* (Tel Aviv: Ministry of Housing, 1977), p. 31.
68 Oren Yiftachel, 'Ethnocracy, Geography and Democracy: Comments on the Politics of
    the Judaization of Israel', *Alpayim*, 19 (2000), 78–105.
69 Neve Girdibm 'How Israel's Occupation Shifted From a Politics of Life to a Politics
    of Death' (*The Nation*, 05.06.17), available at www.thenation.com/article/israels-
    occupation-shifted-politics-life-politics-death (accessed 10.11.17).
70 Udi Shaham, 'Erdan in East Jerusalem: Our Sovereignty Begins Here' (*Jerusalem Post*,
    28.08.17) www.jpost.com/Israel-News/Erdan-in-east-Jerusalem-Our-sovereignty-
    begins-here-503585 (accessed 28.08.17).

71 The 1967 line delineated between Israel, East Jerusalem and West Bank. See United
   Nations Office for the Coordination of Humanitarian Affairs, available at www.
   ochaopt.org/theme/west-bank-barrier (accessed 10.04.16).
72 'The Separation Barrier' (B'Tselem, 11.11.17), available at www.btselem.org/
   separation_barrier (accessed 12.11.17).
73 See, among others, Oren Yiftachel, 'Israeli Society and Jewish-Palestinian
   Reconciliation: "Ethnocracy" and Its Territorial Contradictions', Middle East Journal,
   51:4 (1997), 505–19; and Oren Iftachel, 'Neither Two States Nor One', Arab World
   Geographer, 8:3 (2005), 125–9.
74 See Yehudit Kirstein Keshet, Checkpoint Watch: Testimonies from Occupied Palestine
   (London: Zed Books, 2006); Mariam Barghouti, 'Palestinian Women Are Harassed
   and Humiliated at Checkpoints. Here Are a Few of Their Stories' (Forward, 17.10.17),
   available at http://forward.com/opinion/israel/385062/palestinian-women-are-
   harassed-and-humiliated-at-checkpoints-here-are-a-few (accessed 18.10.18);
   Ronit Lentin, Traces of Racial Exception: Racializing Israeli Settler Colonialism
   (London: Bloomsbury, 2019).
75 Hannah Arendt, Essays in Understanding, 1930–1954 (New York: Harcourt Brace)
   (1994), p. 143.
76 Rassem Khamaisi, 'Resisting Creeping Urbanization and Gentrification in the
   Old City of Jerusalem and Its Surroundings', Contemporary Arab Affairs, 3:1
   (2010), 53–70.
77 Interview with Saudi-Syrian academic, 2017.
78 The Palestinian camp of Belata in the city of Nablus is one such example of a site that
   is self-regulating, yet also subjected to intermittent raids by Israeli security forces amid
   fears of political unrest. The camp is on land that has a ninety-six-year lease, which is
   due to run out in 2046.
79 Perhaps the most incongruent I encountered were environmental slogans in Dahiyya,
   written in both Arabic and English.
80 Such remarks were made in interviews with people across the region, including an
   Iraqi analyst and film-maker, Lebanese journalists, a Syrian academic, Yemen analyst
   and others between 2015 and 2018.
81 Ghada Hashem Talhami, Palestinian Refugees: Pawns to Political Actors
   (New York: Nova Science, 2003), p. 147.
82 'Lebanon: Events of 2017' (Human Rights Watch, 2017), available at www.hrw.org/
   world-report/2018/country-chapters/lebanon (accessed 12.12.18).
83 Nasser Abourahme, 'Assembling and Spilling-Over: Towards an "Ethnography of
   Cement" in a Palestinian Refugee Camp', International Journal of Urban and Regional
   Research, 39:2 (2015), 207.
84 Ramadan and Fregonese, 'Hybrid Sovereignty'.
85 Urbicide in the Lebanese context was not a new phenomena, as Sara Fregonese
   suggests, having taken place across Beirut during the course of the Lebanese civil war
   as geopolitical meaning was 'multi-sited' and renegotiated across urban spaces. See
   Fregonese, 'The Urbicide of Beirut?'. This process of renegotiation continues across
   Beirut today amid competition over the institutionalisation of memory.
86 Ramadan, 'Destroying Nahr el-Bared'.
87 Luigi Achilli, 'Disengagement from Politics: Nationalism, Political Identity, and the
   Everyday in a Palestinian Refugee Camp in Jordan', Critique of Anthropology, 34:2
   (2014), 234–57.

88 David Urqhart, quoted in Augustus R. Norton, *Amal and the Shi'a: Struggle for the Soul of Lebanon* (Austin, TX: University of Texas Press, 1987).

89 Norton, *Amal and the Shi'a*, p. 18.

90 Mabon, 'Circle of Bare Life'.

91 Fuad I. Khuri, 'The Social Dynamics of the 1975–1977 War in Lebanon', *Armed Forces and Society*, 7 (Spring 1981), 383–408.

92 Interview with Iraqi analyst, 2017.

93 Interview with Iraqi film-maker 2017.

94 'Building a House on Shifting Sands: Iran's Influence In Iraq's Center-South, (WikiLeaks, 20.07.05), available at www.wikileaks.org/plusd/cables/ 05BAGHDAD3015_a.html (accessed 12.10.15).

95 '"The Street Is Stronger Than Parliament": Sadrist Vows Opposition to LTSR, (WikiLeaks, 27.01.08), available at https://wikileaks.org/plusd/cables/ 08BAGHDAD239_a.html (accessed 12.10.15).

96 'Iraqi Views on Events in Iran and Impact on Iraq' (WikiLeaks, 05.01.10), available at https://wikileaks.org/plusd/cables/10BAGHDAD22_a.html (accessed 12.10.15).

97 Mabon and Royle, *The Origins of ISIS*, p. 79.

98 Interview with Iraq analyst, 2017.

99 See Dilken, 'Zones of Indistinction'; and Edkins and Pin-Fat, 'Introduction: Life, Power, Resistance'.

6

The people want the fall of the regime

Al-sha'b yurıd isqāṭ al-nizā̄ m
[The people want the fall of the regime]

I see a decaying temple, almost collapsing … it will fall sooner than later.

Mohammed ElBaradei

In the opening chapter of *The Wretched of the Earth*, Franz Fanon suggests that decolonisation, with its world changing aspirations, is

> a program of complete disorder. But it cannot come as a result of magical practices, nor of a natural shock, nor of a friendly understanding. Decolonization, as we know, is a historical process: that is to say that it cannot be understood, it cannot become intelligible nor clear to itself except in the exact measure that we can discern the movements which give it historical form and content. Decolonization is the meeting of two forces, opposed to each other by their very nature, which in fact owe their originality to that sort of substantification which results from and is nourished by the situation in the colonies.[1]

Much like decolonising movements, those who engaged in political protest, taking to the streets across the recent past, also seek to change the order of their world. Such change is a historical process, shaped and given meaning by context and the specificity of contingency. With this in mind, we must not view the uprisings that broke out across the region in late 2010 as independent phenomena. Instead, we must locate the protests within the context of state-building processes – where regimes have sought to maintain sovereign control amid an array of challenges – but also within the history of political protest across the Middle East. Ultimately, the uprisings are the latest manifestation of the long-running politics of resistance. This chapter traces this history of protest and resistance, locating the uprisings within a broader narrative of the contestation of sovereign power, arguing that protest movements which emerged in 2011 should not be viewed as isolated incidents. To do this I look at historical examples of unrest, before turning to a consideration of socio-economic factors and finally, exploration of the impact of environmental degradation that brought about rapid transformations of social and political landscapes in the years leading up to the uprisings.

The emergence of uprisings across the region demonstrates the widespread rejection of political, social and economic conditions that people had faced. The conditions prior to the uprisings should not be viewed solely as a by-product of political life, an accident or the unavoidable consequence of the interaction between nationalist and globalising forces. Instead, as previous chapters have argued, political, social and economic situations were carefully designed as mechanisms of control, resulting in the cultivation of a form of bare life. Although not necessarily the literal manifestation of Agamben's bare life, political meaning had been stripped from groups across the region, wherein individuals are bound by the laws of the state yet not protected by such laws. For Agamben, once in this position, there is no escape and one should accept the position of 'being thus'.[2] Yet looking across the region in the early months of 2011, it was difficult to view events as the acceptance of the status quo. Instead, what quickly became known as the Arab Uprisings was seen as the *rejection* of being thus and the demonstration of agency – seen to be possible even within bare life[3] – amid efforts to improve political life.

After decades of political marginalisation where ruling elites had created political and social conditions tantamount to bare life, there was little hope of lasting change. Although the decade prior to the uprisings had been punctured by political protest, these efforts were largely unsuccessful as instruments of state security pervading all aspects of society were able to crush the protesters. At this point, grievances and resentment continued to fester, as regimes used all manner of mechanisms of control and techniques of government to prevent the emergence of protest movements. Yet by 2011, protesters in a number of states were successful in their demands for political transformation, albeit in a range of different forms, escaping bare life and rejecting 'being thus' in the process.

This rejection was driven by expressions of agency and resistance, which required huge courage and a desire to transform all aspects of political life. As Charles Tripp notes, this was not an immediate phenomenon, but one that emerged over time and space. Much like historical accounts of protest, latent structural grievances began to manifest, resulting in challenges to mechanisms of control. For Tripp, 'the public had been brought into resistance and this had been made possible not only by the immediate performances of resistance, but by the underlying, gradual reversal of the flow of capillary power itself that had been going on for years'.[4]

As we shall see, the rejection of 'being thus' served as a source of possibility: a disjunctive moment where people across the region could either continue with their existence in bare life or to challenge the status quo. In many cases, the latter was chosen as a moment of possibility served to inspire expressions of political agency. This hope was combined with an increased awareness of the latent socio-political-economic structures that had facilitated oppression, while allowing those who benefitted from (neo)patrimonialism to gain vast wealth. The publication of US diplomatic cables from the Middle East in 2010 was one such means through which knowledge of events was distributed and while the cables did not reveal anything that the people of the region didn't know, they added to the psychological damage, impacting on national pride. Although it was generally accepted that corruption played a prominent role in accruing wealth, when documented by WikiLeaks, this placed an additional psychological burden on individuals, prompting many to exert agency through resistance.[5]

In Arabic, the closest transliteration to the concept of resistance is, for many, *muqawamah*, literally understood as 'to stand up'. For Larbi Sadiki, the concept of *muqawamah* is comprised of a broad range of norms and values, driven by agency and shaped by an Islamic and communal ethos. Moreover, although it is context specific, reflecting language and idioms, it also transgresses spatial and temporal dynamics.[6] Ultimately, *muqawamah* is

> a way of thinking, being, and acting, and an ever-widening site of holistic struggle in which the AK-47 is not, in the scheme of resistance, more important than piety, charity, schooling, propaganda or music. It simultaneously constitutes and embodies a normative imaginary for enacting emancipation at various levels, beginning with inner self-transformation through resistance against religious, moral, and intellectual laxity, and ending with creative protest.[7]

To understand why such events took place we must not only look at the uprisings themselves but also place them within broader contexts of resistance and political opposition.

A history of unrest

Protest movements rarely occur as independent phenomena; they are typically shaped by events that have come before. The political history of the twentieth-century Middle East is one of contestation, driven by efforts to exert power and manifestations of resistance. With this in mind, to understand the uprisings that broke out in late 2010, we must consider the residue of historical unrest that shaped performances of resistance. Such reflections allow us to identify broad structural factors that cultivate latent grievances, along with the evolution of state security apparatus that continued to serve within mechanisms of control.

Our exploration of state building began prior to the Treaty of Versailles with acts of resistance and the Arab Revolt, wherein people sought to challenge the power of the Ottoman Empire. Egyptian history across the twentieth century has been shaped by the interaction of political movements, seeking to exercise power and engage in acts of resistance. Driven by decolonisation efforts, the struggle for Egypt is central in understanding political life across the Middle East and shaped by the Egyptian Revolution of 1919, unrest in the 1930s, the 1952 Young Officers Coup and unrest in the late 1970s. In all, mass movements took to the streets, rallying against structural grievances and characterised by regional pressures. The 1919 revolution was driven by anti-imperialist sentiment and economic concerns, wherein thirteen thousand landowners owned 40% of cultivated land, while the poorest 80% held less than 20% of privately owned land.[8] Egyptian intellectuals sought to capitalise on British inertia after the First World War, at a time when key staff and goods were being transferred to Palestine. The revolution began the processes of gaining independence, during which thousands of Egyptians were killed, injured and arrested.[9]

The establishment of the modern Egyptian Republic in 1952 occurred amid decolonisation movements, alongside widespread anti-British sentiment and capitalising on increasingly prominent class tensions. Anti-imperial attacks took place across Cairo, while the Muslim Brotherhood gained prominence. Mass protests stemmed from the expression of multifaceted grievances that spread across the region with the development of Arabism. Political transition from Sadat to Mubarak was triggered by an act of violence, when a member of Islamic Jihad – who also served in the army – assassinated Sadat as a consequence of the peace treaty with Israel. After his death, Sadat was succeeded by his Vice President, Hosni Mubarak.

Life under Mubarak was aptly described by the economist Samer Suleiman 'of regime success and state failure'.[10] In spite of early nods towards democratisation, Mubarak quickly fell into line with regional practices. Having come to power after the assassination of his predecessor Anwar Sadat, early signs of reform and apparent rapprochement with the Muslim Brotherhood quickly dissipated amid perceived threats to his rule. In 1992, Mubarak responded with force writ large across Islamic groups in Egypt as a consequence of the emergence of a violent Islamist insurgency that had committed terrorist attacks in Cairo.

Domestic events continued to be shaped by regional factors and the Palestinian cause, although once described to me as a 'political football', was one such issue. Beginning with the Arab–Israeli wars, the cause continued with the *intifada* of 1987, which much like other incidents, had broader regional ramifications. Across the 1990s, following the fall of the Berlin Wall and end of the Cold War, many states across the Middle East experienced the growth of civil society organisations, yet in several instances, these reforms were restricted by authoritarian tendencies, such as in Jordan where reform was a strategy to maintain control amid economic crisis.[11]

In Syria, Hafez Assad violently suppressed an Islamist uprising across the state (1976–82), resulting in the deaths of around thirty thousand people and widespread repression of Islamist movements[12] in what Patrick Seale referred to as a 'long campaign of terror'.[13] Moreover, in an attempt to maintain order, it was forbidden to discuss events in Hama. As one Syrian recounted, when she asked her father about what happened in Hama, he threatened her with violence if she ever asked again, out of a fear of potential repercussions. Similar incidents were recounted when talking to others about Syria.[14]

A British man travelling to Damascus in the 1980s was asked by his Arabic teacher to take a pair of shoes to a local man in the suburbs. Although no house number was given, this was hardly surprising and, assuming that he would be able to find someone who knew the old man, he went to the area with confidence. After an afternoon of searching, resulting in countless claims not to know the man and an increased sense of suspicion, an old woman took pity on the Brit, telling him to leave as the person he was looking for no longer lived there; in fact, 'he no longer lived at all'.[15] All that remained of him was a pair of shoes. While Robin Yassin Kassab and Leila Al Shami suggest that Hama was 'traumatised for a generation', the Syrian psyche more broadly was devastatingly damaged.[16]

In Iraq, to quash domestic unrest, Saddam Hussein used chemical weapons against the state's Kurdish population[17] and also committed 'atrocities on a predictably massive scale' against both Kurdish and Shi'a dissidents.[18] The most prominent of the Shi'a opposition parties, Al Dawla, fled to Iran after the execution of their spiritual guide, Ayatollah Muhammad Baqir Al Sadr. Disaffection among the Shi'a community was seen by many in Iran as a means of increasing their influence, resulting in the establishment of the SCIRI out of members of Al Da'wa to export Khomeini's revolutionary goals.[19]

Following unification in 1989, Yemen experienced a period of political crisis that continues to shape its future. The struggle to meet basic needs was a prominent characteristic of daily life, exacerbated by the absence of national security infrastructure, health care and limited local governance across the state's 333 districts. Although living within the Yemeni state, individuals in rural areas may have little sense of the state as a political entity beyond the presence of political posters. Across peripheral districts, life is regulated by tribal sheikhs – often competing with one another – where state mechanisms have little influence amid the power of *turath* and normative structures of tribal and religious life.[20] Within such conditions, protests, strikes, riots and bombs were a routine part of life across the state. Dire economic conditions were aggravated by the return of migrant workers expelled from Kuwait.[21]

A history of civic activism within the fabric of the Kuwaiti state has created the most vibrant political sphere in the Gulf, albeit resulting in a number of instances of unrest. The importance of politics within Kuwait should not be understated. As Kristin Diwan suggests, the National Assembly is central to Kuwait's national identity.[22] Since the 2006 succession, the assembly has been characterised by political unrest as groups vie for influence within the political realm. Yet the nature of political life in Kuwait means that a struggle for influence in the National Assembly also results in 'extra-parliamentary' strategies and mobilisation, feeding into a climate of unrest.[23]

Similar events occurred in Bahrain, as decades of political unrest prompted the abolishment of emergency laws and the establishment of a new national charter to replace the country's democratic constitution suspended in 1975. The State Security Law was enacted in 1975 and helped enforce the Al Khalifa's rule across the archipelago, while the State Security Court – established in 1995 – was responsible for sentencing hundreds of activists. The abolition of emergency laws was a key part of reconciliation efforts between the regime and Shi'a opposition groups.[24]

Even the conservative Saudi kingdom was not immune from such pressures as a number of groups challenged the Islamic credentials of the Al Saud. Al Sahwa al Islamiyya Sahwa, an influential group of Muslim Brotherhood activists was joined by the Committee for the Defence of Legitimate Rights, who both criticised the Al Saud's domestic and foreign policies.[25] In the following years, the *sahwa*, perhaps the best organised political group in the kingdom, offered the most likely political challenge particularly after the groups' successes in the 2005 municipal elections, drawing on

Islam to offer resistance to the Al Saud. Yet even this was largely superficial, curtailed by the co-option of the group into the institutional structures of the state.[26]

Beyond isolated incidents, a number of issues occurred in the decade prior to the uprisings that had an incendiary impact regional politics, with repercussions felt across the domestic realm. The first was the US actions in the aftermath of Saddam's invasion of Kuwait, which opened up schisms between regimes and their societies as people were largely opposed to government support for US military action against Iraq. A second issue was the War on Terror, which possessed a degree of Arab complicity, while the third was the onset of the second *intifada*, which was quickly framed as part of the War on Terror. A fourth was the 2005 Cedar Revolution in Lebanon, which was the catalyst for the Syrian withdrawal, while the fifth was the Green Revolution in Iran, which demonstrated the capacity of people to challenge their regimes. Such factors fed into a region-wide mass mobilisation, facilitated by technological developments and the emergence of Al Jazeera. Regional events shaped domestic contexts and vice versa. In this context, local movements had to capitalise on local conditions and regional factors[27] as efforts to create order had implications for spatial borders, as domestic and regional challenges collided.

At this time regional forces exerted a great deal of influence on localised *nomoi*. Both Yemen and Jordan had spoken out against the US military action, responding to public demands, but not without cost, as both were hit economically by the loss of US and Saudi financial support. Jordan at this time had begun a move towards political liberation, seemingly in a pre-emptive move by King Hussein to retain power. In doing this, the country underwent the most competitive parliamentary elections in over forty years.

In the mid 2000s, many believed that reform was likely in the Hashemite kingdom facilitated by the Jordanian National Agenda, cutting across political, economic, social and administrative lines, seeking to restructure parliamentary elections and essentially, offering a radical redistribution of power across Jordanian society. The stated aim of the agenda was

> to achieve sustainable development through a transformative program that puts Jordan on a trajectory path towards fast economic growth and greater social inclusion, resulting in comprehensive strategies and initiatives developed to realise social, economic and political development, evaluate and monitor progress of its implementation according to detailed performance indicators.[28]

Yet amid increasing pressure from conservative aspects of society who feared the erosion of tradition and *turath* amid the trappings of modernity, the Jordanian National Agenda was withdrawn, replaced by the far less progressive 'All for Jordan' initiative.

This example demonstrates the importance of balancing different pressures and agendas both within society and among supporters. Those regimes that had survived the tumultuous 1970s, a period beset by parabolic ideological forces and a spate of *coups d'état* had developed a strong ability to balance competing pressures while preventing the emergence of opposition groups through the penetration of society.

This was perhaps, as Marc Lynch argues, because the Jordanian state had 'perfected the art of pervasive social and political surveillance and control'.[29] The biopolitical state machinery was fully operational, monitoring all aspects of society and preventing the creation of organised opposition movements. Those opposition parties that did emerge typically did so from within the context of the current political system, resulting in a complicit form of dissent. As governmental penetration of society increased, mass urban protests during the 1990s decreased, ultimately feeding into the cultivation of structural grievances.[30] Yet this did not put an end to resistance, nor to the brutal methods of control used by rulers that were argued to be necessary to prevent a spiral into chaos similar to the Lebanese civil war.

There is little doubt that political life in Lebanon was shaped by the fifteen-year long civil war that drew in all aspects of society. During the civil war, Shi'a groups gained greater representation as seen in the establishment of Hizballah in 1982, reflecting both the socio-economic conditions facing Shi'a Muslims in the country but also the failings of Amal who, at that time, dominated political representation of the Shi'a.[31]

As we have seen, although initially an armed militia with an explicit resistance agenda shaped by Shi'a history, the group evolved into a political entity, becoming one of the most influential parties in Lebanon.[32] For the group's leader Hassan Nasrallah, resistance is holistical, involving force and politics. It is 'a complete organism with a thinking brain, eyes, veins, ears that listen, a tongue that utters, and a heart filled with affection or full of anger'.[33] This point is echoed by Hizballah's Deputy Secretary General, Shaykh Na'im Qasim who suggests that resistance is 'military, cultural, political and informational resistance. It is resistance by the people as well as by the mujahidin; it is resistance by the ruler and by the ummah'.[34] In spite of such remarks, the Cedar Revolution served as a spectacle of possibility, resulting in the withdrawal of Syrian troops but also demonstrating the capacity to bring about political change without requiring a descent into civil war.[35]

A year later, war with Israel secured the group's popularity across the region. At the time, Nasrallah and Ahmadinejad were the most popular leaders in the Middle East due to their anti-Israeli stance. This popularity created serious challenges for Sunni Arab rulers who had long viewed the Party of God with suspicion, but after the destruction of Dahiyeh in 2006 they were forced to provide support to the group out of fear that they would lose credibility domestically.

As political space was restricted and groups failed to find traction within electoral processes, the political and social fabric holding the nature of the social contract became increasingly frayed, creating conditions of uncertainty and *fitna* (civil strife). At this point, old divisions within society became increasingly prominent, as economic hardship worsened, while latent tensions across society began to manifest in protest.

Wealth and poverty

The idea that the Arab world is 'richer than it is developed' is one that resonates with many.[36] Reflecting on the Arab Uprisings, Christine Lagarde, Managing Director of the IMF, noted that while top-line numbers often looked good, 'too many people were being left out'.[37] Development is inherently liked with empowerment and to understand the roots of the uprisings, we must consider not just economic or political factors, but the relationship between wealth and power.[38] This relationship manifests in the establishment of (neo)patrimonial systems of governance and the cultivation of so-called 'deep states' across the region, which prevent moves towards regime accountability.[39]

To understand this, we must consider the impact that governance structures have had on people across the region. Although bare life is typically considered as the restriction of human agency through recourse to political and legal structures, normative and economic structures also have a restrictive capacity. As we have seen in earlier chapters, the nature of social contracts – particularly those underpinned by rentier bargains – and the emergence of (neo)patrimonial mechanisms of control have created societies underpinned by marginalisation. As Gilbert Archar suggests, all Arab monarchies are patrimonial regimes, along with Ba'ath regimes in Syria and formerly Iraq. Both Egypt and Yemen are neopatrimonial, where regimes possess autonomy from rulers, who can later be replaced. Thus, neopatrimonial societies possess strong organisational structures that can survive the removal of rulers where particular economic interests and power are more important than governing.[40] Put another way, in a neopatrimonial system there is no distinction between the public and private as states are run in a form of feudal enterprise. Reflecting this, when protesters took to the streets, the term *izba* (fiefdom) was levied at ruling elites and as the uprisings took place, the emergence of gangs and militias along economic lines would become commonplace.[41]

As a consequence, political regimes not only occupied a central role within the economy at the cost of the private sector, but also subsumed the state itself in its quest for survival. States such as Lebanon and Bahrain began to rely on external funds to prop up regimes and national economies. In 2006, Kuwait and Saudi Arabia donated $1.5 billion to the Lebanese Central Bank to support the bank's currency chest, while two years later the bank received a further $1 billion from Saudi Arabia, helping maintain the Lebanese pound's peg to the dollar which had become increasingly precarious.[42] In Bahrain, the Al Khalifa family's personal fortune was supported by finances from Saudi Arabia. In both cases, economic interest was tied to broader political and geopolitical concerns.

As regimes found themselves unable to regulate political life, society became increasingly polarised, leading to the politicisation of the allocation and distribution of resources, while states also became extractors, predatory and clannish.[43] At this point, the security sector received disproportionately large amounts of financial support compared to other aspects of society, along with greater political influence and ability to act without regulation.[44] Arab Human Development Reports in the years leading up to the uprisings paint a gloomy picture of unbalanced development, systematic exclusion and structural neglect.[45] Reports routinely detailed governance failures and the absence of mechanisms to effectively hold political elites to account. Institutional weakness was routinely identified as 'one of the most important causes of socio-economic and political exclusion in the Arab region'.[46] It was regularly stressed that this exclusion resonated across the region because it was 'inclusive', in so much as it affected people across different classes, in both rural and urban areas, and the poor.[47]

In 2004, the authors of *Towards Freedom in the Arab World* referred to the state as a 'black hole', where the centrality of power in the hands of a few results in a situation where 'nothing moves and from which nothing escapes'.[48] The report suggested that the key issue behind political failings 'lies in the convergence of political, social and economic structures that have suppressed or eliminated organised social and political actors capable of turning the crisis of authoritarian and totalitarian regimes to their advantage'.[49]

While it is correct not to reduce the democratic deficit to purely cultural factors, we should not dismiss the importance of history and values in defining contingency and shaping the decisions taken by those in power.[50] Indeed, as the Executive Summary suggests – acknowledging the power of the *nomos, nomoi* and norms – 'freedoms in Arab countries are threatened by two kinds of power: that of undemocratic regimes, and that of tradition and tribalism, sometimes under the cover of religion'.[51] The interaction of the two – a form of *ordnung* and *ortung* – facilitated the creation of systems of governance, both formal and normative, which restrict the capacity of agency. As Amartya Sen argues, cultural factors have a hugely important impact on political and economic behaviour, shaping participation in activities and civil society, mutual support and solidarity.[52]

Socio-economic differences had a detrimental impact on the democratic tradition.[53] In the 2008 *State of Reform in the Arab World* report, Jordan was ranked as the highest performing Arab state in terms of democratic practice and the rule of law, while, Saudi Arabia had the lowest general index and Yemen the lowest rank in terms of application of the rule of law. Palestine had the highest rank of equality and social justice, while Lebanon had the highest rank for respect for rights and freedoms.[54] Yet in a positive analysis of regional dynamics at the time, Bassma Kodami suggested that the region was experiencing a 'constitutional moment', noting the opening of a space of expression, albeit not participation.[55] As the following years would prove, such optimism was ultimately misplaced.

Although the discovery and extraction of oil pumped money into domestic economies there was widespread stagnation in per capita GDP between the 1970s and the 1990s. At the same time the region experienced the world's highest population growth, placing additional pressure on society. This increased growth rate was a consequence of *infitah* policies that led to social reforms and improvements across the health care sector, yet as we have previously seen, the private sector lagged behind, lacking development amid state dominance of economies. At this point, it was estimated that while the private sector accounted for less than half of the GDP across the region, corruption was rife.[56]

Adding to such challenges were enormous levels of capital flight. At the height of the 2008 economic crisis, contracts worth $958 billion and $354 billion were cancelled in the UAE and Saudi Arabia respectively,[57] while an estimated $247.5 billion was removed from the Middle East.[58] Although many analysts reduced the uprisings to a lack of a 'middle class', this is perhaps inaccurate; instead, as Gilbert Archar argues, it should be viewed as a form of private capitalism that operates independent of the state but dependent on wider socio-economic forces, helping to understand the inclusivity of the exclusion.[59] In addition, tensions between public and private sector workers have long been rife, manifesting in the emergence of class struggles.[60] Such factors have been escalated by the relatively high population growth rates, while both standards of living and per capita income have stagnated since the 1980s.[61]

Underpinning all of this, and indeed political life more broadly, were gender issues and questions about the role of women in society. High levels of female underemployment fed into such economic situations, shaped by interpretations of culture, tradition and *nomos*. As a World Bank report on gender and development notes, although there are achievements in a number of areas of well-being, key challenges emerge in economic participation and political empowerment.[62] Moreover, women face widespread discrimination across the private sector, once again stemming from cultural prejudice and bias, resulting in many working for lower wages. The 2009 Arab Human Development Report documents how the interaction of a range of different factors has established structural 'social biases against women',[63] perhaps most obviously seen in the recently lifted ban on women driving in Saudi Arabia. Discrimination has been a direct consequence of the reduction of the number of women in the workforce, leading to higher fertility rates, lower levels of education and less influence in the family. Furthermore, this restricts the type of interactions that occur, limiting the exchange of information and lowering the desire for political agency.[64]

We should not view economic structures independently from political contexts. In the case of the Trucial States, it is easy to see how British colonial policies were essential in establishing political structures that were later necessary for their economic development.[65] Such an approach resulted in the immediate penetration of domestic politics by external actors, but over time, a more centralised economic system was developed, facilitating nationalist projects and the perpetuation of exclusionary forms of social contract. One of the reasons for this identified by the UNDP was the

> inability of the state to co-opt the educated youth into what used to be a relatively well-paid civil service that acted as a mechanism for upward social mobility. In country after country since 1980, the public sector was no longer able to absorb ever-increasing numbers of graduates produced by the educational system.[66]

The failure to provide jobs or to stimulate a vibrant private sector meant that by 2011 41% of people across the Middle East were living 'in need' and in 2015 53% required financial assistance from non-state actors as informal networks began to play a more important role within the state. This was exacerbated by endemic corruption, which is estimated to have amounted to around $1 trillion in the past fifty years.[67] As a consequence of the need to look for alternative sources of economic support, 56% of people viewed the economy of their home country as overly negative.

The cultivation of particular forms of political life and social contract between rulers and ruled had a dramatic impact upon political participation. In the decade prior to the uprisings, voter turnout in elections across the region was low. In Saudi Arabia, for example,

> [p]eople were reluctant to register and vote, as was clear in Riyadh (the Saudi capital and home to 2,692,780 citizens), where the number of registered voters did not exceed 18% of those eligible to vote, i.e., 86,462 voters out of a potential electorate of approximately 470,000 persons – representing just two percent of the total population of the city.
>
> The small number of registered voters was expected to lead a relatively high rate of participation on election day (February 10, 2005). The rate of participation in the capital, however, barely reached 65 percent (i.e. a little bit more than 1 percent of the total population of Riyadh).[68]

Even in elections deemed 'free and fair', low turnout provided scope for regime candidates to win easily.

History and culture must not be ignored when considering the means through which economic allocation facilitate (neo)patrimonialism. Such values played an important role in the establishment of the very structures at the heart of political projects.[69] Although a number of rights were secured by constitutions, there were regular instances of states not fulfilling obligations to international conventions or indeed, not being signatories of such conventions.[70] This feeds into the perception of a gap between the law in theory and the law in practice, with people trapped in a zone of indistinction between the two. The weakness of civil society organisations and widespread restrictions in application of justice only served to fuel a loss of confidence in the state and its institutions. Faith in electoral processes and turnout in elections both rapidly diminished across the years preceding the uprisings.[71] In the 2010 elections in both Egypt and Jordan, the main opposition group, the Islamic Action Front, boycotted the elections, resulting in a climate of despair.[72] It is within this context that people across the Middle East took to the streets in what became known as the Arab Uprisings.

The stories of Khaled and Mohammed

The emergence of protests in late 2010 should not be seen as independent phenomena, but rather the most recent manifestation of long-running politics of resistance from the formal and subaltern. The power of the Arab Uprisings can be traced to the influence of ideas, narratives, sacrifice and human actions against repressive regimes. The stories of two individuals in particular are worth noting, as their behaviour had a dramatic impact upon regional politics. For many, there had been little hope of political or economic reform, as the imposition of emergency laws in the previous decades had prevented any serious reform beyond token nods to elections or economic handouts facilitated by (neo)patrimonial systems inherent within political projects. The process of state building had left people marginalised with little political agency, essentially in a form of bare life, lacking recourse to legal protection yet bound by the laws of the land. The construction of particular forms of political and legal structures prevented expressions of agency, establishing authoritarian structures that were regulated by (neo) patrimonial systems as a mechanism of retaining power. Here governance strategies include economic disenfranchisement and the closure of economic systems, removing channels through which political and legal disenfranchisement and marginalisation could be escaped.

The uprisings must then be seen as the response to existential crises, the visible contestation of sovereign power. Following the self-immolation of Mohammad Bouazizi, Arab populations faced a disjunctive moment wherein they could accept their position within political communities or they could reject being thus. Within this moment, one of the most enduring aspects of the uprisings emerged. Ordinary people who had not been politically active challenged decades of repression, marginalisation and structural violence, emerging from years of bureaucratic inertia with a new form of political agency. From their unique – yet remarkably similar – experiences, a form of collective agency was developed and a shared hope and responsibility was created across the region.

In 2010, an Arab Human Development Report outlined the obstacles to political participation in Egypt. Central to the increasing disillusionment was a perceived political apathy among the Egyptian youth. After noting issues with political structures, the report suggested that an additional factor is 'the apathy among youth towards political participation, borne of the conviction that that their voice will largely remain ignored'.[73] Only months later, people took to the street as the uprisings spread across Egypt. While apathy was certainly a factor, this was a regime construct, stemming from political fatigue and the belief that political change could not happen, all underpinned by fear.

For Wael Ghonim, a prominent opposition figure but at this time a Google employee, the regime lived in fear of opposition, projecting a façade of democracy while vanquishing dissidents.[74] While a number of opposition groups operated across the decade prior to the uprisings, few had a lasting impact, restricted by the power of the emergency laws. Other civil society actors fared little better, leaving the Muslim Brotherhood as the main source of organised opposition to the Mubarak regime, albeit facing widespread discrimination and a ban from electoral politics. In spite of this, the Brotherhood had firmly established themselves as a force across Egypt, wielding vast power and influence across society.[75]

Beyond the *ikhwan*, optimism about opposition parties was placed in the likes of Mohamed ElBaradei who was viewed by many as a means through which lasting change could be engendered. Upon returning to the country in February 2010, his Facebook page documented seven demands:

1. Terminate the state of emergency.
2. Grant complete supervision of elections to the judiciary.
3. Grant domestic and international civil society the right to monitor the elections.
4. Grant equal time in the media for all candidates running for office.
5. Grant expatriate Egyptians the right and ability to vote.

6. Guarantee the right to run for president without arbitrary restrictions, and set a two-term limit.

7. Vote with the national identity card.[76]

These demands required dramatic structural changes across Egyptian society. It also marked the point at which social media began to play a prominent role in political life across Egypt and the wider Middle East. At this point, Ghonim took on responsibility for running both the ElBaradei and Kullena Khaled Said (We Are All Khaled Said) Facebook pages. His account of events in *Revolution 2.0* reveals how such platforms were used as a means of spreading information and government fears at their perceived 'revolutionary power'.

Posting anonymously on Kullena Khaled Said, Ghonim provided followers with contemporary updates from the case and other acts of state repression across Egypt. Followers of the Facebook page organised a 'silent stand' protest to take the disenchantment to the street and express anger at the Ministry of Interior, in a non-violent way. Despite regime attempts to prevent it, protests took place across a number of Egyptian cities, while dissent also spread across the 'echo chamber' resulting in protests on the corniche in Doha; this was 18 June 2010.

In the months that followed, a set of organic, grassroots movements using the Internet gained momentum across Egypt. It was a time in which political agency began to manifest across the country, in spite of the perceived apathy of the Egyptian youth. Independently of Ghonim, a Facebook page was established calling for the monitoring of the 2010 elections, which were later argued to be fraudulent, suggesting that the ensuing parliament was illegitimate.[77] On 30 December 2010, Ghonim posted: 'January 25th is Police Day and it's a national holiday … I think the police have done enough this year to deserve a special celebration … What do you think?'

After the toppling of Ben Ali in Tunisia, Egyptians were hopeful about what could happen next. While contexts were different, there were a number of similarities between the two cases; it was hoped that just as Tunisians had rejected their positions within bare life, so too might others. On 25 January, Egyptians took to the streets, occupying Tahrir Square in a collective demonstration of political agency and frustration at the Mubarak regime and his intention to transfer power to his son, Gamal. Although the Brotherhood was the leading opposition party, their view of events across the country was mixed, with the older generation taking a watching brief, while younger Brothers and Sisters took to the streets.

Somewhat counter-intuitively, the support of the Egyptian army was integral for the success of the revolution, facilitating the transition away from Mubarak. In the coming years, the army took on an increasingly prominent role in political life, but in an attempt to retain influence across the country's future, military personnel supported the protesters in Tahrir against their former sponsor, Hosni Mubarak. On 10 February, Mubarak transferred power to the Supreme Council of Armed Forces (SCAF), a standing military committee with its roots in the Free Officers' Movement, which ruled in Egypt during times of severe crisis. A day later, Mubarak fled to the Red Sea resort of Sharm el-Sheikh.[78] In the following months, the Muslim Brotherhood would play an increasingly influential role in Egyptian politics, as befitted the unofficial opposition party that had strong networks of influence across the state. This culminated in the election of the Mohammed Morsi – the Brotherhood's Freedom and Justice Party candidate – as the first democratically elected President of Egypt, albeit not without serious schisms within the *ikhwan* about how to rule.

Across the region, a number of common factors were found in protest movements. Fridays became days of protest, requiring little or no communication through channels that had routinely been monitored or regulated by the state, while the mosque served as a focal point. Protest movements used the cityscape around them as an integral part of their political action, seizing public spaces and transforming them into spaces of possibility. Online spaces were used as a means of spreading images and messages across the region. Central to the movements were slogans such as *irhal* (leave) or *al-shaab yureed isqat al-nizam* (the people want the fall of the regime) and events across the region were eagerly watched by those protesting in different countries across the region.

Collective empowerment and realisation of possibility born out of the toppling of Ben Ali and Mubarak facilitated widespread mobilisation across the region. Ideas quickly spread across space, resonating with local grievances and a spirit of empowerment and hope emerged. People who had long been pushed to the margins of political life began to believe in the possibility of change and took to the streets to express their political will.[79] Across the region, people watched, encouraged and emulated each other, from the squares of Cairo to Sana, from Manama to Damascus. Ideas spread across state borders, aided by technological developments and the establishment of hashtags across social media that facilitated investment in shared projects and bound people together across a region in turmoil, supported with a clear narrative of struggle, replete with expectations, heroes and villains.

Although often ignored, protests in Jordan began on 14 January, with a day of rage that focused upon the Prime Minister Samir Al Rifai. At this point, the protesters were predominantly the traditional opposition parties, who had experienced two decades of repression and negotiation with the regime over their place within the political system. As a consequence, the regime had become well versed in counter-revolutionary tactics, designing an urban architecture that prevented large-scale mobilisation, along with the widespread penetration of opposition groups. In spite of this, the protesters' demands were met and the Prime Minister was dismissed.[80]

Protests in Yemen began in early February inspired by events in Tunisia and Egypt, but once again drew upon a long history of local discontent. A day of rage was called for on 3 February, which drew a crowd of thousands in protest against Ali Abdullah Saleh's rule. In the early stages, the protesters were a combination of civil society actors who had long been critical of the regime and youth activists. Networks were informal, grassroots movements that largely bypassed formal opposition groups. In Sanaa, *irhal* was baked into bread while in Taiz, it was painted on banners. For one observer, 'That single Arabic word has united Yemen's fractured political opposition, turning old enemies into temporary allies and pushing President Ali Abdullah Saleh's regime to the brink of collapse'.[81]

On 25 February pro-regime supporters clashed with protesters and on 19 March regime snipers opened fire, leading to an escalation of violence and a rapidly increasing death count as Saleh struggled to retain control. After efforts to reshuffle his cabinet, implement a new constitution and a number of announcements about transition to his Vice President, on 3 June Saleh was injured in a bomb blast at the presidential compound and taken to Saudi Arabia to be treated. On 4 June, Abdrabbuh Mansour Hadi was appointed as Acting President, but amid a range of competing tribal, religious and political factions, a Houthi insurgency and active Al Qa'ida franchise, along with a range of regional actors, Yemen was drawn into a seemingly intractable war, shaped by geopolitical considerations with devastating humanitarian consequences.

In Bahrain, protesters designated 14 February as a day of rage. Much like protesters elsewhere, activists moved into Pearl Roundabout and transformed the space into a site of possibility. Two days later, regime forces cleared the square and destroyed the site, in doing so removing one of the prominent symbols of Bahrain history; a six-hundred-fils coin that also depicted the roundabout was removed from circulation. Protesters differed greatly in their approaches, which ultimately proved detrimental to their cause. Chants referring to not being Sunni or Shi'a 'just Bahraini'[82] evoked memories of political protests from the 1990s yet played a prominent role in the uprisings. Some called for peaceful protest, requesting political reform while others demanded the end of Al Khalifa rule. The regime's response across Manama was swift following clashes between protesters and security forces. The restriction of political space that followed later was hardly surprising but was the beginning of the counter-revolution.

On 14 March, after the Crown Prince's failed efforts to facilitate dialogue with the protesters, Saudi-led GCC forces under the guise of the Peninsular Shield Force entered Bahrain, leading to a widespread crackdown on civil society, political space and opposition groups. Across the island, the Al Khalifa rule had become increasingly challenged by long-standing political grievances, predominantly from Shi'a parties such as Al Haq and Al Wefaq. A public sphere that facilitated dialogue about political reform had emerged in the late 1990s, but efforts to regulate political debate in the kingdom had resulted in arrests of prominent human rights and political activists. As we shall see in the following chapter, regime figures quickly framed the 2011 uprisings along sectarian lines, adding in an existential dimension by playing into fears about Iranian expansionism and of the 'Persian other'. Fundamentally, the protests became the site of contestation between *ortung* and *ordnung*.

In Oman, protests began in earnest on 18 February, taking on a vastly different character to that in other states. For many, the uprisings in the sultanate came as a surprise as it had long been isolated from broader regional currents and possessed a well-respected leader, a long and proud history and financial resources to provide a comfortable life. In spite of this, a spate of protests occurred across February, spread by text message and the Internet, resulting in the closure of schools across the country.[83] Initially small, the protests gained traction when they reached the city of Sohar where they escalated, resulting in regime forces using tear gas, rubber bullets and suggestions of one fatality.[84] On 4 March, the largest demonstration in the history of the state took place, stimulating further protests throughout the month along with military aggression against those politically active.

Grievances were similar to other states, as protesters sought to eradicate corruption and called for the removal of a number of prominent ministers, yet protesters expressed 'confidence in the sultan that he will respond to our demands'.[85] On 21 March, a crowd of around seven thousand in Muscat handed a letter to the public prosecutor calling for the immediate investigation into ministerial finances. Recognising the severity of the protests, the sultan acquiesced and later in the year held parliamentary elections for the first time. Although the sultan's rule was never in serious danger, the protests exposed underlying structural tensions within the state. Unlike other instances of unrest across the region, protesters issued a public apology to the sultan for damaging the state.[86] While concerns were assuaged, questions about succession in the sultanate post-Qaboos continue to plague political life.[87]

On 25 February, demonstrations took place across Iraq as activists sought to use the popular momentum as a means through which to stimulate political progress and end the deadlock that had frozen political life. As violence broke out, six protesters were killed. Protests became a weekly occurrence but, unlike other states across the region, the uprisings failed to find the popular support to affect political change. This lack of support is predominantly seen as a consequence of two reasons. First, divisions within Iraqi society and all-too recent memories of war and violence meant that there was a distinct lack of popular will to take to the streets.[88] Second, a number of Iraqis felt that they had democracy and as a consequence many believed that 'we're ok'.[89] A more convincing argument, however, suggests that although disenfranchised and marginalised, Sunnis lacked representation and popular leadership, preventing wide-scale mobilisation.[90]

The biggest prize for the revolutionaries was Saudi Arabia. As we have seen, the very fabric of the Saudi state is bound up with the Al Saud tribe, whose conservative alliance with Wahhabi clerics and rentier bargain meant that political participation was limited. In spite of this, the kingdom faced a number of serious pressures in the years prior to the uprisings, leading to Madawi Al Rasheed, a prominent Saudi scholar to suggest that Saudi Arabia was 'ripe for change'.[91]

Despite deep structural grievances, few turned up to a day of rage in Riyadh, with the majority of those who attended from news outlets. One of those who did was Khaled Al Johani, a Saudi teacher who spoke to the BBC before being arrested. His words reflect much of what was happening across the Arab world at this time: 'I am here to say we need democracy. We need freedom. We need to speak freely. We need no one to stop us from expressing our opinions ... Freedom ... there is no freedom. Dignity ... there is no dignity. Justice ... there is no justice'.[92] The Saudi response to Al Johani's words would serve as a premonition of what was to follow across the region.

Both Syria and Palestine set 15 March as their day of rage. While some Palestinians called for expressions of frustration and non-violent resistance against both the Israelis and Palestinian Authority, divisions between West Bank and Gaza, and Hamas and Fatah meant that no serious opposition could be organised. In contrast to the burgeoning optimism across the region, few in Syria believed that the regime of Bashar Al Assad could be seriously affected as a consequence of decades of repression and restrictions of political space. The strength of the Syria state and its repressive apparatus seemed impregnable, but regime violence inspired protests and mobilised the body politic.[93]

The tragedy of events across Syria is widely documented in a number of prescient accounts. Perhaps the most powerful is by Yassin Al Haj Saleh, whose account of the fragmentation of Syria documents the rise of war machines that were supported by the Assad regime in a move that helped regulate all aspects of the Syrian population.[94] Protests broke out across the state where they were met with disproportionate force. In Deraa, regime forces opened fire on protesters and the ensuing brutality created a cycle of escalation that drew in more and more people as family and friends were killed or injured. Grievances grew rapidly, as tales of the horrors of the regime's brutality spread. Events escalated following the arrest of fifteen schoolboys in Deraa who had sprayed walls with revolutionary slogans picked up on TV. While in detention the children were tortured as their fingernails were ripped out. The parents of the children went to plead for their release from the local branch of political security, led by a cousin of the President, where they were told, 'Forget your children. Go sleep with your wives and make new ones or send them to me and I'll do it.' It was hardly surprising that in response, thousands of people gathered in front of the Omari Mosque and demanded their release.[95]

The escalation and emerging intractability of the conflict was in part a consequence of the burgeoning regional importance of events in Syria. The geopolitical aspirations of Iran, Saudi Arabia, Qatar, Russia, the United States and groups such as Hizballah coalesced in Syria, aligning themselves with either regime or opposition groups. As a consequence, each side became emboldened, provided with weapons, finances and international political support in international forums such as the UN, leaving the people of Syria paying a truly abhorrent price.[96]

In Kuwait, the government marked the fiftieth anniversary of independence and the twentieth anniversary of the liberation of the country from Iraqi forces with large handouts given to all except *bidoon*. On 18 January, protests broke out in the country and although events would not dramatically escalate until June, where thousands took to the streets of Kuwait City, discontent began to spread. Amid growing political turmoil, a number of MPs refused to sit on committees with colleagues who were perceived to be corrupt and following the defection of a number of government MPs, the opposition was able to win a vote of no confidence in the Prime Minister. One of the main goals of the opposition MPs was to gain the opportunity to question the Prime Minister about political activity and perceived corruption in the country. Allegations of corruption included the suggestion that sixteen MPs had received bribes of around $350 million to support government policies and that the Prime Minister was also involved, having diverted public funds to personal accounts abroad.

Shortly after, the Constitutional Court decreed that the Prime Minister could not be held to account for violations committed by his ministers, only those violations under his direct authority. Amid widespread allegations of corruption, this was seen by opposition figures as 'a clear attempt to prevent the lawmakers from exercising their constitutional right to question the Prime Minister' and to avoid accountability.[97]

Despite this setback, protest groups were not deterred. One opposition group, the Popular Action Bloc, stressed that 'no medium of escalation would be spared', while another opposition figure tweeted that 'no solution will come from within the parliamentary halls of Abdullah Al Salem, but instead must come to it'.[98] In response to such inertia, protesters stormed the parliament on 16 November. There, in a nod to democracy, Musallam Al Barrack – a prominent opposition leader – proclaimed that protesters have 'entered the house of the people'.[99] In response, the National Action Bloc stated that 'the storming of the parliament is no less dangerous than what the government is doing'[100] and revealing the surprise at the turn of events, one interviewee referred to them as a 'rare incident'.[101]

Protesters were careful to frame the uprisings as a defence of the constitution. In doing this, protest movements were able to draw support from a range of disparate groups including Islamists, Shi'a and *bidoon*, along with those who had expressed desires for greater democratic accountability. Galvanised by successfully storming the parliament, red lines imposed by the Al Sabah were breached, notably insulting and taunting the Emir and ruling family. One protester proclaimed: 'In the name of the nation, in the name of the people, we will not let you, your Highness, practice autocratic rule'.[102] Such comments were not beyond reproach and a number of opposition figures were arrested, including Al Barrack.[103]

Much like other states across the region, protests began within the fabric of current political structures. Aware of the potential repercussions of expressing dissent against the ruling family, but also with the idea that change could only be brought about from within the system, political anger was expressed carefully. As Al Barrack suggested, 'People do not dispute the Al Sabah family's right to the presidency, but the Al Sabah family is disputing the people's right to manage the state and its wealth'.[104] Instead, ire was directed towards the government, as it was felt that Kuwaitis have 'a government that doesn't listen, doesn't see and all it does is deceiving the people'.[105] Yet as a caveat to such incendiary comments, Al Barrack was careful to express support for the Al Sabah family.

The Prime Minister resigned on 28 November 2011 and a new Prime Minister, Jaber Al Mubarak Al Sabah, was appointed amid serious political challenges. Legislative elections in February 2012 returned thirty-five of fifty seats in the National Assembly to opposition candidates, the largest grouping of which was the Shi'a National Islamic Alliance movement. Parliamentarians elected in February, led by Musallam Al Barak, advocated the idea of a parliamentary government for Kuwait and widespread political reform, including a law guaranteeing the independence of the courts. Eight days before a vote on this law, the Constitutional Court – appointed by the Emir – dissolved parliament.[106] Protesters stressed that they would continue 'under the umbrella of the constitution' using 'all peaceful and constitutional tools'.[107] In a nod to the power of the exception, Sheikh Salman Al Humoud, the Information Minister, proclaimed that the ruling enhanced the 'durability of the democratic system' and 'demonstrates the strength our democratic institutions and our judicial system'.[108]

While the uprisings spread across the Arab world, on its periphery, Iran, Turkey and Israel were all also affected by events. In Israel, 400,000 out of a population of around

7.7 million took to the streets to express solidarity with Tahrir Square. In the summer of 2011 outrage at the rising cost of living resulted in protests, demonstrating the move from a quietist social welfare Zionism of the formative stages of the state to the more hawkish but economically liberal interpretations of Zionism. In response, a tent was pitched in Habima Square on Rothschild Boulevard in Tel Aviv, triggering a mass protest. Facebook once again proved a platform to spread ideas, helping to develop a tent city that straddled differences across Israeli society as people were ultimately united in search of social justice. In spite of the scale of the protests, as 2011 ended, so too did the movement, amid reform of aspects of society including restrictions on benefits given to the Haredi community.[109]

In Turkey, the ruling AKP discourse stressed 'historical responsibilities' to the region, stemming from deep collaboration and personal relationships with political leaders. Prominent figures in the party, including President Recep Tayyip Erdogan, viewed the AKP model as one that could be applicable across the Arab world. Indeed, Turkish historical experience and record of parliamentary democracy offered a vision of political and democratic stability for the region, driven by Ataturk's secular vision, albeit eroded by Erdogan's Islamic party.[110] In spite of this, over the coming years Turkey was not immune from protests.

Protests in Turkey erupted in Istanbul's Taksim Gezi Park, stemming from the violent eviction of protesters who were demonstrating against the planned destruction of the park.[111] The protests rapidly escalated, bringing together broader concerns over the political vision of the Turkish state, environmental challenges, the erosion of secular ideals, the freedom of the press and freedom of expression.[112] Rising authoritarianism was perhaps the main driving force, triggering protests across the state after the occupation of the park. The park was later cleared using tear gas and rubber bullets amid claims from the Prime Minister that 'Taksim is not Turkey'.[113]

For many in Iran, events across the Arab world were framed as a continuation of one of two possible narratives. Regime figures viewed the uprisings as a continuation of the 1979 revolution, while opposition figures framed the protests movements as a continuation of the 2009 Green Movement. As we shall see in the following chapter, the Islamic Republic's response to the uprisings was rife with contradiction and shaped by geopolitical calculations. In 2009, Iranian citizens demanded political change in the aftermath of a contested presidential election that returned the incumbent Mahmoud Ahmadinejad to office. In the so-called Green Movement, protestors used social media as a tool to mobilise people across the state, facilitating demonstrations and getting information about events outside of Iran. While triggered by the electoral crisis, the protests must also be placed into historical context.[114] Images of Iranian men and women in squares, on university campuses and major roads were transmitted internationally, as protesters began to support reformist candidates Mir Hossein Mousavi and Mehdi Karoubi.[115]

While the protest movements spread across the region, a number of states were largely able to avoid unrest, as will be discussed in the following chapter, with a number of Gulf states using patrimonial networks and rentier economies to placate protest movements. Surprisingly, in spite of serious societal schisms, Lebanon also remained largely free from protests. In part this was a consequence of such societal schisms, preventing the emergence of a coherent protest movement under strong leadership, but the memory of the civil war remained central in the minds of many.[116] Yet only a few years later, protests erupted across Beirut as people from a range of sects expressed frustration at governance failures and bureaucratic inertia that prevented collection of rubbish across the city in what became known as the #YOUSTINK movement.

While Gulf states were largely unaffected by events in 2011, their rulers faced a serious challenge only three years later with a dramatic fall oil prices. Uncertainty following the Arab Uprisings had driven the price of oil up from just over $60 in 2010 to a peak of $115 in 2014 but this was not sustainable, driven down by increased supply facilitated by the rapid expansion of North American crude oil. This fall in in oil prices had a serious impact on those states that exported oil. In 2013, oil rents amounted to 53.8% of GDP in Kuwait[117] along with 90% of government income and 88% of exports in Saudi Arabia.[118]

Vast reserves of natural resources allowed Gulf regimes to placate populations through rentier social contracts, along with the welfare benefits and subsidies that come with such a social contract.[119] Although difficult to estimate, break-even oil prices differed greatly across the Gulf, from $52 in Kuwait to $126.9 in Bahrain,[120] while Saudi Arabia required the price of oil to be above $84.3 to break even. Maintaining social cohesion amid serious economic pressure placed additional pressure on regimes across the Gulf, already wary after the events of 2011.

Demands for an improved quality of life were at the heart of protest movements, as chants such as 'ish, huriya, karama insaniya' (bread, liberty and human dignity) were heard from Cairo to Manama, revealing seismic schisms within political structures.[121] The rapid emergence of protest movements revealed a great deal about the political nature of contemporary societies and also the strength of belief and agency, as people took to the streets in defiance of emergency laws that had previously been tools of restriction and repression. The overwhelming images of the first part of the uprisings were the scenes of hope and possibility that political change could be achieved. For the first time in political protests, there was no reference to slogan such as 'Islam is the solution', or 'Arab unity is the solution'. The protesters truly were grassroots organisations, driven by a desire to change the order of their worlds but in the months and years to come, such movements would be hijacked by a range of different actors.

Spaces and performances of resistance

As Frantz Fanon argued, changing one's world is a violent process that leads to disorder. This violence need not necessarily be direct but can take place in a range of different forms, through a range of different objects and subjects. One such transformative aspect occurred in public spaces, where expressions of agency facilitated the metamorphosis of space that had previously been a mechanism of sovereign power into a site of possibility. As we have seen, space is simultaneously the arena and the canvas, the area in which politics was played out and the means through which political agendas were also expressed. Urban landscapes had long been sites and spaces of expressions of political power but also mechanisms of control, drip-feeding civilian populations with a sense of sovereign control and ultimate authority.

The fabric of space, as we saw earlier, both demonstrates and enacts power. Such visible – yet unseen – techniques of power fed into the construction of myths and narratives that were used as mechanisms of control. These mechanisms helped normative structures to be accepted by those who are subjugated. The uprisings demonstrated a widespread rejection of the ordering of space. Essentially, as Hamid Dabashi argued, protesters were 'creating a new geography of liberation, which is no longer mapped on colonial or cast upon postcolonial structures of domination … a restructuring [that] points to a far more radical emancipation'.[122]

As a consequence, a range of tactics were employed and graffiti became both voice and action of dissent against ruling elites. It became a medium of communication when the mainstream media 'ignored the dissenters' and exploded across urban environments in response to Orwellian surveillance of creative figures.[123] Acts of graffiti helped facilitate the reappropriation of public space, serving as 'unsanctioned aesthetic modes of self-expression in dialogue with the urban environment', transforming space from sites of neutrality to those demonstrating potential and revolutionary change.[124] Graffiti as art became resistance in and of itself, reflecting protest narratives but also interjecting, reframing the urban environment according to the creativity of the protesters. Squares became sites of possibility, gymnasiums of civic activism, as new meaning was given to all manner of arenas.[125] Transformative processes fed into and developed anti-systemic protests and the appetite for democratic process, as Larbi Sakiki suggests, through 'sustained and creative mass protest'.[126]

After seizing public space, protest movements sought to reclaim it, transforming meaning beyond its previous message of repression. This transformative process went some way to dismantling authoritarian regimes, rejecting the visibility of power and in doing so, creating space and possibility for the new. In dismantling the physical world, protesters created space to be shaped into something new. Space thus became a zone of indistinction where the remnants and residue of the *ancien régime* remained, but were subsumed by transformative possibility.

In rejecting authoritarianism, citizens regained control of territory, purging regime forces and symbols from space and time, transforming the geographical area into a site of possibility. The presence of crowds in Tahrir was symbolic not only in their defiance of state legislation, but also in their presence in the square itself, wherein previous relations between regime and square – or urban architecture broadly – that had previously served to reinforce power were severed.[127] In a more powerful move, it was the scene of a new becoming, as an opportunity emerged to reframe the nature of Egyptian politics. It also fuelled protests across the region, demonstrating the power and possibility of collective action.

The transformation of space in an existentially liberating way was characteristic of the uprisings. In such a climate, artists became the targets of persecution. One particular instance of regime brutality that became a prominent work of art saw an Egyptian woman wearing an abaya being dragged through the street, revealing a blue bra. An image of a blue bra would later become used as a symbol of revolution. The image took on symbolic importance, becoming a symbol of the struggle for freedom against oppression, viewed through the lens of gender-related issues.[128] The image of the blue bra was later banned by the UAE.

In Bahrain, public spaces that were in tourist areas became canvasses to disseminate political messages. Competing narratives played out on the streets, with black paint used to cover up earlier messages. The images of martyrs and political prisoners adorned the walls, annotated with comments written in both Arabic and English to get coverage from the international press visiting to cover the Formula 1 race. Amid an increasingly violent conflict, space became contested as protesters were met by counter-demonstrations and security forces, as the Al Khalifa regime sought to prevent further escalation. Protests quickly moved across space, from the urban environments of the suq in Manama to rural villages across the island and as a consequence, highways took on a security dimension with military and police personnel stationed at intersections. Similar scenes were found in Yemen, Syria and Egypt.

Authoritarian regimes were not only draconian but also resilient. Their penetration of all aspects of society, domination or destruction of opposition movements and regulation of public space made few optimistic about lasting change. Decades of authoritarian rule, facilitated by (neo)patrimonial structures and underpinned by normative structures limited political space and civil society, restricting the capacity of people to express grievances, yet making the expression of a political voice all the more powerful.

The words used by protesters were imbued with meaning: hope, possibility and a desire to challenge seemingly endemic despotism.[129] Words became tools of empowerment rather than repression and songs took on political importance.[130] In one of the more powerful Egyptian protest songs, engineering student Ramy Essam wrote the song 'Irhal', a call and response song in Tahrir Square, featuring the lyrics: 'We are not leaving; He will leave; As one; We demand one thing; Leave, leave, leave'. Nationalist songs historically used by regimes were transformed as lyrics were rewritten to express loyalty to protest movements and people, rather than regimes. In addition to the tangible fabric of the state, protesters also sought to alter the metaphysical construction of the state. As one Syrian woman observed, songs that had been symbols of nationalist pride were rewritten to express possibility, solidarity and hope.[131]

Virtual space also became a site of contention as technological developments allowed anyone with a smartphone to become a journalist. This rise of the citizen journalist allowed events to be documented, stories to be verified and hegemonic narratives to be challenged. Moreover, amid widespread restrictions on the freedom of press, the Internet provided a means to circumvent regulation but also created a new space for divisions and dissent to emerge as friends and families became bitterly divided.[132] In Egypt, token nods to reform meant little, leaving the press under regime control in what one analyst called a 'truly Orwellian nightmare for reformists'.[133]

Emergency laws gave Mubarak licence to cut off the Internet which, counter intuitively for the regime, pushed more people out on to the street. Yet the Internet made awareness of the uprisings immediate and grounded it in the present. Ultimately, Tahrir became the focal point: the epicentre of protests and the site of performance, as individuals engaged in collective action. As Judith Butler argues, these actions 'collect the space itself, gather the pavement, and animate and organize the architecture'.[134]

Ultimately, the transformation of public space into sites of possibility was an essential aspect of the uprisings. The prominent rejection of previously embedded authoritarian regimes offered an alternative vision to people who had been trapped in bare life. Moreover, graffiti and street art served as a non-violent method of transformation, dramatically altering and reclaiming space while also having the capacity to speak to a range of audiences regardless of language. Fundamentally, graffiti was a way of 'defending and occupying the street'.[135] Over time, this transformative process took on a holistic nature as both the formal power of regimes and normative practices were identified and transformed.

Degradation and transformation

While a great deal of this chapter has discussed transformation in the run up to the uprisings, perhaps the most important form of change was demographic. Transformation from rural to urban has been a prominent feature of political development across the history of the Middle East, changing the nature of urban environments and placing additional pressures on political elites to both meet basic needs and to regulate life. In the years leading up to the uprisings, the most important transformative movement from rural to urban was a consequence of environmental degradation, stemming from the inability of farmers to tend to land and produce food.

In the Levant, environmental change enforced by anthropogenic developments increased the likelihood and occurrence of droughts and in Syria, the length and intensity of droughts as experienced between 2006 and 2011 was two to three times as likely.[136] Such changes had a dramatic impact upon migration in Syria and across the Levant broadly, as individuals sought water and sustenance, while arable land became increasingly rare. In the run up to the uprisings in Syria, 75% of farmers suffered total crop failure and in the north east, 85% experienced loss of livestock. Ultimately, the drought affected 1.3 million people, bringing the number of Syrians in poverty over the 2 million mark, also resulting in 800,000 Syrians losing their livelihoods and migration to cities.[137] The price of bread rose 87% in public bakeries while families had to spend between 50% and 80% of income on basic food.[138] Of course, the impact on state infrastructure was undeniable, with a generation of Syrians existing without schooling and institutional support. Such conditions remain, exacerbated by conflict, leaving 9.8 million Syrians as food insecure while 6.8 million of those are severely food insecure.[139] Making matters worse, recent estimates suggest that one in three houses in Syria have been destroyed, while the country lost 80% of its GDP between 2010 and 2016.[140]

Environmental degradation should not be seen as a neutral phenomenon. As Francesca de Châtel argues, such events must be placed in the context of Syrian mismanagement of moves towards a market economy and the failure of the Assad regime to respond appropriately to drought. As de Châtel asserts, drought is a structural feature of the Levant that need not necessarily result in such widespread unrest.[141]

We should then place it in a broader context of events at the time. While some argue that drought should be viewed through the lens of a 'threat multiplier',[142] it is perhaps the inadequate regulation of such issues and the failure of the move from centrally planned economy to market liberalisation[143] that meant that serious humanitarian issues emerging from the drought were mismanaged. Some estimates suggest that around 50% of the Syrian workforce was involved in agriculture at this time.[144] As a consequence, an estimated three hundred thousand people migrated from the north-east of the country[145] and by 2009 an estimated 60–70% of villages in the governorates of Deir ez-Zor and Hassakeh had been deserted.[146] Drought appeals failed to meet targets and the government sought to downplay the severity of the crisis, fearing the potential consequences of decades of economic and resource mismanagement.[147]

As a 2016 Arab Human Development Report noted, 'the events of 2011 and their ramifications are the outcome of public policies over many decades that gradually led to the exclusion of large sectors of the population from economic, political and social life'.[148] At this time there was a low level of support for formal institutions and a widespread lack of confidence in legislatures, particularly in its ability to hold the executive to account, to protect liberties and to treat all societal groups equally. Indeed, by 2014 only 21% viewed the rule of law to be applied universally and a year later this figure rose to 25%. As a consequence, over 50% of people had a negative view of the political situation along with their economic circumstances.[149]

In 2011, 41% of people in the region were living 'in need' and although this number dropped by 2015, 53% of people required financial assistance from other actors such as families, friends and other groups, as informal networks took on an increasingly important role and the need for support remains.[150] Indeed, 56% of people asked had an overly negative view of the economy of their home country, with Lebanon worst at 71%. These sentiments were exacerbated by endemic corruption, estimated to be in the region of $1 trillion in the past fifty years.[151] Ultimately, in such conditions of uncertainty and instability, those able to provide support were seen in a positive way, giving them a great deal of influence across the region, which helps to explain the popularity of groups such as the Muslim Brotherhood, Hamas, Hizballah and even Da'ish.[152]

Conclusions

Placing the Arab Uprisings in the context of political, economic and social unrest across the Middle East provides valuable insight in understanding why, when and how the protests took place. The proliferation of ideas, grievances and ultimately protest across time and space reveals two important aspects. First, that state-building processes have created structures that have a detrimental impact on life, manifesting in tensions between rulers and ruled, along with existential and often competing visions of political organisation. Second, amid a shared normative environment what happens in one state can have regional repercussions. Protest movements have always been shaped by domestic context and regional pressures meaning that the two are often intertwined, with serious consequences for the ordering of space. From Nasser's manipulation of the pan-Arab cause to the multifarious agendas and groups involved in the Arab Uprisings, political agendas have served to undermine real political progress across the region. The complexity of such factors and inter-relation of themes and issues has created a new political dynamic, wherein space became a site of possibility and in the months that followed, the region was characterised by a struggle to shape this possibility in a range of different ways.

The uprisings of 2011 should not be viewed as qualitatively new phenomena but instead, the continuation and manifestation of revolt and resistance against embedded authoritarian movements. With this in mind, we see that although the protest movements demonstrated the ability to reject being thus, seeking to move away from the creation of bare life in political, legal and socio-economic forms, similar expressions of agency had been occurring over time, albeit without the success of the Arab Uprisings. Although Agamben argues that escaping bare life is impossible, across the region, expressions of agency and resistance served as a mechanism of rejecting being thus. This is, however, part of a bigger narrative account of the Arab Uprisings, which should be split into two. The first part, as documented above, is a story of hope and resistance, where autocratic, authoritarian regimes were deposed in Egypt and Yemen (and Tunisia and Libya, although these are beyond the scope of our analysis) but regimes in Bahrain and Syria were seriously challenged. The second part of the broader narrative considers the response of the state, to see how regimes fought back against the protesters.

The uprisings reveal the depth of political dissatisfaction and the fissures that were inherent within political projects. These divisions were also prevalent in opposition groups whose views on how best to respond to regimes vastly differed even within sites of protest. From calling for peaceful pro-democracy marches to the violent toppling of regimes, the range of competing visions of protest ultimately restricted their capacity for change. Although people took to the street to express this displeasure, little changed. Structural grievances remained and although token reform would take place, the underlying factors that caused the uprisings endure, leaving a very real possibility of future unrest.

Notes

1 Frantz Fanon, *The Wretched of the Earth* (London: Penguin, 1967 [1961]).
2 Agamben, *Homo Sacer*.
3 Owens, 'Reclaiming "Bare Life"?'.
4 Tripp, *The Power and the People*, p. 142.
5 Simon Mabon, 'Aiding Revolution? WikiLeaks, Communication and the "Arab Spring" in Egypt', *Third World Quarterly*, 34:10 (2013), 1843–57.
6 Ibid.
7 Larbi Sadiki, 'Reframing Resistance and Democracy: Narratives from Hamas and Hizbullah', *Democratization*, 17:2 (2010), 27.
8 Peter Mansfield, *The British in Egypt* (London: Weidenfeld & Nicolson, 1971), p. 111.

9 Great Britain, Army, Egyptian Expeditionary Force, Court of Enquiry on the Alexandria Riots, 'Minutes of Proceedings and Report of the Military Court of Enquiry into the Alexandria Riots, May 1921', in *A Brief Record of the Advance of the Egyptian Expeditionary Force* (London: His Majesty's Stationery Office, 1919).

10 Samer Suleiman, *Al Nizam al-qawi wa al-dawa al-dha'ifa* (The Strong Regime and the Weak State) (Cairo: Dar Merit, 2005), p. 271.

11 Quintan Wiktorowicz, 'The Limits of Democracy in the Middle East: The Case of Jordan', *Middle East Journal*, 53:4 (1999), 606–20.

12 Dara Conduit, 'The Syrian Muslim Brotherhood and the Spectacle of Hama', *Middle East Journal*, 70:2 (2016), 11–226.

13 Patrick Seale, *Asad, the Struggle for the Middle East* (Berkeley: University of California Press, 1989), pp. 336–7.

14 Interview with Syrian academic, 2017.

15 Interview with former British diplomat, 2017.

16 Robin Yassin-Kassab and Leila Al Shami, *Burning Country: Syrians in Revolution and War* (London: Pluto Press, 2016), p. 51.

17 Joost R. Hilterman, *A Poisonous Affair: America, Iraq, and the Gassing of Halabja* (Cambridge, UK: Cambridge University Press, 2007).

18 'Endless Torment: The 1991 Uprising in Iraq And Its Aftermath' (Human Rights Watch, 1992), available at www.hrw.org/reports/1992/Iraq926.htm (accessed 01.04.16).

19 Soren Schmidt, 'The Role of Religion in Politics. The Case of Shia-Islamism in Iraq', *Nordic Journal of Religion and Society*, 22:2 (2009), 123–43.

20 Interview with Yemen analyst, 2018.

21 Robert Burrowes, 'The Republic of Yemen', in Michael Hudson (ed.), *The Middle East Dilemma* (New York: Columbia University Press, 1991), p. 192.

22 Kristin Smith Diwan, 'Kuwait's Constitutional Showdown' (*Foreign Policy*, 17.11.11), available at http://foreignpolicy.com/2011/11/17/kuwaits-constitutional-showdown (accessed 17.11.13).

23 Ibid.

24 'Bahrain Lifts Key Security Law' (BBC News, 18.02.01), available at http://news.bbc.co.uk/1/hi/world/middle_east/1177690.stm (accessed 17.11.16).

25 Clive Jones, 'Saudi Arabia After the Gulf War: The Internal-External Security Dilemma', *International Relations*, 12:6 (1995), 31–51.

26 Stephane Lacroix, *Awakening Islam: The Politics of Religions Dissent in Contemporary Saudi Arabia* (Cambridge, MA: Harvard University Press, 2011).

27 Marc Lynch, *The New Arab Wars: Uprisings and Anarchy in the Middle East* (New York: Public Affairs, 2016), p. 56.

28 Quoted in Rami G. Khouri, 'Reform in the Mashreq Set Back by Warfare, Ideological Battles and Regime Resistance', in The Arab Reform Initiative, *The State of Reform in the Arab World 2008* (Arab Democracy Index, 2008), p. 66.

29 Lynch, *New Arab Wars*, p. 44.

30 Asef Bayat, 'Activism and Social Development in the Middle East', *International Journal of Middle East Studies*, 34 (2002), 1–28.

31 Norton, *Hezballah*.

32 Mabon, 'The Circle of Bare Life'.

33 Sayyid Hassan Nasrallah, 'Keynote Speech', Ramadan 'Iftar' Ceremony Held by the Society for the Support of the Islamic Resistance (22 November 2001).

34 Na'im Qasim, 'Kalimat Al-Iftitah' [Key Note or Opening Speech], in *Qiyam Al-Muqawamah: Khiyar Al-Shahadah wa Al-Hayat* [The Values of Resistance: The Choice of Martyrdom and Life], ed. Shafiq Jaradi et al. (Beirut: Dar Al-Hadi and Ma 'had Al-Ma 'arif Al-Hakimah, 2008), pp. 5–12 at p. 6.

35 Michael Kerr, *The Arab Cold War*.

36 United Nations Development Programme (UNDP), *Arab Human Development Report 2002: Creating Opportunities for Future Generations* (New York and Amman: Regional Bureau for Arab States, 2002).

37 Christine Lagarde, 'The Arab Spring, One Year On' (IMF, 06.12.11), available at www.imf.org/external/np/speeches/2011/120611.htm (accessed 07.12.11).

38 See Adam Przeworski and Fernando Limongi, 'Political Regimes and Economic Growth', *Journal of Economy Perspectives*, 7:3 (1993); and Arab Human Development Reports in 2004, 2005 and 2009. Although such reports have been denounced by a number of Arab commentators for self-denigration and scapegoating. See Michael Trebilcock, 'Between Institutions and Culture: The UNDP's Arab Human Development Reports, 2002–2005', *Middle East Law and Governance*, 1 (2009), 212. See also Asef Bayat, 'Transforming the Arab World: The Arab Human Development Report and the Politics of Change', *Development and Change*, 36 (2005), 1225–37.

39 Bassma Kodmani, 'The Awakening of Societies as Engine of Change', in The Arab Reform Initiative, *The State of Reform in the Arab World 2008* (Arab Democracy Index, 2008), p. 55.

40 Gilbert Archar, *The People Want: A Radical Exploration of the Arab Uprising* (London: Saqi, 2013), p. 78.

41 Baghat Korany, *Arab Human Development in the Twenty-First Century* (Cairo: American University Cairo Press, 2014), p. 7. A similar theme came out of interviews in a number of different contexts.

42 Hannes Baumann, 'The Different Risks of Saudi and Iranian Aid to Lebanon', in Simon Mabon (ed.), *Saudi Arabia and Iran: The Struggle to Shape the Middle East* (London: Foreign Policy Centre, 2018).

43 Korany, *Arab Human Development*, p. 9.

44 Kodmani, 'The Awakening of Societies as Engine of Change', p. 57.

45 UNDP, *Arab Development Challenges Report: Towards the Developmental State in the Arab Region* (UNDP, 2011), p. 2.

46 Ibid., p. 13.

47 Ibid., p. 62.

48 UNDP, *Arab Human Development Report: Towards Freedom in the Arab World* (UNDP, 2004), p. 15.

49 Ibid., p. 11.

50 See Lawrence Harrison, *The Central Liberal Truth: How Politics Can Change a Culture and Save it from Itself* (New York: Oxford University Press, 2006).

51 'Executive Summary: Arab Human Development Report' (United Nations, 2004), available at www.arab-hdr.org/reports/2004/english/execsummary-e%202004.pdf?download (accessed 10.06.15).

52 Amartya Sen, 'How Does Culture Matter', in Vijayendra Rao and Michael Walton (eds), *Culture and Public Action* (Palo Alto, CA: Stanford University Press, 2004).

53 The Arab Reform Initiative, *The State of Reform in the Arab World 2008* (Arab Democracy Index, 2008), p. 24.

54 Ibid. pp. 25–6.
55 Kodmani, 'The Awakening of Societies as Engine of Change', pp. 52–3. See also, Khouri, 'Reform in the Mashreq', pp. 60–1.
56 Archar, *The People Want*, p. 62.
57 UNCTAD, *World Investment Report 2012: Towards a New Generation of Investment Policies* (Geneva: UNCTAD, 2012), p. 48.
58 Dev Kar and Karly Curcio, *Illicit Financial Flows from Developing Countries: 2000–2009* (Washington DC: Global Financial Integrity, 2011).
59 Archar, *The People Want*, p. 77.
60 Kristin Diwan, 'Kuwait's Impatient Youth Movement' (*Foreign Policy*, 29.06.11), available at http://foreignpolicy.com/2011/06/29/kuwaits-impatient-youth-movement (accessed 30.06.11)
61 Trebilock, 'Between Institutions and Culture', p. 228.
62 MENA Development Report, *Gender and Development in the Middle East and North Africa* (Washington, DC: World Bank, 2004), p. 1.
63 UNDP, *Arab Human Development Report 2009: Challenges to Human Security in the Arab Countries* (New York: UNDP/Regional Bureau for Arab States, 2009).
64 Michael Ross, 'Oil, Islam and Women', *American Political Science Review*, 102 (2008), 107.
65 Archar, *The People Want*, p. 88.
66 'Strategy of Response to Transformative Change Championed by Youth in the Arab Region' (UNDP), available at www.arabstates.undp.org/content/dam/rbas/doc/arab_transformations1/UNDP%20Strategy%20of%20Response%20to%20 Transformative%20Changes%20in%20the%20Arab%20Region-Final%20(2).pdf (accessed 10.06.15), p. 4.
67 United Nations, *Arab Human Development Report 2016*, p. 19.
68 Pascal Menoret, 'The Municipal Elections in Saudi Arabia 2005: First Steps on a Democratic Path', in *Arab Reform Brief* (Paris: Mubadarat al-Islah al-'Arabi/Arab Reform Initiative, n.d.), p. 2.
69 Korany *Arab Human Development*, p. 30.
70 Ibid., p. 33.
71 M. Malki, 'Al-Barlaman fi al-Maghrib', In al-Barlman fi al-dawla al-'arabiya (Beirut: Beirut Arab Centre for the Development of the Rule of Law and Integrity and UNDP, 2007).
72 Korany, *Arab Human Development*, p. 45.
73 UNDP, *Egypt Human Development Report 2010: Youth in Egypt: Building our Future* (UNDP, 2010), available at http://hdr.undp.org/sites/default/files/reports/243/egypt_2010_en.pdf (accessed 11.02.16).
74 Wael Ghonim, *Revolution 2.0: The Power of the People IS Greater Than the People in Power: A Memoir* (New York: Houghton Mifflin Harcourt, 2012), p. 3.
75 At this point, intelligence agencies had identified nine hundred companies that belonged to the Brotherhood, in Archar, *The People Want*, p. 124.
76 Ghonim, *Revolution 2.0*, pp. 44–5.
77 Ibid., p. 120.
78 Jean-Pierre Filiu, *From Deep State to Islamic State: The Arab Counter-Revolution and its Jihadi Legacy* (London: Hurst, 2015), pp. 151–3.
79 Lynch, *New Arab Wars*, p. 101.

80 See Curtis Ryan, *Jordan and the Arab Spring: Regime Survival and Politics Beyond the State* (New York: Columbia University Press, 2018).

81 Gregory Johnsen, 'See Ya Saleh' (*Foreign Policy*, 23.03.11), available at https://foreignpolicy.com/2011/03/23/see-ya-saleh-2 (accessed 05.08/19).

82 Interview with Bahraini student, 2014.

83 James Worrall, 'The Forgotten Corner of the Arab Spring', *Middle East Policy*, 19:3 (2012), 98–115.

84 James Worrall, 'Protest and Reform: The Arab Spring in Oman', in Larbi Sadiki (ed.), *Routledge Handbook of the Arab Spring* (London: Routledge, 2014).

85 Sunil K. Vaidya, 'Oman Protesters Apologise to Ruler' (*Gulf News*, 01.03.11), available at https://gulfnews.com/world/gulf/oman/oman-protesters-apologise-to-ruler-1.769812 (accessed 02.03.11).

86 Ibid.

87 Interview with Omani academic, 2017.

88 Interview with Iraqi filmmaker, 2017.

89 Ibid.

90 Ibid.

91 Madawi Al Rasheed, 'Yes It Could Happen Here' (*Foreign Policy*, 28.02.11).

92 'Where Is Khalid?', available at www.youtube.com/watch?v=mxinAxWxXo8 (accessed 06.04.11).

93 Lynch, *New Arab Wars*, p. 118.

94 Al Haj Saleh, *The Impossible Revolution*.

95 Samar Yazbek, *A Woman in the Crossfire: Diaries of the Syrian Revolution* (London: Haus Publishing, 2011).

96 Phillips, *The Battle for Syria*.

97 Diwan, 'Kuwait's Constitutional Showdown'.

98 Ibid.

99 'Protesters Storm Kuwaiti Parliament' (BBC News, 16.11.11), available at www.bbc.co.uk/news/world-middle-east-15768027 (accessed 16.11.11).

100 Ibid.

101 Interview with Kuwaiti academic, 2018.

102 'Kuwait Court Hand Down Two Years Jail Sentence for Insulting Emir' (Reuters, 22.02.15), available at www.reuters.com/article/us-kuwait-court/kuwait-court-hands-down-two-years-jail-sentence-for-insulting-emir-idUSKBN0LQ09N20150222 (accessed 22.02.15).

103 'Kuwait Court Sentences MPs to Jail Terms for Storming into Parliament' (Reuters, 27.11.17), available at https://uk.reuters.com/article/uk-kuwait-court-parliament/kuwait-court-sentences-mps-to-jail-terms-for-storming-into-parliament-idUKKBN1DR1TG (accessed 27.11.17).

104 Mussallam Al Barrack, 'Kuwait's Democracy Is Being Undermined: That's Why Its People Are Protesting' (*Guardian*, 25.11.12) www.theguardian.com/commentisfree/2012/nov/25/kuwait-democracy-at-risk-protests (accessed 25.11.12).

105 'Kuwait Protest at Court Ruling Dissolving Parliament' (BBC, 27.06.12) www.bbc.co.uk/news/world-middle-east-18606540 (accessed 27.06.12).

106 Sylvia Westall and Mahmoud Harby, 'Kuwait Court Orders Dissolution of Parliament, New Elections' (Reuters, 16.06.13), available at www.reuters.com/article/us-kuwait-court-ruling-idUSBRE95F04320130616 (accessed 16.06.13).

107 'Kuwait Opposition Demands New Assembly Scrapped' (*Gulf News*, 02.12.12), available at https://gulfnews.com/world/gulf/kuwait/kuwait-opposition-demands-new-assembly-scrapped-1.1113406 (accessed 02.12.12).

108 'Constitutional Court's Ruling Enhances Durability of Democratic System: Info Minister' (Kuwait News Agency, 16.06.13), available at www.kuna.net.kw/ArticlePrintPage.aspx?id=2317163&language=en (accessed 16.06.13).

109 Alan Craig, 'The Israel Tent Protests', in Sadiki (ed.), *Routledge Handbook of the Arab Spring*, pp. 538–46.

110 Derya Göçer and Marc Herzog, 'Turkey and the Arab Uprisings', in Sadiki, *Routledge Handbook of the Arab Spring*, p. 509.

111 Yesim Arat, 'Violence, Resistance, and Gezi Park', *International Journal of Middle East Studies*, 45 (2013), 807–9.

112 'Protesters Are Young, Libteratian and Furious at Turkis PM, Says Survey' (*Hurriyet Daily News*, 05.06.13), available at www.hurriyetdailynews.com/protesters-are-young-libertarian-and-furious-at-turkish-pm-says-survey-48248 (accessed 05.06.13).

113 Constanze Letsch and Ian Traynor, 'Turkey Unrest: Violent Clashes in Istanbul as Erdogan Holds Rally' (*Guardian*, 16.06.13), available at www.theguardian.com/world/2013/jun/16/turkey-unrest-clashes-istanbul-erdogan (accessed 16.06.13).

114 Shabnam J. Holliday, 'Iran's Own Popular Uprising and the Arab Spring', in Sadiki, *Routledge Handbook of the Arab Spring*, pp. 527–37.

115 It must be stressed that these candidates are reform minded *within the context* of the Islamic Republic.

116 Interviews with a number of people from Lebanon (including journalists and policy advisors) noted the importance of memory in shaping political action (2017–18).

117 Natural Resource Governance Institute (2015), available at www.resourcegovernance.org/countries/middle-east-and-north-africa/saudi- arabia/overview (accessed 07.10.16).

118 IMF Middle East and Central Asia Department, *Regional Economic Outlook Update, Statistical Appendix May 2014* (Washington, DC: IMF, 2014).

119 In discussions with a colleague who taught a number of prominent Bahrainis at university in the UK, the very concept of the rentier state and its workings was unfamiliar to them before studying in the UK.

120 Sovereign Wealth Fund Institute (2015), available at www.swfinstitute.org/fund-rankings (accessed 10.02.16).

121 Zaki Moheb, 'Civil Society and Democratisation in the Arab World', *Annual Report* (Ibn Khaldoun Center for Development Studies, 2007), p. 15.

122 Hamid Dabashi, *The Arab Spring: The End of Postcolonialism* (London: Zed Books, 2012).

123 Hakki Tas, 'Street Arts of Resistance in Tahrir and Gezi', *Middle Eastern Studies*, 53:5 (2017), 802–19.

124 Ibid., pp. 802–6.

125 Tripp, *The Power and the People*.

126 Sadiki, *Routledge Handbook of the Arab Spring*, p. 4.

127 Judith Butler, *Bodies in Alliance and the Politics of the Street* (EIPCP, European Institute for Progressive Cultural Policies, 2011).

128 Charlotte Schriwer, 'Graffiti Arts and the Arab Spring', in Sadiki, *Routledge Handbook of the Arab Spring*, p. 384.

129 Akeel Abbas, 'Deconstructing Despotic Legacies in the Arab Spring', in Sadiki, *Routledge Handbook of the Arab Spring*, p. 412.

130 For a historical account of the importance of music see Mark Levine, *Heavy Metal Islam: Rock, Resistance and the Struggle for the Soul of Islam* (New York: Crown, 2008); and in the Arab Uprisings, see Mark Levine, 'The Revolution Never Ends: Music, Protest and Rebirth in the Arab World', in Sadiki, *Routledge Handbook of the Arab Spring*, pp. 354–65.

131 Interview with Syrian academic, 2017.

132 Sossie Kasbarian and Simon Mabon, 'Contested Spaces and Sectarian Narratives In Post-Uprisings Bahrain', *Global Discourse*, 6:4 (2016), 677–96.

133 Hani Morsi, 'The Virtualisation of Dissent: Social Media as a Catalyst for Social Change Part Two: From Reanimating the Social Discourse on Reform to a Grassroots Revolt for Change' (Blog posted 17.02.11 in Egypt), available at www.hanimorsi.com/blog (accessed 18.02.11).

134 Butler, *Bodies in Alliance and the Politics of the Street*, p. 627.

135 Hakki Tas, 'Street Arts of Resistance', p. 810.

136 Colin P. Kelley, Shahrzad Mohtadi, Mark A. Cane, Richard Seager and Yochanan Kushnir, 'Climate Change in the Fertile Crescent and Implications of the Recent Syrian Drought', *Proceedings of the National Academy of Sciences of the United States of America*, 112:11 (2015), 3241–6.

137 Robert Worth, 'Earth Is Parched Where Syrian Farms Thrived' (*New York Times*, 14.10.14), available at www.nytimes.com/2010/10/14/world/middleeast/14syria.html?adxnnl=1&adxnnlx=1330449407-yAiPXrD1kQsKbG2Bb5A61A&pagewanted=1 (accessed 05.05.17); 'Drought Driving Farmers to the Cities' (IRIN, 02.09.09), available at www.irinnews.org/feature/2009/09/02/drought-driving-farmers-cities (accessed 05.05.17).

138 Food and Agriculture Organization of the United Nations and World Food Programme, *Special Report: FAO/WFP Crop and Food Security Assessment Mission to the Syrian Arab Republic* (FAO, 2015), available at www.fao.org/3/a-i4804e.pdf (accessed 05.05.17).

139 Ibid.

140 Aron Lund, 'Dispossession or Development? The Tug of War Over Syria's Ruined Slum Dwellings' (IRIN, 04.07.18), available at www.irinnews.org/analysis/2018/07/04/dispossession-or-development-tug-war-over-syria-s-ruined-slum-dwellings (accessed 05.07.18).

141 Francesca De Châtel, 'The Role of Drought and Climate Change in the Syrian Uprising: Untangling the Triggers of the Revolution', *Middle Eastern Studies*, 50:4 (2014), 521–35.

142 Sarah Johnstone and Jeffrey Mazo, 'Global Warming and the Arab Spring', in Caitlin E. Werrel and Francesco Femia (eds), *The Arab Spring and Climate Change* (Washington, DC: Center for American Progress, 2013), p. 15.

143 R. Hinnebusch, 'Syria: From "Authoritarian Upgrading" to Revolution?', *International Affairs*, 88:1 (2012), 95–113.

144 H. Harding, 'Working in the Grey Zone' (*Syria Today*, May 2010).

145 United Nations Office for the Coordination of Humanitarian Affairs, *Syria Drought Response Plan 2009–2010 Mid-Term Review* (New York: United Nations Office for the Coordination of Humanitarian Affairs, 2010).

146 United Nations, *Office for the Coordination of Humanitarian Affairs, Syria Drought Response Plan 2009* (New York: United Nations Office for the Coordination of Humanitarian Affairs, 2009).
147 De Châtel, *The Role of Drought.*
148 United Nations, Arab Human Development Report 2016, p. 17.
149 See Arab Center for Research and Policy Studies, *Arab Opinion Index* (Doha, Qatar: Doha Institute, 2014); and Arab Center for Research & Policy Studies, *Arab Opinion Index* (Doha, Qatar: Doha Institute, 2015).
150 Ibid.
151 United Nations, *Arab Human Development Report 2016*, p. 19.
152 See *Arab Opinion Index 2015*, p. 1. See also Mabon, 'Sovereignty, Bare Life and the Arab Uprisings'.

7

The regime fights back

The regime in Egypt is waging war against the young who dare to dream of a bright future for themselves and their country. Somewhere there are still peoples and herds, but not with us, my brothers: here there are states. A state? What is that? Well! Open now your ears to me, for now will I say to you my word concerning the death of peoples. State is the name of the coldest of all cold monsters. Coldly lies it also; and this lie creeps from its mouth: 'I, the state, am the people'.

Family of Alaa Abd el-Fattah, detained in June 2015

On 3 July 2013, the Egyptian army engineered a *coup d'état* against Mohammad Morsi, the region's first democratically elected Islamist President.[1] Following a spate of protests that culminated in an estimated twenty million people taking to the streets of Egypt to voice their displeasure at Morsi's 'ordinary' transition,[2] the army forced the Freedom and Justice Party from power. On 14 August, some four weeks after Morsi's government was toppled, over eight hundred supporters of the Muslim Brotherhood were killed near the Rabaa al-Adawiya mosque in Cairo in what Human Rights Watch called a likely 'crime against humanity'.[3] It was in Rabaa where Egypt's revolutionary dream died.

Over the course of twelve hours, Egyptian security personnel used a range of tactics and weapons including bulldozers and supported by snipers, security personnel entered the square to disperse protesters to devastating effect. Yet the Rabaa massacre was not an isolated incident. Shortly afterwards, protesters were dispersed from al-Nahda in a similar manner, while further Brotherhood protests were also ended with violence.

The Human Rights Watch investigation into events in Rabaa documents a systematic attack against 'unarmed persons on political grounds', where lethal force was used indiscriminately.[4] Kenneth Roth, the executive director of Human Rights Watch, referred to it as one of the world's largest killings of demonstrators in a single day in recent history, a violent crackdown planned 'at the highest levels of the Egyptian government'.[5] The report names Abdul Fatal Al Sisi, the Egyptian President, as one of the individuals complicit in events.

In the weeks that followed, some of the remaining members of the Brotherhood fled to London, Doha and Istanbul, while others were imprisoned or killed; over the course of the following year, over 2,500 civilians were killed and 17,000 injured,[6] while 40,000 were arrested.[7] The following year, an Egyptian court sentenced 529 Muslim Brothers to death and, a year later, Mohammad Morsi also received a death sentence in a systematic repression of the *ikhwan* – both party and ideology – driven by domestic and regional concerns, driven by the concerns of Saudi Arabia and the UAE.[8] Morsi later died in an Egyptian court.

In Bahrain, where regional concerns were equally prevalent, the regime's response framed protestors as fifth columnists doing the nefarious bidding of Iran, resulting in the widespread restriction of political space across the island. In this climate, opposition groups and a number of journalists were imprisoned and in a number of instances, killed. The case of Eman Salehi, a Bahraini sports journalist who was killed by a member of the royal family reveals a great deal about the political climate in Bahrain.[9] The Salehi case also evokes memories of Agamben's *homo sacer*, the individual who can be killed with impunity, revealing the potentiality at the heart of political projects; at the time of writing, her killer remains free.

In contrast to Egypt and Bahrain, events in Syria and Yemen erupted in violent conflict, pitting protest movements against regimes in ferocious fighting that rapidly consumed political dynamics across each state. Following the fragmentation of political organisation, ferocious hostilities began to shape life across the two states as local grievances interacted with national events, which all took place within a struggle for supremacy across the Middle East. As existential fear began to take hold, politics began to play out in what the Syrian intellectual Yassin Al Haj Saleh has termed a 'state of nature'. Evoking the work of Thomas Hobbes, Al Haj Saleh's description of events in Syria bear a number of hallmarks with those in Yemen as politics became characterised by 'social dispersion, direct reactive responses, violence – all characteristics of a society losing its self-control and its ability to act uniformly'.[10]

Al Haj Saleh's portrayal of the state of nature is perhaps bleaker than Hobbes', suggesting that there is a 'natural' transformation into this state of nature as a consequence of the increasingly repressive and sect-based politics of survival that challenge the very existence of the Syrian people. This approach stems from regimes following their instincts, their neuroses and 'their madness'. In such conditions, groups develop narratives of superiority and victimhood as a means of ensuring their survival. As a consequence, politics is reduced to a 'sectarian war, in which murder leads to murder, *asabiyyah* activates *asabiyyah*, and hatred animates hatred'.[11]

The events of early 2011 that eviscerated regime–society relations across the Middle East were a widespread rejection of the political, economic, social and legal status quo, pushing people into localised forms of *asabiyyah* and challenging the relationship between *ordnung* and *ortung* in the process. Having had political meaning stripped from their lives and the regulation of this limited form of existence embedded within the fabric of the state, protests were an expression of agency in the face of seemingly insurmountable structures. Contestation was met with a fierce response from the governance structures of the state as regimes attempted to regain control over the situation, using a range of draconian strategies. The rejection of 'being thus', in turn, created a situation wherein both regime and peoples sought to define the ordering of political life and, as a consequence, the very limits of political space. This process of contestation resulted in the emergence of war machines and a struggle to exert control over them.

Regime responses to the protests emerged from state-building processes, which facilitated the widespread repression that followed the uprisings. Although a number of regimes created bare life in an attempt to end the protest movements, this was not always successful. Instead, because of the existence of strong normative currents across the region, further mechanisms of control were deemed necessary. This chapter traces regime responses in the aftermath of the Arab Uprisings, beginning with the declaration of emergency powers before moving to consideration of securitising moves – the linguistic framing of particular issues as threats – which once again demonstrates the conflation of domestic and regional factors. It argues that regional affairs had a profound impact on regime responses to protest movements, while in turn, regime responses had regional repercussions.

States (and spaces) of emergency and exception

As protesters took to the streets in early 2011, political organisation was renegotiated amid the reconceptualisation of protest and resistance. This biopolitical machinery helped regimes control life, stripping it of political meaning but when this was deemed insufficient, sovereign power was exerted by controlling life through death. Regimes quickly declared states of emergency, suspending political structures and the rule of law as a consequence of perceived existential threats to their rule. Recourse to such methods was hardly surprising, yet as the repeal of emergency legislation was a prominent feature of protestor's demands, such action only served to escalate tensions. Once again, the state of exception had become the paradigm of government, the new norm.

The historical use of emergency legislation across the Middle East set a precedent for constitutional powers to be used in times of domestic unrest, embedding potentiality within the fabric of political organisation. Yet with the onset of the uprisings, regimes derogated from legal responsibilities to ensure their survival. The uprisings had a seismic impact upon regional dynamics as millions of people were displaced from their homes amid widespread instability and violence across the region. Widespread migration both within and between states impacted not only on state infrastructures but also their economies, as refugee populations were comprised of large numbers of professionals and highly qualified workers. The flow of people across state borders placed huge strains upon host countries such as Jordan, Lebanon and Turkey, while also having a serious impact upon the construction of societies and their very survival.

These actions occurred in space that quickly took on new political meaning, opening up new sites for regulation.[12] While sites of opportunity, they were also sites of the mundane, where the theatre of the spectacle was also the everyday landscape of life's routines, making the evolution of space more powerful. Amid contested societies and environments, public spaces became the battleground. Across the region, people articulating political messages occupied public spaces where they were quickly met with counter-narratives, protests and often, the security mechanisms of the state. As Mona El-Ghobashy suggests, 'the streets had become parliaments, negotiating tables and battlegrounds rolled into one'.[13] Public space quickly became a zone of indistinction: a site of contestation and exception, where regime and opposition discourses clashed, while repressive force was a mechanism of control.

The uprisings triggered a fundamental shift in the way of *doing* politics. Beyond the mobilisation and direct action seen in the squares of the region, politics became a topic that was readily discussed as the shackles of authoritarian restrictions were thrown off. Debate about political life was everywhere but with such debate came divisions. As securitising moves took place, political divisions both online and in person between family and friends became increasingly heated, resulting in ostracisation and separation.[14] It was a time of uncertainty for regimes and peoples, but it was a time when regimes fought back.

Derogation from constitutional clauses and establishment of emergency powers gave regimes seemingly unlimited power to respond to protest movements in whatever way was deemed necessary. Although a number of constitutions possessed clauses that limited the time under which emergency legislation could be imposed without review, such powers were rarely challenged.[15] Through derogating from legal obligations, regimes were given power to respond to protests with violence, both direct and structural, destroying political space and reshaping the nature of societal dynamics. Such moves allowed for the repression of a range of different political and religious groups across the Middle East with regional repercussions.

Emergency laws were deeply unpopular and often cited by protestors as one of their main grievances. Perhaps the most prominent example of the draconian use of such laws was in Egypt. Although emergency laws in Egypt were lifted in the final days of the Mubarak regime – for the first time since 1980 – they were quickly reinstalled by the SCAF amid the uncertainty of post-revolutionary life. In response, rights organisations were vocal in their condemnation of the move. In response to Decree 193/2011, which not only revived the powers but also expanded their scope, an open letter was written that noted how the legislation highlighted the gulf between aspirations for democracy and the legacy of the old regime that continued to administer Egyptian affairs.[16]

Although Mohammad Morsi had promised to remove emergency laws, when faced with serious threats to his regime he derogated from the rule of law, returning to a paradigm of government that had become the all too common norm. In support of the sovereign decision, Morsi stated: 'I am against any emergency measures, but I have said that if I must stop bloodshed and protect the people then I will act.'[17]

After the *coup d'état* that deposed Morsi in the summer of 2013, Decree 136 permitted military personnel to stand by police forces to protect buildings.[18] Such a decision was supported by the move to allow civilians to be tried in military courts, once more depriving people of political rights.[19] Two years on from the uprisings, concern at the behaviour of the security services remained, amid widespread corruption and endemic violence, with policemen remaining 'above the law and immunized from criminal accountability'.[20]

In conditions of increasing uncertainty, it was argued that 'police continue to deploy excessive violence and torture systematically as it was during the Mubarak regime'.[21] In the following years, the human rights situation worsened, amid 'massive and systematic violations of basic rights and freedoms despite starting the year with a promising new constitution'.[22] The spectre of a terrorist threat in Sinai from a group that had declared allegiance to Da'ish only served to strengthen the Sisi regime's proclamations of the necessity of such legislation. This move also located Egypt within a Saudi-led coalition of Sunni states in the fight against terrorism, which had broader geopolitical repercussions beyond the fight against Da'ish, drawing on a burgeoning anti-Iranian sentiment along with cultivation about the Shi'a – and Persian – other.

In the early days of the uprisings in Syria, emergency laws were repealed in a token nod towards the protest movements. Imposed in 1963 to legislate for the prolix war with Israel the laws were used to support efforts to counter internal dissent, feeding into narratives that dissent was an attempt to emasculate the nation or collude with the enemy.[23] On 20 April 2011, Decree 161 lifted the emergency legislation, but the state of emergency was later replaced with Decree 54. Upon its implementation Mohammed Al Shaar, the Interior Minister, was explicit in his warnings to protestors stressing that they must 'refrain from taking part in all marches, demonstrations or sit-ins under any banner whatsoever'.[24]

Amid unrest across the Bahrain, on 15 March 2011, the Al Khalifa declared a state of emergency in accordance with Article 36(b) of the Bahraini Constitution. Coming a day after GCC troops crossed the King Fahd causeway, emergency legislation was imposed to restrict political activity and support counter-revolutionary efforts, coupled with the use of military courts to try protestors. Three days later, Yemen's President Ali Abdullah Saleh declared a thirty-day state of emergency, suspending the constitution. In Kuwait, regime efforts to regulate political life involved handing out prison sentences to those who stormed the parliament along with those who insulted the Emir.[25]

In a similar move, Saudi Arabia sought to regulate political activity through recourse to counter-terror laws that restricted access to the Internet and freedom of speech.[26] Such efforts resulted in the establishment of new anti-terror legislation, which meant that acts of peaceful dissent could be defined as terrorist crimes. In addition to such manoeuvring, Riyadh employed other strategies to regulate political dissent and opposition. The Ministry for Culture and Information placed legal requirements on anyone wishing to blog to have a licence; those wishing to apply for a licence had to be in possession of a college degree and be over the age of twenty.[27]

Another mechanism of control that became increasingly prominent at this time was the regulation of citizenship, where the politics of identity and ensuing revocation of citizenship rights from individuals became increasingly important in times of crisis.[28] Such a tactic has been routinely used across the Gulf, provoking not only philosophical questions about the nature of citizenship, but also exploration of the legal mechanisms through which such strategies can be undertaken. As Zahra Bashar notes, the importance of historical and cultural dynamics has created a particular form of citizenship and stringent restrictions upon those who can claim nationality. With this in mind, after the uprisings, states across the Gulf amended legislation to allow for the removal of citizenship through recourse to either anti-terrorism legislation or nationality laws[29]and between 2011 and 2018, 738 Bahrainis had their citizenship revoked.[30] One former MP told me that he found out that he had lost his nationality while in London, via Al Jazeera.[31]

In such conditions, lives are deemed 'expendable' through the cultivation of bare life, through recourse to Law Number 58 of 2006 for Protecting Society from terrorism Acts and the Citizenship Law of 1963. In Bahrain it is illegal to be a stateless individual, a crime routinely punished under the Asylum and Immigration Law. As a consequence of their position in society, the stateless are unable to appeal against the charges as they possess no legal protection or ability to give lawyers power of attorney. The law denies individuals access to employment, marking them as migrant workers requiring sponsorship, along with the right to own property. It also denies health care and excludes children from formal education. By the summer of 2018, of the 738 individuals stripped of their citizenship, many remained in Bahrain as 'illegal residents', reduced to bare life: abandoned by the law yet bound to it.[32]

Beyond physical space, protests also took place online, prompting regime efforts to regulate the Internet and arresting a number of individuals such as Nabeel Rajab, a Bahraini human rights activist, for criticising the Al Khalifa. While social media is often heralded as the means through which the uprisings took place, such a position denies local agency[33] and the widespread regulation of the Internet meant that some narratives were restricted. Supporting this position, Derek Gregory acknowledges that Westerners in positions of privilege tend to reduce political action in the Middle East to the digital repertoire, ignoring the importance of 'brave bodies in alliance installing new spaces'.[34]

The uprisings demonstrated once more that space matters, highlighting the power of the street, of collective consciousness and the possibility of becoming, as the intimately tiny collided with hegemonic regional pressures. Yet the process of negotiating the uprisings – the clash between regimes and societies – reminded many that ownership of space had not been fully transformed from elites to publics. Efforts to demonstrate control through architecture continue as violence is embedded within urban structures. The erasure of symbolic sites was supplemented with an increasingly militarised regulatory force and an increase in symbolic violence. Across the Gulf, the presence of ruling families in public spaces, along highways and within hotels, increased in the aftermath of the protests; regime power was seemingly all encompassing.

Other efforts were undertaken to regulate life and manage images. News channels took on political meaning, where Al Jazeera was seen as the mouthpiece not only of Qatar but of the uprisings themselves. As the protests spread, regimes worked carefully to control and manipulate flows of information. A struggle quickly emerged over music and literature: nationalist songs were played day and night in ministries and other public buildings while opposition groups sang modified versions of the same songs in the streets.[35] On state TV channels across Syria, prominent pro-regime religious leaders and intellectuals were interviewed, along with members of the public who were vocal in their praise for the President and military, while also baying 'for the blood of the "terrorists" '.[36]

The struggle to regulate space also includes intellectual debates. At the 2014 World Congress on Middle East Studies Conference in Ankara, those attending a panel on the politics of the UAE were met by a row of TV cameras and an armed security presence. Breaking with academic convention, the Chair introduced a Sheikha from the Emirates who proceeded to give a presentation on the merits of life in – and the politics of – the UAE. Again, breaking from the norm, the Chair refused to allow for questions and, in spite of a small amount of heckling from the floor, the session passed without further event. Although hardly remarkable in the grand scheme of Middle Eastern soft-power strategies, regime efforts to shape academic discourse have become increasingly prominent. The conference has routinely been a space of contestation. Four years earlier, the former Crown Prince of Jordan, Hassan bin Talal, publicly condemned a Malaysian journalist who had criticised the Hashemite kingdom, saying, in English, 'Fuck you. People in glass houses shouldn't throw stones'.

The regulation of physical borders became increasingly important.[37] Prominent journalists and academics, including a number of my own colleagues, were turned away from the states that they worked on and in, while others were also targeted, followed and hacked.[38] Urban landscapes became contested sites of political representation, a battleground within which actors embroiled in conflict express their views and attempt to garner support for people who witness such scenes.

News coverage of events beyond regional outlets has also taken on a political agenda. In the Syrian context, intellectual exploration has increasingly become populated by conspiracy theories and ideological agendas at the cost of rigorous empirically driven analysis.[39] This has helped to facilitate a position where the narrative that the secular Syrian regime is fighting Islamist extremists – as part of the War on Terror – is taken with little critical engagement. Ultimately, this creates a position that results in international inaction, policy confusion[40] and the death of thousands, justified within the global *nomos*.

The sectarianisation of political life

Amid the contestation of sovereign power, regimes have sought to ensure their survival by closing off a community against an outside, increasingly done along sect-based lines. Parallels can be drawn across the region as regimes sought to solidify their support bases by creating existential fears about the other. In such conditions, political life took on a sectarian dimension while also becoming imbued with geopolitical meaning. By framing opposition groups as an existential threat to the very survival of the *polis*, regimes not only strengthened their support bases internally and externally, but also framed their responses as *necessary* to defend the state, speaking to domestic and international audiences in the process.[41]

The emergence of politically charged sectarian narratives reveals the spatial aspects at play in the relationship between politics and Islam, as domestic politics clash with the geopolitical aspirations of regional powers. By locating national events within (geo)sectarian narratives, regimes derive legitimacy and security from co-religious kin within their states and beyond in what has become known as *sectarianisation*, the *securitisation* of *sect-based difference*. As we shall see below, sectarianisation was a key weapon in the armoury of a number of regimes, opening up questions about the ordering of space in the process.

For Nader Hashemi and Danny Postel, *sectarianisation* is

> an active process shaped by political actors operating within specific contexts, pursuing political goals that involve the mobilisation of popular sentiments around particular identity markers. Class dynamics, fragile states, and geopolitical rivalries also shape the sectarianization process.[42]

The thesis is underpinned by the prevalence of authoritarian rule, creating a crisis of legitimacy that requires the manipulation of sect-based identities as a means of ensuring regime survival. When placed in the context of geopolitical currents, most importantly the rivalry between Saudi Arabia and Iran, efforts to ensure survival draw upon – and feed into – regional security. Yet beyond this elite process, it also occurs in different guises as groups seek to close themselves off against an outside, exacerbating sectarian differences in the process.

Processes of sectarianisation seek to ensure survival by mobilising communities around a shared identity, framing the predetermined other as an existential threat. This framing has been a prominent feature of the state-building process, where loyalty is forged from a complex web of identities across the region. Amid the separation of regime and society in the aftermath of the Arab Uprisings, opportunities have emerged to ensure survival through the (re)shaping of space and ordering of life, driven by the interaction of regional forces with local actors.

Such processes refer to the cultivation and manipulation of seemingly violent divisions between – and within – groups by individuals with a vested interest in communal supremacy in pursuit of political or economic aims. Through these approaches, sect-based difference becomes a vehicle through which subjectivity, prejudice and politics gain traction. From this, grievances develop, and as political structures are put in place to regulate life such sentiments become both institutionalised and generational. As we have seen in Lebanon, Iraq, Israel, Egypt, Saudi Arabia and Iran (among others), processes of state formation have regularly created antagonistic grievances between sectarian groups as a means of maintaining control and ultimately, survival.[43]

In many cases, the survival of the state has been conflated with the survival of the regime and, as such, actors seek to frame particular issues as *existential threats* – those requiring extraordinary measures – in a process typically known as securitisation.

Securitisation seeks to understand how particular issues are moved from the realm of 'normal politics' and framed in such a way that 'justifies the use of extraordinary measures to handle them'.[44] These processes require the linguistic framing of events for particular audiences, which take place within domestic, regional and international contexts that support the move to extraordinary measures.[45]

Securitising approaches take place within spaces shaped by the interaction of the global with the 'intimately tiny'. Regional politics provides context within which such moves take place, combined with the contingency of local factors, giving meaning to particular approaches that may differ in neighbouring states. To justify this suspension of rules and order, regimes speak to audiences to legitimise and frame their behaviour, yet the complexity of state building and identity construction finds traction among intended and unintended audiences.[46] Amid a shared normative environment, securitising moves have implications across the Middle East, taking place within and across spaces that are shaped by the interaction of the global with the local.

The context in which sectarianisation occurs is integral. While sectarianisation takes place *within* political projects, it also derives a great deal of traction from geopolitical contexts. In recent years, a key component of sectarianisation and securitisation processes is a fear about nefarious Iranian activity among Shi'a communities, perhaps most explicitly addressed in remarks about the Shi'a Crescent. Demonstrating the success of such framing, a commonly held view across the region is that Iran has sought to destabilise states as a means through which they can increase their influence, capitalising on moments of crisis to manipulate domestic populations whose loyalty has long been questioned.[47]

To understand the contemporary roots of these processes we must return to Iraq after the 2003 invasion. Although most Arab regimes were apathetic to events in Iraq, Iranian forces capitalised on the vacuum that emerged after the fall of Saddam.[48] In the years that followed, Iranian agents began to exert influence across Iraq through Qassem Soleimani, the influential head of the Iranian Revolutionary Guards Corps.[49] Fearing Iranian gains, Saudi officials urged the United States not to 'leave Iraq until its sovereignty has been restored, otherwise it will be vulnerable to the Iranians'.[50] The King was a staunch critic of increasing Iranian expansionism, regularly urging US military action. One diplomatic cable recounts the King's exhortations to 'cut off the head of the snake', with a clear nod to the regime in Tehran.[51] Moreover, Abdullah stressed that he had 'no confidence whatsoever in Maliki', proclaiming that he had no credibility. Moreover, Maliki was 'an Iranian agent' who had 'opened the door for Iranian influence in Iraq' since taking power.[52] Abdullah's comments echo those made by previous Saudi officials, pre-dating the revolution, yet the increased influence of Iranian actors escalated these fears.[53] At this time, US diplomatic cables are dominated by Saudi and Bahraini efforts to securitise the Iranian threat to US audiences, calling on Washington to suspend normal politics and prevent rapprochement with Iran.[54]

Life in Iraq became increasingly precarious with many fearing for their lives amid widespread violence and seemingly routine persecution. Within such a landscape, Sunni tribes across Anbar found themselves in bare life, trapped between Shi'a militias, Al Qa'ida franchises, coalition forces and the sectarian politics of Baghdad.[55]

Struggling to meet basic needs and facing threats to their lives from Shi'a militias who were seemingly acting with impunity and without recourse to political or legal structures, a number of Sunni tribes were left with little option but to find protection from groups such as Da'ish.[56] Fragmentation of state structures across Iraq resulted in narratives of sectarian conflict consuming the political sphere, yet as Fanar Haddad has presciently argued, such claims fall wide of the mark.[57] Instead, fragmentation revealed a complex and fluid set of interactions around communal identities that may coalesce around sectarian identities but were far more nuanced, with repercussions beyond the borders of Iraq.

Similar strategies of political marginalisation can be seen across Saudi Arabia's response to the Arab Uprisings.[58] Fragmentation of political organisation created spaces of possibility for increased involvement of a range of actors, prompting the kingdom to cultivate and mobilise allies, typically along sectarian lines. The sectarianisation of geopolitics served as a means of securing influence across the region while simultaneously reducing the influence of their rivals.

For Saudi Arabia, action was necessary to curtail the burgeoning threat posed by Iran.[59] Supporting this, Prince Saud Al Faisal, the late Foreign Minister of Saudi Arabia, was reported as saying, 'You can't feast and leave your neighbours hungry'.[60] In contrast, for many in Iran, widespread anti-Iranian sentiment was a consequence of Saudi and American actions. According to Javad Zarif, 'Iranian "aggression" is a myth, easily perpetuated by those willing to spend their dollars on American military equipment and public-relations firms, and by those promising to protect American interest rather than those of their own people'.[61]

In these geopolitical conditions, regimes sought to circumvent domestic unrest through sectarianisation. As protest movements challenged the survival of authoritarian rulers, regimes began the process of closing communities off against the sectarian other, drawing on history and geopolitical fears as a means of ensuring their survival.

In Bahrain, sectarianisation has been taken alongside emergency laws in an attempt to regulate life, which has long been shaped by the exercise of power by the ruling Sunni minority over the Shi'a majority amid allegations of divided loyalties and long-standing Iranian claims to the island.[62] The history of violent opposition in Bahrain fueled such suspicions, particularly with regard to the Islamic Front for the Liberation of Bahrain (IFLB) and rhetoric from Tehran.

In an attempt to ensure the survival of the regime, the Al Khalifa regime excluded Shi'a from the security services[63] and prominent ministries, although a number still held senior positions in the private sector, much like other states who experience 'sectarian violence'.[64] A second strategy was to reduce the demographic influence of the Shi'a, while the third strategy was to mobilise Sunni identities against their Shi'a counterparts to secure the regime's support base, a domestic move aimed at securing regional support.[65]

Shortly after the protests began, Saudi-led GCC forces of the Peninsular Shield Force crossed the King Fahd causeway and entered Bahrain. The force was instrumental in crushing the protest movements and in the months to follow, a widespread crackdown on opposition figures – including MPs – ensued. In an attempt to secure support from

Sunnis in Bahrain and beyond, Shi'a groups were framed as fifth columnists, allies of Iran and part of a Shi'a crescent. Securitising moves helped cultivate such fears among Sunni Bahrains, creating a climate where one Sunni businessman claimed that 'the Persians are everywhere'.[66] Such sentiments are also held by a number of state officials, revealed after the publication of an article by Fawaz bin Mohammad Al Khalifa that articulated the 'expansionist ambitions of the Persian Shia establishment', laying blame for unrest in Bahrain, Lebanon, Kuwait and Yemen at the door of Iran.[67]

Such fears had routinely been expressed to US officials. In 2006, Bahraini officials argued that 'as long as Khamenei has the title of Commander-in-Chief, Bahrain must worry about the loyalty of Shia who maintain ties and allegiance to Iran'.[68] Among the island's Shi'a populations, such views are deeply offensive. One Bahraini Shi'a cleric declared that 'it is an insult to accuse me of following an Iranian agenda or being part of an Iranian vision of the region just for being from a Shi'a background'.[69] Fears of increased Shi'a involvement in political life resulted in widespread gerrymandering, the manipulation of electoral borders as a means of ensuring Sunni dominance in electoral districts as much as possible.

Fundamental to this adherence of this anti-Iranian sentiment were concerns in Manama that 'the Saudis would turn off the tap', revealing the collapse of distinctions[70] between (geo)politics and religion, where identities begin to play a dual role, demonstrating both nationalist and religious loyalties, leaving Bahrainis caught within a regional struggle between Saudi Arabia and Iran and their own domestic issues. Sectarianisation efforts drew upon both Bahraini history – notably long-standing Iranian claims to the island and the actions of the IFLB – and broader geopolitical fears. Amid such fears, sectarianising narratives found traction among many Sunni Bahrainis, quickly exacerbating divisions across the island, meaning that the Al Khalifa retained power and Shi'a opposition groups were largely marginalised from political, social and economic life.[71]

In Yemen, a similar story unfolded. While typically (inaccurately) reduced to a conflict over sectarian difference, Yemen is perhaps the best example of how a conflict gains sectarian meaning through taking on geopolitical importance. Prior to 2014, there was little talk of sectarian difference in a country whose complex divisions occur along tribal or political lines. Yet following the *coup d'état* against Abd Rabbu Mansour Hadi and the rapidly increasing influence of the Houthi movement, this dramatically changed to the point that Saudi soldiers fighting in Yemen are told they are fighting against Shi'a heretics.

Saudi Arabia responded to the threat of growing Iranian influence in Yemen by building an alliance with the UAE, Bahrain and Egypt, which sought to eradicate the Houthis, resulting in massive humanitarian consequences and allegations of war crimes.[72] The complexity of political and security factors within the civil war created ample space for external actors to work towards their own geopolitical aspirations. The presence of a melange of actors laying claim to political legitimacy and authority fed into the fragmentation of the state, amid strong tribal currents, the presence of a powerful Al Qa'ida franchise, and burgeoning secessionist movements.[73] Amid allegations of Iranian support for the Houthis – given credibility by the Houthis firing Iranian-made missiles at targets in Saudi Arabia – Saudi Arabia's Crown Prince Mohammed bin Salman accused Iran of 'direct military aggression', suggesting that Tehran's actions 'may be considered an act of war against the Kingdom'.[74] Yet in later incidents in 2019, more restraint was shown.

For Adel Al Jubeir, 'Iranian interventions in the region are detrimental to the security of neighbouring countries and affect international peace and security. We will not allow any infringement of our national security'.[75] Moreover, 'Iran's role and its direct command of its Houthi proxy in this matter constitute a clear act of aggression that targets neighbouring countries, and threatens peace and security in the region and globally'.[76] Although Saudi involvement in Yemen can be traced back to 1978 and the establishment of networks of patronage in support of its aims, the provision of financial support since 2007 to help the Yemeni state to buy wheat on global markets has left many in Riyadh with the belief that they have a say in Yemeni politics, which is increasingly viewed through a sectarian lens. While many in the kingdom hold the view that Yemeni politics 'should not be in opposition to Riyadh', the dominance of the Houthis have proved detrimental to the success of this strategy.[77] Saudi influence was traditionally exerted through 'bags of cash', although this was also matched by military support during the six Saada wars and while many were critical of Saudi involvement it is generally accepted that 'Iran will never pay the food bill for Yemen'.[78]

In contrast, Iranian involvement in Yemen can be traced back to around 2006 when members of the Islamic Revolutionary Guard Corps (IRGC) provided Houthis and members of the southern Yemen population with weapons, tactics, financial resources and PR strategies. This led to collusion with Hizballah and the establishment of a strong network of informants, spies, developmental strategists, soldiers and politicians, which provided Iran with a strong degree of leverage and influence, albeit at very little expense. In spite of this involvement, US diplomatic cables from the years before the uprisings acknowledge that Houthi weapons were originally Yemeni army weapons bought on the black market.[79] There was no evidence of Iranian support at this time, although in the years that followed, Tehran offered a great deal more support to the Houthis.

The sectarianisation of regional politics took a different form with Saudi efforts to convert members of the Yemeni Zaydi community to Wahhabism. Reflecting the construction of space – as regional forces interact with the local factors – tribal leaders also saw this as a means through which they could circumvent the historical legacy of the *sayyid* (descendants of the Prophet) facilitating the fracturing of the Shi'a body politic.[80] Religious groups provided possibilities for achieving political ends in such conditions. In Bahrain where the Muslim Brotherhood and Salafi groups were used to counter the threat posed by Shi'a groups and, although this policy was used after the uprisings, by 2014 pressure from Riyadh prevented its continued use.[81] The same year, demands from Saudi Arabia and the UAE placed pressure on the Bahraini government to give key ministerial positions to independent politicians with strong links to the military and security sector who were recruited into politics after retiring to serve as independents in support of the Al Khalifa.[82]

In Egypt, the securitisation of the Muslim Brotherhood built upon long-standing repression of the Brothers – and Sisters – as the Sisi regime sought to destroy the group's political capacity, violently rejecting and crushing their beliefs in the process. As the family of one protester jailed in Egypt claimed, 'The regime in Egypt is waging war against the young who dare to dream of a bright future for themselves and their country.'[83] In the months that followed the toppling of Morsi, regime forces used force to destroy the infrastructure of the Muslim Brotherhood, killing thousands of its members in the process.

In Syria, although protests initially began around demands for political reform, the Assad regime constructed narratives of sectarian difference, as part of a mechanism of control. As protests escalated, a civil war broke out broadly although not exclusively[84] along sectarian lines,[85] as the Assad regime supported violent Sunni groups such as Al Qa'ida in an attempt to deepen such divisions and exacerbating the conflict. In a survey by *The Day After*, almost three-quarters of people asked responded that they had experienced sectarian discrimination.[86] This behaviour was not new. As Haider Al Khoei argued, the Syrian regime had long manipulated violent extremist agendas for their own ends, particularly after the 2003 invasion of Iraq when Sunni jihadists were incited to fight in Iraq.[87]

Elements of the Syrian opposition initially sought to maintain the peaceful character of the revolution into the summer of 2011, rejecting the call to arms politically, nationally and ethically.[88] Yet as the regime became increasingly violent in its repression of events, the protestors armed themselves to protect their families and neighbourhoods amid huge power disparities with the regime.[89]

With the emergence of protest movements across the country, Assad quickly sought to frame them as jihadists, part of an Al Qa'ida movement determined to topple his regime. Although this narrative quickly found traction, it faced a serious problem as most of the jihadists present in Syria were imprisoned. In an attempt to strengthen the regime narrative, a number of these prisoners were discretely released in the spring and summer of 2011, whereupon many joined groups including the forerunner of Da'ish. Reflecting on such events, then Foreign Secretary Boris Johnson argued that the British position was that it was Assad's 'decision to let Daesh out of the jails to create this alternative for the West'.[90]

After this manipulation of divisions within the fabric of Syrian society, fear quickly began to take hold and violence became a prominent feature of political life. As Yassin Al Haj Saleh suggests, the descent into fear was a prominent strategy of *tashbih* – a sense of collective paranoia – as regimes murder 'the very concept of truth'.[91] In such conditions, it was hardly surprising that protestors took up arms in self-defence. The conflict quickly gained an international dimension through the construction and manipulation of sect-based networks that transcended the Syrian state,[92] while the presence of Iranian, Russian and Hizballah figures further eroded sovereign power.[93] As societal schisms deepened, the fighting intensified, leading to mass casualties across the state and a descent into an intractable conflict.

Beyond the violence, a number of other strategies were used to retain the support of people across Syria. Public space took on existential importance and cities became battlegrounds. Urban environments underwent rapid transformation as they endured massive military bombardment in places such as Aleppo, while others were scarred by the scale of fighting between rival groups. In places where violence had not escalated as far, urban landscapes were transformed in different ways, taking on increasingly militarised characteristics. Conflict also took place over contested historiographies and culture, as protestors challenged the meaning of poetry, narratives and music previously used by the regime in an effort to develop an emancipatory identity and to erode support for the Assad regime.[94]

Similar events unfolded in Yemen, where fighting had a deleterious impact upon both the state and also the ability of people to meet their basic needs. Amid serious environmental challenges, water reserves rapidly depleted, 18.8 million people need some kind of humanitarian assistance while 17 million people are considered to be food insecure.[95] Politically, the unification of north and south looks increasingly precarious, particularly as southern separatists declare a state of emergency and reject the legitimacy of the Saudi supported government.[96]

Political and structural repression of opposition groups across the Middle East was supported by people who feared that the escalation of conflict – albeit one that began in a quest to secure better democratic rights – would end in a similar situation to that found in Syria. Moreover, the sectarianisation of political life fuelled suspicions that democratic movements were cover for seditious activity, orchestrated by Iran. And with these fears, democratic aspirations were renounced by many in favour of security and stability.[97]

Yet not all efforts to exacerbate sectarian divisions resulted in violence. A 2015 Da'ish attack on a mosque in Kuwait City was met by widespread condemnation while Sunni and Shi'a prayed together in a demonstration of unity. In an attempt to maintain this unity, hate speech was criminalised and in a number of speeches, the Emir made repeated pleas for unity, condemning those wishing to create discord. Claims to unity were echoed by a group of *diwaniyahs* – the Kuwaiti traditional 'gathering lounges' – who stressed the Kuwaiti spirit of devotion and togetherness,[98] while Shi'a political groups occupied a prominent role in the political system as a bulwark against other opposition groups.[99]

Events such as this in Kuwait City and others such as the attack on a Shi'a Mosque in the eastern province of Saudi Arabia reveal the collapse of political and theological tensions. While many are quick to blame Hizballah-type organisations – and by extension Iran – for such actions, in recent years they have been conducted by groups such as Da'ish who wish to capitalise on burgeoning sectarian tensions. Anti-Shi'a rhetoric from Saudi leaders creates a climate where such attacks can take place. This strategy seeks to trap Sunni Arab regimes: either to demonstrate nationalist unity with Shi'a groups and risk alienating Sunni supporters, or to risk further instability by alienating Shi'a groups further.

The increasing sectarianisation of political life has other serious implications. Economic dimensions of sectarian difference are clearly seen in Syria, Lebanon and Bahrain and although events have been framed as sectarian struggles, a more nuanced analysis positions class within socio-political difference. In Lebanon, where society is still recovering from the civil war that left a deep scar on the psyche of the country, along with the more visible aspects of bullet holes across streets around the 'Green

Line', political life is organised along sectarian lines.[100] Yet within such sectarian blocs, economic factors are perhaps the real drivers of division, as wealthy business leaders cultivate difference as a mechanism of ensuring support from their constituencies, while also benefitting from divisions financially.[101] Indeed, in recent years a number of cross-sectarian alliances have emerged,[102] perhaps as a result of the power-sharing agreement. Thus, to reduce political divisions to a theological base wilfully ignores how divisions are being manipulated to suit the needs of a wealthy few.

Returning to the concept of *nomos*, we can see how sectarianisation processes seek to create order over space, but also to close off an inside against an outside, shaped by historical experience. This process of closing is different to previous processes, achieved through the displacement and exclusion of individuals from the inside, essentially closing them off from the community. This takes place through the framing of Shi'a groups as an existential threat to the survival of the community whose loyalties lie with a group that has been closed off against the inside. As a consequence, securitisation and sectarianisation moves seek to solidify the closing off of the inside against an outside, but also to strengthen the bonds of the inside against the outside from within, reordering regional politics in the process.

Necropolitics and war machines

Amid conditions of uncertainty and increasing violence, regimes sought to retain power through a plethora of strategies. While some reformed political structures, others sought to control life by stripping it of political meaning. In some cases, the fragmentation of the state meant that these strategies were not viable, leading to the emergence of necropolitics and mobilisation of war machines in a final attempt to exert sovereign power and ensure regime survival. In a number of states, regimes embarked on a dangerous yet calculated gambit designed to secure their rule by mobilising jihadist movements to create – and escalate – sectarian violence. Within such environments, regimes used excessive violence to regulate life, resulting in catastrophic loss of life and devastating humanitarian conditions. One consequence of this is the mobilisation of war machines – the manifestation of disruption against sovereign power – as an expression of agency.

The case of Da'ish offers a good example of the emergence of war machines out of fragmentation and the contestation of sovereign power in the years after the 2003 war.

An array of mistakes from Iraqi, US, UK and Iranian governments empowered Sunni militancy and amid conditions of marginalisation, securitisation and existential crises they drew support from people marginalised from political and economic structures. Fundamentally, the group was able to emerge as a consequence of the failure of Sunnis to find political representation, either formally or informally,[103] yet it is now generally accepted that the key strategists in the group were ex-Ba'athists, operating beyond state structures.

In conditions of uncertainty, around 50 PMUs emerged, with membership estimated to be between 60,000 and 140,000 people.[104] The identities of the PMUs provided opportunities for external actors to become involved in political life, raising questions about Iranian involvement and, in the longer term, debates about integration. In the struggle against Da'ish, militias played a key role in the liberation of Mosul and as such, Baghdad's efforts to curtail the power and influence of the groups bringing them into the institutional machinery of the state – many of whom had 'given blood' for Iraq – was met with a great deal of resistance.

This move sought to end the existence of the PMUs as war machines, although the level of criminality involved with such groups means that Baghdad may not be fully able to put an end to them. Yet the move evoked questions about the groups more broadly and the role of clerics such as Iraq's leading Shi'a cleric Grand Ayatollah Ali Sistani, who issued a number of fatwas calling on Iraqis to engage in political life in a number of often contradictory ways in the fifteen years after the US-led invasion. These not only mobilised Iraqis, but imbued lives with meaning, taking them from conditions of bare life into a more qualified political existence, revealing the impact of religious figures on political life.

In Yemen, the fragmentation of political organisation created space for countless groups and factions – often with competing agendas – to operate within the territorial shell of the state.[105] Underpinning the social fabric of the state was a complex and malleable tribal network that was shaped by the concerns of their respective leaders, leading to a range of transient alliances that cut across society. Groups possessed a range of different political aspirations that were driven by the contexts in which they were operating, where poverty, corruption and civil war were rife. Although external borders of the state have proved somewhat durable, internally a number of 'mini-states' each held together by its own internal logic, economy and political ecosystem.[106] The failure of the 2014 National Dialogue appears to contradict such a view, particularly amid the secessionist demands, which remain prevalent.[107] In such conditions, war machines shape Yemeni politics, in many cases often competing and funded by external actors, adding to the complexity and ferocity of the fighting.[108]

The Houthi movement fought six wars with the Saleh regime between 2004 and 2010, during which time the group evolved from small cadre of fighters comprised of the family and friends of Hussein Badr Al Din Al Huthi, the group's leader, into an organisation that would pose an existential challenge to Saleh's leadership. Although routinely referred to an Iranian proxy, the Houthis were formed as an independent entity operating with national goals, yet Tehran's influence has increased in recent years.

The Houthi movement – which took on the formal name Ansar Allah, the Partisans of God, in 2011 – is one that is comprised of a range of fluid alliances, both overt and covert, but predicated on a 'precise knowledge' of tribal dynamics, albeit supported by Iran and Hizballah.[109] The fluidity of their alliances is seen in their willingness to work with Saleh, which allowed Ansar Allah to co-opt forces loyal to the former President, to capture Sana'a on 21 September 2014. Less than six months later, the group also overran the Yemeni government's 'fallback' capital of Aden in the longest-range operation ever conducted by the group, reflecting its ability to draw upon local grievances and create alliances in an incredibly complex set of political dynamics. In such conditions of fragmentation, war machines took on more formal characteristics of state power, losing some of their fluidity in the process, while regimes took on characteristics of war machines, leading to increased instability and Saudi-led intervention.

Similar complexity is found in conflict zones across the region. As political life fragmented, war machines continued to emerge, capitalising on the elasticity of political structures. With the erosion of sovereign power, groups began to offer support and protection to communities across the region. Such conditions were exacerbated by the sectarianisation of regional politics, which imbued local politics with new meaning, often derived from geopolitical struggles. External support for proxies increased the contestation of sovereign power, adding to the conflation of regional and domestic politics that began to collapse into each other, along with the emergence of war machines that challenged political projects in Iraq, Syria, Lebanon, Gaza and Yemen.

Of course, the emergence of a war machine is not a new phenomenon. Indeed, if we look at the history of the region, when sovereignty fragments, war machines emerge, further adding to the contestation of power. Within the context of sectarianisation, the manifestation of this type of war machine often serves to reproduce sectarian difference, particularly when they are sponsored by external actors propagating their own agendas. The emergence of increasingly violent war machines documents the weakness of sovereign power and the strength of *asabiyyah* amid political fragmentation. In such conditions, the sect emerges as a new form of life as regimes practice necropolitics on marginalised masses, along sect-based lines. In pursuit of such an aim, war machines from the same *asabiyyah* are often co-opted, subsumed into state structures as a mechanism of control. Although seemingly against the deterritorialised nature of the concept, this reveals the fluidity of sovereign power and complexity of different logics deployed to regulate life. Such an approach also serves as a mechanism to colonise life 'from below', defining the inside against an outside, restricting and regulating life in the process.

Beyond the manifestation of war machines, other regimes have sought to maintain sovereign power through recourse to necropolitics. The brutality of the Assad regime was seen in the early days of the uprisings but by this point, it was well versed in dealing with challenges to its rule, much like a number of its neighbours. Since Hafez Al Assad came to power in 1971, political activity was limited through the violent regulation of life and subjugation of it to death in times of crisis, such as in Hama. In 2011, protestors stressed the peaceful nature of their actions, offering flowers, food and water to soldiers that had been sent to crush their expressions of political dissent. In response, a number of prominent individuals were arrested, tortured and killed; their mutilated bodies were later returned to their families for burial. Tens of thousands of protesters were 'disappeared' into government prisons, where tales of torture and inhumane cruelty continue to be told. This was, as Al Haj Saleh notes, the action of a colonial aggressor, internal to the very structure of the state.

In Syria, death became a consequence of torture, not a by-product of it, and as a consequence necropolitics became the logic of governmentality through which the Syrian state exerted power and subjected large segments of the population to 'political and symbolic extermination'.[110] With the escalation of the conflict, the Syrian regime used chemical weapons on its own population, seeking to regulate life by subjugating it to death. This was not an isolated incident, but as UN war crimes investigators suggested, by April 2018, there were thirty-four confirmed cases of the use of chemical weapons.[111]

The Assad regime used all possible mechanisms to regulate life and death, drawing on a range of issues including the exclusionary ideas of 'Absolute Arabism', sectarian difference and the socio-economic climate that had created the Shabiha, a militia with close links to the Assad family. The Shabiha operates as an example of the war machine, regulating life through repression and restriction and making money through appropriation, although in this case war machines were hiding behind the mask of the state. In such conditions, repression transforms into business, a new model of governance that rewards those who are loyal to the regime, allowing Shabiha to make money through appropriating the production of others, while creating – and capitalising upon – conditions of *tashbih* (typically understood in the Syrian context as 'thuggishnesss') that found traction amid sectarian biases and divisions within communities. As violence increased and the regime faced increasingly existential challenges, the Shabiha took on a prominent role in the defence of the regime as security was privatised. Unlike other manifestations of the war machine, this is not just an armed militia. Instead, and this point should be carefully stressed, it is a powerful state actor with responsibilities that is using its regulatory force to subjugate life to death in support of the regime's goal: survival at all costs.

Rent and reform

In contrast to regimes who used political and legal strategies that were underpinned by the use of violence, others responded in different ways. Those predicated upon the rentier bargain were able to draw upon a variety of methods to placate protest movements, essentially buying off protest movements within the context of the current social contract. Yet a number of regimes also engaged in reform of political systems and those involved in political life.

The largest of all reform packages was in Saudi Arabia – representing the fear felt by many in the Al Saud about the consequences of protests breaking out across the kingdom – where a welfare package of around $130 billion was announced. Bigger than the state's 2007 budget, it contained a raft of new jobs in the Ministry of Interior – adding to the burgeoning public sector employment problem – along with five hundred thousand new houses, an increased minimum wage and general infrastructural improvements.[112] It was supplemented by a number of reforms, including permitting women to vote and run in municipal elections.[113] In Bahrain, twenty thousand new jobs were promised in the Ministry of Interior.[114] The UAE offered around $2 billion for new housing loans, dwarfed by Qatar's pledge of $8 billion for salary and benefit payments. In the UAE, around $1.55 billion was invested into infrastructural projects and commitments to keep food prices low. In Kuwait, around $3,500 was given to each national along with a promise that basic food items would be free for two years.[115]

In March 2011 a GCC fund was established for Bahrain and Oman that saw Manama and Muscat receiving $10 billion each over a ten-year period to facilitate infrastructure developments. It was later announced that the GCC fund would also provide developmental assistance worth $5 billion to both Jordan and Morocco, alongside debate about expanding the GCC.[116] It was through the provision of financial assistance that Saudi Arabia began to take on an increasingly prominent regional role, using its financial might to influence actors amid widespread instability.

While few Gulf states suffered serious damage in the uprisings, the situation worsened in 2014, when the price of oil dropped around 70% over the previous year. The impact was felt across the region, where spending was dramatically cut and harsh austerities measures were imposed in Saudi Arabia after an IMF report suggested that the kingdom would run out of money within five years at its current rate.[117] This prompted a raft of new policies aimed at invigorating the kingdom's economy, spearheaded by a new Crown Prince, Mohammad bin Salman. While Saudi Arabia was the outlier, other states across the region were also affected, requiring serious reconsideration of social contracts and political organisation. Ultimately, the Gulf states – Bahrain aside – were largely able to circumvent unrest by updating their social contracts but this required ongoing demonstrations of responsibility towards citizens.

Others undertook minor reform as a mechanism of placating protesters. In Jordan, forty-two minor constitutional amendments were issued,[118] along with changes to electoral laws. Electoral laws were also changed in Kuwait[119] while religious figures were banned from standing in elections in Bahrain.[120] In Oman, a number of ministers were removed from office following protester demands to eradicate corruption. Constitutional reform in the aftermath of the uprisings both acquiesced to protester demands as in Egypt and Oman, but also reverted back to characteristics of the *ancien régime*, as in Yemen, where following the removal of Ali Abdullah Salah, the country returned to single-candidate elections for the office of president. Constitutional reform in moments of disjuncture is a characteristic feature of the Middle East. During the 1950s and 1960s, amid a period of political turmoil, constitutions became malleable documents through which political agendas were expressed. Yet although agendas were expressed in a number of states, the complexity of political situations and deep grievances created conditions that could be triggered into mass violence.

The uprising and the *coup d'état*

The story of the Muslim Brotherhood's rise – and fall – in the years after the Arab Uprisings is perhaps emblematic of the struggle over political life in the Middle East and competing visions of the ordering of space.[121] After the toppling of Hosni Mubarak, the military retained control under the leadership of SCAF, revoking emergency legislation[122] and holding parliamentary and presidential elections across 2011–12 that resulted in the election of the Muslim Brotherhood candidate, Mohammad Morsi, and a number of candidates from the Freedom and Justice Party. While in power, many expressed concerns at the extent to which Morsi and the Brotherhood had been able to undertake serious change within state institutions and infrastructure. As Nathan Brown noted, the power of the deep state in Egypt meant that Morsi was unable to exert serious influence over the military and security services, leaving him without real power.[123]

Although in the early stages of the uprisings the official line of the Brotherhood was to remain neutral, younger members of the organisation played an integral role in driving events.[124] In spite of deep schisms within the *ikhwan* between those who advocated neutrality and those who desired more involvement, prior to the 'Day of Rage', the group announced that it was endorsing the protest movements, calling on its members to join protesters in the streets.[125] This decision was essential in increasing the legitimacy of the *ikhwan*, where the group's members were praised for their courage.[126]

After almost sixty years of political marginalisation, the Muslim Brotherhood was invited into the SCAF-supervised interim administration to participate in a nation dialogue to shape the future of Egypt.[127] In presidential elections, the Ikhwan sought to 'participate, not to dominate' with the goal of working towards a vision of national unity.[128] A spokesperson for the group stressed that they were 'wiling to form an alliance with the political forces that agree to our principles, whether they are socialists, liberals, or other Islamist forces and all forces concerned about this homeland'.[129]

The founding statement of the Freedom and Justice Party, the Brotherhood's political wing, stressed the goal of inclusion, working to rebuild state institutions and aspiring to cultivate the Egyptian political community.[130] On 24 June 2012, Mohammed Morsi was appointed as President of Egypt with 51.7% of the vote, the first time an Islamist had been democratically chosen to lead a modern Arab state.

In spite of inclusive aspirations, Morsi's rule was not without problems. For some such as Asef Bayat, this was to be expected as the group experienced the transition to 'post-Islamism',[131] yet it was the creation of a new constitution[132] that gave Morsi and the Brotherhood increasingly authoritarian powers – and emergency powers that went beyond those of Mubarak – which was ultimately the cause of their downfall as they failed to live up to their promise of inclusion and creating an Egypt for all.[133] Ultimately, the constitution sought to strengthen the Brotherhood's position as a means of overcoming the political deadlock that had consumed the country.[134]

In protest at the new constitution, sit-ins and marches quickly followed the constitutional decree and Morsi's intention to hold a referendum on its application. Once again, thousands of people entered Tahrir Square to protest against the regime where they were met by *ikhwan* supporters.[135] In early December, clashes took place across Cairo between protesters and supporters of the *ikhwan* while chants reminiscent of early 2011 rang out.[136] In the months leading up to the *coup d'état*, Morsi's government lost what little support it had retained after the constitutional crisis and on 3 July 2013, Morsi was forced from power.[137] In the aftermath of the *coup d'état*, the military once again seized power, demonstrating the power and prevalence of the 'deep state'.

Reflecting increased insecurity following the coup, Emergency Law No. 162 of 1958[138] was reinstated by presidential decree on 13 August 2013. Derogation occurred to allow for the clearing of two Muslim Brotherhood camps[139] leaving six hundred dead and four thousand injured in what would become known as the Rabaa Massacre, where sovereign power was exerted by controlling death.[140]

Conclusions: the failure of the uprisings?

On 2 March 2017, an Egyptian court of appeal found former President Hosni Mubarak innocent of a number of charges including complicity in the murder of protesters in 2011 and corruption. Although sentenced to life in prison in 2012 for conspiracy to murder 239 demonstrators, the case offers a symbolic 'closing of the circle' with the continuation of the deep state that once had Mubarak as its figurehead.[141] Over a year later the Egyptian parliament ratified a draft bill giving immunity and unprecedented privileges to key military officials involved in the Rabaa massacre at the discretion of the President.[142]

In contrast, on 27 November 2017, a Kuwaiti court sentenced fifty people to prison for storming parliament in 2011, including the prominent opposition figure Musallam Al Barrack. Al Barrack, who had previously spoken about how the Al Sabah's response to the uprisings risked dragging the country into 'a dark abyss', was sentenced to nine years, while other protesters received sentences ranging from one to five years. The defendants were comprised of Salafis, members of the Muslim Brotherhood, youth activists and secular figures who had colluded in an anti-corruption protest in November 2011.

Political discourse centred around democracy and governance, while political reform was deemed central to improving the quality of life, but reform was viewed with suspicion by many. As regimes responded to protest movements with violence and Syria and Yemen descended into intractable violence, debate quickly moved away from democracy to focus upon security and stability.[143] As one individual recounted, 'We can't say we have full democracy, but we are educated and progressing. But people don't necessarily want democracy immediately. We saw what happened in Iraq.'[144] Similar arguments continue to be made about events in Syria and Yemen, where regimes across the region are framing democracy and participatory politics as a slippery slope into intractable conflict. Another individual noted that regimes propagate narratives of choice: 'Do you want Syria or us?'[145] As one Omani stressed, 'after the escalation of violence in Syria, people now think that stability is more important'.[146]

The aftermath of the uprisings was a struggle to regulate political life and the struggle between life and death more broadly. Although previous efforts to exert sovereign control were focused on the regulation of life and *letting life live*, in such contested periods, a number of regimes sought to exert control by subjugating life to death. The struggle to regulate life and impose order over space, over *ordnung* and *ortung*, became the central feature of the post-uprisings Middle East. Efforts to retain power through regulating and taking life challenged the territorial organisation of space within the context of the spatialised exception. As sovereign power became contested, the localisation of the exception and the order that regulated it were also challenged. From this, new spaces of possibility emerged, zones of indistinction that could be moulded according to a particular vision, beyond the borders of the state.

A key part of such strategies was the sectarianisation of political life, where a number of Arab regimes sought to frame events within the context of burgeoning Iranian power. In doing so, they spoke to domestic populations and framed events as a consequence of nefarious Iranian influence. Framing events in such a way was a prominent part of closing off an inside against an outside, albeit an outside that had previously been inside, securing the community and contributing to the reorganisation of regional politics. Yet as we shall see, this was not unproblematic amid the complex polarity of the region and the influence of Qatar, Turkey and Israel.

The evolution of sovereign power reveals a great deal about the nature of political organisation within a particular time and space. In Syria and Yemen, where political projects had dramatically fragmented, the recourse to necropolitics and mobilisation of war machines was hardly surprising. As political projects had been embedded within – and shaped by – parabolic regional pressures, the creation of new political spaces was almost inevitable, as a number of actors sought to ensure their own survival and improve their standing by dramatically altering the ordering of regional space. In doing this, the struggle to regulate life and define spatial boundaries became even more incendiary, with repercussions across the Middle East.

Notes

1 Some Iranian colleagues reject this claim, instead suggesting that Khomeini's election in 1979 was the first example of this type.
2 Shadi Hamid and Meredith Wheeler argue that the evolution of political life in Egypt was neither 'wholly autocratic nor wholly democratic'. Shadi Hamid and Meredith Wheeler, 'Was Mohammed Morsi Really an Autocrat?' (*Atlantic*, 31.03.14), available at www.theatlantic.com/international/archive/2014/03/was-mohammed-morsi-really-an-autocrat/359797 (accessed 31.03.14). Instead, Hamid suggests that the Morsi regime was reflective of the Brotherhood broadly: a reform-minded organisation but one that advocated gradualism rather than revolution in an attempt to 'wrest control' from the bureaucratic structures of the deep state. Hamid, *Islamic Exceptionalism*.
3 'All According to Plan: The Rab'a Massacre and Mass Killings of Protesters in Egypt' (Human Rights Watch, 12.08.14), available at www.hrw.org/report/2014/08/12/all-according-plan/raba-massacre-and-mass-killings-protesters-egypt (accessed 12.08.14).
4 Ibid.
5 Ibid.
6 Michelle Dunne and Scott Williamson, 'Egypt's Unprecedented Instability by the Numbers' (Carnegie Endowment for International Peace, 24.03.14), available at https://carnegieendowment.org/2014/03/24/egypt-s-unprecedented-instability-by-numbers-pub-55078 (accessed 01.08.19).

7 'UN Human Rights Council: Adoption of the UPR Report on Egypt' (Human Rights Watch, 20.03.15), available at www.hrw.org/news/2015/03/20/un-human-rights-council-adoption-upr-report-egypt (accessed 01.08.19).

8 In the UK, pressure from the Gulf resulted in calls to proscribe the Brotherhood as a terrorist organisation, which was ultimately rejected.

9 Raf Sanchez and Associated Press, 'Journalist in Bahrain was "Murdered by Member of Royal Family", Activists Claim' (Telegraph, 29.12.16), available at www.telegraph.co.uk/news/2016/12/29/journalist-bahrain-murdered-member-royal-family (accessed 16.05.17).

10 Al Haj Saleh, The Impossible Revolution, p. 65.

11 Ibid., p 75.

12 Lefebvre, The Production of Space, p. 26.

13 Mona El-Ghobashy, 'The Praxis of the Egyptian Revolution', Middle East Report, 258 (2011), 2–13.

14 Kasbarian and Mabon, 'Contested Spaces'.

15 Derogation from constitutional responsibilities is permitted under Article 4 of the International Bill of Human Rights.

16 'The Mubarak Regime Persists' (Egyptian Initiative for Personal Rights, 20.09.11), available at https://eipr.org/en/press/2011/09/mubarak-regime-persists (accessed 04.10.14).

17 'Egyptian Constitution Approved in Referendum' (BBC News, 23.12.12), available at www.bbc.co.uk/news/world-middle-east-20829911 (accessed 23.12.12).

18 See Presidential Decree No. 136 of 2014. See also 'Egypt: Decree Allowing Armed Forces to Assist Law Enforcement Agencies in Protecting Government and Public Facilities' (Global Legal Monitor, 06.11.14), available at www.loc.gov/law/foreign-news/article/egypt-decree-allowing-armed-forces-to-assist-law-enforcement-agencies-in-protecting-government-and-public-facilities (accessed 01.08.19).

19 Ibid.

20 '25 January 2013: The Revolution Two Years On … Injustice Continues State Crimes Remained Unpunished: The Interior Ministry Is Above the Law and the Public Prosecution is Missing in Action' (Egyptian Initiative for Personal Rights, 22.01.13), available at https://eipr.org/en/publications/25-january-2013-revolution-two-years-injustice-continues-state-crimes-remained (accessed 22.01.13).

21 Ibid.

22 'Egypt Where Impunity Is Entrenched and Accountability Is Absent' (Egyptian Initiative for Personal Rights, 31.12.14), available at https://eipr.org/en/press/2014/12/egypt-where-impunity-entrenched-and-accountability-absent (accessed 31.12.14).

23 Al Haj Saleh, The Impossible Revolution, p. 96.

24 'Syria protests: Assad to Lift State of Emergency' (BBC News, 20.04.11), available at www.bbc.co.uk/news/mobile/world-middle-east-13134322 (accessed 04.10.14).

25 See Reuters, 'Kuwait Court Hand Down Two Years Jail Sentence for Insulting Emir'.

26 Mabon, 'Kingdom in Crisis'.

27 Georgina Enzer, 'Saudi Arabia Forces All Bloggers to get a License' (ITPnet, 13.01.11); and 'Reactions to Amended Saudi Press and Publications Law Banning Insults to Public Figures' (MEMRI, 31.05.11).

28 See Audrey Macklin, 'Citizenship Revocation, the Privilege to Have Rights and the Production of the Alien', Queen's Law Journal, 40:1 (2014), 1–54; S. Lavi, 'Punishment

and Revocation of Citizenship in the United Kingdom, United States, and Israel', *New Criminal Law Review*, 13:2 (Spring 2010), 404–26; Mathew J. Gibney, 'Should Citizenship be Conditional? The Ethics of Denationalization', *Journal of Politics*, 75:3 (July 2013), 646–58.

29 Zahra Babar, 'The "Enemy Within": Citizenship-Stripping in the Post-Arab Spring GCC', *Middle East Journal*, 71:4 (2017), 525–43.

30 'Bahrain: Hundreds Stripped of Citizenship' (Human Rights Watch, 27.07.18), available at www.hrw.org/news/2018/07/27/bahrain-hundreds-stripped-citizenship (accessed 27.07.18). Such a move has serious implications across all aspects of life, including discrimination in the right to labour markets, advisory rights and capital control rights.

31 Interviews with former Bahraini MP, 2014, 2018, 2019.

32 Zeinab Al Sabeegh, 'Bahrain's Citizenship Policy of Inclusion and Exclusion', in Nils A. Butenschon and Roel. Meijer (eds), *The Middle East in Transition: The Centrality of Citizenship* (Cheltenham: Edward Elgar, 2018), pp. 133–57.

33 Mabon, 'Aiding Revolution'.

34 Gregory, 'Tahrir', p. 244.

35 Interview with Syrian academic, 2017.

36 Yassin-Kassab and Al Shami, *Burning Country*, p. 40.

37 A website provided by the Ministry of Justice provides updates on any travel restrictions from Execution Courts: 'Travel Ban Services' (eGovernment), available at https://services.bahrain.bh/wps/portal/!ut/p/a1/jZBND4IwDIZ_iweutI4B09vEKPhFjCHiLgbNnBpkBlH8-SI3E0V6a_M86duCgBhEljxOKilOOkvSdy-cLWNjr0sYmYR0MUIe9Uhoo2shdSpgUwE2I54_fQMWtZHT6XIQhb6FIbbzvTH3qTtDRMoIBsOBP3R7c8TAaefjj-J_969kBmsQNdZ0RQ00xayBhhwTECrVu_qnG57tLKZA5PIgc5mb97waH4vieusba GBZlqbSWqXS3OuLgd-Uo74VEH-ScL1EUfwMznb6mHHe6bwAiFnolA!!/dl5/d5/L2dBISEvZ0FBIS9nQSEh (accessed 21.10.18).

38 For a full list of those denied entry see 'Access Denied' (Bahrain Watch), available at https://bahrainwatch.org/access (accessed 21.10.18).

39 One interviewee (Syria analyst, 2017) recounted daily arguments with pro-Assad 'trolls' over narratives of the conflict.

40 This is perhaps best seen in British policy towards Syria. In 2013, parliament voted against military strikes against regime targets but in 2015 it voted to strike against Da'ish targets in the country. This inertia was not limited to military action. In an evidence session for the International Relations Committee, then Foreign Secretary Boris Johnson 'flip-flopped' about British policy towards Bashar Al Assad when asked if he should be permitted to stay on in the event of the war ending.

41 Interview with Syria analyst, 2017.

42 Nader Hashemi and Danny Postel, 'Sectarianization: Mapping the New Politics of the Middle East', *Review of Faith and International Affairs*, 15:3 (2017), 3.

43 Ibid. See also Abdo, *The New Sectarianism*.

44 Ibid.

45 Matt McDonald, 'Securitization and the Construction of Security', *European Journal of International Relations*, 14:4 (2008), 570–1.

46 Simon Mabon, 'Muting the Trumpets of Sabotage: Saudi Arabia, the US and the Quest to Securitise Iran', *British Journal of Middle Eastern Studies*, 45:5 (2018), 742–59.

47 Interview with Saudi policy advisor. Stemming from the Iran–Iraq War, there is long-standing suspicion about the loyalty of Shi'a Iraqis. Fear pervaded other arenas – a common theme among interviews.

48 Testimony, Neil Crompton.

49 Sune Engel Rasmussen, 'Iran General's Profile Rises as Tehran Flexes Mideast Muscle' (*Wall Street Journal*, 20.02.18).

50 WikiLeaks, 'Saudi Moi Head Says if U.S. Leaves Iraq, Saudi Arabia will Stand with Sunnis'.

51 'Saudi King Abdullah and Senior Princes on Saudi Policy Towards Iraq' (WikiLeaks, 20.04.08), available at https://wikileaks.org/plusd/cables/08RIYADH649_a.html (accessed 16.11.16).

52 'Counterterrorism Adviser Brennan's Meeting with Saudi King Abdullah' (WikiLeaks, 22.03.14), available at https://wikileaks.org/plusd/cables/09RIYADH447_a.html (accessed 16.11.16).

53 Bruce Riedel, *Kings and Presidents: Saudi Arabia and the United States Since FDR* (Washington, DC: Brookings, 2018).

54 Mabon, 'It's a Family Affair'; Simon Mabon, 'End of the Battle of Bahrain', *Middle East Journal*, 73:1 (2019), 29–50.

55 Ibid.

56 See Mabon and Royle, *Origins of ISIS*; and Simon Mabon, Nationalist Jahiliyyah and the Flag of the Two Crusaders, or: ISIS, Sovereignty, and the Owl of Minerva', *Studies in Conflict and Terrorism*, 40:11 (2017), 966–85.

57 Haddad, ' "Sectarianism" and Its Discontents'.

58 Madawi Al Rashed, 'Sectarianism as Counter-Revolution: Saudi Responses to the Arab Spring', in Hashemi and Postel, *Sectarianization*, pp. 143–58.

59 Mabon, 'The Kingdom and the Glory'.

60 Interview with Saudi journalist, 2017.

61 Javad Zarif, 'Iranian Foreign Minister: "Arab Affairs Are Iran's Business" ' (*Atlantic*, 9 October 2017), available at www.theatlantic.com/international/archive/2017/10/iran-persian-gulf-jcpoa/542421 (accessed 09.10.17).

62 'Bahrain Reacts Angrily to Iranian Territorial Claim on Bahrain' (WikiLeaks, 12.07.07), available at https://wikileaks.org/plusd/cables/07MANAMA650_a.html (accessed 16.11.16). See also Toby Matthiesen, 'Sectarianization as Securitization' in Hashemi and Postel, *Sectarianization*, pp. 199–214.

63 Laurence Louër, 'Sectarianism and Coup-Proofing Strategies in Bahrain', *Journal of Strategic Studies*, 36:2 (2013), 245–60.

64 Interview with Bahraini oil executive, 2013.

65 Gengler, 'Royal Factionalism'. See also Matthiesen, 'Sectarianization as Securitization'.

66 Interview with Bahraini businessman, 2013.

67 Fawaz bin Mohammad Al Khalifa, 'The Gulf States Are Stuck between Isil and Iran' (*Telegraph*, 21.01.16), available at www.telegraph.co.uk/news/worldnews/middleeast/bahrain/12113355/The-Gulf-states-are-stuck-between-Isil-and-Iran.html (accessed 21.01.16).

68 'Luncheon with King Hamad' (WikiLeaks, 15.03.06), available at https://wikileaks.org/plusd/cables/06MANAMA409_a.html (accessed 16.12.15).

69 Interview with Shi'a Bahraini cleric, 2014.

70 Interview with Bahraini oil executive, 2013.

71 Matthiesen, 'Sectarianization'.

72 Josh Halliday and Anushka Asthana, 'Met Police Look at Allegations of Saudi War Crimes in Yemen' (*Guardian*, 02.04.17), available at www.theguardian.com/world/2017/apr/02/met-police-examine-allegations-saudi-arabia-war-crimes-yemen (accessed 02.04.17).
73 Interview with Yemen analyst, 2018.
74 Saeed Kamali Dehghan, 'Saudi Arabia Accuses Iran of "Direct Aggression" Over Yemen Missile' (*Guardian*, 07.11.17), available at www.theguardian.com/world/2017/nov/07/saudi-arabia-accuses- iran-of-supplying-missile-to-houthi-rebels-in-yemen (accessed 07.11.17).
75 Siraj Wahab, 'Missile Attack on Riyadh "an Act of War" by Iran' (*Arab News*, 07.11.17), available at www.arabnews.com/node/1189476/saudi-arabia (accessed 07.11.17).
76 Ibid.
77 Interview with Yemen analyst, 2018.
78 Ibid.
79 Ibid.
80 Stacey Philbrick Yadav, 'Sectarianization, Islamist Republicanism, and International Misrecognition in Yemen', in Hashemi and Postel, *Sectarianization*, p. 188.
81 Interview with Bahraini academic, 2018.
82 Ibid.
83 'The "Arab Spring": Five Years On' (Amnesty International), available at www.amnesty.org/en/latest/campaigns/2016/01/arab-spring-five-years-on (accessed 16.06.16).
84 One should be careful with claims such as this, which once again bely the complexity of events on the ground, where wealthy Sunni families, Sunni Kurds and Turkmen can support the Assad regime for a range of different reasons.
85 See 'Syrian Opinions and Attitudes Towards Sectarianism in Syria: Survey Study' (*The Day After*, 22.02.16), available at http://tda-sy.org/en/publications/english-sectarianism-in-syria-survey-study.html (accessed 07.03.16).
86 Ibid.
87 Testimony, Hayder Al Khoei.
88 Yassin Kassab and Al Shamli, *Burning Country*, p. 77.
89 While a number of Western analysts have criticised the move to violence, this is done from a privileged position of safety, espousing a sense of moral superiority that is both misplaced and damaging.
90 Testimony, Boris Johnson.
91 Al Haj Saleh, *The Impossible Revolution*, p. 61.
92 Testimony, Haid Haid.
93 Interview with Lebanese journalist, 2017.
94 Interview with Syrian academic 2017.
95 'Statement to the Security Council on Missions to Yemen, South Sudan, Somalia and Kenya and an Update on the Oslo Conference on Nigeria and the Lake Chad Region' (United Nations Office for the Coordination of Humanitarian Affairs, 10.03.17), available at https://reliefweb.int/sites/reliefweb.int/files/resources/ERC_USG%20Stephen%20O%27Brien%20Statement%20to%20the%20SecCo%20on%20Missions%20to%20Yemen%2C%20South%20Sudan%2C%20Somalia%20and%20Kenya%2C%20and%20update%20on%20Oslo%20Conference%20-%2010%20March%202017.pdf (accessed 21.01.18).
96 Interview with Yemeni-Emirati student, 2018. See also Mohammed Mukhashaf, 'Southern Yemen Separatists want Saudi-Backed Government Overthrown' (Reuters,

21.01.18), available at https://uk.reuters.com/article/uk-yemen-security-southerners/
southern-yemen-separatists-want-saudi-backed-government-overthrown-
idUKKBN1FA0WT (accessed 21.01.18).

97 A common view expressed in the 'young persons roundtable'.

98 'Kuwaiti "Diwaniyahs" Unite in Condemnation of Mosque Attack, (Kuwait
News Agency, 27.06.15), available at www.kuna.net.kw/ArticleDetails.
aspx?id=2448700&Language=en (accessed 27.06.15).

99 Madeline Wells, 'Sectarianism, Authoritarianism, and Opposition in Kuwait', in
Postel and Hashemi, *Sectarianization*, pp. 235–58.

100 Hannes Baumann, 'Social Protest and the Political Economy of Sectarianism in
Lebanon', *Global Discourse*, 6:4 (2016), 634–49.

101 See interviews with Lebanese journalists, Lebanese policy analysts, Syrian author
2017 and 2018.

102 Interview with Lebanese journalist, 2017.

103 Interview with Iraqi film-maker, 2017.

104 Renad Mansour and Faleh A. Jabar, 'The Popular Mobilisation Forces and Iraq's
Future' (Carnegie Middle East Center, 28.04.17), available at http://carnegie-mec.
org/2017/04/28/popular-mobilisation-forces-and-iraq-s-future-pub-68810 (accessed
28.04.17).

105 One prominent example of this concerns the emergence of strong factions within
the army that had been created by Saleh in an attempt to silo the institution and to
maintain loyalty in times of crisis. As the uprisings escalated, factions in the military
cultivated alliances with tribal groups in pursuit of their own economic interests. The
interaction of military forces with tribal groups reveals both the complexity of civil–
military relations, but also suggests that the very structure of the military that Saleh
had created to ensure his survival would work against him. See Michael Knights, 'The
Military Role in Yemen's Protests: Civil–Military Relations in the Tribal Republic',
Journal of Strategic Studies, 36:2 (2013), 261–88.

106 Peter Salisbury, 'Yemen: National Chaos, Local Order' (Chatham House, 20.12.17),
available at www.chathamhouse.org/publication/yemen-national-chaos-local-order
(accessed 21.12.17).

107 Peter Salisbury, *Yemen: Stemming the Rise of a Chaos State* (London: Royal Institute
of International Affairs, 2016), available at www.chathamhouse.org/publication/
yemen-stemming-rise-chaos-state (accessed 21.12.17).

108 Interview with Yemen analyst, 2018.

109 Michael Knights, *The Houthi War Machine: From Guerrilla War to
State Capture* (Washington, DC: CTC Sentinel, Washington Institute, September
2018), p. 17.

110 Ibid., p. 73.

111 Stephanie Nebehay, 'Syrian Government Forces Used Chemical Weapons More
Than Two Dozen Times: U.N.' (Reuters, 06.09.17), available at www.reuters.
com/article/us-mideast-crisis-syria-warcrimes/syrian-government-forces-used-
chemical-weapons-more-than-two-dozen-times-u-n-idUSKCN1BH18W (accessed
06.09.17). Although the Organisation for the Prevention of Chemical Weapons
received a Nobel Prize for their work getting WMDs out of Syria, in conversation
with a member of the team it was widely acknowledged that they did not get the
whole cache.

112 Steffen Hertog, 'The Cost of the Counter Revolution in the GCC' (Middle East Channel, 31.05.11), available at http://mideast.foreignpolicy.com/posts/2011/05/31/the_costs_of_counter_revolution_in_the_gcc (accessed 01.06.11)

113 Caryle Murphy, 'GCC to Set Up $20bn Bailout Fund for Bahrain and Oman' (National, 11.03.11), available at www.thenational.ae/news/world/middle-east/gcc-to-set-up-20bn-bail- out-fund-for-bahrain-and-oman (accessed 11.03.11).

114 Hertog, 'The Cost of the Counter Revolution in the GCC'.

115 Lin Noueihed and Alex Warren, The Battle for the Arab Spring: Revolution, Counter-Revolution and the Making of a New Era (New Haven, CT: Yale University Press, 2012).

116 'KSA to Finance Morocco Projects Worth $ 1.25 bn' (Arab News, 18.10.12); 'Saudi Arabia to Provide Jordan with $487 million for Development Projects' (Jordan News Agency (Petra), 28.11.12).

117 World Economic and Financial Surveys, Regional Economic Outlook: Middle East and Central Asia (International Monetary Fund, 2015), available at www.imf.org/external/pubs/ft/reo/2015/mcd/eng/pdf/menap1015.pdf (accessed 10.10.16).

118 Zoltan Barany, The 'Arab Spring' in the Kingdoms (Arab Center for Research & Policy Studies, 2012), p. 30, available at www.dohainstitute.org/en/lists/ACRPS-PDFDocumentLibrary/The_Arab_Spring_in_the_Kingdoms.pdf (accessed 11.10.18).

119 Habib Toumi, 'Bahrain MPs Ban Mixing of Politics and Religion' (Gulf News, 11.10.18), available at http://gulfnews.com/news/gulf/bahrain/bahrain-mps-ban-mixing-of-politics-and-religion-1.1830097 (accessed 11.10.18).

120 Ibid.

121 Al Anani, K., 'Upended Path: The Rise and Fall of Egypt's Muslim Brotherhood', Middle East Journal, 69:4 (Autumn 2015), 532; E. Trager, Arab Fall: How the Muslim Brotherhood Won and Lost Egypt in 891 Days (Washington, DC: Georgetown University Press, 2016); E. Balir, P. Taylor and T. Perry, 'Special Report: How the Muslim Brotherhood Lost Egypt' (Reuters, July 2013), available at www.reuters.com/article/us-egypt-mistakes-specialreport-idUSBRE96O07H20130726 (accessed 01.08.13).

122 Marc Lynch, 'Ending Egypt's State of Emergency (Sort Of)' (Foreign Policy, 24.01.12), available at http://mideast.foreignpolicy.com/posts/2012/01/24/ending_egypts_state_of_emergency_sort_of (accessed 24.01.12). See also Al Masry Al Youm, 'EU Urges Egypt to Lift State of Emergency before Elections' (Egypt Independent, 16.05.12), available at www.egyptindependent.com/news/eu-urges-egypt-lift-state-emergency-elections (accessed 16.05.12).

123 Nathan J. Brown, 'Mrs Lincoln's Egyptian Constitution' (Foreign Policy, 20.08.13), available at http://mideast.foreignpolicy.com/posts/2013/08/20/mrs_lincoln_s_egyptian_constitution?wp_login _redirect=0 (accessed 20.08.13).

124 C. Wickham, The Muslim Brotherhood: Evolution of an Islamist Movement (Princeton, NJ: Princeton University Press, 2013), p. 155.

125 S. Brooke and S. Hamid, 'The Muslim Brotherhood's Role in the Egyptian Revolution', CTC Sentinel, 4:2 (February 2011), 2.

126 Dina Ezzat, 'Tactical Gains' (Al-Ahram Weekly, No. 1034, 2011), available at http://weekly.ahram.org.eg/Archive/2011/1034/sc51.htm (accessed 21.12.17).

127 Tarek Osman, *Egypt on the Brink* (New Haven, CT: Yale University Press, 2013). p. 119.
128 Ikhwan Web, 'MB Chairman: We Seek to Participate Not to Dominate' (Ikhwan Web, April 2011), available at www.ikhwanweb.com/article.php?id=28432 (accessed 01.05.15).
129 Zaid, M., 'El Erian to Political Parties: Win Votes Than Discuss Power' (Ikhwan Web, June 2011), available at www.ikhwanweb.com/article.php?id=28713 accessed 01.05.15).
130 The Founding Statement of the Freedom and Justice Party, available at www.fjponline.com/view.php?pid=1.
131 Ibid.
132 'English Text of Morsi's Constitutional Declaration' (Ahram Online, 22.11.12), available at http://english.ahram.org.eg/News/58947.aspx (accessed 22.11.12).
133 Muge Aknur, 'The Muslim Brotherhood in Politics in Egypt: From Moderation to Authoritarianism?', *Uluslararası Hukuk ve Politika*, 9:33 (2013), 11. See also Ibrahim El Houdaiby, 'From Prison to Palace: The Muslim Brotherhood's Challenges and Responses in Post-Revolution Egypt', *FRIDE*, 117 (February 2013).
134 Marc Lynch, 'Morsi's Mixed Moves', in *POMEPS Briefings: The Battle for Egypt's Constitution* (January 2013), pp. 10–12; M. Revkin, 'Egypt's Untouchable President', in *POMEPS Briefings: The Battle for Egypt's Constitution* (January 2013), pp. 13–15; M. Mabrouk, 'The View from a Distance: Egypt's Contentious New Constitution', in *Brookings: Middle East Memo, No. 28* (January 2013).
135 Haroon Siddique, 'Mohamed Morsi Supporters and Opponents Clash in Cairo' (*Guardian*, 05.12.12), available at www.theguardian.com/world/2012/dec/05/morsi-supporters-opponents-clash-cairo (accessed 05.12.12).
136 'Egypt Crisis: fatal Cairo Clashes amid Constitutional Row' (BBC News, 06.12.12), available at www.bbc.com/news/world-middle-east-20605134 (accessed 06.12.12).
137 Abigail Hauslohner, William Boot and Sharaf Al Hourani, 'Egyptian Military Ousts Morsi, Suspends Constitution' (*Washington Post*, 03.07.13), available at www.washingtonpost.com/world/egypts-morsi-defiant-under-pressure-as-deadline-looms/2013/07/03/28fda81c-e39d-11e2-80eb-3145e2994a55_story.html (accessed 03.07.13).
138 Emergency Law no. 162/1958: Official Gazette of 28 September 1958, no. 28, Bis.; 'State of Emergency: What Does It Imply?' (Ahram Online, 14.08.13), available at http://english.ahram.org.eg/NewsContent/1/64/79036/Egypt/Politics-/State-of-emergency-What-does-it-imply-.aspx; 'Emergency Law [no. 162/1952 in translation]' (Carnegie Endowment for International Peace, 14.08.13), http://egyptelections.carnegieendowment.org/2010/09/09/emergency-law (accessed 06.03.13).
139 David D. Kirkpatrick, 'Hundreds Die as Egyptian Forces Attack Islamist Protesters' (*New York Times*, 14.08.13), available at www.nytimes.com/2013/08/15/world/middleeast/egypt.html?pagewanted=all &_r=0. (accessed 14.08.13).
140 See www.hrw.org/report/2014/08/12/all-according-plan/raba-massacre-and-mass-killings-protesters-egypt. See also Maggie Michael, 'Death Toll Soars to 638 in Egypt

Violence' (Associated Press, 15.08.13), available at http://bigstory.ap.org/article/after-hundreds-killed-egypt-faces-new-uncertainty.

141 'Mubarak Acquitted in Final Ruling on Egypt's Arab Spring Deaths' (*Guardian*, 02.03.17), available at www.theguardian.com/world/2017/mar/02/hosni-mubarak-acquitted-in-final-ruling-on-egypts-arab-spring-deaths (accessed 02.03.17).

142 Rami Galal, 'Sisi Grants Privileges, Immunity to Egypt's Military Brass' (*Al-Monitor*, 11.07.18), available at www.al-monitor.com/pulse/originals/2018/07/bill-armed-forces-senior-commanders-immunity-privileges.html (accessed 11.07.18). It also circumvents potential challenges from the military as it allows the President to call all such individuals back to active service.

143 Roundtable testimony.

144 Ibid.

145 Ibid.

146 Ibid.

8

Houses built on sand

The crisis consists in the fact that the old [order] is dying and the new cannot be born; in this interregnum a large variety of morbid symptoms appear.

Antonio Gramsci, *Passato e presente*

Ana wa akhi ala ibn ammi, ana wa ibn ammi ala algharib.
[My brother and I against our cousin, my cousin and I against a stranger.]

An old Beouin saying

In the fallout from the Arab Uprisings, a number of parallels have been drawn with the Thirty Years' War across Europe in the seventeenth century.[1] Take the opening lines of an article by Richard Haas, President of the Council on Foreign Relations:

It is a region wracked by religious struggle between competing traditions of the faith. But the conflict is also between militants and moderates, fueled by neighboring rulers seeking to defend their interests and increase their influence. Conflicts take place within and between states; civil wars and proxy wars become impossible to distinguish. Governments often forfeit control to smaller groups – militias and the like – operating within and across borders. The loss of life is devastating, and millions are rendered homeless. That could be a description of today's Middle East. In fact, it describes Europe in the first half of the seventeenth century.[2]

Although the parallels are obvious, this argument reveals a great deal about analysis of the region, drawing upon Eurocentric approaches and linear trajectories of development. Moreover, as Lorenzo Kamel suggests, this is part of a broader project of 'medievalising' the region, reducing identities to sectarian schisms that have their roots in what Barack Obama referred to as 'ancient hatreds' that have defined the history of

Islam.[3] This approach is part of a broader Orientalist strategy to 'other' the Middle East and neglects the multifarious factors that underpin the emergence of different types of involvement and relationships that are shaping the region.

Others have sought to categorise recent events as efforts to bring congruence to nation and state amid the alleged imposition of Western conceptions of statehood.[4] Efforts to exert power and regulate life amid the presence of powerful movements has had a devastating impact on regional politics. The spread of ideas and ideologies across state borders routinely opened up schisms between regimes and societies and, in turn, shaped the spatial landscape. Amid the presence of a shared normative environment populated by a melange of identities and ideologies within and across state borders, what happens in one state has the capacity to impact upon political life in another. Thus, regime efforts to maintain domestic power are predicated upon regional machinations, which may also impact upon domestic politics.

Central to such fusion is a concern with creating order and regulating space. Agamben's global *nomos*, the spatialised localisation of the unlocalisable exception shapes international politics. Conditioned by neo-liberal modernity, the emergence of political projects fall in line with such visions. Yet as we have seen, conditions that facilitate *ordnung* and *ortung* have become increasingly contested, creating new spaces that challenge the organisation and ordering of space. State-building projects created zones of indistinction, which are simultaneously spaces of restriction and spaces of possibility to be moulded in accordance with local context and contingency. With the complex relationship between *ordnung* and *ortung*, new possibilities emerge for the reorganisation of political life.

Zones of indistinction and possibility emerge in numerous forms, perhaps most obviously as a consequence of competing theological and political interpretations of sovereign power. In discussions with people across the region about the nature of statehood, prominent themes included legitimacy deficits and the erosion of the sovereign state.[5] Amid the presence of a wide range of groups exerting power and influence within and across territorial borders, legitimate claims to sovereign control and authority become increasingly complex. In a number of cases, two or more groups exert regulatory power over people in particular territorial areas, not necessarily spatially bounded, leading to competition domestically and regionally.[6]

With the onset of the uprisings, new arenas of competition emerged which brought together local and regional actors, simultaneously serving as zones of possibility and restriction as international players sought to manipulate domestic affairs often for their own ends.[7] Yet the increasingly securitised and politicised role of religion, particularly within the context of the rivalry between Saudi Arabia and Iran has left regimes open to criticism while state security is undermined by the ability of clerics in one state to speak to audiences in another. When domestic audiences are framed as a security threat, it is hardly surprising that some communities are perceived to have sought guidance and support from co-ethnic or sectarian kin.[8] Evoking memories of Paul Noble's regional echo chamber, this chapter shows how the fallout from the Arab Uprisings has consequences for the organisation of the contemporary Middle East.

Echo chambers and zones of possibility

Most scholars typically agree that the arrangement of Middle Eastern politics and security is fundamentally different to the 2003 landscape, where new ways of ordering space have emerged, appearing to take on sectarian characteristics and underpinned by anti-Iranian sentiment. Yet it is easy to misrepresent such change. As the late Fred Halliday noted, 'There are two predictable, and nearly always mistaken, responses to any great international upheaval: one is to say that everything has changed; the other is to say that nothing has changed.'[9] The answer, of course, is somewhere in-between, albeit contingent on time, place and space.

The toppling of Saddam Hussein created a 'new' space of competition between Saudi Arabia and Iran, which escalated after the uprisings of 2011.[10] As we saw earlier, Morten Valbjørn and André Bank argue that it is generally accepted that the region is 'qualitatively different from earlier days', yet in spite of this difference, they argue that the Middle East is still shaped by a form of Arab nationalism and shared ethnic experiences.[11] Jerrold Green's comments in a 1986 article that 'Arab politics is still Arab'[12] remains true, documenting that although nationalist concerns remain, they are located within geopolitical machinations and the framing of a 'Persian other' alongside sectarianisation to argue that recent events are still shaped by nationalist concerns. This view has clear resonance in 'high politics', but has also found traction within states, particularly those who are sites of direct competition between the Saudis and the Iranians. With this in mind, Paul Noble's comments about the Middle Eastern echo chamber as 'a set of interconnected organisms separated only by porous membranes, or, alternatively a large-scale domestic system divided into compartments of varying degrees of permeability' remain relevant.[13]

Central to the organisation of regional politics is the ability of religion to shape the conflation and calibration of space and politics, driven both by local and regional contexts.[14] While the 2003 war in Iraq facilitated the emergence of violence along sect-based lines – driven by the vociferously anti-Shi'a rhetoric of Abu Musab Al Zarqawi, the leader of Al Qa'ida in Iraq – the 2006 Hizballah war with Israel brought sectarian politics into regional calculations. Breaking norms in the 'Arab game of politics', Saudi Arabia, Jordan and Egypt publically rebuked Hizballah's decision to go to war, demonstrating concern at the popularity of Hassan Nasrallah and the group more broadly.[15] In spite of these concerns, in the aftermath of war the kingdom used its financial reserves to help rebuild Dahiyeh, in spite of sectarian difference, perhaps suggesting that the kingdom was held hostage by the remnants of Arab nationalist norms and its enmity towards Israel. Twelve years later, it is hard to envisage such behaviour from the Al Saud.

The fallout from the Arab Uprisings once again demonstrated the collapse of the distinction between internal and external as actors from across the region became embroiled in the domestic affairs of other states. Of course, this is hardly a new phenomenon, as we saw with Arab nationalism, but in recent years this has taken on increasing sect-based dimensions. As a consequence, when political crises emerge, they are also located within broader regional dynamics. Events in Syria offer a good example of this, transforming, as Bassell Saloukh suggests, from a Leviathan to a weak state, penetrated by regional actors as a consequence of the interplay between domestic and regional forces.[16] In spite of this weakness, the Assad regime has exercised brutal force over its population, using all manner of strategies to regulate life and to subjugate life to death.

As the war escalated, it took on regional and international importance as a zone of indistinction, caught in competition between Iran and Saudi Arabia, and Russia and the United States. A range of networks were mobilised to shape the conflict, along sectarian, ethnic, tribal and familial lines, creating a situation that was far more complex than the reductive analysis of 'ancient hatreds' or 'proxy wars' suggest. The collapsing distinction of internal and external is not limited to Syria as events in Lebanon, Bahrain, Yemen and Iraq reveal. Although this distinction is predominantly a consequence of security calculations, economic factors remain important both independently and as a part of security calculations concerns, amid the provision of support for communal groups across state borders.[17] Fundamentally, it is about regimes wanting to create order and stability.

While sovereignty and respect for the sanctity of territorial borders is routinely used as a mechanism to both justify and criticise political action across the region, the extent to which the norm of sovereignty is sacrosanct is contingent upon context.[18] For many, external interference in the domestic affairs was seen as a 'tool of repression'[19] as networks were mobilised across state borders. Yet in order to mobilise these networks, political and socio-economic conditions must facilitate interactions between local and global. Here, we see how contingent factors shape different contexts, even within shared normative environments. For instance, although a growing number of young people advocate the separation of religion and politics,[20] the power of religion within informal power structures is undeniable, shaping social, economic and political landscapes, with repercussions for spatial ordering.[21]

As a consequence, the need to contextualise events is paramount, requiring the location of events within local and regional environments and the identification of contingent factors that shape action. Of course, such contexts are underpinned by broader economic trends, as a consequence of globalisation and neoliberal agendas that collapse the distinction between internal and external.[22] Such neoliberal forces also play an important role in shaping the political landscape, both economically and socially. Widespread investment in Lebanon has fed into increasingly visible economic divides across urban environments, which in turn have political and social consequences.[23] Such economic divides have political and social dimensions resulting in the reproduction of sectarian identities alongside the emergence of powerful mafias such as the Shahiba in Syria who capitalise on local contexts for their own ends.[24]

Amid the melange of identities across the Middle East, how a regime behaves towards one group will have repercussions with regard to how such a group behaves in response. The spread of identities creates space for – and the perception of – external involvement and manipulation of particular causes; local grievances and agendas quickly become imbued with regional meaning. In Syria, Sunni groups are said to frame themselves as Salafi in an attempt to secure money from Saudi Arabia, as members often changed their names to something more 'appropriate' to derive money from the kingdom.[25]

Reform in one state is also seen to have implications for groups in another. In Bahrain, a Saudi-imposed red line is alleged to have prevented the emergence of a democratically elected second chamber to thwart the proliferation of democratic aspirations into the eastern province of Saudi Arabia.[26] This same red line also resulted in the removal of the Crown Prince from the public eye after an ill-fated effort to facilitate dialogue between opposition groups and the ruling family.[27]

The conflation of internal and external agendas also shaped the character of institutional structures, as fragmenting sovereignty left institutions open to the influence of regional actors. In Iraq, for instance, the police were perceived by some to be 'controlled not by the Ministry of the Interior (MOI) but by the Islamic Supreme Council of Iraq (ISCI)/Badr, particularly in Karbala, Diwaniyah and Nasiriyah'.[28] Moreover, the evisceration of state infrastructure in post-2003 Iraq left many Sunnis unemployed amid social and political chaos, and increasing the target of Shi'a militias.[29] In early 2017, PMUs such as Badr were integrated into formal state structures with the establishment of a parallel military force, much to the chagrin of Sunni communities whose experiences of marginalisation and violence at the hands of the PMUs appear to have been ignored.[30]

Sectarianisation as geopolitics *by other means*

On 2 January 2016, Saudi Arabia executed the Shi'a cleric Nimr Al Nimr for his involvement in protests in the eastern province. Sheikh Nimr had long been an advocate of political reform in Saudi Arabia, a staunch critic of authoritarian rule and a prominent figure in the uprisings in 2011. In response, protests broke out across the eastern province, in Kashmir, Pakistan, and protesters stormed the Saudi consulate in Tehran as Nimr's execution was met with global condemnation.[31] A few months earlier, in a much less covered event, Kuwaiti officials arrested a number of nationals amid suggestions that they had been planning an attack against the state;[32] it was alleged that the group was supported by Iran. Of course, most forms of domestic unrest across the region, particularly after the uprisings, have been framed as a consequence of nefarious Iranian behaviour.

Following the fragmentation of sovereign structures, power has shifted away from a number of regimes, providing scope for the emergence of powerful war machines in the guise of militias, mafias and gangs, often underpinned by sectarian identities.[33]

This transformation has provided opportunities for actors to seek to shape the region in accordance with their own image, with repercussions for domestic politics in the process. Thus, geopolitical ambitions have seen actors mobilising and harnessing the power of religious identities and groups along sectarian lines across the region in what has become known as the sectarianisation of politics.[34]

This type of strategy served to support narratives of Iranian manipulation and interference. Narratives supporting sectarianisation have had a serious impact on people across the region, not only in terms of their political performances but also concerning their own identities within the context of an evolving and increasingly precarious environment. There are regional and domestic repercussions of the sectarianisation of political life. As political contexts become imbued with sectarian tensions, the ordering of space takes on a geopolitically charged meaning, with Saudi Arabia at the vanguard of efforts to counter the Iranian threat. Efforts to challenge this ordering creates a precarious environment, as we shall see below.

In a changing geopolitical environment, narratives espousing the construction of a Shi'a crescent and cultivating fears of the Persian other became more prominent, as regimes sought to frame domestic events as a consequence of regional machinations. For a large number of Sunni Arabs across the Gulf, Iranian activity is the source of instability across the Middle East, resulting in the increasing politicisation and securitisation of the region.[35] Regime responses to protest movements were framed as necessary retorts to perfidious action from fifth columnists supported by Tehran. Conflicts emerging from the fragmentation or weakness of state structures took on new meaning as they became shaped by geopolitical agendas. Local groups became embroiled in regional dynamics and vice versa, albeit the capacity of regional actors to affect change locally was determined by both power and perceptions of legitimacy.[36] In the early stages of protests, events in Bahrain and Yemen were largely free of sectarian traits, but as external actors became more prominent, local context was given new meaning by incoming actors. In some cases there were suggestions that local groups took advantage of such events, moulding their identities according to the perceived wishes of external actors in search of funding, although this suggests a rather transient and instrumentalised view of identity.[37]

A wide range of tactics have been used to achieve sectarianisation, shaped by context-specific contingent factors. Although the prominence of religion provides scope for politicians to use religious and sectarian discourses for their own ends, this is seen to offer a means to 'to mobilise and manipulate their people', and we must locate broader narratives within local contexts.[38] Yet as Haid Haid stresses, we must distinguish between the motives of local and regional actors, which may coalesce at times but may not have the same objectives.[39] By doing this, we are better placed to see how geopolitical aims have been achieved through recourse to sectarian membership. This distinction also helps us consider how sectarian identities have been manipulated by sectarian *entrepreneurs*, those who are able to manipulate sectarian boundaries and who 'profit from these boundaries become the defining markers of a particular segment of society'.[40] While sectarian entrepreneurs play a prominent role in shaping socio-political climates, they are conditioned by the interaction of local context and contingency, and the rhythms of regional forces, facilitating the *sectarianisation* of political life.

The sectarianisation of political life has serious implications for the regulation of life more broadly, for both states and their peoples. One journalist suggested that viewing events through a sectarian prism is how people have had to define themselves in order to survive. Essentially, 'it is a way of saying I am less likely to be killed by this person than if I align with that person'.[41] While such analysis may appear reductive, the conflation of politics, economics and sect has loaded sect-based identities with existential importance, to the extent that the interaction of each facet shapes the other. In places such as Lebanon, sectarian dimensions risk becoming all encompassing, providing business elites – both legitimate and mafias – with the mechanisms to increase their profit margins and political elites with mechanisms of control. Quickly this became an existential issue, not because of sectarian difference itself, but because of the political and economic manifestations of this difference and the ways in which this plays out across all aspects of life.[42]

One possible response to such issues is to move to a federal model, such as in Lebanon, or to formalise the quasi-federalism in operation across Iraq, yet this too is problematic.[43] While the current Prime Minister Haider Al Abadi recognises decentralisation as a mechanism to empower local communities within the context of a nationalist project, his predecessor Nouri Al Maliki viewed decentralisation as a 'hidden plot' and part of an agenda to divide the country. Others suggest that opening Iraq – and indeed Syria will 'open Pandora's box', resulting in 'a race to the bottom in each individual canton [over] who is more Sunni, who is more Shia who is more Kurdish'.[44] Supporting this perception, Haider Al Khoei argued that unlike a century ago, if Iraq were to be partitioned, 'it is not going to be white men in suits meeting in London and Paris drawing lines on a piece of paper and imposing them; it is going to be young, angry armed men on the ground who will impose, change or redraw those lines with their blood'.[45] Acknowledging the concern about increasing instability and Iranian influence in Iraq, Saudi Arabia has attempted to build alliances with a number of Shi'a parties who are seen as 'nationalist', including with Moqtada Al Sadr.[46]

Much like in Iraq, the fragmentation of Syria drew in regional and international actors working towards their own geopolitical goals.[47] The provision of support to a range of different sides in a multi-faceted conflict served to entrench divisions that quickly took on sectarian dimensions through a policy of sect-coding by the Assad regime, creating an intractability that prevents the swift resolution of the conflict. In contrast to events in Bahrain and Yemen, where Saudi efforts sought to preserve the status quo, in Syria – much like Iraq – Riyadh attempted to topple the Assad regime to reduce Iranian influence across the Levant. As Madawi Al Rasheed notes, Saudi policy in Syria can be described as an attempt to 'win Syria back to the Arab fold', in doing so, dramatically reducing Iranian influence across the region. Yet the internationalisation of the conflict geographically and through the spread of Wahhabism helped to secure the survival of the Assad regime while also making the conflict increasingly intractable.

In Egypt, the election of Mohammad Morsi as President posed a different kind of challenge to Saudi Arabia and the UAE. The *ikhwan* has long challenged Saudi Arabia's Wahhabi vision of Islam, in spite of members of the group being brought into the state apparatus during the 1960s. The Morsi government, the first democratically elected Islamist President, offered an alternative vision of the ordering of political life to that propagated by the Al Saud, while their social activity was seen as a threat in the UAE. At this time, Qatar offered public support to the Morsi government, causing a great deal of irritation to their Gulf neighbours. Fuelling the concerns of many, Morsi's government appeared willing to improve relations with Iran, much to the chagrin of Saudi Arabia. As a consequence, it was hardly surprising that the toppling of the Brotherhood was well received and shortly after the coup, Saud Arabia, the UAE and Kuwait pledged $12 billion in aid to Abdul Fatah Al Sisi's 'new', *ancien régime.*

Bahrain has largely managed to control unrest, albeit at a price. In seeking to address demographic imbalances, naturalisation processes gave Bahraini passports to Sunnis from the Asian subcontinent and Africa, while members of the Shi'a community were framed as fifth columnists doing the bidding of Tehran. The societal implications of such a reframing may not be seen in the very near future, but schisms between different societal groups will emerge. In Lebanon, the influx of Syrian refugees has led to increasing xenophobia and the amorphous alignment of a number of indigenous Lebanese parties against the refugees.[48] Similar forms of anti-refugee xenophobia are also found in Turkey as a consequence of the political, social and economic pressures placed on the state in order to accommodate those displaced from Syria.[49]

Fundamentally, such moves have positioned Arab and Sunni concerns front and centre within regional security calculations. Although a number of rulers have sought to cultivate new nationalisms, these are all too often predicated upon an exclusive view of national identity based upon shared communal characteristics of ethnicity and sect, defined against the other, cultivating racisms, fear and hatred in the process. Within this strategy, networks are mobilised and while traditionally along sect-based lines, it begins to take the form of regional patronage as richer states distribute financial resources in pursuit of their own ends.

Geopolitical realignment

Given the region's geopolitical importance it was hardly surprising that events took on an international dimension, becoming imbued with additional complexity and contradiction in the process. The most obvious example of this is in Syria, where fighting between regime and opposition figures was complicated by the presence of external actors providing support to a range of groups. While the United States, Saudi Arabia, Qatar and Turkey provided support to rebel groups, Russia, Iran and Hizballah supported the regime,[50] yet it would be remiss to suggest that Tehran and Moscow agree on longer-term goals.[51]

Debate about how best to respond to the uprisings was shaped not only by events in the region but also by the domestic contexts of international states. The administration of US President Donald Trump was dominated by anti-Iranian sentiment, reflecting a marked shift from his predecessor Barack Obama, whose administration had taken a more conciliatory position towards Tehran.[52] In a wide-ranging interview with Jeffrey Goldberg published in *The Atlantic*, Obama's views on the Middle East were articulated:

> The competition between the Saudis and the Iranians – which has helped to feed proxy wars and chaos in Syria and Iraq and Yemen – requires us to say to our friends as well as to the Iranians that they need to find an effective way to share the neighborhood and institute some sort of cold peace.[53]

It was hardly surprising that Obama's words were not received well in Riyadh:

> The Kingdom's 80 years of constant friendship with America to an Iranian leadership that continues to describe America as the biggest enemy, that continues to arm, fund and support sectarian militias in the Arab and Muslim world, that continues to harbor and host Al-Qaeda leaders, that continues to prevent the election of a Lebanese president through Hezbollah, which is identified by your government as a terrorist organization, that continues to kill the Syrian Arab people in league with Bashar Assad?[54]

Saudi Arabia's perception of Iranian foreign policy was made explicit through a number of newspaper opinion pieces. In one, Adel Al Jubeir argued that Iran sought to 'obscure its dangerous sectarian and expansionist policies, as well as its support for terrorism, by leveling unsubstantiated charges against the Kingdom of Saudi Arabia'.[55] Al Jubeir also stressed that Iran is 'the single-most-belligerent-actor in the region, and its actions display both a commitment to regional hegemony and a deeply held view that conciliatory gestures signal weakness either on Iran's part or on the part of its adversaries'.[56]

Such comments reveal a great deal about the alliance between Riyadh and Washington during the Obama administration. Once a mutually beneficial relationship driven by the strength of the personalities involved, cooperation between the two had become increasingly frayed. The extent of such fears prompted consecutive Saudi figures to frame Iran as an existential threat to Western audiences, including through the funding of a number of universities and think tanks across Washington, DC.[57] Although ultimately unsuccessful in persuading the United States to strike against Iranian targets, Saudi securitisation moves fed into a regional realignment.

As a consequence of existential fears about the Iranian nuclear crisis and the ensuing framing of protest movements along sectarian lines, the balance of power across the region shifted. Decades-old suspicion and enmity between Sunni Arab states and Israel began to thaw at a state level – although data suggests that this is far less popular with domestic populations[58] – as anti-Iranian sentiment brought long-time rivals together in a classic example of realpolitik.

Post 2011, changes in the organisation of regional security provided scope for a number of peripheral regional actors to take a more prominent role in regional affairs. A more pro-active Turkish foreign policy was matched by Qatar, seeking to establish itself as a regional force. While Israel continued to play a peripheral role in the region, happy to maintain the status quo and wary of instability brought by the uprisings, changing currents across the Middle East supported growing moves towards rapprochement with Saudi Arabia and other Gulf powers amid shared security concerns.[59] While such moves gained momentum after 2011, diplomatic cables recall observations from King Hamad of Bahrain calling for 'real peace' with Israel so that 'we can all face Iran'.[60]

Amid such fears, it was hardly surprising that the Joint Comprehensive Plan of Action (JCPOA) agreed by the P5+1 and Iran was viewed with a great deal of consternation by many, who saw it as an agreement that would empower Tehran and its allies across the region. Fearing that Iran might develop a 'breakout capacity' while also leading to and an emboldened Hizballah, many in Israel, the Gulf and the United States were critical of the deal,[61] leading to a range of securitisation efforts designed to suspend the 'normal politics' of diplomatic efforts and calling for a military strike against the Islamic Republic.[62] Such calls reflect the growing uncertainty across the Middle Eastern security environment while also stressing the extent to which regional events possess international importance.

The election of Donald Trump as President of the United States in 2016 had a dramatic impact on the Middle East. On Trump's first official foreign trip as President, he visited Saudi Arabia and Israel to set out a bolder foreign policy, where his anti-Iranian message was well received in both states. The legacy of anti-Iranian sentiment from the Iraq War featured prominently in Trump's cabinet, with Mike Pompeo and John Bolton – two vehemently anti-Iranian hawks – holding prominent portfolios along with setting the scene for future policy trajectories. The anti-Iranian sentiment fed into the Trump administration's policy decisions, choosing to swiftly withdraw from the JCPOA, much to the concern of many across the world.

Although the rivalry between Riyadh and Tehran has come to occupy a central role in regional machinations, there are added complexities at play. A by-product of the policy of geopolitics by other means is the recent tension between Saudi Arabia – and the UAE and Bahrain – and Qatar. Tensions between the two have historical roots but became increasingly fractious amid debates over who was responsible for coordinating support to rebel groups in Syria. Tensions rapidly escalated, prompting the withdrawal of Saudi, Bahraini and Emirati ambassadors from Doha, along with a threat to close Qatar's only land border and putting out tenders to turn the border into a canal. Although these tensions were defused, ambassadors were withdrawn again in June 2017 amid continued support for a number of Islamist groups such as the Muslim Brotherhood and Hamas – alongside perceived rapprochement with Iran – that underpinned the decision.[63] As a consequence, air and sea borders were closed and Qatari citizens were given fourteen days to return home.

A thirteen-point list of demands was given to Qatar and met with great scorn in Doha, where it was viewed as an attack on Qatari sovereignty. In conversation with a US TV show, Emir Tamim stated that, 'Our sovereignty is a red line. We don't accept anybody interfering with our sovereignty'. He later suggested that the blockade was a consequence of Doha's engagement with the Arab Uprisings, where a serious difference was exposed wherein Qatar 'stood by the people. They stood by the regimes'.[64]

The blockade was a consequence of Doha's support for actors across the region deemed unpalatable to the Saudi bloc, including links with Iran, the Muslim Brotherhood and subversive activity in Bahrain. The leader of Bahrain's Al Wefaq, Ali Salman, was framed as a Qatari agent on the basis of a phone call between Salman and the Qatari Foreign Minister.[65] Qatar has long played host to Islamist groups such as Hamas, the Taliban and the Muslim Brotherhood in an attempt to wield political influence across the Middle East. It has also provided support to groups across the region, both formally through foreign policy channels and informally, through Al Jazeera, much to the chagrin of Saudi Arabia. Amid existential concerns about regime survival, Islamist groups are seen to be a serious threat to regimes in Riyadh and Abu Dhabi.[66] Yet in spite of this, a number of GCC states have empowered Salifist groups and the Muslim Brotherhood in an attempt to counter the threat from Shi'a groups.[67]

In response to Saudi actions, images of Emir Tamim drawn by the Qatari artist Ahmen bin Majed Amaaheed sprung up across Doha. The image, captioned 'glorious Tamim', appeared on skyscrapers, cars and T-shirts and the cult of personality was almost tangible. Although the blockade was seen to disrupt life across Qatar, preventing the development of the state amid the development of national infrastructure of the 2022 World Cup, the ability to import cows from the United States,[68] olive trees from Italy, support from allies and the development of a 'blockade busting port'[69] meant that the impact of the Saudi-led actions was mitigated. Speaking to a hotel manager in September 2017, I asked about the impact of the blockade, to which the manager replied, 'Is that still happening?' The financial might of Qatar has left it with the capacity to circumvent external challenges, along with the repressive technologies to quell potential domestic unrest.

Yet as it fragments, the Gulf continues to be a region of international importance, not only because of the location of natural resources but also as a consequence of widespread diversification and integration into global supply chains.[70] Increased foreign direct investment followed, while the region's prestige has been augmented by links with global sporting brands such as Arsenal, Barcelona and Manchester City, not to mention Qatar hosting the World Cup in 2022. Although demand for Gulf oil from the West has decreased following the establishment of fracking programmes in the United States, Russian and Chinese demand increases.[71]

Gulf leaders face a number of important challenges in balancing domestic agendas with regional relations, along with international obligations and increasing domestic discontent.[72] Writing in 2011, Kristian Coates Ulrichsen suggested that Gulf states found themselves in the delicate position of navigating both the evolution of geoeconomic changes and the diffusion of power in the global economy and increased domestic uncertainty from pro-democracy and violent Islamist groups.[73] Beyond the economic challenges of 2014, little has changed. While GCC states were largely able to circumvent dissent, structural conditions remain that leave regimes vulnerable in the longer term to demands for greater political accountability, while recourse to Islamic legitimacy leaves regimes open to criticism from the religious groups who also seek to capitalise on societal differences.

Within the context of such machinations, Bahrain and Oman find themselves struggling to exert influence and agency, caught in the shadow of their far more powerful neighbours. As a consequence, the two have sought creative responses to structural challenges, along with recourse to diplomatic efforts. In Bahrain there have been serious moves towards fracking amid concerns about depleting oil reserves and a brain drain to the Emirates and Saudi Arabia.[74] In contrast, Oman has sought to use its strategic location as a means of creating influence by upgrading ports in Sohar, Duqm and Salalah, allowing cargo to bypass the Strait of Hormuz.

Omani developments take place amid rising friction with their neighbours and domestic economic concerns stemming from questions of succession. Fundamental to such decisions are desires to maintain independence and reduce vulnerability to political pressure from Saudi Arabia and the UAE, particularly in light of Muscat's relationship with Tehran. Yet Omani developments have broader repercussions for the GCC, with Saudi investments in infrastructure building seen by some as a means of reducing the Emirati monopoly on Gulf trading roots.[75] Such competition takes place within an increasingly militarised Gulf and proliferation into the Horn of Africa, which adds Chinese and Egyptian aspirations into an already volatile mix.

Moments of indistinction

According to Wahhabi traditions, when Muslims die they are buried in an unmarked grave to prevent idolatry. Such protocols are observed by rulers and ruled alike. It was no surprise that when King Abdullah of Saudi Arabia was buried on 24 January 2015, it was in such a grave at an austere public cemetery named El Ud. Abdullah's funeral was attended by a number of Middle Eastern leaders, yet Oman's well-respected ruler Sultan Qaboos was not present, prompting questions about his health. Omanis are not alone in fearing for the health of their much-loved ruler, particularly as he is yet to publicly anoint a successor, leading to political and economic uncertainty.[76] Across the Gulf, questions of succession plague a number of monarchies amid concerns of the repercussions of political reform.

Almost two and a half years after the death of Abdullah, Mohammad bin Salman, the son of King Salman was named as Crown Prince of Saudi Arabia, replacing the former incumbent Mohammad bin Nayef. Known across the region as MbS, the young Crown Prince rapidly progressed through the kingdom's upper echelons, leaving his mark on political life. One apocryphal story recounts how MbS gained the nickname Abu Rasasa – the father of the bullet – after sending a bullet in the post to a man who refused to help him appropriate property.[77]

Although initially installed as Minister of Defence, during which time he launched efforts to restrict Houthi military action, MbS was soon positioned as Crown Prince, heir apparent to the throne. Seemingly reform minded and seeking to facilitate the transition to a 'post-oil' economy, the Crown Prince's moves risk opening the deep fissures within the fabric of the Saudi state amid efforts to curb the power of the clerics and prevent the spread of violent Wahhabi thought.[78]

The Crown Prince quickly embarked on an anti-corruption drive across the kingdom, resulting in the arrests of eleven prominent royals and two hundred members of the Saudi business elite, in a move referred to by Madawi Al Rasheed as a 'theatrical performance'. Although framed as an effort to reduce corruption, it was clear that this was also an attempt to secure his position amid the uncertainty and shifting sands of political allegiance and ambitions within the Al Saud.[79] The anti-corruption drive was largely well received by young Saudis, with strict legislation preventing the proliferation or acknowledgement of extremist ideologies on social media.[80] Yet faith in the Saudi economy had dwindled as a consequence of the level of corruption. As one official told the *New York Times*, 'Corruption is at every level, and there are hundreds of billions of riyals that are lost from the national economy every year … The point here was mainly to shock the system, to send a message that this will not be tolerated anymore and that nobody is immune.'[81]

MbS was also a vocal supporter of the need to diversify the kingdom's economy, driven by Vision 2030. Central to this vision was a move away from a reliance on oil, along with the development of NEOM, a $500 billion megacity, viewed as the new commercial capital of the kingdom,[82] as part of a privatisation designed to create more jobs for Saudis and to facilitate the transition to the post-oil age. Although comprised of territory in Saudi Arabia, Egypt and Jordan, the new city will be under Saudi jurisdiction.[83] In support of this – and with the aim of attracting tourists from the kingdom and beyond – greater importance has been given to the kingdom's pre-Islamic history, with a number of heritage sites being protected with United Nations Educational, Scientific and Cultural Organization (UNESCO) status. Tourism was also mooted as a potential source of income, yet the impact of this – and recognition of pre-Islamic sites – upon the kingdom's social contract remains to be seen.[84]

The Crown Prince also announced a move towards a 'more tolerant' form of Islam, threatening to crack down on members of the *ulema* who opposed his programme of reforms and professed that he wanted to 'destroy' extremist ideologies, evoking memories of Faisal in the process.[85] It was also supported by the aforementioned anti-terrorism coalition, comprised entirely of Sunni states but seemingly dominated by Pakistani 'boots on the ground', before outright rejection from the Pakistani government.

Beyond the kingdom's borders, the Crown Prince embarked on a more proactive foreign policy that sought to reassert Saudi Arabia's dominance across the Middle East, restricting Iranian influence and continuing the burgeoning rapprochement with Israel.[86] Foreign policy has been driven by an explicitly anti-Iranian agenda, leading to military escalation in Yemen – a view used to justify the war particularly in the Emirates[87] – while in Lebanon, a working relationship between Saad Hariri and Hizballah officials resulted in a bizarre series of events in late 2017. Amid Saudi concerns about the Lebanese political climate, Hariri was summoned to Riyadh and forced to resign before being held under house arrest. After his release Hariri returned to Lebanon, where he rescinded his resignation.

Yet the kingdom continued to rely on key allies to help achieve its aims. The close friendship between Mohammed bin Salman and Mohammed bin Zayed[88] – the Crown Prince and de facto ruler of the UAE – meant that Saudi military efforts in Yemen were also supported by the UAE, along with Egypt, Bahrain and Qatar, although the latter was expelled from the Saudi-led coalition amid escalating tensions between the two.[89] Relations with the United States rapidly thawed under Trump and Riyadh was the first official trip made by the new President after coming to office, demonstrating the importance of not only relations with Saudi Arabia but his personal relationship with the Crown Prince. In an unofficial account of time in the Trump White House, it was reported in June 2017 that the President said, 'We've put our man on top', after King Salman removed Mohammed bin Nayef as Crown Prince and replaced him with his son.[90] In the months that followed, Trump was vocal in his support of Salman and his son, on one occasion tweeting, 'I have great confidence in King Salman and the Crown Prince of Saudi Arabia, they know exactly what they are doing'.[91]

The close relationship between Trump and MbS makes criticism of the kingdom in the United States more powerful. MbS' father, King Salman, had previously been identified as 'Fund-Raiser in Chief' of Saudi funding for violent extremism across the world, where an estimated $90 billion was given to mosques and clerics in the twenty years before 9/11, many of whom used the money to finance extremist motivated violence. While Saudi Arabia does not tolerate extremist thought within the kingdom, it is widely accepted that 'it is openly backing, funding and arming radical Islamic jihadists outside the Saudi Kingdom'.[92] Tackling this perception was a key goal of the new leadership in Riyadh, yet the murder of Jamal Khashoggi, a Saudi dissident, provoked a great deal of international condemnation not only concerning the death of Khashoggi but over the kingdom's domestic and foreign policy.

Old questions, new answers?

On 6 December 2017, US President Donald Trump broke with decades of US policy and stated that it was 'time to officially recognise Jerusalem as the capital of Israel'.[93] The move to recognise Jerusalem as Israel's capital seemingly ended the moribund peace process. If a US administration had acted in such a manner in the past, Arab leaders would have vehemently rejected the move, and the possibility of widespread violence would have been high. Yet in spite of pockets of unrest across the region – again stemming from grassroots movements – there was little in the way of a coordinated response. The old question about Palestinian autonomy was populated with new apathy.

Although most states across the Arab world have played with the 'Palestinian football', the cause has long been removed from their strategic priorities. In spite of strong domestic anti-Israeli sentiment, Egyptian leaders tacitly accepted the embassy move.[94] Although clerics at Al Azhar were critical, most followed government guidelines, choosing to focus their Friday sermons on 'family values' rather than events in Jerusalem.[95] Unsurprisingly, Saudi Arabia was largely quiet on the matter. On visiting the Washington Institute, MbS offered 'mild rebuke' of the decision and presented an optimistic vision of Saudi–Israeli relations, but only when asked.[96] Yet the Crown Prince was vociferous in his criticism of the Palestinian leadership. At a meeting with Jewish leaders in the United States, it was reported that MbS said, 'It's about time that the Palestinians accept the offers, and agree to come to the negotiating table – or they should shut up and stop complaining'.[97]

Such a response is hardly unexpected given Saudi manoeuvres in recent years. Shortly after publicly rebuking Saad Hariri, Mahmoud Abbas, the leader of the Palestinian Authority (PA) was called to Riyadh to hear a Saudi peace plan. Reports suggested that the Saudi plan was presented to Abbas along with an ultimatum: accept it or resign.[98] As the outline was comprised of a number of concessions that no Palestinian leader could accept, Abbas was furious. The plan did allow for the establishment of a Palestinian 'entity', but this would include non-contiguous parts of territory in Gaza, parts of the West Bank (Areas A, B and 10% of C), leaving limited territorial sovereignty. Moreover, the vast majority of Israeli settlements across the West Bank would remain. The most troublesome parts of the plan suggested that there would be no right of return for Palestinian refugees and the capital of this entity would be in Abu Dis or Ramallah, not Jerusalem.[99]

In response to both Trump's decision and the Saudi ultimatum, Abbas was steadfast: 'Now we say "No" to Trump, we won't accept his plan – we say the "deal of the century" is the slap of the century'.[100] The PLO Executive Committee was urged to 'suspend recognition of Israel until it recognises the State of Palestine on the 1967 borders' while the PLO stated that the Oslo Agreements 'no longer stand'.[101] Two days after the Jerusalem announcement, Yoav Galant, the Israeli Construction and Housing Minister, announced plans to build fourteen thousand new 'units' in settlements across the West Bank and East Jerusalem.

Later that year, the Knesset passed a 'nation state law' that was framed by Prime Minister Benjamin Netanyahu as 'a defining moment in the history of the state',[102] which offers a legal response to existential questions about Israel, codifying 'the basic principle of our existence'. The law enshrined the right to exercise national self-determination in Israel as unique to the Jewish people, establishing settlement as a national value and labouring to 'encourage and promote its establishment and development', making spatial ordering and transformation a key part of the Israeli sovereign project.[103]

Coming home to roost

In recent years, cartoons have appeared in a number of regional newspapers portraying Saudi Arabia as the ideological founder and sponsor of violent Salafist extremism. One cartoon depicts King Salman placing money into a jihadi piggy bank, while another shows the King throwing a boomerang with the face of a jihadi away from the kingdom towards Syria. By their very nature boomerangs return to where they were thrown from, suggesting that such problems will return to Saudi Arabia in the future.

State policy in the face of regional and international challenges has only served to support such perceptions. Amid a range of political, economic and ideological challenges, regimes have firmly positioned themselves within broader normative and security environments in the quest for legitimacy and ultimately survival. Driven by sectarianisation, in some cases, this has resulted in alliances that will ensure regime survival in the face of particular threats but that are unpalatable to domestic populations. The collapse of the distinction between regional and domestic is escalating, with potentially dire consequences for people, the ordering of space and territorial borders. As sectarianisation narratives find traction, sectarian conflict risks becoming a self-perpetuating truth, with devastating repercussions, posing serious challenges to those aiming for *desectarianisation*.

The fragmentation of the region post 2011 has posed a number of existential challenges to regime survival. In an effort to ensure survival, state-building projects have become increasingly exclusionary, defining themselves against an outside, leading to widespread marginalisation, repression and disenfranchisement. Yet amid widespread uncertainty and instability, (politically charged) religion offers a semblance of certainty for both regimes and individuals amid these struggles.

Recourse to religion and tradition to circumvent opposition created a zone of possibility to be shaped by the interaction of various groups. The struggle to exert influence, lay claim to legitimacy or implement democracy led to accusations of state failure or weakness. Some even predicted the collapse of the Gulf regimes, most obviously in Christopher Davidson's *After the Sheikhs*.[104] Although Davidson's claims were ultimately premature, his initial premise has some merit. Although traditionally secure states such as Saudi Arabia, Kuwait, Qatar and the UAE have largely escaped from the problems of the Arab Uprisings, this position is not tenable in the medium to long term, feeding into the crisis of legitimacy and instability that drives sectarianisation processes.

In such conditions, the struggle to shape political life becomes increasingly important, while groups and individuals face precarious futures. In an article in the *Financial Times*, the former Jordanian Finance Minister Marwan Muasher suggested that the problems facing the Arab world were increasing, with societal fissures deepening and economic challenges escalating. For Muasher, fractures in society are 'the biggest problem, and unfortunately very few leaders are paying attention to it'. One potential outcome is 'another Arab Spring … the status quo is not sustainable'.[105] One additional consequence, for Shadi Hamid, is that amid such conditions and increasing repression, Islamist groups move towards violent escalation as they are pushed to the periphery of political projects.[106]

The complexity of contemporary political life underpinned by often competing geopolitical agendas means that regimes across the Middle East operate with a profound sense of insecurity. Such conditions are hardly new, yet the perceived severity of the threats facing the region's rulers have multiplied, challenging stability from a range of different vantage points. As scholars of International Relations are aware, existential fear breeds a security dilemma, which, without careful management, increases instability. Regimes across the Middle East now face a number of often competing security dilemmas, including the traditional dilemma between states but also occurring *within* states. A number of these internal security dilemmas have regional repercussions, particularly when embedded within shared normative environments.[107] In such precarious conditions, maintaining security or reassuring those whose security is to be guaranteed is increasingly difficult. As fear permeates the region, along with sectarianisation processes, it facilitates the descent into violent conflict and makes the possibility of de-escalation increasingly unlikely.

Conclusions

In one of the more powerful analyses of the Arab Uprisings, Hamid Dabashi argues that the post-uprisings landscape has been defined by the struggle between domestic tyranny and globalised disempowerment.[108] In this moment, a new geography emerges as states seek to reimagine the 'moral map' of the Middle East away from the colonial legacy of 'the West', essentially 'altering the very geography of how we think and fathom the world'.[109] Moreover, the spread of identities and ideologies across state borders resulted in the collapse of the distinction between internal and external. This conflation of national and regional dynamics obfuscates the counter-revolutionary factions at play, while also establishing a new cosmopolitan geography.

Within this new geography, spatial borders have been eroded as a new means of ordering life, while schisms within and across states have deepened. Debate about the resolution of domestic unrest involved discussions of a move towards federalism, underpinned by power-sharing agreements such as those seen in Lebanon. An increasingly popular view suggested that an ethno-sectarian redistribution across the region would bring stability to the region.[110] Indeed, for many, the centrifugal forces shaping the region were interpreted as the rearrangement of populations in an attempt to 'better fit the nation states'.[111] After the uprisings, these centrifugal forces challenged the spatial organisation of politics through the emergence of a new system of ordering life, increasingly along sectarianised lines, eroding the sovereign power of the state in the process.

The geography of ideas and ideologies also transcend the construction of national borders. Ideas of liberation and empowerment served as a source of possibility and inspiration, providing a compelling means through which to reject 'being thus'. As Dabashi argued, the uprisings also served as a means of creating a new geography of hope, challenging the colonial legacy of external actors and the counter-revolutionary forces that had regulated spatial dynamics across the Middle East. In spite of this optimism, following the initial successes of the revolutionary groups, a more restrictive and counter-revolutionary set of forces began to shape the region.

Political life is shaped in accordance with the context and contingency of space yet underpinning a great deal of recent events is the increasingly toxic rivalry between Saudi Arabia and Iran that capitalises on – and drives – the fragmentation of political projects. Although a number of organisations have sought to embark on track II diplomatic processes, there appears little scope for rapprochement at present given the conflation of political issues with geopolitical concerns and efforts to cultivate

Islamic legitimacy. As a consequence, while the two states have sought to capitalise on opportunities that present themselves, this feeds into the fragmentation of political organisation and supports sectarianisation processes.

Where authority and legitimacy have been seriously challenged, the move to more community grounded identities that often share some form of identity or ideology with external actors has supported such claims. Such counter-revolutionary forces were supported by external actors, whose own interests did not align with those who took to the streets across the region to express political goals. Although his optimism appears misguided, we should not ignore Dabashi's words, which urge us to look beyond the clash of imperialism, Orientalism and lazy journalism. Doing so results in the construction of 'truth' posited upon 'the grid of prosaic normativity, a reading of reality by way of sustaining the power and the benefits of imperial domination'.[112]

Yet as counter-revolutionary forces prevail, the dreams and hopes of those who took to the streets have been crushed by the bureaucratic systems of biopolitical machinery designed to regulate life and, where necessary, to subjugate it to death. Ultimately, amid widespread devastation and humanitarian crises, the people of the region have paid the heaviest price.

Notes

1   See Michael Axeworth and Patrick Milton, 'A Westphalian Peace for the Middle East' (*Foreign Affairs*, 10.10.16), available at www.foreignaffairs.com/articles/europe/2016-10-10/westphalian-peace-middle-east (accessed 11.10.16); Richard N. Haas, 'The New Thirty Years' War' (Project Syndicate, 21.07.14), available at www.project-syndicate.org/commentary/richard-n--haass-argues-that-the-middle-east-is-less-a-problem-to-be-solved-than-a-condition-to-be-managed?barrier=accessreg (accessed 11.10.16); Greg R. Lawson, 'A Thirty Years' War in the Middle East' (*National Interest*, 16.04.14), available at http://nationalinterest.org/feature/thirty-years-war-the-middle-east-10266 (accessed 11.10.16); Brendan Simms, Michael Axworth and Patrick Milton, 'Ending the New Thirty Years War' (*New Statesman*, 26.01.16), available at www.newstatesman.com/politics/uk/2016/01/ending-new-thirty-years-war (accessed 11.10.16); David Rothkopf, 'A Time of Unprecedented Instability?' (*Foreign Policy*, 21.07.14), available at http://foreignpolicy.com/2014/07/21/a-time-of-unprecedented-instability (accessed 21.07.14); Bernard Lewis, 'Rethinking the Middle East' (*Foreign Affairs*, 1992), available at www.foreignaffairs.com/articles/middle-east/1992–09–01/rethinking-middle-east (accessed 21.07.14).
2   Testimony, Richard Haas.
3   Lorenzo Kamel, 'Reshuffling the Middle East: A Historical and Political Perspective', *International Spectator* 51:3 (2016), 132–41.
4   Joshua Landis, 'The Great Sorting Out: ethnicity and the Future of the Levant' (Qifa Nabki, 18.12.13), available at https://qifanabki.com/2013/12/18/landis-ethnicity (accessed 18.12.13); Robert Bowker, *Ending Sykes-Picot: The Arab World and the West After 2011* (HH Sheikh Nasser al-Mohammad al-Sabah Publication Series 2013), available at www.dur.ac.uk/resources/alsabah/al-SabahPaperBowkerSeptember2013.pdf (10.08.19).

5 See interviews with Iraqi film-maker, Syrian academic, Syrian analysts, Yemen analysts, Iraqi analyst, Lebanese journalists, Bahraini MPs, Bahraini cleric, 2014–2018.
6 Interview with Yemen analyst, 2018.
7 Phillips, *Battle for Syria*.
8 Interview with Bahraini academic, 2018.
9 Fred Halliday, 'A New Global Configuration', in Ken Booth and Timothy Dunne (eds), *Worlds in Collision – Terror and the Future of Global Order* (New York: Palgrave Macmillan), p. 235.
10 See Richard N. Haass, 'The New Middle East', *Foreign Affairs*, 85 (2006), 2–12; Alexander T. J. Lennon (ed.), *The Epicenter of Crisis. The New Middle East* (Cambridge, MA: MIT Press, 2008); Robert Malley and Peter Harling, 'Beyond Moderates and Militants', *Foreign Affairs*, 89 (2010), 18–29; Vali Nasr, *The Shia Revival: How Conflicts Within Islam Will Shape the Future* (New York: Norton, 2007); Ottaway et al., *The New Middle East*; Nicolas Pelham, *A New Muslim Order: The Shia and the Middle East Sectarian Crisis* (London: I. B. Tauris, 2008); Philip Seib, *New Media and the New Middle East* (New York: Palgrave Macmillan, 2009).
11 Morten Valbjørn and André Bank, 'The New Arab Cold War: Rediscovering the Arab Dimension of Middle East Regional Politics', *Review of International Studies*, 38 (2012), 3–24.
12 Jerrold Green, 'Are Arab Politics Still Arab?', *World Politics*, 38 (1986), 611–25.
13 Paul Noble, 'The Arab System: Pressures, Constraints, and Opportunities', in Bahgat Korany and Ali E. Hillal Dessouki (eds), *The Foreign Policies of Arab States* (Boulder, CO: Westview, 1991), p. 57.
14 Hashim, S. *Al-Intifadhat al-'Arabiya 'ala Dhaou Falsafit at-Tarikh* [The Arab Uprising in Light of the Philosophy of History] (Beirut: Dar al-Saqi, 2013).
15 Shibley Telhami, *Anwar Sadat Chair for Peace and Development University of Maryland/Zogby International 2006 Annual Arab Public Opinion Survey* (8 February 2007).
16 Bassel F. Salloukh, *Overlapping Contests and Middle East International Relations: The Return of the Weak Arab State* (Project on Middle East Political Science, 2015), available at https://pomeps.org/2015/08/12/overlapping-contests-and-middle-east-international-relations-the-return-of-the-weak-arab-state (accessed 13.08.15).
17 Interview with Saudi political theorist, 2018.
18 Interview with Syrian analyst, 2017.
19 Interview with Bahraini Shi'a cleric, 2018.
20 In 2011 43% either agreed or strongly agreed with the statement 'it would be better for my home country if religion were separated from politics' and in 2015 this number had risen to 52%. See *Arab Opinion Index 2015*, p. 23.
21 This was a prominent theme across a number of interviews.
22 Archar, *The People Want*.
23 Interview with Lebanese journalist, 2017.
24 Baumann, 'Social Protest'. The term mafia was routinely used by interviewees to describe life in Lebanon, Syria and Iraq.
25 Interview with Syrian author, 2018.
26 Simon Mabon 'The Battle For Bahrain: Iranian-Saudi Rivalry', *Middle East Policy*, 19:2 (2012), 84–97.
27 Interview with ex-Bahraini MP.
28 See WikiLeaks, 'The Street is Stronger Than Parliament'.

29 Mabon and Royle, *Origins of ISIS*. See also Mabon 'Nationalist Jahiliyya'.
30 Alex MacDonald, 'Controversial Iraqi Militias Now Part of Army after Parliament Vote' (*Middle East Eye*, 26.11.16), available at www.middleeasteye.net/news/iraqs-parliament-legalizes-controversial-pmus-566417926 (accessed 26.11.16).
31 Ali Khamenei, Supreme Leader of Iran called for 'divine vengeance'. 'Iran Furious Over Saudi Arabia's Execution of Shi'ite Sheikh Nimr Al-Nimr' (Memri, 01.04.16), available at www.memri.org/reports/iran-furious-over-saudi-arabias-execution-shiite-sheikh-nimr-al-nimr (accessed 04.01.16).
32 'Iran says Ambassador to Remain in Kuwait Despite Row' (Reuters, 24.07.17), available at www.reuters.com/article/us-iran-kuwait-diplomacy/iran-says-ambassador-to-remain-in-kuwait-despite-row-idUSKBN1A91CC?il=0 (accessed 24.07.17).
33 Testimony, Hamli.
34 Hashemi and Postel, *Sectarianization*. Although most visible in conflicts in Iraq, Syria and Yemen, it is also a feature of Lebanon, Bahrain, Saudi Arabia, Kuwait and Iran.
35 Testimony, Hamli.
36 Interview with Turkish activist, 2017.
37 Christopher Phillips and Morten Valbjørn, ' "What Is in a Name?": The Role of (Different) Identities in the Multiple Proxy Wars in Syria', *Small Wars & Insurgencies*, 29:3 (2018), 414–33.
38 Testimony, Haider Al Khoei.
39 Testimony, Haid Haid.
40 Matthiesen, *Sectarian Gulf*, p. 127.
41 Testimony, Danahar.
42 This was a point made by several interviewees from Lebanon. Similar issues also appear in Syria and Iraq.
43 Testimony, Haider Al Khoei.
44 Testimony, Haid Haid.
45 Testimony, Haider Al Khoei.
46 Interview with Kurdish policy advisor. See also 'Iraq's Muqtada al-Sadr Makes Rare Saudi Visit' (*Al Jazeera*, 21.07.17), available at www.aljazeera.com/news/2017/07/iraq-muqtada-al-sadr-rare-saudi-visit-170731073908238.html (accessed 21.07.17).
47 Phillips, *Battle for Syria*.
48 Interview with Lebanese journalist, 2017.
49 Ibid.
50 Phillips, *Battle for Syria*.
51 Testimony, Trenin.
52 Mabon, 'Muting the Trumpets'.
53 Jeffrey Goldberg, 'The Obama Doctrine' (*Atlantic*, April 2016), available at www.theatlantic.com/magazine/archive/2016/04/the-obama-doctrine/471525/#5 (accessed 26.11.16).
54 Turki Al Faisal, 'Mr. Obama, We Are Not "Free Riders" ' (*Arab News*, 14.03.16) www.arabnews.com/columns/news/894826 (accessed 15.03.16).
55 Adel Bin Ahmed Al Jubeir, 'Can Iran Change?' (*New York Times*, 19.01.16), available at www.nytimes.com/2016/01/19/opinion/saudi-arabia-can-iran-change.html?_r=2 (accessed 20.01.16).
56 Ibid.
57 Mabon, 'Muting the Trumpets'.
58 The 2016 Arab Opinion Index found that 86% of respondents 'disapproved of their countries' recognition of Israel' while 80% stated that Israel 'certainly' posed a threat to

the Arab region. See http://arabcenterdc.org/wp-content/uploads/2017/04/2016-Arab-Opinion-Index-Executive-Summary-for-web.pdf (accessed 26.11.16).

59 See Adham Saouli, *Middle Powers* (London: Hurst, 2018); Clive A. Jones and Guzarsky, Yoel, 'Israel's Relations with the Gulf states: Toward the Emergence of a Tacit Security Regime?' *Contemporary Security Policy*, 38:3 (2017), 398–419.

60 'King Hamad Supports Gulf Security Dialogue' (WikiLeaks, 01.11.06), available at https://wikileaks.org/plusd/cables/06MANAMA1849_a.html (accessed 26.11.16).

61 See Merom, Gil. 'Israeli Perceptions of the Iranian Nuclear Threat', *Political Science Quarterly*, 132:1 (2017), 87–118; Ehud Eiran and Martin B. Malin, 'The Sum of all Fears: Israel's Perception of a Nuclear-Armed Iran', *Washington Quarterly*, 36:3 (2013), 77–89; Scott Peterson, 'Imminent Iran Nuclear Threat? A Timeline of Warnings Since 1979', *Christian Science Monitor*, 8 (2001), available at www.csmonitor.com/World/Middle-East/2011/1108/Imminent-Iran-nuclear-threat-A-timeline-of-warnings-since-1979/Earliest-warnings-1979-84 (accessed 02.08.19); 'Netanyahu's Claim that Iran is "Six Months" from Having Nuclear Bomb Material' (*Washington Post*, 16.09.12).

62 Amir Lupovici, 'Securitization Climax: Putting the Iranian Nuclear Project at the Top of the Israeli Public Agenda (2009–2012)', *Foreign Policy Analysis*, 12:3 (2016), 413–32; Hossein Pour-Ahmadi and Sajad Mohseni, 'The Obama and Securitization of Iran's Nuclear Energy Program', *Iranian Review of Foreign Affairs*, 3:2 (Summer 2012), 143–74; Jarrod Hayes, 'Identity and Securitization in the Democratic Peace: The United States and the Divergence of Response to India and Iran's Nuclear Programs', *International Studies Quarterly*, 53 (2009), 977–99.

63 Patrick Wintour, 'Gulf Plunged into Diplomatic Crisis as Countries Cut Ties with Qatar' (*Guardian*, 05.06.17), available at www.theguardian.com/world/2017/jun/05/saudi-arabia-and-bahrain-break-diplomatic-ties-with-qatar-over-terrorism (accessed 05.06.17).

64 'Qatari Emir: Our Sovereignty Is a Red Line' (*Al Jazeera*, 30.10.17), available at www.aljazeera.com/news/2017/10/qatar-emir-blockading-countries-regime-change-171029194842654.html (accessed 30.10.17).

65 Interview with Shi'a Bahraini cleric 2018.

66 Courtney Freer, 'Same But Different: The GCC Continues to Clash Over Islamists' (Middle East Centre, 06.06.17), available at http://blogs.lse.ac.uk/mec/2017/06/06/same-same-but-different-the-gcc-continues-to-clash-over-islamists (accessed 26.11.16).

67 Interviews with Bahraini academic 2018.

68 Patrick Wintour, 'Land of Milk and Money: Qatar Looks to Farms to Beat the Gulf Boycott' (*Guardian*, 20.10.17), available at www.theguardian.com/world/2017/oct/20/land-of-milk-and-money-qatar-looks-to-farms-to-beat-the-gulf-boycott (accessed 21.10.17).

69 'Qatar Launches "Blockade-Busting" Port, One of Region's Largest' (*New Arab*, 05.09.17), available at www.alaraby.co.uk/english/news/2017/9/5/qatar-launches-blockade-busting-port-one-of-regions-largest (accessed 05.09.17).

70 Yamada, 'Gulf–Asia Relations as "Post-Rentier" Diversification? The Case of the Petrochemical Indus- try in Saudi Arabia', *Journal of Arabian Studies*, 1 (2011), 101–3.

71 Ben Simpfendorfer, *The New Silk Road: How a Rising Arab World is Turning Away From the West and Rediscovering China* (Basingstoke, UK: Palgrave Macmillan, 2009), pp. 30–2.

72 Kristian Coates Ulrichsen, 'Links Between Domestic and Regional Security', in Kristian Coates Ulrichsen, *The Changing Security Dynamics of the Persian Gulf* (London: Hurst, 2014), pp. 23–41.

73 Kristian Coates Ulrichsen, 'Repositioning the GCC States in the Changing Global Order', *Journal of Arabian Studies*, 1:2 (2011), 231–47.

74 Interview with Bahraini oil executive 2014.

75 Camille Lons, 'Battle of the Ports: Emirates Sea Power Spreads from Persian Gulf to Africa' (*Newsweek*, 08.03.18), available at www.newsweek.com/battle-ports-emirates-sea-power-spreads-persian-gulf-africa-1051959 (accessed 08.03.18).

76 A position that is quickly apparent in conversations with those Omanis willing to talk about succession.

77 Dexter Filkins, 'A Saudi Prince's Quest to Remake the Middle East' (*New Yorker*, 09.04.18), available at www.newyorker.com/magazine/2018/04/09/a-saudi-princes-quest-to-remake-the-middle-east (accessed 09.04.18).

78 Mabon, 'Family Affair'; Al Rasheed, *Salman's Legacy*.

79 Al Rasheed, *Salman's Legacy*.

80 Interviews with Saudi academic 2017.

81 Thomas Freedman, 'The Upstart Saudi Prince Who's Throwing Caution to the Winds' (*New York Times*, 14.11.17), available at www.nytimes.com/2017/11/14/world/middleeast/saudi-arabia-mohammed-bin-salman.html?action=click&contentCollection=Middle%20East&module=RelatedCoverage&region=Marginalia&pgtype=article (accessed 15.11.17).

82 Vivian Nereim and Alaa Shahine, 'Saudi Arabia Crown Prince Details Plans for New City: Transcript' (Bloomberg, 26.10.17), available at www.bloomberg.com/news/articles/2017-10-26/saudi-arabia-crown-prince-details-plans-for-new-city-transcript (accessed 26.11.16).

83 Ibid.

84 Interview with Saudi analyst who advises Saudi embassy 2017 and with Saudi academic. See also Mabon, 'Family Affair'.

85 Sam Meredith, 'Saudi Arabia Promises a Return to "Moderate Islam"' (CNBC, 25.10.17), available at www.cnbc.com/2017/10/25/saudi-arabia-promises-a-return-to-moderate-islam.html (accessed 26.10.17).

86 Jones and Guzansky, 'Israel's Relations with the Gulf States'. Following the international condemnation of the murder of the Saudi dissident Jamal Khashoggi, Israeli Prime Minister Benjamin Netanyahu suggested that the Kingdom should 'get a pass' because the larger problem is 'Iran, and we have to make sure that Iran does not continue the malign activities that it has been engaged in'. See Yaron Steinbuch, 'Netanyahu: Saudi Arabia Deserves a Pass for Khashoggi Murder' (*New York Post*, 02.11.18), available at https://nypost.com/2018/11/02/netanyahu-saudi-arabia-deserves-a-pass-for-khashoggi-murder (accessed 03.11.18).

87 One interviewee told me that 'we went to war in Yemen because we are next', referring to fears about Iranian expansionism that began to pervade Emirati society, including the mother of one Emirati soldier killed in Yemen speaking on TV and saying that 'we have to stop them there', referring to Iran. Moreover, it was also suggested that ideas of Arab nationalism were only now evoked in reference to Iran.

88 Declan Walsh, 'Tiny, Wealthy Qatar Goes Its Own Way, and Pays for It' (*New York Times*, 22.01.18), available at www.nytimes.com/2018/01/22/world/middleeast/qatar-saudi-emir-boycott.html (accessed 23.01.18).

89 Many in Oman have been critical of the 'Yemen adventure', including Sultan Qaboos,
    who are concerned about the destabilising impact of the conflict upon the region.
    Giorgio Cafiero and Theodore Karasik, 'Yemen War and Qatar Crisis Challenge
    Oman's Neutrality' (Middle East Institute, 06.07.17), available at www.mei.edu/
    content/article/oman-s-high-stakes-yemen (accessed 06.07.17).

90 '"We Put Our Man on Top", Trump said on MBS, Book Claims' (Al Jazeera, 05.01.18),
    available at www.aljazeera.com/news/2018/01/put-man-top-trump-mbs-book-claims-
    180105124054629.html (accessed 05.01.18).

91 Tweet (Twitter, 06.11.17, 11.03 pm), available at https://twitter.com/realDonaldTrump/
    status/927672843504177152 (accessed 26.11.16).

92 Testimony, Haider Al Khoei.

93 The White House, 'Statement by President Trump on Jerusalem'.

94 David D. Kirkpatrick, 'Tapes Reveal Egyptian Leaders' Tacit Acceptance of Jerusalem
    Move' (New York Times, 06.01.2018), available at www.nytimes.com/2018/01/06/
    world/middleeast/egypt-jerusalem-talk-shows.html (accessed 08.01.18); 'Egypt Denies
    Report That It Accepts Trump's Jerusalem Recognition' (Times of Israel, 07.01.2018),
    available at www.timesofisrael.com/egypt-denies-report-that-it-accepts-trumps-
    jerusalem-recognition (accessed 08.01.18).

95 Shahira Amin, 'Sisi Performs Balancing Act in Wake of Trump's Jerusalem Move' (Al-
    Monitor, 12.12.2017), available at www.al-monitor.com/pulse/originals/2017/12/egypt-
    sisi-balance-trump-decision-jerusalem-israel-azhar.html (accessed 16.12.12).

96 Robert Satloff, 'Mohammed bin Salman Doesn't Want to Talk About Jerusalem'
    (Foreign Policy, 14.12.2017), available at http://foreignpolicy.com/2017/12/14/
    mohammad-bin-salman-doesnt-want-to-talk-about-jerusalem (accessed 16.12.12).

97 TOI Staff, 'Palestinians Must Make Peace or Shut Up, Saudi Crown Prince Said to Tell
    US Jews' (Times of Israel, 29.04.18), available at www.timesofisrael.com/palestinians-
    must-make-peace-or-shut-up-saudi-crown-prince-said-to-tell-us-jews (accessed
    30.04.18).

98 Sue Surkes, 'Saudis Told Abbas to Accept Trump Peace Plan or Resign – Report'
    (Times of Israel, 12.11.17), available at www.timesofisrael.com/saudis-told-abbas-to-
    accept-trump-peace-plan-or-resign-report (accessed 12.11.17); Adnan Abu Amer,
    'Details of Abbas' Mysterious Saudi Trip Still Scarce' (Al-Monitor, 16.11.17), available
    at www.al-monitor.com/pulse/originals/2017/11/palestine-saudi-arabia-abbas-
    resignation-pressure-peace-us.html (accessed 17.11.17).

99 Anne Barnard, David M. Halbfinger and Peter Baker, 'Talk of a Peace Plan That
    Snubs Palestinians Roils Middle East' (New York Times, 03.12.17), available at
    www.nytimes.com/2017/12/03/world/middleeast/palestinian-saudi-peace-plan.
    html (accessed 04.12.17); Samia Nakhoul, Stephen Kalin and Suleiman Al Khalidi,
    'Despite Furor Over Jerusalem Move, Saudis Seen on Board with U.S. Peace
    Efforts' (Reuters, 8.12.17), https://news.yahoo.com/despite-furor-over-jerusalem-
    move-saudis-seen-board-183218008.html?guce_referrer=aHR0cHM6Ly93d3cu
    ZWNvc2lhLm9yZy9zZWFyY2g_cT1OYWtob3VsJTJDK0thbGluK2FuZCthbC
    1LaGFsaWRpJTJDKyVFMiU4MCU5OERlc3BpdGUrRnVyb3JlK092ZXIrSmVy
    dXNhbGVtK01vdmUlRTIlODAlOTkmYWRkb249c2FmYXJp&guce_referrer_
    sig=AQAAAM24PuZt60THRktfl1MTfOG6Ge3KrFiP4bTw_AEGFbMipcMebvW_
    GDo4dn1Yu5DPD_v46Xg-PSxUSvB4QJFjGpCAM9A-rsghg
    PtV0eKUZ9IYLsdKNgmUXpIt8qbmI5F8iMWxkBrbqaofdjObKSHPy
    DCOXAgBssF9yY3hbWdtQMaa&guccounter=2 (accessed 10.08.19).

100 'Mahmoud Abbas Slams Trump Over "Slap of the Century"' (*Al Jazeera*, 14.01.18), available at www.aljazeera.com/news/2018/01/mahmoud-abbas-slams-trump-slap-century-180114195614715.html (accessed 14.01.18).

101 'Palestinian Leaders Reconsider Recognition of Israel' (*Al Jazeera*, 15.01.18), available at www.aljazeera.com/news/2018/01/palestinian-leadership-revokes-recognition-israel-180116060200939.html (accessed 15.01.18).

102 'Read the Full Jewish Nation-State Law' (*Jerusalem Post*, 19.07.18), available at www.jpost.com/Israel-News/Read-the-full-Jewish-Nation-State-Law-562923 (accessed 19.07.18).

103 Ibid.

104 Davidson, *After the Sheikhs*.

105 Andrew England and Heba Saleh, 'How the Middle East Is Sowing Seeds of a Second Arab spring' (*Financial Times*, 05.03.18), available at www.ft.com/content/a6229844-1ad3-11e8-aaca-4574d7dabfb6 (accessed 05.03.18).

106 Hamid, *Islamic Exceptionalism*.

107 Mabon, *Saudi Arabia and Iran*.

108 Dabashi, *The Arab Spring*, p. 3.

109 Ibid., p. 6.

110 R. Wright, 'Imagining a Remapped Middle East' (*New York Times*, 28.09.13), available at www.nytimes.com/2013/09/29/opinion/sunday/imagining-a-remapped-middle-east. html?pagewanted=all&_r=0 (accessed 28.09.13); J. Stavridis, 'It's Time to Seriously Consider the Partition of Syria' (*Foreign Policy*, 09.03.16), available at http:// foreignpolicy.com/2016/03/09/its-time-to-seriously-consider-partitioning-syria (accessed 09.03.16); D. Pipes, 'Like-to-Like Ethnic Migration in the Middle East' (*Washington Times*, 25.02.15), available at www.washingtontimes.com/news/2015/feb/25/daniel-pipes-like-to-like-ethnic-migration- in-the- (accessed 09.03.16); Landis, 'The Great Sorting Out'.

111 Landis, 'The Great Sorting Out'.

112 Dabashi, *The Arab Spring*, p. 224.

Conclusion: The end of the dream

The story of our struggle has finally become known. We lost our home, which means the familiarity of daily life. We lost our occupation, which means the confidence that we are of some use in this world. We lost our language, which means the naturalness of reactions, the simplicity of gestures, the unaffected expression of feelings ... *Once we were somebodies about whom people cared.*

Hannah Arendt, We Refugees (emphasis added)

On 2 October 2018, Jamal Khashoggi, a Saudi journalist, walked into the kingdom's consulate in Istanbul where he was murdered by senior intelligence officers, allegedly with the approval of Crown Prince Mohammad bin Salman. In the days that followed, questions about what happened to Khashoggi dominated news cycles around the world, while diplomats from the kingdom's allies pulled out of an investment conference due to take place in Saudi Arabia. Following in the footsteps of Raif Badawi and many others, the incident reveals a great deal about the extent to which authoritarian leaders will go in order to silence critics and maintain power, much like in the aftermath of the Arab Uprisings where violence was used to crush protest movements, seemingly whatever the cost.

The fragmentation of sovereign borders and retreat into communal identities collapsed domestic and regional politics into new spaces of the political that placed regime survival above human security, albeit not curtailed by territorial borders. Following regime responses to the uprisings, intractable conflicts have emerged, becoming all-encompassing, dividing societies and communities along political lines. Socio-economic contexts add additional characteristics to these divisions, creating conditions that give rise to mafia groups who are able to capitalise on marginalisation and instability. The allocation of resources and jobs becomes a mechanism through which control is exerted and as such, performing identity becomes essential to ensuring survival.

With the fragmentation of the state and emergence of competing claims to sovereignty, the biopolitical regulation of life provided the mechanisms of control to regulate life through stripping it of its political meaning. Across the region, the creation of bare life was a mechanism of sovereign power, designed to ensure order and compliance. Yet in a number of cases, the creation of bare life was an insufficient expression of sovereign power. Instead, we see regimes choosing to exert sovereign power through necropolitics, with war machines emerging as a consequence of widespread fragmentation.

In such conditions, localised manifestations of the global *nomos*, defined by a spatialised exception and underpinned by conditions of modernity have become increasingly contested by the contingency of daily life. Amid such contestation, definitions of the outside against an inside become increasingly complex, while regime efforts to maintain sovereign power shifted from the regulation of life to the subjugation of life to death. In conditions of necropolitics, replete with death zones and war machines, human life operates in a Hobbesian state of nature, a war of all against all.[1] There is little doubt that the crises in Syria and Yemen have become humanitarian tragedies on a devastating scale, driven by the mobilisation of war machines seeking to exert power in the face of – and hiding behind the mask of – state power. Regulating life through controlling death, regimes seek to maintain power regardless of the human cost.

The evolution of sovereign projects meant that wars were waged for societies not the sovereign, to devastating effect. With that in mind, such a view alludes to the emergence of a battle between races, resulting in the emergence of state racism. As Foucault argues in *Society Must Be Defended*, 'a racism that society will direct against itself, against its own elements and its own products ... the internal racism of permanent purification, and it will become one of the basic dimensions of social normalization'.[2] While the Israeli–Palestinian conflict particularly in the aftermath of the nation-state law, is a prime example of such a racial struggle, as documented by the likes of Eyal Weizman and Achille Mbembe, events in Iraq, Bahrain, Syria and Yemen possess a number of similar characteristics. Yet with the collapse of the distinction between internal and external, along with the framing of sect as a main point of difference within political life, we see similar processes emerging along sectarian lines, where such difference becomes all consuming.

In states such as Lebanon that have attempted to rectify societal divisions through democratic means, schisms within society have become embedded within political structures that have prevented the descent into all-out violence. A survey conducted by the Arab Barometer found that 52% of Lebanese participants reported that no party is close to representing their political, social and economic aspirations.[3] Additionally, only the army is seen as a trustworthy public institution, while only 8% of respondents trusted the government, 10% trusted parliament and 17% trusted the courts and legal system. In Beirut, these figures are dramatically lower, with only 1% trusting the government, 2% parliament and 6% trusting the courts and legal system.[4] Unsurprisingly the economic situation is identified as one of the two major challenges facing Lebanon according to 64% of respondents, while 43% of respondents viewed the presence of Syrian refugees in the country as one of the two major challenges.[5]

Education plays a powerful role in such matters. One interviewee recalled a lack of historical awareness through the curriculum,[6] while another suggested that only recently have Gulf states started to teach on ideas of nationalism.[7] The focus upon community rights places greater emphasis upon the power of particular groups within society at the expense of individual rights, regardless of the text and indeed sentiment of constitutions or Basic Laws. Instead, groups derive power and legitimacy from history and culture that provide a reservoir of norms to facilitate the ordering of life, albeit with implications for spatial borders. Yet stressing the dominance of communities only serves to reify divisions, whereas a move towards greater acceptance of individual rights can facilitate a move beyond community divisions. Of course, such an approach is easy to discuss in theory but in practice, far harder to implement, particularly amid civil war or serious political, theological and socio-economic tensions.

Strategies to retain control amid myriad competing pressures has ultimately contributed to the evisceration of state sovereignty and the fragmentation of the regional order. The rejection of national identities, securitisation of sectarian identities and decision to view events through the lens of communitarian – or indeed sectarian – interests has created a political environment that contributes to the entrenchment and replication of division at the cost of human safety and well-being. Although sectarian narratives have been applied and writ large across the region, the manifestation of sectarian difference is contingent upon context. We must remember the importance of context-specific contingent factors when conducting this analysis, which can lead to different regional manifestations of sectarian difference as a consequence of different political contexts.

Just as the construction of space is a consequence of the interaction of the intimately small with the global – and all in-between – political life in the Middle East is shaped by the interaction of local, regional and international forces. Domestic affairs occur within the context of broader events, while regional and international actors capitalise on internal affairs in pursuit of their own agendas. Amid a climate of fear and the descent into *asabiyyah*, ensuring support from more powerful actors is of paramount importance, yet in doing so, events become imbued with new meaning, adding to the challenge of working towards reconciliation.

In failing to respond to the deep structural grievances that drove the protests in 2011, regimes remain in a precarious situation. At the time of writing, protests are breaking out across Algeria – following Sudan and Iraq – amid frustration at similar socio-economic conditions that resulted in the events of 2011. Those closely watching the Middle East were not surprised, as economic instability and uncertainty continue to plague the region. A piece in the *Financial Times* titled 'How the Middle East Is Sowing the Seeds of a Second Arab Spring' suggested that conditions that gave rise to the protest movements of 2011 had not been addressed. Instead, rising youth unemployment, huge public sector wage bills, heavy subsidies on food and fuel and declining foreign direct investment underpinned by continued repression left the region ripe for further revolution.[8]

These fundamental challenges were supported by the findings of the 2018 Arab Barometer, which revealed that 30% of people in the Arab region continue to live 'in need', meaning that household incomes fail to cover necessary expenditures. Economic pressures mean that 55% of those living in need require financial support, with 17%

requiring handouts and charitable assistance from family and friends and a further 15% on charitable organisations. Of those asked, 55% had negative views of their home country's political situations, with 33% of people suggesting that economic issues were the most pressing challenges. Some 22% suggested that political issues and governance were the most pressing, while only 10% suggested that safety and security were the biggest threat. The rule of law was widely criticised. Only 28% of Arab publics felt the rule of law was applied universally, while 52% of respondents believed that some groups were shown preferential treatment.[9]

Underpinning such factors is latent structural discrimination against women. In a survey conducted by Pew Research, five of the bottom six countries with the lowest percentage share of females in the workforce were from the Middle East. While the global median female share of the workforce is 45.4%, in Qatar, the lowest ranked state, it is 13.4%.[10] In economic performance, it is hardly surprising to see Israel ranked highest out of all Middle Eastern states, followed by states from the Gulf.

The Arab region has the highest youth unemployment rate in the world, along with increasing birth rates. It also has one of the largest public sector wage bills, deepening dependence on foreign debt and bond markets. One consequence is the redrawing of social contracts. The 2018 Arab Youth Survey documented a widespread frustration at recent events. When asked if things in the Arab world as a region have moved in the right direction or in the wrong direction over the past ten years, 55% answered in the negative. Within those respondents were 89% of people from Lebanon, 88% from Jordan and 83% from Palestine. In contrast, across the Gulf, 57% of people answered that things had moved in the right direction.[11]

Western (in)action

In spite of routinely espousing the values and merits of freedom, justice and democracy, Western responses to the uprisings were characterised by indecision, first over whether to support the protest movements, second over intervention and third with regard to maintaining links with regimes that are routinely considered to be abusers of human rights. Although the Arab Uprisings were driven by demands for greater democratic accountability, world leaders were largely uncertain on how to respond, caught between providing support to autocratic allies or endorsing demands for greater political equality. Comments from Barack Obama, Hillary Clinton and former British Prime Minister David Cameron were replete with uncertainty and, over time, rife with contradiction, perhaps best seen in the White House's responses to events in Egypt and Bahrain.

As regimes fought back against protesters, Western governments continued to support their allies in a triumph of realpolitik over normative concerns. Supplementing this were arms sales to Saudi Arabia and Bahrain, in spite of concerns that these weapons were being used in Yemen against civilians and allegations of war crimes. Underpinning Western policy towards the uprisings were long-standing fears about both Political Islam and Iran. These views were routinely inaccurate, with one former official suggesting that the ideologies of the Brotherhood and Al Qa'ida were 'all the same'.[12] Such views meant that violence was often reduced to 'ancient hatreds'. From Obama and other world leaders, to respected analysts such as Richard Haas, this Orientalist thesis is deeply problematic and has facilitated the deaths of hundreds of thousands through inaction. We should not view inaction solely as the lack of military intervention, but rather as the failure to do anything at all.[13]

Similar views were echoed by Carla Del Ponte, a UN War Crimes Prosecutor, who resigned following the inaction of her employer, arguing that 'everyone in Syria is now bad'.[14] This is, of course, a seismic oversimplification. There is no doubt that violence in Syria has escalated to a devastating level yet providing support to groups who were working to overthrow authoritarian leaders was deemed to run contrary to the realpolitik of national interest. Engagement with the conflict is replete with generalisations,[15] alongside what have been alleged as racist views of the Syrian opposition, most devastatingly seen in the case of the White Helmets and their association with various Al Qa'ida organisations, which resulted in serious funding cuts.[16] Of course, a great deal of this is predicated on the predominance of the state as the vanguard of sovereign power amid a broader struggle between the homogenising powers of globalisation and the nation state itself, between global and local *nomoi*.

Theoretical reflections

Although predominantly driven by empirical questions, the project has raised a number of theoretical points. Sovereign power has been at the centre of our inquiry, which allows us to understand the regulation of life and space, along with the way in which contestation emerges. As we have seen, the ideas of Agamben, Mbembe and Arendt offer strong theoretical support to understand the process through which human life is regulated by the sovereign. The struggle to regulate life has taken place in a number of different forms, shaped by local context, from stripping life of political meaning to controlling life by subjugating it to death. Running alongside all of this is the continued presence of war machines that contest state power.

The regulation of life has implications for the ordering of time and space, with the concept of *nomos* central in helping us understand the manifestation of sovereign power on human agency. Questions about spatial ordering and normative visions of organisation – *ordnung* and *ortung* – are central to discussions of *nomos*. Myriad factors shape the interaction of *ordnung* and *ortung*, from competing visions of how to live as set out by Peter Berger and Robert Cover, to the geopolitical pressures that feature prominently in space across the Middle East. Fundamental to both dimensions are questions about sovereign power and the interaction between *ordnung* and *ortung* that creates the localised *nomos*. Tensions between these competing visions and spatial borders have had clear implications for the ordering of space and for political life in the hundred years since the end of the Ottoman Empire, from the Arab nationalist movement to the construction of a Shi'a crescent and will continue to do so as communities seek to define themselves.[17]

In the global *nomos* of the spatialised exception, the struggle to order such localised spaces is a prominent feature of political life. From the creation of a state of exception and as the normalisation of this exception becomes permanent, zones of indistinction are created. Distinction between *zoe* and *bios* blurred with the emergence of a nation state and as a consequence, 'human life is politicised only through an abandonment to an unconditional power of death'.[18] Amid such conditions of competing and contested sovereignty, the spatially defined and ordered *nomos* locates the exception within context and contingency, but in ordering life challenges the very relationship between *ordnung* and *ortung*, along with the broader spatial aspects of political organisation that become contested amid competing visions of the organisation of life. In engaging with these questions, Geneive Abdo's comments about the primacy of the state and role of religion opens up a zone of indistinction between competing visions of sovereign power, creating space for dissent to emerge. In such conditions, the sovereign makes decisions not just about the life and death of human beings but over who is a human being at all. As such, to paraphrase Agamben, within bare life the *homo sacer* stands outside of the law while simultaneously being abandoned by it, relating to the law through their exclusion from it.

Whither the dream

In the aftermath of the uprisings, the relationship between rulers and ruled has been shaken amid contrasting conditions across the region. From an evolving rentier bargain in the Gulf to the ongoing war in Syria and Yemen, the nature of political organisation appears dramatically different. We should not be surprised at regime responses to the Arab Uprisings. Consideration of state-building processes reveals a history of regimes acting in pursuit of their survival, deploying governance structures of (neo) patrimonialism and, when conditions call for it, regulating life through subjugating it to death. Amid seemingly existential fragmentation that has consumed societies, the implications of such conflicts will be felt long after battles are over, spilling out beyond the borders of sovereign states and subsuming others in broader regional struggles.

While the fallout from the uprisings and conflict is perhaps the most pressing challenge to peace and stability across the Middle East, there are a number of other issues confronting regimes. With a population increase of 53% between 1991 and 2010,[19] the pressure on regimes across the region to provide job opportunities increased dramatically, yet the inability to provide employment either in the public sector or to create a vibrant private sector, fed into a lack of trust in politics. Projected growth rates suggest that by 2020 it is estimated that there will be over three hundred and fifty million people living in countries 'vulnerable to conflict', which is expected to double by 2050. Such deep structural conditions are exacerbated by the growth of an increasingly vocal middle class making serious demands on the state,[20] where the capacity of Gulf states to act was reduced by a fall in oil prices. Changes in the demographic construction of states and the fluidity of peoples across the region resulted in serious challenges for the management of space, particularly in urban environments. The struggle to regulate life has led to increased political violence and repression as the (re)construction of society after a moment of disjuncture threatened to – and in many cases did – rupture relations between rulers and ruled.

The speed of environmental change poses additional challenges that require structural responses to ensure access to water and to maintain stability in times of chaos. Ensuring the governance of such rapid urban expansions poses a serious challenge to local and national elites, whose legitimacy is bound up in the provision of security. Underpinning all of this is a burgeoning sense of frustration at the other. With the increasingly fractious relationship between *ordnung* and *ortung*, new sites of contestation emerge. Amid an influx of people from different backgrounds, latent racism increases, often resulting in acts of violence against incoming residents. The emergence of an increasingly tech-savvy generation poses a new set of challenges for ruling elites, particularly across urban environments.

There are also longer-term implications for those displaced from their homes within the context of the collapse of internal and external politics. Those forced to flee from Syria, Yemen or Iraq typically find themselves in states that are not signatories of UN conventions on refugees and, as a consequence, lack the necessary infrastructure to protect people. A generation of Syrians will grow up without proper schooling and health care, at home and abroad, struggling to assimilate into increasingly xenophobic environments made more so by continued violence and sectarian narratives and latent trauma.[21] Beyond Syria, those stripped of nationality face similar challenges, abandoned by the law yet bound by it, while the intergenerational nature of statelessness poses a challenge to future generations.

The process of post-war reconstruction – albeit before the war has officially ended – provided the Asad regime with a further opportunity to ensure his survival. Recognising the need to attract foreign direct investment (FDI), Urban Law Renewal 10 allows for the mass confiscation of refugee property, offering areas for potential redevelopment and valuable urban real estate.[22] Although some frame it as 'reconstruction legislation', the political dimensions are easily seen. Legislation prevents people from returning to their homes while unrealistic demands for paperwork in the midst of a conflict zone makes it difficult to prove ownership. All of which serves as a means of expropriating land for political, religious and economic reasons. The first areas to be redeveloped under Law 10 are Barzeh, Jobar, Qaboun and Yarmouk, all of which had previously been besieged rebel areas of Damascas. Estimates suggest that one in three homes across Syria have been destroyed, posing serious challenges to lasting – and peaceful – redevelopment.

Similar issues plague Yemen, where almost eighteen million are in dire need of humanitarian assistance. As fighting continues to devastate the state, getting aid into Yemen is increasingly difficult. The port city of Hudaydah, where 80% of the country's aid is received, continues to be the scene of fierce conflict. Beyond Syria and Yemen, fragmentation of political organisation continues to have a devastating impact in Iraq and Gaza. Those displaced from their homes within and beyond state borders face countless challenges amid reconciliation efforts and survival efforts that are jeopardised by the cultivation of normative environments that breed racism. On the Greek island of Lesbos, Kurdish refugees are persecuted by groups pledging allegiance to Da'ish on ethnic grounds.[23] Post-conflict reconstruction is traditionally a precarious process, but increasingly poisonous regional dynamics add an extra challenge.

Of course, all (in)action has consequences and within the consequences of the securitisation of sectarian identities, people are left to pay the price. Across the region the repercussions of dealing with politics through communal identities creates a volatile environment where individual rights are sacrificed for the benefit of regime survival. With anti-Shi'a rhetoric becoming commonplace in the region and beyond, there are serious implications for Shi'a minorities and, conversely, for Sunni communities when Shi'a groups respond. Yet there are a number of instances where such binary politics is challenged. In Kuwait, Da'ish attacks on Shi'a mosques prompted displays of intra-sectarian unity and although the sectarianisation of political life has created exclusionary politics and the establishment of communitarian networks that transcend state borders, others have responded to questions of sectarian allegiance by stressing national identity.[24]

While uncertainty is viewed by many with trepidation, it also remains a source of possibility. The existence of biopolitical modes of governance restrict the capacity for political expression and action, yet the regulation of life also creates zones of indistinction that can also be seen as zones of possibility. Although political, social and economic situations are bleak, residue of protest and resistance remains in the *nomos* and thus, the dreams of the Arab Uprisings remain. Demonstrations of political agency in the face of oppressive structural factors have been a common feature of the past decade as regimes attempt to retain sovereignty and the right to take life or let it live. As long as there is scope to express agency there is hope; and where there is hope, there is uncertainty and an imaginative geography of liberation, justice and dignity, effervescent in the minds of revolutionaries and documented in art, poetry and song.

Yet like the unity of *nomos*, such optimism is but a fleeting glance, eradicated in the minds of people as they are abandoned by the outside world. Dreams occur within the context of rampant authoritarianism – supported by Western powers – and seemingly unchecked efforts to restrict human agency, either through the regulation of life or through the subjugation of life to death. As we have seen, maintaining sovereign power is the ultimate goal of regimes, apparently regardless of the economic or human cost. Political contestation is a consequence of long-standing repression and marginalisation, a struggle to exert and control political agency that has transcended the borders of the sovereign state. Amid precarious conditions, political futures look bleak. As contestation escapes territorial borders, the fight for survival occurs within a broader struggle for regional supremacy where people are sacrificed in in the name of political projects and, ultimately, regime survival.

Notes

1   Al Haj Saleh, *The Impossible Revolution*.
2   Michel Foucault, *Society Must Be Defended* [Lecture Series at the Collège de France, 1975–76] (D. Macey, trans.) (London: Allen Lane, 2003), p. 62.

3 'What Are the Political Attitudes of Citizens in Lebanon?' (*Arab Barometer*, 24.04.18),
   available at www.arabbarometer.org/2018/04/what-are-the-political-attitudes-of-
   citizens-in-lebanon (accessed 24.04.18).

4 Ibid.

5 'The Concerns of Lebanese Citizens and Their Opinions About Politics' (*Arab
   Barometer*, 01.05.18), available at www.arabbarometer.org/2018/05/what-are-the-
   main-concerns-of-lebanese-citizens-what-are-their-opinions-about-politicians-
   political-participation (accessed 01.05.18).

6 Interview with Yemeni-Emirati student 2018.

7 Interview with Saudi academic, 2017.

8 Andrew England and Heba Saleh, 'How the Middle East is Sowing the Seeds of a
   Second Arab Spring' (*Financial Times*, 05.03.18), available at www.ft.com/content/
   a6229844-1ad3-11e8-aaca-4574d7dabfb6 (accessed 05.03.18).

9 'The 2017–2018 Arab Opinion Index: Main Results in Brief' (Arab Center for
   Research and Policy Studies), available at www.dohainstitute.org/en/Lists/ACRPS-
   PDFDocumentLibrary/2017-2018%20Arab%20Opinion%20Index%20Main%20
   Results%20in%20Brief%20-%20final%20(002).pdf (accessed 19.07.19).

10 Janell Fetterolf, 'In Many Countries, at Least Four in Ten in the Labor Force Are
   Women' (Pew Research Center, 07.03.17), available at www.pewresearch.org/fact-tank/
   2017/03/07/in-many-countries-at-least-four-in-ten-in-the-labor-force-are-women
   (accessed 10.03.17).

11 Arab Youth Survey, *Top 10 Findings* (Dubai, UAE: ASDA'A Burson-Marsteller, 2018),
   available at http://arabyouthsurvey.com/findings.html (accessed 02.01.19).

12 David D. Kirkpatrick, 'The White House and the Strongman' (*New York Times*,
   27.07.18), available at www.nytimes.com/2018/07/27/sunday-review/obama-egypt-
   coup-trump.html (accessed 02.08.19).

13 Yassin Al Haj Saleh, 'The Conscience of Syria' (*Boston Review*, 12.03.14), available at
   http://bostonreview.net/world/postel-hashemi-interview-syrian-activist-intellectual-
   yassin-al-haj-saleh (accessed 15.03.14).

14 'War Crimes Expert Carla Del Ponte Resigns From U.N.'s Syria Inquiry' (NPR,
   08.08.17), available at www.npr.org/2017/08/08/542164025/war-crimes-expert-carla-
   del-ponte-resigns-from-u-n-s-syria-inquiry/english/news/2017/8/7/war-crimes-
   prosecutor-quits-un-syria-abuses-panel (accessed 10.08.17).

15 John L. Esposito and Faisal Kattan, 'Generalising About the Arab Spring Is Playing
   with Fire' (*Middle East Eye*, 24.01.15), available at www.middleeasteye.net/essays/
   generalising-about-arab-spring-playing-fire-585127162 (accessed 24.01.15).

16 Interview with Syrian author, 2017.

17 Mabon, 'The World Is a Garden'.

18 Agamben, *Homo Sacer*, p. 90.

19 International Labour Organization, 'Rethinking Economic Growth'.

20 In Syria this was 56.5%, in Egypt 55% and in Yemen 31.6%.
   See United Nations, 'Arab Middle Class: Measurement and Role in Driving Change'
   (UNESCWA, 2014), available at www.unescwa.org/sites/www.unescwa.org/
   files/publications/files/arab-middle-class-measurement-role-change-english.pdf
   (accessed 01.05.16).

21 Wendy Pearlman, *We Crossed a Bridge and It Trembled: Voices from Syria*
   (New York: Harper Collins, 2017).

22 'The New Urban Renewal Law in Syria' (*Syrian Law Journal*, 14.05.18), available at www.syrianlawjournal.com/index.php/new-urban-renewal-law-syria (accessed 14.05.18).

23 Anna Lekas Miller and Salem Rizk, 'Attacks on Kurds in a Greek Camp raise fears that conflict in Syria has followed refugees abroad' (*Intercept*, 25.07.18), available at https://theintercept.com/2018/07/25/lesbos-moria-kurdish-refugees-isis (accessed 25.07.18).

24 Interview with Bahraini student, 2014.

Selected bibliography

This bibliography is by no means a complete record of all the sources I have consulted in this volume. Instead, it indicates the substance and range of reading that helped forge my ideas and is intended to serve as a resource for those readers who wish to explore these topics further.

Abdo, G. *The New Sectarianism: The Arab Uprisings and the Rebirth of the Shi'a-Sunni Divide* (Oxford: Oxford University Press, 2017).

Agamben, G. *Homo Sacer, Sovereign Power and Bare Life.* (Palo Alto, CA: Stanford University Press, 1995).

Agamben, G. *State of Exception* (Chicago: Chicago University Press, 2005).

Ahmed, S. *What Is Islam? The Importance of Being Islamic* (Princeton, NJ: Princeton University Press, 2016).

Ajami, F. *The Arab Predicament: Arab Political Thought and Practice Since 1967* (Cambridge, UK: Cambridge University Press).

Al Haj Saleh, Y. *The Impossible Revolution: Making Sense of the Syrian Tragedy* (London: Hurst, 2017).

Anderson, L. 'The State in the Middle East and North Africa', *Comparative Politics*, 20:1 (1987) 1–18.

Arendt, H. *The Origins of Totalitarianism* (London: Harcourt, 1958).

Asad, T. and R. Owen (eds) *The Middle East* (Basingstoke, UK: Palgrave Macmillan, 1983).

Aybui, N. N. *Over-Stating the Arab State* (London: I. B. Tauris, 1995).

Ayubi, N. N. *Political Islam: Religion and Politics in the Arab World* (London: Routledge, 1991).

Barnett, M. *Dialogues in Arab Politics: Negotiations in Regional Order* (New York: Columbia, 1998).

Batatu, H. *The Old Social Classes and the Revolutionary Movements of Iraq: A Study of Iraq's Old Landed and Commercial Classes and of its Communities, Ba'athists and Free Officers* (Princeton, NJ: Princeton University Press, 1978).

Baumann, H. *Citizen Hariri: Lebanon's Neo-Liberal Reconstruction* (London: Hurst, 2017).

Bayat, A. *Revolution without Revolutionaries: Making Sense of the Arab Spring* (Palo Alto, CA: Stanford University Press, 2017).

Brown, N. J. 'Shari'a and State in the Modern Muslim Middle East', *International Journal of Middle Eastern Studies*, 29 (1997), 359–76.

Burgis, M. 'Faith in the State? Traditions of Territoriality and the Emergence of Modern Arab Statehood', *Journal of the History of International Law*, 11:1 (2009), 37–79.

Cover, R. 'The Supreme Court, 1982 Term – Foreword: *Nomos* and Narrative', *Faculty Scholarship Series* (1983) Paper 2705.

Deleuze, G. and F. Guattari, *Nomadology: The War Machine* (South Pasadena, CA: Semiotext(e), 1986).

Dodge, T. '"Bordieu Goes to Baghdad": Explaining Hybrid Political Identities in Iraq', *Journal of Historical Sociology*, 31 (2018), 25–38.

Fromkin, D. *A Peace to End All Peace: The Fall of the Ottoman Empire and the Creation of the Modern Middle East* (New York: Henry Holt, 1989).

Gause, F. G. *The International Relations of the Persian Gulf* (Cambridge, UK: Cambridge University Press, 2010).

Ghobadzadeh, N. and S. Akbarzadeh, 'Sectarianism and the Prevalence of "Othering" in Islamic Thought', *Third World Quarterly*, 36 (2016), 691–704.

Haddad, F. ' "Sectarianism" and Its Discontents in the Study of the Middle East', *Middle East Journal*, 71:3 (2017), 363–82.

Halliday, F. *The Middle East in International Relations: Power, Politics and Ideology* (Cambridge, UK: Cambridge University Press, 2005).

Hashemi, N. and D. Postel (eds) *Sectarianization: Mapping the New Politics of the Middle East* (London: Hurst, 2017).

Hudson, M. C. *Arab Politics: The Search for Legitimacy* (New Haven, CT: Yale University Press, 1977).

Jurkevics, A. 'Hannah Arendt Reads Carl Schmitt's *The Nomos of the Earth*: A Dialogue On Law and Geopolitics From the Margins', *European Journal of Political Theory*, 16:3 (2017), 345–66.

Kamrava, M. *Inside the Arab State* (London: Hurst, 2018).

Kamrava, M. *The Modern Middle East: A Political History Since World War 1* (Berkeley: University of California Press, 2013).

Kerr, M. *The Arab Cold War: Gamel 'Abd Al-Nasir and His Rivals, 1958–70* (Oxford: Oxford University Press, 1972).

Khoury, P. S. and J. Kostiner (eds), *Tribes and State Formation in the Middle East* (Berkeley: University of California Press, 1990).

Korany, B. *Arab Human Development in the Twenty-First Century* (Cairo: American University Cairo Press, 2014).

Lefebvre, H. *The Production of Space* (Oxford: Blackwell, 1991).

Lindahl, H. 'Give and Take: Arendt and the *nomos* of Political Community', *Philosophy & Social Criticism*, 32:7 (2006), 881–901.

Lynch, M. *The Arab Uprising: The Unfinished Revolutions of the New Middle East* (New York: Public Affairs, 2012).

Mabon, S. 'The Circle of Bare Life: Hizballah, Muqawamah and Rejecting "Being Thus"', *Politics, Religion and Ideology*, 18:1 (2017), 1–22.

Mabon, S. 'Muting the Trumpets of Sabotage: Saudi Arabia, the US and the Quest to Securitize Iran', *British Journal of Middle Eastern Studies*, 45:5 (2018), 742–59.

Mabon, S. *Saudi Arabia and Iran: Soft Power Rivalry in the Middle East* (London: I. B. Tauris, 2013).

Mabon, S. 'Sovereignty, Bare Life and the Arab Uprisings', *Third World Quarterly*, 38:8 (2017), 1782–99.

Mabon, S. 'The World Is a Garden: *Nomos* and the (Contested) Ordering of Life', *Review of International Studies* (forthcoming).

March, A. F. 'Genealogies of Sovereignty in Islamic Political Theology', *Social Research* (Special Issue on Political Theology), 80:2 (Spring 2013), 293–320.

Massey, D. *For Space* (London: Sage, 2005).

Matthiesen, T. *The Other Saudis: Shiism, Dissent and Sectarianism* (Cambridge, UK: Cambridge University Press, 2014).

Matthiesen, T. *Sectarian Gulf: Bahrain, Saudi Arabia and the Arab Spring That Wasn't* (Palo Alto, CA: Stanford University Press, 2013).

Mbembe, A. 'Necropolitics', *Public Culture*, 15:1 (2003), 11–40.

Owen, R. *State, Power and Politics in the Making of the Modern Middle East* (Oxford: Routledge, 1992).

Parvin, M. and M. Sommer, 'Dar al-Islam: The Evolution of Muslim Territoriality and its implications for Conflict Resolution in the Middle East', *International Journal of Middle East Studies*, 11(1980), 1–21.

Phillips, C. 'The Arabism Debate and the Arab Uprisings', *Mediterranean Politics*, 19:1 (2014), 141–4.

Phillips, C. *The Battle for Syria* (New Haven, CT: Yale University Press, 2016).

Salame, G. (ed.) *The Foundations of the Arab State* (Oxford: Routledge, 1987).

Salloukh, B. F. 'The Arab Uprisings and the Geopolitics of the Middle East', *International Spectator*, 48:2 (2013), 32–46.

Sand, S. *The Invention of the Jewish People* (London: Verso, 2010).

Sand, S. *The Invention of the Land of Israel: From Holy Land to Homeland* (London: Verso, 2014).

Searle, P. *The Struggle for Syria: A Study of Post-War Arab Politics 1945–1958* (London: I. B. Tauris, 1965).

Shafir, G. and Y. Peled, 'Citizenship and Stratification in an Ethnic Democracy', *Ethnic and Racial Studies*, 21:3 (1998), 412–3.

Smooha, S. 'The Model of Ethnic Democracy: Israel as a Jewish and Democratic State', *Nations and Nationalism*, 8:4 (2002), 475–503.

Tripp, C. *A History of Iraq* (Cambridge, UK: Cambridge University Press, 2007).

Tripp, C. *The Power and the People: Paths of Resistance in the Middle East* (Cambridge, UK: Cambridge University Press, 2013).

Tripp, C. 'The State as an Always-Unfinished Performance: Improvisation and Performativity in the Face of Crisis', *International Journal of Middle East Studies*, 50 (2018), 337–42.

Valbjørn, M. and A. Bank, 'The New Arab Cold War: Rediscovering the Arab Dimension of Middle East Regional Politics', *Review of International Studies*, 38:1 (2012), 3–24.

Weizman, E. *Hollow Lands: Israel's Architecture of Occupation* (London: Verso, 2007).

Index

Al Abadi, Haider 217
Abdullah II, King of Jordan 51
Abu Dhabi 130, 221
Agamben, Giorgio 5, 8–9, 13–15, 17–18,
    22, 32–3, 62, 66, 82–3, 86, 119, 138–9,
    150, 173, 182, 212, 239–40, 243
Ahmadinejad, Mahmoud 52, 155, 167
AKP (Justice and Development Party) 76,
    167
Alawi 63, 74
Aleppo 193
Amal movement 139, 155
ancient hatreds 4, 211, 214, 239
Arab Human Development Report 22, 24,
    156, 158, 160, 172
Arab League 34–5, 37, 46, 47
Arab nationalism 34–5, 42–3, 45–6, 48–9,
    52, 67, 71, 80, 103, 106, 213–14, 232
    see also pan-Arabism
Arab Revolt 34–5, 151
Arab Uprisings 2, 5–7, 22, 33, 52, 53, 95,
    103, 108, 150, 155, 159, 168, 172–3,
    183, 188, 199, 211, 213–14, 221,
    226–7, 235, 238, 240, 242
Arendt 5, 8, 9, 13, 19, 20, 29–30, 64, 67,
    85–6, 147, 235, 239
Ashura 111
Assad, Bashar 1, 6, 113, 135, 164–5, 171,
    193–4, 197–8, 214, 217, 219
Assad, Hafez 42, 74, 152, 197
authoritarianism 47–8, 63–4, 101, 167, 169,
    242

Ba'ath party 42, 44, 74
Badr organisation 102, 113, 215
Baghdad 36, 44–5, 50, 69, 129, 139, 141,
    189, 196
Bahrain
    domestic unrest 52, 153, 163
    economics 130, 133, 156, 168, 194, 199,
    222

migrant workers 81, 133
    passports 218
    political Islam 192
    political repression 48, 54, 81–3, 153,
    163, 170, 182, 185–6, 190–1
    Qatar crisis 53, 198, 221
    reform 65, 153, 199
    relations with Iran 82, 113, 163, 189–91
    claims to 48
    relations with Israel 220
    relations with Saudi Arabia 156,
    215–17
    role of religion 107, 199
    sectarianism 81, 163, 182, 190–1,
    216, 236
    USA and WikiLeaks 189
    Yemen war, involvement in, 224
Al Banna, Hassan 37–8, 41, 100–1, 105
bare life 13–14, 16, 22, 24–5, 54, 62, 64,
    67–8, 81–2, 96, 139–41, 143, 150, 156,
    160–1, 171, 173, 183, 186, 189, 196,
    236, 240
Al Barrack, Mussallam 166, 201
basij 77
Beirut 1, 34–5, 52, 128–9, 133, 140–1, 168,
    236
bidoon 67, 80–1, 165–6
blockade 53, 220, 221
Bush, George W. 51, 111

Cedar Revolution 33, 129, 154–5
chemical weapons 153, 210
Christianity 34, 43, 106, 137
civil war 1, 45–7, 64, 69, 106, 140, 147, 155,
    163, 168, 191, 193–4, 196, 237
Cold War 44, 152
Communism 23, 33, 44, 71
consociationalism (power sharing) 25,
    63–5, 69, 106, 195, 227
Cover, Robert 5, 9, 19, 75, 157, 170, 194,
    237, 239

Al Da'wa 107, 153
Damascus 152, 162
day of rage, 162–4, 200, 225
deep state 41, 200–2
Deleuze, Gilles 5, 8, 9, 16, 18
desectarianisation 226
Doha 130, 161, 182, 220–1
Dubai 67, 130

Egypt
  corruption 201
  deep state 41, 132, 188, 200
  economy 43, 65, 156
  elections 63, 159
  emergency laws 24, 64, 83, 184
  foreign policy 4–5, 46, 185, 191, 213, 222
  formation 35, 41, 44, 151, 152
  pan-Arabism 23, 44–6, 103
  relations with Iran 45, 54
  relations with Israel 46–7
  relations with Muslim Brotherhood 38,
    100, 105–6, 152, 160, 162, 181–2, 192,
    193, 200, 217
  relations with Saudi Arabia 45, 185, 191,
    213, 223, 224
  religion 48, 93, 100, 105
  unrest 24, 52, 160–1, 169, 170, 173,
    181–2, 199, 201, 238
emergency laws 24, 64, 78, 83, 153, 159–60,
    168, 170, 185, 190
environment 126, 150, 167, 171, 206, 241
Erdogan, Recep Tayyip 167, 178

fatwa 104, 114, 196
fitna 155

GCC (Gulf Co-Operation Council) 53,
    163, 185, 190, 199, 221–2
Ghonim, Wael 160–1
Gulf Co-Operation Council see GCC

Hadi, Mansour 163, 191
hadith 20
hajj 112
Hama massacre 42, 152–3, 197
Hamas 118, 131, 164, 172, 220–1
Hariri, Rafik 52, 60, 129
Hariri, Saad 223, 225

Hizballah
  formation 94, 155
  governance 1, 83, 131, 143, 223
  Hariri assassination 52
  links with Iran 49, 194, 220
  regional activity 3, 53, 165, 192–3,
    196, 218
  social programmes 102, 131, 139,
    141, 172
  war with Israel 50, 52, 213
Houthi 163, 191–2, 196, 222
Hussein, Saddam 50–1, 74, 142, 153–4, 213

IFLB (Islamic Front for the Liberation of
    Bahrain) 190, 203
Iran
  activity in Yemen 191–2, 196
  domestic policy 24, 44, 63, 77, 93, 102,
    134, 154, 167
  foreign policy 2, 45, 50–3, 95, 107, 111,
    202, 218
    Iranian 'influence' 36, 50, 54, 81–2, 94,
      107, 113, 131, 182, 189, 194, 202,
      215–17, 219
  identity 77
  IRGC (Islamic Revolutionary Guard
    Corps) 189, 192, 204
  nuclear issue 219
    JCPOA (Joint Comprehensive Plan of
      Action) 220
  Persia 39
  relations with Bahrain 107, 163, 182,
    190–1
  relations with Hizballah 52–3, 141,
    196, 220
  relations with Iraq 66, 69, 107, 113, 131,
    141, 153, 189, 195–6
  relations with Popular Mobilisation
    Units 53, 107, 153, 189
  relations with Syria 165, 192–3, 214,
    217–18
  religion 3, 48–9, 77, 111–12
  revolution 33, 77, 95, 107, 111
  rivalry with Saudi Arabia 48–52, 112,
    165, 185, 188, 190–2, 212–14, 216–17,
    219, 223, 227, 238
  rivalry with United States 51, 53, 189,
    218–20

Iraq
  2003 invasion of 33, 95, 132, 154, 195,
    220
  economy 70, 75, 156
  formation and development of 36–7, 44,
    63, 69, 74, 102, 142
  geopolitics 2, 113–14, 165, 189, 197, 214,
    219
  relations with Iran 50, 189, 215
  sectarianism 82, 102, 107, 131, 139, 188,
    190, 196, 213, 217
  Sunni extremism 51, 53, 141, 190, 195,
    213
  unrest 24, 83, 140, 153, 164, 196, 201,
    236–7, 241
Islamic Front for the Liberation of Bahrain
  see IFLB
Islamic Revolutionary Guard Corps see
  Iran, IRGC
Islamic Supreme Council of Iraq see SCIRI
Israel 1–2, 23, 202
  Arab wars with 44–7, 52, 152, 155, 185,
    213
  Camp David Accords 47, 50
  economics 64, 238
  elections 63
  embassy move 224
  establishment of
    process 40–1, 188
    repercussions 33, 39–41
    transformation of land 115–16,
      133–8
  IDF (Israeli Defence Force) 41, 47, 138
  invasion of Lebanon 50
  law 82–3, 136
  political life 114–15
  protests 166, 167
  relations with Gulf states 219–20, 223,
    225
  relations with Palestinians 47, 50, 78, 79,
    135–7, 140, 164, 236
  religion 11, 20, 66, 78, 98, 114
  Zionism 40, 78, 115
Israeli Defence Force see Israel, IDF

Al Jazeera 53, 154, 186, 221
JCPOA (Joint Comprehensive Plan of
  Action) 219–20

Jerusalem 47
  control of 40, 45
  embassy 224–5
  transformation of 135–8
Joint Comprehensive Plan of Action see
  JCPOA
Jordan
  Bedouin 134
  domestic unrest 162
  economics 154, 157, 199, 223, 226
  elections 65, 159
  Israel 154
  mandate and Hashemite 37
  networks of patronage 70
  Palestinians 47, 102
  political life 63, 83, 152, 154–5, 183, 199
  regional pressures 45, 83, 187, 213
  religion 4, 105–6
  role of military 74
Al Jubeir, Adel 192, 219
Judaism 11, 79, 115–16
Justice and Development Party see AKP

Khaldun, Ibn 3, 5, 9, 19, 20, 30, 70, 85, 109
Khalifa family 9, 82, 153, 163, 170, 185–6,
  190–2
Khamenei, Ali 1, 131, 142, 191, 230
Khomeini, Ruhollah 1, 49, 50, 77, 93,
  111–13, 131, 141–2, 153, 202
Kurds 50, 63, 69, 76–7, 153, 217, 241
Kuwait
  Battle of Jahra 38
  bidoon 67, 81, 165
  east of Suez 48, 130
  elections 63–4
  Iraq invasion 50, 83, 154, 165
  Muslim Brotherhood in 80
  political life 80, 81, 106, 125, 130, 165,
    168, 194, 199
  political unrest 153, 166, 185, 199, 201,
    215
  regional support 156, 199, 218
  sectarian relations 54, 82, 191, 194

Lebanon
  Christians 106
  civil war 155, 194–5
  communalism 227

Lebanon (*cont.*)
  drugs 142
  economics 141, 156, 172, 214, 236
  elections 63–4
  geopolitical competition 49
  Israeli invasion (1982) 50
  Israeli invasion (2006) 52
  Palestinians 47, 139
  political repression 83
  refugee camps 139–40
  religion 3, 66
  role of Iran 191
  role of Saudi Arabia 223
  Salafis 113
  sectarianism 4, 106, 188, 217
    cross-sectarian unity 223
    political economy 194–5
  Syrian refugees 139, 183, 218
  Syrian withdrawal 52
  Ta'ifa 69

Mahabad Republic 69
Al Maliki, Nouri 113, 189, 217
Manama 133, 162–3, 168, 170, 191, 199
mandate period 12, 35–7, 39, 41, 78, 82, 98,
    102, 110, 128, 133, 138
Mecca 35, 49, 94, 112, 134
military
  acceptance into/exemption from 36,
    78, 116
  activity in politics 76, 82, 115, 137,
    140, 155, 161, 164, 170, 184–5, 192,
    199–201
  military aid and spending 45,
    73–5, 190
  military structures 38, 70–1, 73–5, 132,
    141, 199–200, 215
Morsi, Mohammad 24, 162, 181–2, 184,
    193, 199–200, 217–18
Mubarak, Hosni 105, 132, 152, 160–2, 170,
    184–5, 199–201
Muhasasa 69
muqawamah 151
Muscat 164, 199, 222
Muslim Brotherhood (Ikhwan)
  formation and evolution 37, 38, 41, 44
  religious views 3, 23, 37, 100, 109, 217
  repression 45, 152, 181–2, 193, 200–1

role in politics 24, 42, 80, 105–6, 152–3,
    160–2, 192, 199–200
social programmes and civil society 41,
    47, 74, 80, 102, 105–6, 131, 141, 143,
    160, 172
support for 53, 220

Nasrallah, Hassan 1, 52, 141, 155, 213
necropolitics 7, 13, 21, 24, 42, 54, 139, 195,
    197, 202, 236
neopatrimonialism 43, 70–1, 73–5, 82, 84,
    126, 150, 156, 159, 160, 167, 170, 240
Netanyahu, Benjamin 225
nomos 6, 17–22, 25, 32–4, 36, 54, 63, 66,
    70, 76, 82, 84–5, 94, 96, 109, 115, 117,
    126, 129, 131, 157–8, 187, 195, 212,
    236, 239, 240, 242

Obama, Barack 4, 211, 219
oil 12, 37–41, 44, 48, 50, 52, 80, 102, 109,
    110, 129, 157, 168, 199, 222–3, 240
Oman
  domestic unrest 163, 199, 201
  political structures 68, 199
  ports 222
  regional tensions 222
  religion in 20, 94
  support for 199
  transition 222
Ottoman Empire 9, 33, 35–6, 38–40, 72, 76,
    95, 102, 109, 128, 151, 239

Palestine
  Arab nationalism 44
  attacks on 11
  Balfour Declaration 39–40
  citizenship 67
  control of 133, 134, 138
  domestic conditions 157
  domestic unrest 164
  intifada 50, 165
  mandate 37, 39–41, 82, 102
  nakba 41
  Oslo Accords 12, 50, 225
  partition 40
  PLO (Palestine Liberation Organization)
    and resistance 47, 50, 140, 225
  refugees 102, 105, 139, 140

Palestine (*cont.*)
  relations with Israel 115
  Saudi peace plan 224–5
  settlements 136–7
  transformation of 115, 135
  UN General Assembly Council
    Resolution 181 40
Palestine Liberation Organization *see*
  Palestine: PLO and resistance
pan-Arabism 3, 11, 22–3, 41, 43–4, 48, 102,
  106, 173
pan-Islamism 6, 11, 23, 49, 54, 67
PMUs *see* Popular Mobilisation Units
political Islam
  concept of 102
  Islamist revival 95–6
  in power 107
  Western views of 238
  see also Muslim Brotherhood (Ikhwan)
Popular Mobilisation Units (PMUs) 53,
  196, 215

Qaboos, Sultan 164, 222
Qassim, Isa 107
Qatar
  blockade 53, 220–1
  economics 125, 198, 226, 238
  formation and transformation
    125, 130
  politics 65, 226
  regional role 165, 186, 202, 218–20, 224
  regulation of life 54, 83
  religion 103
Qutb, Sayyid 100–1, 107

Rabaa massacre 181, 201
rentierism 63–4, 67, 71, 79, 156, 164,
  167–8, 198, 240
resistance 7, 15, 20, 38, 47–8, 50, 80, 94,
  131, 135, 140, 149–51, 154–5, 159,
  164, 168–9, 173, 183, 196, 242
  see also muqawamah
revolution 19, 22, 24, 32–3, 38–9, 45–6
  concepts 19, 22
  counter-revolution 162–3, 170, 185, 227,
    228
  Egypt 151–2, 161, 181, 184
  future scope for 237, 242
  Iran 39, 48–50, 77, 81, 93–4, 111, 167

  Iraq 141
  Lebanon 154–5
  Palestinian 140
  regional trends 24, 46, 49, 50, 95, 107,
    112–13, 153–4
  Syria 165, 193
  tools of 169–71
  transformations 32–3, 164
  Turkey 38
  Yemen 45
Riyadh 72, 104, 112, 159, 164, 185, 191,
  219–21, 223–4, 226
Russia
  demand for oil 221
  involvement in Syria 165, 193,
    214, 218
  Russian Jews 78
  war against Da'ish 53
  see also Soviet Union

Al Sabah family 50, 80, 106, 166, 201
Sadat, Anwar 47, 65, 102, 105, 152
Sadr family
  Muhammad Baqir 107, 153
  Muqtada 217
  Sadrist movement 113
Saleh, Ali Abdullah 162, 185, 199
Salman, Ali 221
Al Saud family
  Abdulaziz 37, 74, 94, 104
  Abdullah 189, 222
  Faisal 102, 223
  Mohammad bin Salman (MbS) 192, 199,
    222–5, 235
Saudi Arabia
  domestic politics 4, 24, 65–6, 74, 83,
    104, 125, 164, 185, 198, 222, 226,
    235
    economics 157, 168, 198–9
    elections 159
    seizure of Grand Mosque 49, 94
    state building 37, 103, 130, 222–4
  gender 79, 158
  involvement in Lebanon 156, 213, 225
  involvement in Syria 113, 165, 214–15,
    217–18
  involvement in Yemen 45, 163, 190, 192,
    194, 223–4
  involvement with Palestine 224

Saudi Arabia (*cont.*)
  relations with Bahrain 163, 190–2, 215, 217, 220
  relations with domestic Shi'a 82, 112–13, 215
  relations with Iraq 52, 66, 213, 217
  relations with Israel 220
  relations with Qatar 220–1
  relations with US 52, 219, 224, 238
  religion 4, 20, 23, 49, 66, 94
    Organisation of Islamic Cooperation 113
    pan-Islamism 103
    political Islam 182, 217–18, 220–1, 226
  rivalry with Iran 48–52, 112, 165, 185, 188, 190–2, 212–14, 216–17, 219, 223, 227, 238
  tribalism 70, 94
SCAF (Supreme Council of Armed Forces) 161, 184, 199–200
SCIRI (Islamic Supreme Council of Iraq) 113, 153, 215
sectarianism
  ancient hatreds 4, 211, 214, 239
  communalism 2, 4, 69, 106, 190, 194, 237
  concept of 4, 94–5, 190
  in foreign policy 48–9, 52, 112, 114, 187, 189–92, 197, 202, 213–14, 219, 226, 228
  in legal structures 81, 96, 106, 114, 117, 141, 190, 215–17
  othering 81, 107, 112, 114, 117, 182, 188, 190, 202, 213, 227, 241
  political economy of 4, 107, 126, 131, 142, 190, 194, 198, 213–17
  roots of 111
  sectarian unity 11, 163, 194, 242
  sectarian violence 1, 2, 94, 141, 182, 190, 192–4, 198, 217, 227, 236
  sectarianization 96, 163, 187–95, 216, 237
  securitisation of 54, 94, 237
  spaces of 127, 131, 139, 142, 189, 192, 216, 226
secularism 38, 43, 66, 73, 76, 78, 80, 102, 106–8, 115, 167, 187, 201
security services 73, 116, 133, 185, 190, 200
Shahiba 214

Shi'a crescent 51, 189, 191, 239
Sisi, Abdul Fatah 182, 185, 218
Soleimani, Qassim 69, 141, 189
Soviet Union 37, 46, 116
state of exception 12–16, 18, 22, 24–5, 32–3, 51, 62, 64, 68, 82–5, 92, 111, 125, 137, 139–40, 143, 166, 183–4, 201–2, 212, 236, 239–40
Supreme Council of Armed Forces *see* SCAF
Sykes–Picot 12, 35, 53
Syria 44, 63–5, 170, 187, 202, 218, 220, 236, 240–1
  actions in Lebanon 2, 52, 154–5
  Ba'athism 45, 156
  Da'ish 53
  drugs 142
  economics 156, 172, 198, 214
  environmental degradation 171–2
  political unrest 24, 42, 164–5, 173, 182, 217
  relations with Iran 165, 193, 217, 219
  relations with Saudi Arabia 113, 165, 193, 215, 217, 219
  religion 66
    sectarianism 183, 185, 193–4, 214
  repression 54, 74, 135, 152, 165, 182, 193, 197–8, 201
  UAR (United Arab Republic) 45
  war 1, 4, 165, 182, 193, 201, 214
  wars with Israel 47, 83

tribe 9, 20, 33, 37–8, 69, 70–2, 74–6, 80–1, 94, 96, 109–10, 142, 164, 189–90
Trump, Donald 218, 220, 224–5
Turkey 53, 83, 140, 183
  elections 63–4, 76
  geopolitics 167, 218
  irredentism 24
  military 73, 218
  political transformation 38, 76, 129
  political unrest 166–7
  refugees 183, 218
  role of religion 66, 76, 102

UAE (United Arab Emirates)
  economics 157
  geopolitics 191–2, 218
  independence 48

UAE (United Arab Emirates) (*cont.*)
  involvement in Yemen 224
  political Islam 182, 192, 217
  political repression 54, 170, 187, 226
  relations with Oman 222
  relations with Qatar 220
  rentierism 81, 198
UAR (United Arab Republic) 42, 44
UK 6, 20, 35, 41, 44, 53, 195
United Arab Emirates *see* UAE
United Arab Republic *see* UAR
USA
  crude oil 168
  relations with Iran 190
  relations with Saudi Arabia 219

war
  (1948) 40, 41, 78
  (1967) 33, 45–7, 83, 103, 135–7, 140, 225
  (1982) 50
  (2006) 1, 52, 155–6, 213
  invasion of Iraq 2, 33, 52, 69, 95, 107,
    141–2, 189, 193, 195, 213
  invasion of Kuwait 50, 83, 154

war machines 16, 24–5, 139, 165, 183,
    195–8, 202, 215, 236, 239
Al Wefaq 82, 108, 163, 221

Yemen
  domestic unrest 52, 75, 83, 162–3, 170,
    173, 182, 201, 240, 241
  economics 142, 153, 156–7
  humanitarian crises 142, 153, 163, 182,
    194, 236, 238, 241
  Iranian involvement in 192, 196, 217
  National Dialogue 196
  North Yemen 45
  People's Republic of South Yemen 46
  political life 63, 68, 125, 153
  religion 113–14, 191–2, 216
  Republic of North Yemen 46
  Saudi involvement in 191–2, 217,
    223–4
  secessionism 24
  site of geopolitical competition 2, 5, 53,
    154, 191, 192, 202, 214, 219
  tribalism 163
  war 46

EU authorised representative for GPSR:
Easy Access System Europe, Mustamäe tee 50,
10621 Tallinn, Estonia
gpsr.requests@easproject.com